As this appalling ocean surrounds the verdant land,

so in the soul of man there lies one insular Tahiti,

full of peace and joy, but encompassed by

all the horrors of the half-known life.

God help thee! Push not off from that isle,

thou canst never return.

— Herman Melville

TAHITI
-POLYNESIA
HANDBOOK

TAHITI
-POLYNESIA
HANDBOOK
THIRD EDITION

DAVID STANLEY

MOON
PUBLICATIONS INC.

TAHITI-POLYNESIA HANDBOOK
THIRD EDITION

Published by
Moon Publications, Inc.
P.O. Box 3040
Chico, California 95927-3040, USA
tel. (916) 345-5473, fax (916) 345-6751

Printed by
Colorcraft Ltd., Hong Kong

ISBN: 1-56691-037-4
ISSN: 1082-4855

Editor: Charles Mohnike
Copy Editors: Elizabeth Kim, Asha Johnson
Production & Design: Carey Wilson
Cartographers: Bob Race, Brian Bardwell
Index: Valerie Sellers Blanton

Front cover photo: Tom Servais

Tahiti-und Polynesien-Handbuch. A German translation of this book is published by Verlag Gisela E. Walther,
Oppenheimerstr. 26, D-28307 Bremen, Germany.

Distributed in the U.S.A. by Publishers Group West
Printed in Hong Kong

Please send all comments,
corrections, additions,
amendments, and critiques to:

**DAVID STANLEY
MOON PUBLICATIONS, INC.
P.O. BOX 3040
CHICO, CA 95927-3040, USA
e-mail: travel@moon.com**

Printing History
   1st edition — September, 1989
      Reprinted, June 1991
   2nd edition — November 1992
      Reprinted, August 1994
   3rd edition — January 1996

CONTENTS

MAPS

MAP SYMBOLS

———— HIGHWAYS, ROADS, STREETS
– – – – FOOT TRAILS
═══ BRIDGE

▲ MOUNTAIN
WATERFALL
WATER
REEF

O ■ SIGHTS, POINTS OF INTEREST
O TOWNS, CITIES
o VILLAGES
● HOTEL/ACCOMMODATION

CHARTS AND SPECIAL TOPICS

ABBREVIATIONS

4WD—four-wheel drive
A$—Australian dollars
a/c—air conditioned
B.P.—Boîte Postale
C—centigrade
C$—Canadian dollars
CDW—collision damage waiver
CFP—French Pacific francs
cm—centimeters
E.U.—European Union
I.—island

Is.—islands
kg—kilogram
km—kilometer
kph—kilometers per hour
LDS—Latter-day Saints
(Mormons)
LMS—London Missionary
Society
mm—millimeters
MV—motor vessel
No.—number

NZ—New Zealand
OW—one way
PK—point kilométrique
pop.—population
pp—per person
RT—round trip
tel.—telephone
U.S.—United States
US$—U.S. dollars
WW II—World War Two

IS THIS BOOK OUT OF DATE?

Travel writing is a little like trying to take a picture out the side of *le truck:* time frustrates the best of intentions. Things change fast—you'll understand how hard it is for us to keep up. A strong hurricane can blow away half the tourist facilities on an island overnight! So if something in this book doesn't sound quite right, please let us hear about it. Did anything lead you astray or inconvenience you? In retrospect, what sort of information would have made your trip easier?

Unlike many other travel writers, this author doesn't solicit "freebies" or announce who he is to one and all, and at times that makes it difficult to audit the expensive resorts. Thus we especially welcome comments from readers who stayed at upscale places, particularly when the facilities didn't match the rates. Legitimate complaints will most

certainly influence future coverage in this book, and no hotel or restaurant is exempt from fair criticism.

When writing, please be as precise and accurate as you can. Notes made on the scene are far better than later recollections. Write comments into your copy of *Tahiti-Polynesia Handbook* as you go along, then send us a summary when you get home. You can recycle travel brochures by sending them to us when you're done with them. If this book helped you, please help us make it even better. Address your letters to:

David Stanley
c/o Moon Publications Inc.
P.O. Box 3040,
Chico, CA 95927, U.S.A.
e-mail: travel@moon.com

THE LATEST TROUBLE IN PARADISE

In June 1995, French President Jacques Chirac ordered a resumption of underground nuclear testing at Moruroa Atoll in the Tuamotu Islands, 1,200 km southeast of Tahiti. Deadly radiation, the result of 175 nuclear explosions between 1966 and 1992, could already be leaking into the sea from dumps and cracks at the French facilities on Moruroa, and the leakage of radioactive materials up through the atoll's coral cap could eventually contaminate the Pacific Ocean.

Chirac ordered the resumption of testing without bothering to consult the Polynesians, and this unpredictable opportunist has a long history of using Pacific islanders as pawns in personal power games (for a more detailed account of the French imperialist tradition in Tahiti, see "The Rape of Polynesia" under "History" in the main Introduction, and "The Nuclear Test Zone" in the Tuamotu Islands chapter).

Chirac appears determined to proceed with this course of action despite strong objections from the international community and protest actions by the environmental organization Greenpeace.

The release of this book may coincide with the resumption of testing, and we leave it up to the individual reader to decide whether he or she cares to visit Tahiti at that time. If you do go, take the opportunity to ask the Tahitians what they think about all this.

ACKNOWLEDGMENTS

The nationalities of those listed below are identified by the letters which follow their names: AUS (Australia), CDN (Canada), D (Germany), F (France), FI (Fiji), GB (Great Britain), J (Japan), N (Norway), NL (Netherlands), NZ (New Zealand), TP (Tahiti-Polynesia), and USA (United States).

The antique engravings by M.G.L. Domeny de Rienzi are from the classic three-volume work *Oceanie ou Cinquième Partie du Monde* (Paris: Firmin Didot Frères, 1836).

Special thanks to Dr. Peter Bellwood of the Australian National University, Canberra, for pointing out inaccuracies in the archaeology and anthropology sections, to Norm Buske (USA) for information on the leakage of nuclear materials at Moruroa, to Anselm Zänkert (D) for a fascinating report on his trip to Mangareva, Steven Vete (FI), editor of *Pacific AIDS Alert*, for information on AIDS, to Tjalling Terpstra (NL) for help in updating Pacific air routes, to Udo Schwark (D) for arranging my latest research trip, to Bengt Danielsson (who arrived in Polynesia aboard Thor Heyerdahl's famous raft *Kon Tiki* in 1947) for correcting the entire manuscript, and to Ria de Vos (NL) for her continuing assistance, suggestions, and support.

Thanks too to the following readers who took the trouble to write us letters about their trips:

Krenne Aymans (D), Dr. Ross Barnard (AUS), Eric Beauchemin (NL), Joy Bloom (USA), Dr. K. Börger (D), Alexander K. Braden (GB), Andreas Busch (D), Emma Campbell (USA), Teri A. Cleeland (USA), Howard Conant (USA), Hanne Finholt (N), Hans S. Fletcher (USA), Frances Forbes (USA), Sherry Freeman (USA), Claudia Gacek (D), Siegfried Gebel (D), Vera Graf (USA), Lady Hermione Grimston (GB), Jackie Halter (USA), Sandy Harford (USA), Andrew Hempstead (AUS), Claus-Walter Herbertz (D), Ms. B. Hiscock (USA), Manfred Hoffmann (D), Martina Hütten (D), Anita Jackson (GB), L. Konecny (D), Petra Ledwoch (D), Georgia Lee (USA), Ward and Judy LeHardy (USA), Mike Long (USA), Allegra E. Marshall (AUS), Kevin McAuliffe (USA), Mathias Megyeri (D), Ewa Ochimowski (CDN), Will Paine (GB), Jeff Perk (USA), William J. Plumley (USA), Marlene Rain (USA), John Ray (GB), Holger Riess (D), Gerhard Ringer (D), Toru Sasaki (J), Greg Sawyer (USA), Burkhard Schultz (D), Dr. Werner Steinert (D), Douglas P. Stives (USA), Christine Tuttle (USA), and Elizabeth D. Whitbeck (USA).

All of their comments have been incorporated into the volume you're now holding. To have your own name included here next edition, write: David Stanley, c/o Moon Publications Inc., P.O. Box 3040, Chico, CA 95927-3040, U.S.A.

Attention Hotel Keepers,
Tour Operators, Divemasters:
The best way to keep your listing in *Tahiti-Polynesia Handbook* up to date is to send us current information about your business. If you don't agree with what we've written, please tell us why—there's never any charge or obligation for a listing. Thanks to the following island tourism workers and government officials who *did* write in:

Edwina Arnold (USA), Dr. Jean-François Baré (F), Donny Barnhardt (USA), Joanne Batty (USA), René Boehm (D), L. Bonno (TP), Sherrill L. Bounnell (USA), Christa Brantsch-Harness (USA), Marie-Isabelle Chan (TP), Anne and Michel Condesse (TP), Mary Ann Cook (USA), Mary T. Crowley (USA), Catherine Cuny (USA), Wendy Dell (CDN), Pierre Florentin (TP), Professor Francis Dubus (TP), Anne Fairlie (CDN), Taina Fehr (D), Valerie Gadway (USA), Bruno Gendron (TP), Bob Goddess (USA), Michael Ann Harvey (USA), Billy Hawkins (GB), Mary-Lou Hewett (AUS), Karen Jeffery (USA), Richard Johnson (USA), Debora Kimitete (TP), Elisabeth Lajtonyi (D), Evelyn League (USA), Yves Lefèvre (TP), Geneviève Lemaire (TP), April Lief (USA), Donna Oakley (USA), J.C. Perelli (TP), Andria Piekarz (USA), Karine Plouhinec (TP), Susan Reed (USA), Nicolas de Riviere (F), Philippe Robard (TP), Yves Roche (TP), Carl Roessler (USA), Joan A. Serra (USA), Tom Sheehan (USA), Diana Sikora (USA), Pascale Siu-Chow (USA), Andy Turpin (USA), Sandy Wand (USA), Katrina Wards (NZ), Jules C. Wong (USA), and Angélian Zéna (TP).

From the Author
While out researching my books I find it cheaper to pay my own way, and you can rest assured that nothing in this book is designed to repay freebies from hotels, restaurants, tour operators, or airlines. I prefer to arrive unexpected and uninvited, and to experience things as they really are. On the road I seldom identify myself to anyone. In a nutshell, the essential difference between this book and the myriad travel brochures free for the taking in airports and tourist offices around Tahiti-Polynesia is that this book represents travelers and the brochures represent the travel industry. The companies and organizations included herein are there for information purposes only, and a mention in no way implies an endorsement.

FOREWORD

"**A**ll my life I had longed to go to the South Seas. These very words had magic in them, conjuring up primordial memories of palms and coral reefs and sun-drenched sands, of fruits and flowering trees, of women warm in welcome, of peace and isolation, and of a shore where the struggle for existence is unknown."

Thus writes Cecil Lewis, an ordinary, average American, who before the second World War managed to realize his dream and consequently published an enthusiastic account of the happy months he spent in Tahiti and the other Society Islands.

The dream is not dead. But as most South Sea travelers today will sadly discover, the "native" villages they find along their crowded paths are often human zoos, where the athletic guitar players and graceful hula dancers are paid performers, professional natives so to say, with a bank account, a car, and a TV set at home.

So there is a general belief that there is nothing left of the "real" South Seas.

Fortunately, this is not altogether true. During the forty years I have lived in Tahiti, I have received a steady stream of visitors, who are all appalled by the traffic jams, concrete buildings, and frantic life in and around Papeete, and therefore eager to learn the exact location of the primitive, unspoiled island paradises they have been dreaming of, and which do exist in the remote archipelagoes of Tahiti-Polynesia, or French Polynesia, as the colony is officially named.

It has always surprised me that none of the previous guidebooks have supplied this badly needed information, and I am

GÖRAN BURANHULT

Bengt Danielsson

very happy to see that my friend David Stanley has at long last filled this gap and has thus taken a heavy burden off my shoulders. Fortunately, this does not mean, however, that there is nothing in this new-style up-to-date handbook about the central, more sophisticated islands, like Tahiti, Moorea, Raiatea, and Bora Bora.

Actually, this blend of old and new, Polynesian and European cultural elements found today in varying degrees in the majority of the 118 islands is as interesting and fascinating as the "pure" traditional lifestyle in the outer islands. Whereas few other travel guides take notice of these changes, the readers of this handbook will also find much information about all these social, economic, and political consequences due to the long exposure of a stone-age people with a simple subsistence economy and strong family and community solidarity to our Western type of individualistic and commercial civilization.

There are also pertinent notices about the regional differences in French Polynesia which, in fact, consists of five distinct archipelagoes, inhabited by native peoples speaking separate Polynesian tongues and having different cultural traditions.

The last but not the least important feature of this unique handbook is the complete, detailed, and accurate practical information it offers the user about where to stay and what to pay—as well as equally useful advice about how to avoid being overcharged for goods and services.

With sincere congratulations for your fortunate choice of handbook, I guarantee you a happy sojourn, wish you a warm welcome to my islands, and extend to you the traditional greeting, corresponding to a Hawaiian aloha, which in Tahitian is pronounced—

AROHA
Bengt Danielsson
Papehue, Tahiti

INTRODUCTION

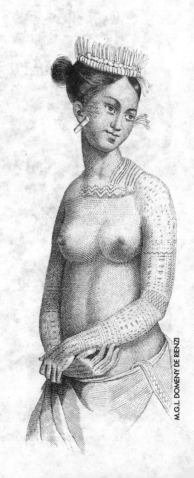

METRO GOLDWYN MAYER

Tarita co-starred with Marlon Brando in the 1962 MGM film Mutiny on the Bounty.

the Tahitian fleet preparing to attack Moorea, 1774 (after William Hodges)

INTRODUCTION

Legendary Tahiti, isle of love, has long been the vision of "la Nouvelle Cythère," the earthly paradise. Explorers Wallis, Bougainville, and Cook all told of a land of spellbinding beauty and enchantment, where the climate was delightful, hazardous insects and diseases unknown, and the islanders, especially the women, among the handsomest ever seen. Rousseau's "noble savage" had been found! A few years later, Fletcher Christian and Captain Bligh acted out their drama of sin and retribution here.

The list of famous authors who came and wrote about these islands reads like a high-school literature course: Herman Melville, Robert Louis Stevenson, Pierre Loti, Rupert Brooke, Jack London, W. Somerset Maugham, Charles Nordhoff and James Norman Hall (the Americans who wrote *Mutiny on the* Bounty), among others. Exotic images of uninhibited dancers, fragrant flowers, and pagan gods fill the pages. Here, at least, life was meant to be enjoyed.

The most unlikely PR man of them all was a once-obscure French painter named Paul Gauguin, who transformed the primitive color of Tahiti and the Marquesas into powerful visual images seen around the world. When WW II shook the Pacific from Pearl Harbor to Guadalcanal, rather than bloodcurdling banzais and saturation bombings, Polynesia got a U.S. serviceman named James A. Michener, who added Bora Bora to the legend. Marlon Brando arrived in 1961 on one of the first jets to land in Polynesia and, along with thousands of tourists and adventurers, has been coming back ever since.

The friendly, easygoing manner of the people of Tahiti-Polynesia isn't only a cliché! Tahiti gets just 140,000 tourists a year (compared to the seven million that visit Hawaii) and many are French nationals visiting friends, so you won't be facing a tourist glut! Despite over a century and a half of French colonialism, the Tahitians retain many of their old ways, be it in personal dress, Polynesian dancing, or outrigger canoe racing. Relax, smile, and say hello to strangers—you'll almost always get a warm response. Welcome to paradise!

THE LAND

Tahiti-Polynesia consists of five great archipelagos, the Society, Austral, Tuamotu, Gambier, and Marquesas islands. The Society Islands are subdivided into the Windwards or *Îles du Vent* (Tahiti, Moorea, Maiao, Tetiaroa, and Mehetia), and the Leewards or *Îles Sous le Vent* (Huahine, Raiatea, Tahaa, Bora Bora, Maupiti, Tupai, Maupihaa/Mopelia, Manuae/Scilly, and Motu One/Bellingshausen).

Together the 35 islands and 83 atolls of Tahiti-Polynesia total only 3,543 square km in land area, yet they're scattered over 5,030,000 square km of the southeastern Pacific Ocean, from the Cook Islands in the west to Pitcairn in the east. Though Tahiti-Polynesia is only half the size of Corsica in land area, if Papeete were Paris then the Gambiers would be in Romania and the Marquesas near Stockholm.

There's a wonderful geological diversity to these islands midway between Australia and South America—from the dramatic, jagged volcanic outlines of the Society and Marquesas islands, to the 400-meter-high hills of the Australs and Gambiers, to the low coral atolls of the Tuamotus. All of the Marquesas are volcanic islands, while the Tuamotus are all coral islands or atolls. The Societies and Gambiers include both volcanic and coral types.

Tahiti, just over 4,000 km from both Auckland and Honolulu, is not only the best known and most populous of the islands, but also the largest (1,045 square km) and highest (2,241 meters). Bora Bora and Maupiti are noted for their combination of high volcanic peaks within low coral rings. Rangiroa is one of the world's largest coral atolls while Makatea is an uplifted atoll. In the Marquesas, precipitous and sharply crenelated mountains rise hundreds of meters, with craggy peaks, razorback ridges, plummeting waterfalls, deep, fertile valleys, and dark broken coastlines pounded by surf. Compare them to the pencil-thin strips of yellow reefs, green vegetation, and white beaches enclosing the transparent Tuamotu lagoons. In all, Tahiti-Polynesia offers some of the most varied and spectacular scenery in the entire South Pacific.

POLYNESIA AT A GLANCE

	POPULATION (1988)	AREA (HECTARES)
WINDWARD ISLANDS	**140,341**	**118,580**
Tahiti	131,309	104,510
Moorea	8,801	12,520
LEEWARD ISLANDS	**22,232**	**38,750**
Huahine	4,479	7,480
Raiatea	8,560	17,140
Tahaa	4,005	9,020
Bora Bora	4,225	1,830
Maupiti	963	1,140
AUSTRAL ISLANDS	**6,509**	**14,784**
Rurutu	1,953	3,235
Tubuai	1,846	4,500
TUAMOTU ISLANDS	**11,754**	**72,646**
Rangiroa	1,305	7,900
Manihi	429	1,300
GAMBIER ISLANDS	**620**	**4,597**
MARQUESAS ISLANDS	**7,358**	**104,930**
Nuku Hiva	2,100	33,950
Hiva Oa	1,671	31,550
TAHITI-POLYNESIA	**188,814**	**354,287**

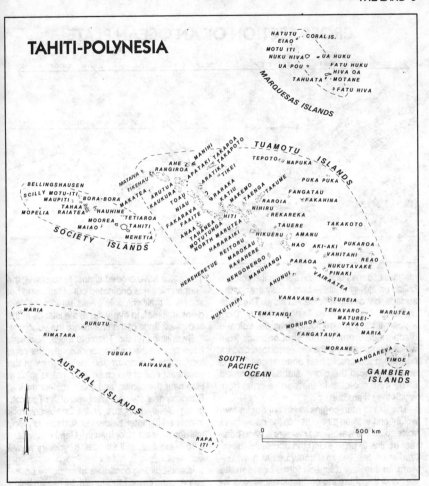

TAHITI-POLYNESIA

Darwin's Theory of Atoll Formation

The famous formulator of the theory of evolution surmised that atolls form as high volcanic islands subside into lagoons. The original island's fringing reef grows into a barrier reef as the volcanic portion sinks. When the last volcanic material finally disappears below sea level, the coral rim of the reef/atoll remains to indicate how big the island once was.

Of course, all this takes place over millions of years, but deep down below every atoll is the old volcanic core. Darwin's theory is well illus- trated at Bora Bora, where a high volcanic island remains inside the rim of Bora Bora's barrier reef; this island's volcanic core is still sinking imperceptibly at the rate of one cm a century. Return to Bora Bora in 25 million years and all you'll find will be a coral atoll like Rangiroa or Manihi.

Hot Spots

High or low, all of the islands have a volcanic origin best explained by the "Conveyor Belt Theory." A crack opens in the earth's mantle and volcanic

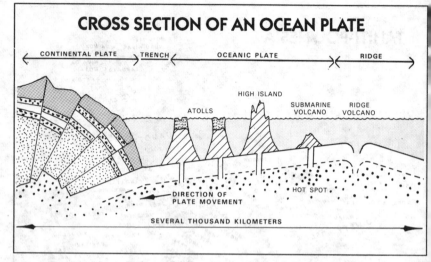

CROSS SECTION OF AN OCEAN PLATE

CONTINENTAL PLATE | TRENCH | OCEANIC PLATE | RIDGE

HIGH ISLAND

ATOLLS

SUBMARINE VOLCANO | RIDGE VOLCANO

DIRECTION OF PLATE MOVEMENT

HOT SPOT

SEVERAL THOUSAND KILOMETERS

magma escapes upward. A submarine volcano builds up slowly until the lava finally breaks the surface, becoming a volcanic island. The Pacific Plate moves northwest approximately 10 cm a year; thus, over geologic eons the volcano disconnects from the hot spot or crack from which it emerged. As the old volcanoes disconnect from the crack, new ones appear to the southeast, and the older islands are carried away from the cleft in the earth's crust from which they were born.

The island then begins to sink under its own weight and erosion also cuts into the now-extinct volcano. In the warm, clear waters a living coral reef begins to grow along the shore. As the island subsides, the reef continues to grow upward. In this way a lagoon forms between the reef and the shoreline of the slowly sinking island. This barrier reef marks the old margin of the original island.

As the hot spot shifts southeast in an opposite direction from the sliding Pacific Plate (and shifting magnetic pole of the earth), the process is repeated, time and again, until whole chains of islands ride the blue Pacific. Weathering is most advanced on the composite islands and atolls at the northwest ends of the Society, Austral, Tuamotu, and Marquesas chains. Maupiti and Bora Bora, with their exposed volcanic cores, are the oldest of the larger Society Islands. The

Tuamotus have eroded almost to sea level; the Gambier Islands originated out of the same hot spot and their volcanic peaks remain inside a giant atoll reef. In every case, the islands at the southeast ends of the chains are the youngest.

By drilling into the Tuamotu atolls, scientists have proven their point conclusively: the coral formations are about 350 meters thick at the southeast end of the chain, 600 meters thick at Hao near the center, and 1,000 meters thick at Rangiroa near the northwest end of the Tuamotu group. Clearly, Rangiroa, where the volcanic rock is now a kilometer below the surface, is many millions of years older than the Gambiers, where a volcanic peak still stands 482 meters above sea level.

Island-building continues at an active undersea volcano called MacDonald, 50 meters below sea level at the southeast end of the Australs. The crack spews forth about a cubic mile of lava every century and someday MacDonald too will poke its smoky head above the waves. The theories of plate tectonics, or the sliding crust of the earth, seem proven in Tahiti-Polynesia.

Life of an Atoll
A circular or horseshoe-shaped coral reef bearing a necklace of sandy, slender islets *(motus)* of debris thrown up by storms, surf, and wind is known as an atoll. Atolls can be up to 100 km

across, but the width of dry land is usually only 200-400 meters from inner to outer beach. The central lagoon can measure anywhere from 1-50 km in diameter; huge Rangiroa Atoll is 77 km long. Entirely landlocked lagoons are rare; passages through the barrier reef are usually found on the leeward side. Most atolls are no higher than four to six meters.

A raised or elevated atoll is one that has been pushed up by some trauma of nature to become a platform of coral rock rising up to 20 meters above sea level. Raised atolls are often known for their huge sea caves and steep oceanside cliffs. The only raised atoll in Tahiti-Polynesia is crescent-shaped Makatea in the northwestern corner of the Tuamotu group. It is 100 meters high, seven km long, and 4.5 km wide.

Where the volcanic island remains there's often a deep passage between the barrier reef and shore; the reef forms a natural breakwater, which shelters good anchorages. Australia's Great Barrier Reef is 1,600 km long and 25-44 km offshore. Soil derived from coral is extremely poor in nutrients, while volcanic soil is known for its fertility. Dark-colored beaches are formed from volcanic material; the white beaches of travel brochures are entirely coral-based. The black beaches are cooler and easier on the eyes, enabling plantlife to grow closer, providing patches of shade; the white beaches are generally safer for swimming, as visibility is better.

The Greenhouse Effect

The gravest danger facing the atolls of Oceania is the greenhouse effect, a gradual warming of earth's environment due to fossil fuel combustion and the widespread clearing of forests. By the year 2030 the concentration of carbon dioxide in the atmosphere will have doubled from preindustrial levels. As infrared radiation from the sun is absorbed by the gas, the trapped heat melts mountain glaciers and the polar ice caps. In addition, seawater expands as it warms up and water levels could rise almost a meter by the year 2100, destroying shorelines created 5,000 years ago.

A 1982 study demonstrated that sea levels had already risen 12 cm in the previous century; in 1993 the United Nations Environment Program predicted a further rise of 20 cm by the year 2030 and 65 cm by the end of the next century. Not only will this reduce the growing area for food crops, but rising sea levels will mean saltwater intrusion into groundwater supplies—a horrifying prospect if accompanied by the droughts that have been predicted. In time entire populations could be forced to evacuate and eventually whole archipelagos like the Tuamotus may be flooded. And if that's not enough, increasing temperatures may already be contributing to the dramatic jump in the number of hurricanes in the eastern South Pacific. Cases of coral bleaching and reefs being killed by rising sea temperatures have been confirmed. (Coral bleaching occurs when an organism's symbiotic algae are expelled in response to environmental stresses, such as changes in water temperature.)

As storm waves wash across the low-lying atolls, eating away the precious land, the entire populations of archipelagos such as the Tuamotus may be forced to evacuate long before they're actually flooded. The construction of seawalls to keep out the rising seas would be prohibitively expensive.

Unfortunately, those most responsible for the problem, the industrialized countries led by the United States, have strongly resisted taking any action to significantly cut greenhouse gas emissions. And as if that weren't bad enough, the hydrofluorocarbons (HFCs) presently being developed by corporate giants like Dupont to replace the ozone-destructive chlorofluorocarbons (CFCs) presently used in cooling systems are far more potent greenhouse gasses than carbon dioxide. This is only one of many similar consumption-related problems, and it seems as if one section of humanity is hurtling down a suicidal slope, unable to resist the momentum, as the rest of our race watches the catastrophe approach in helpless horror. It will cost a lot to rewrite our collective ticket but there may not be any choice.

CORAL REEFS

To understand how a basalt volcano becomes a limestone atoll, it's necessary to know a little about the growth of coral. Coral reefs cover some 200,000 square km worldwide, between 35°

north and 32° south latitude. A reef is created by the accumulation of millions of tiny calcareous skeletons left by myriad generations of tiny coral polyps. Though the skeleton is usually white, the living polyps are of many different colors.

The polyps thrive in clear salty water where the temperature never drops below 18°C. They must also have a base not over 50 meters below the water's surface on which to form coral. The coral colony grows slowly upward on the consolidated skeletons of its ancestors until it reaches the low-tide mark, after which development extends outward on the edges of the reef. Sunlight is critical for coral growth. Colonies grow quickly on the ocean side due to clearer water and a greater abundance of food. A strong, healthy reef can grow four to five cm a year. Fresh or cloudy water inhibits coral growth, which is why villages and ports all across the Pacific are located at the reef-free mouths of rivers.

Polyps extract calcium carbonate from the water and deposit it in their skeletons. All reef-building corals also contain limy encrustations of microscopic algae within their cells. The algae, like all green plants, obtain their energy from the sun and contribute this energy to the growth of the reef's skeleton. As a result, corals behave (and look) more like plants than animals, competing for sunlight just as terrestrial plants do. Many polyps are also carnivorous; with minute stinging tentacles they supplement their energy by capturing tiny planktonic animals and organic particles at night. A small piece of coral is a colony composed of large numbers of polyps.

Coral Types

Corals belong to a broad group of stinging creatures, which includes polyps, soft corals, stony corals, sea anemones, sea fans, and jellyfish. Only those types with hard skeletons and a single hollow cavity within the body are considered true corals. Stony corals such as brain, table, staghorn, and mushroom corals have external skeletons and are important reef builders. Soft corals, black corals, and sea fans have internal skeletons. The fire corals are recognized by their smooth, velvety surface and yellowish brown color. The stinging toxins of this last group can easily penetrate human skin and cause swelling and painful burning that can last

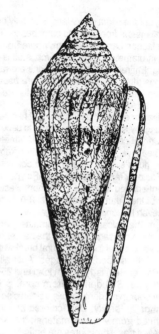

Fewer than 200 specimens of the rare glory-of-the-sea cone (Conus gloriamaris) are known. Some species of cone shells have a deadly stinging dart that can reach anywhere on the shell's outer surface, so never pick one up.

up to an hour. The many varieties of soft, colorful anemones gently waving in the current might seem inviting to touch, but beware: many are also poisonous.

The corals, like most other forms of life in the Pacific, colonized the ocean from the fertile seas of Southeast Asia. Thus the number of species declines as you move east. Over 600 species of coral make their home in the Pacific, compared to only 48 in the Caribbean. The diversity of coral colors and forms is endlessly amazing. This is our most unspoiled environment, a world of almost indescribable beauty.

Exploring a Reef

Until you've explored a good coral reef, you haven't experienced one of the greatest joys of nature. While you cannot walk through pristine forests due to the lack of paths, it's quite possible to swim over untouched reefs—the most densely populated living space on earth. Dive shops throughout the region rent or sell snorkeling gear, so do get into the clear, warm waters around you. Be careful, however, and know the dangers. Practice snorkeling in the shallow water; don't head into deep water until you're sure you've got the hang of it. Breathe easily; don't hyperventilate.

When snorkeling on a fringing reef, beware of deadly currents and undertows in channels that drain tidal flows. Observe the direction the water is flowing before you swim into it. If you feel yourself being dragged out to sea through a reef passage, try swimming across the current rather than against it. If you can't resist the pull at all, it may be better to let yourself be carried out. Wait till the current diminishes, then swim along the outer reef face until you find somewhere to come back in. Or use your energy to attract the attention of someone onshore.

Snorkeling on the outer edge or drop-off of a reef is thrilling for the variety of fish and corals, but attempt it only on a very calm day. Even then it's best to have someone stand onshore or on the edge of the reef (at low tide) to watch for occasional big waves, which can take you by surprise and smash you into the rocks. Also,

beware of unperceived currents outside the reef—you may not get a second chance.

A far better idea is to limit your snorkeling to the protected inner reef and leave the open waters to the scuba diver. Commercial scuba operators know their waters and will be able to show you the most amazing things in perfect safety. Dive centers are operating on Tahiti, Moorea, Tetiaroa, Huahine, Raiatea, Bora Bora, Rangiroa, Manihi, and Tikehau. Rangiroa and Tikehau offer the best diving, followed by Bora Bora and Moorea. Dive centers at all the main resorts operate year-round, with marinelife most profuse July to November.

If you wish to scuba dive you'll have to show your scuba certification card, and occasionally divers are also asked to show a medical report from their doctor indicating that they are in good physical condition. Serious divers will bring along their own mask, buoyancy compensator, and regulator. Many of the scuba operators listed in this book offer introductory "resort courses" for those who want only a taste of scuba diving, and full CMAS, NAUI, or PADI certification courses for those wishing to dive more than once or twice. The main constraint is financial: snorkeling is free, while scuba diving varies from CFP 4500-7500 a dive.

Conservation

Coral reefs are one of the most fragile and complex ecosystems on earth, providing food and shelter for countless species of fish, crustaceans (shrimps, crabs, and lobsters), mollusks (shells), and other animals. The coral reefs of the South Pacific protect shorelines during storms, supply sand to maintain the islands, furnish food for the local population, form a living laboratory for science, and are major tourist attractions. Without coral, the South Pacific would be immeasurably poorer.

Hard corals grow only about 10 to 25 mm a year and it can take 7,000-10,000 years for a coral reef to form. Though corals look solid they're easily broken; by standing on them, breaking off pieces, or carelessly dropping anchor you can destroy in a few minutes what took so long to form. Once a piece of coral breaks off it dies, and it may be years before the coral reestablishes itself and even longer before the broken piece is replaced. The "wound" may become infected by algae which can multiply and kill the entire coral colony. When this happens over a wide area the diversity of marinelife declines dramatically.

We recommend that you not remove seashells, coral, plantlife, or marine animals from the sea. In a small way, you are upsetting the delicate balance of nature, and coral is much more beautiful underwater anyway! This is a particular problem along shorelines frequented by large numbers of tourists, who can completely strip a reef in very little time. If you'd like a souvenir, content yourself with what you find on the beach (though even a seemingly empty shell may be inhabited by a hermit crab). Also think twice about purchasing jewelry or souvenirs made from coral or seashells. Genuine traditional handicrafts that incorporate shells are one thing, but by purchasing unmounted seashells or mass-produced coral curios you are contributing to the destruction of the marine environment.

The anchors and anchor chains of private yachts can do serious damage to coral reefs. Pronged anchors are more environmentally friendly than larger, heavier anchors, and plastic tubing over the end of the anchor chain helps minimize damage. If at all possible, anchor in sand. A longer anchor chain makes this easier and a good windlass is essential for larger boats. A recording depth sounder will help locate sandy areas when none are available in shallow water. If you don't have a depth sounder and can't see the bottom, lower the anchor until it just touches the bottom and feel the anchor line as the boat drifts. If it "grumbles" lift it up, drift a little, and try again. Later, if you notice your chain grumbling, motor over the anchor, lift it out of the coral and move. Not only do sand and mud hold better, but your anchor will be less likely to become fouled. Try to arrive before 1500 to be able to see clearly where you're anchoring—Polaroid sunglasses make it easier to distinguish corals.

There's an urgent need for stricter government regulation of the marine environment, and in some places coral reefs are already protected. Exhortations such as the one above have only limited impact—legislators must write stricter laws and impose fines. Resort developers can minimize damage to their valuable reefs

PAPEETE'S CLIMATE

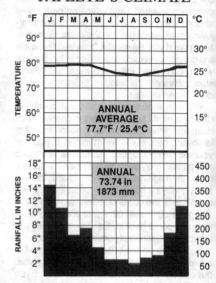

ATUONA'S CLIMATE

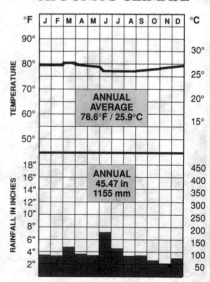

by providing public mooring buoys so yachts don't have to drop anchor and pontoons so snorkelers aren't tempted to stand on coral. Licensing authorities can make such amenities mandatory whenever appropriate, and in extreme cases, especially endangered coral gardens should be declared off limits to private boats. As consumerism spreads, once-remote areas become subject to the problems of pollution and overexploitation: the garbage is visibly piling up on many shores. As a visitor, don't hesitate to practice your conservationist attitudes, and leave a clean wake.

CLIMATE

The hot and humid summer season runs from November to April. The rest of the year the climate is somewhat cooler and drier. The refreshing southeast trade winds blow consistently from May to August, varying to easterlies from September to December. The northeast trades from January to April coincide with the hurricane season.

The trade winds are caused by hot air rising near the equator, which then flows toward the poles at high altitude. Cooler air drawn toward the vacuum is deflected to the west by the rotation of the earth. Tahiti-Polynesia's proximity to the intertropical convergence zone (5° north and south of the equator), or "doldrum zone"—where the most heated air is rising—explains the seasonal shift in the winds from northeast to southeast. The trade winds cool the islands and offer clear sailing for mariners, making May to October the most favorable season to visit.

Hurricanes are relatively rare, although they do hit the Tuamotus and occasionally Tahiti. From November 1980 to May 1983 an unusual wave of eight hurricanes and two tropical storms battered the islands. A hurricane would merely inconvenience a visitor staying at a hotel, though campers and yachties might get blown into oblivion. The days immediately following a hurricane are clear and dry. Tahiti-Polynesia enjoys some of the cleanest air on earth—air that hasn't blown over a continent for weeks.

a waterspout during a tropical cyclone or hurricane

M.G.L. DOMENY DE RIENZI

Rainfall is greatest in the mountains and along the windward shores of the high islands. The Societies are far damper than the Marquesas. In fact, the climate of the Marquesas is erratic: some years the group experiences serious drought, other years it could rain the whole time you're there. The low-lying Tuamotus get the least rainfall of all. Tahiti-Polynesia encompasses such a vast area that latitude is an important factor: at 27° south latitude Rapa Iti is far cooler than Nuku Hiva (9° south).

Winds from the southeast *(maramu)* are generally drier than those from the northeast or north. The northeast winds often bring rain: Papenoo on the northeast side of Tahiti is twice as wet as rain-shadowed Punaauia. The annual rainfall is extremely variable, but the humidity is generally high, reaching 98%. In the evening the heat of the Tahiti afternoons is replaced by soft, fragrant mountain breezes called *hupe,* which drift down to the sea.

FLORA AND FAUNA

FLORA

The variety of floral species encountered in the Pacific islands declines as you move away from the Asian mainland. Although some species may have spread across the islands by means of floating seeds or fruit, wind and birds were probably more effective. The microscopic spores of ferns, for example, can be carried vast distances by the wind. In the coastal areas of Tahiti most of the plants now seen have been introduced by humans.

Here in Polynesia the air is sweet with the bouquet of tropical blossoms such as bursting bougainvillea, camellia, frangipani, ginger, orchids, poinsettia, and pitate jasmine. The fragrant flowers of the Polynesian hibiscus *(purau)* are yellow, not red or pink as on the Chinese hibiscus. A useful tree, the hibiscus has a soft wood used for house and canoe construction, and bast fiber used to make cordage and mats. The national flower, the delicate, heavy-scented *tiare Tahiti (Gardenia tahitiensis),* can have anywhere from six to nine white petals. It blooms year-round, but especially from September to April. In his *Plants and Flowers of Tahiti* Jean-Claude Belhay writes: "The tiare is to Polynesia what the lotus is to India: a veritable symbol." Follow local custom by wearing this blossom or a hibiscus behind your left ear if you're happily taken, behind your right ear if you're still available.

Tahiti-Polynesia's high islands support a great variety of plantlife, while the low islands are restricted to a few hardy, drought-resistant species such as coconuts and pandanus. On the atolls, taro, a root vegetable with broad heart-shaped leaves, must be cultivated in deep organic pits. Rainforests fill the valleys and damp windward slopes of the high islands, while brush and thickets grow in more exposed locations. *Mape* (Tahitian chestnut) grows along the streams. Other trees you'll encounter include almond, candlenut, casuarina (ironwood), flamboyant, barringtonia, *purau* (wild hibiscus), pistachio, and rosewood. Mountain bananas *(fei)* grow wild in the high country. Along the coast fruits such as avocado, banana, custard apple, guava, grapefruit, lime, lychee, mango, orange, papaya, pineapple, watermelon, and a hundred more are cultivated.

Mangroves can occasionally be found along some high island coastal lagoons. The cable roots of the saltwater-tolerant red mangrove anchor in the shallow upper layer of oxygenated mud, avoiding the layers of hydrogen sulfide below. The tree provides shade for tiny organisms dwelling in the tidal mudflats—a place for birds to nest and for fish or shellfish to feed and spawn. The mangroves also perform the same task as land-building coral colonies along the reefs. As sediments are trapped between the roots, the trees extend farther into the lagoon, creating a unique natural environment. The past decade has seen widespread destruction of the mangroves.

MARINELIFE

The South Pacific's richest store of life is found in the silent underwater world of the pelagic and lagoon fishes. Coral pinnacles on the lagoon floor provide a safe haven for angelfish, butterfly fish, damselfish, groupers, soldierfish, surgeonfish, triggerfish, trumpet fish, and countless more. These fish seldom venture more than a few meters away from the protective coral, but larger fish such as barracuda, jackfish, parrot fish, pike, stingrays, and small sharks range across lagoon waters which are seldom deeper than 30 meters. The external side of the reef is also home to many of the above, but the open ocean is reserved for bonito, mahimahi, swordfish, tuna, wrasses, and the larger sharks. Passes between ocean and lagoon can be crowded with fish in transit, offering a favorite hunting ground for predators.

In the open sea the food chain begins with phytoplankton, which flourish wherever ocean upwellings bring nutrients such as nitrates and phosphates to the surface. In the western Pacific this occurs near the equator, where massive currents draw water away toward Japan and Australia. Large schools of fast-moving tuna ply these waters feeding on smaller fish, which consume tiny phytoplankton drifting near the sunlit surface. The phytoplankton also exist in tropical lagoons where mangrove leaves, sea grasses, and other plant material are consumed by far more varied populations of reef fish, mollusks (clams, octopuses, and trochi), and crustaceans (crabs, lobsters, and prawns).

It's believed that most Pacific marine organisms evolved in the triangular area bounded by New Guinea, the Philippines, and the Malay Peninsula. This "Cradle of Indo-Pacific Marine-life" includes a wide variety of habitats and has remained stable through several geological ages. From this cradle the rest of the Pacific was colonized.

Dolphins

While most people use the terms dolphin and porpoise interchangeably, a porpoise lacks the dolphin's beak (although many dolphins are also beakless). There are 62 species of dolphins, and only six species of porpoises. Dolphins leap from the water and many legends tell of their saving humans, especially children, from drowning (the most famous concerns Telemachus, son of Odysseus). Dolphins often try to race in front of ferries and large ships.

Sharks

The danger from sharks has been greatly exaggerated. Of some 300 different species, only 28 are known to have attacked humans. Most dangerous are the white, tiger, hammerhead, and blue sharks. Fortunately, all these inhabit deep water far from the coasts. An average of only 50 shark attacks a year occur worldwide, so considering the number of people who swim in the sea, your chances of being involved are pretty slim. In Tahiti-Polynesia shark attacks are extremely rare.

Sharks are not aggressive where food is abundant, but they can be very nasty far offshore. You're always safer if you keep your head underwater (with a mask and snorkel), and don't panic if you see a shark—you might attract it. Even if you do, they're usually only curious, so keep your eye on the shark and slowly back off. The swimming techniques of humans must seem very clumsy to fish, so it's not surprising if they want a closer look.

Sharks are attracted by shiny objects (a knife or jewelry), bright colors (especially yellow and red), urine, spearfishing, blood, and splashing (divers should ease themselves into the water). Sharks normally stay outside the reef, but ask local advice. White beaches are safer than dark, and clear water safer than murky. Avoid swimming in places where sewage or edible wastes enter the water, or where fish have just been cleaned. You should also exercise care in places where local residents have been fishing with spears or even hook and line that day.

Never swim alone if you suspect the presence of sharks. If you see one, even a supposedly harmless nurse shark lying on the bottom, get out of the water calmly and quickly, and go elsewhere. Recent studies indicate that sharks, like most other creatures, have a "personal space" around them which they will defend. Thus an attack could be a shark's way of warning someone to keep his/her distance and it's a fact that over half the victims of these incidents are not eaten, but merely wounded. Sharks are much less of a problem in the South Pacific than in colder waters because marine mammals (commonly hunted by sharks) are rare here, so you won't be mistaken for an otter or seal.

Let common sense be your guide, not blind fear or carelessness. Many scuba divers come actually *looking* for sharks, and local divemasters seem able to swim among them with impunity. If you're in the market for some shark action, many

The sea urchin feeds on seaweed and uses tubular feet on its underside for locomotion. The long protective spines do not always protect it from hungry snails and fish.

LOUISE FOOTE

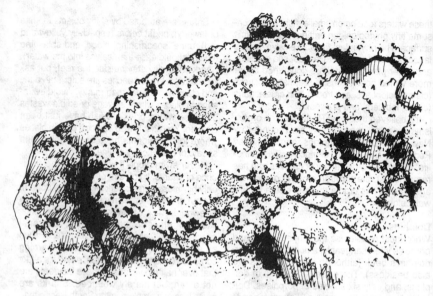

The highly camouflaged stonefish (Synanceia verrucosa) rests on reef flats waiting for the chance to strike small fish. The deadly venom in the stonefish's dorsal fin causes excruciating pain and even death to anyone who happens to step on one.

dive shops can provide it. Just be aware that getting into the water with feeding sharks always entails some danger, and a divemaster who admits this and lays down some basic safety guidelines (such as keeping your hands clasped or arms folded) is probably a safer bet than the guy who simply says he's been doing it for years without incident. Like all other wild animals, sharks deserve to be approached with respect.

Sea Urchins

Sea urchins (living pincushions) are common in tropical waters. The black variety is the most dangerous: their long, sharp quills can go right through a snorkeler's fins. Even the small ones, which you can easily pick up in your hand, can pinch you if you're careless. They're found on rocky shores and reefs, never on clear, sandy beaches where the surf rolls in.

Most sea urchins are not poisonous, though quill punctures are painful and can become infected if not treated. The pain is caused by an injected protein, which you can eliminate by holding the injured area in a pail of very hot water for about 15 minutes. This will coagulate the protein, eliminating the pain for good. If you can't heat water, soak the area in vinegar or urine for a quarter hour. Remove the quills if possible, but being made of calcium, they'll decompose in a couple of weeks anyway—not much of a consolation as you limp along in the meantime. In some places sea urchins are a favorite delicacy: the orange or yellow urchin gonads are delicious with lemon and salt.

Others

Although jellyfish, stonefish, crown-of-thorns starfish, cone shells, eels, and poisonous sea snakes are hazardous, injuries resulting from any of these are rare. Gently apply methylated spirit, alcohol, or urine (but not water, kerosene, or gasoline) to areas stung by jellyfish. Harmless sea cucumbers (bêche-de-mer) punctuate the lagoon shallows. Stonefish also rest on the bottom and are hard to see due to camouflaging; if you happen to step on one, its dorsal fins inject a painful poison, which burns like fire in the blood. Treat the wound by holding it, along with an opposite foot or hand, in water as hot as you can stand for 30 minutes (the opposite extremity prevents scalding due to numbness). If a hospital or clinic is nearby, go there immediately. Fortunately, stonefish are not common.

Never pick up a live cone shell; some varieties have a deadly stinger dart coming out of the pointed end. The tiny blue-ring octopus is only five cm long but packs a poison that can kill a human. Eels hide in reef crevices by day; most are dangerous only if you inadvertently poke your hand or foot in at them. Of course, never tempt fate by approaching them (fun-loving divemasters sometimes feed the big ones by hand and stroke their backs).

REPTILES

Five of the seven species of sea turtle are present in Polynesia (the green, hawksbill, leatherback, loggerhead, and olive ridley turtles). These magnificent creatures are sometimes erroneously referred to as "tortoises," a land turtle. All species of sea turtle now face extinction due to overhunting and egg harvesting. Turtles are often choked by floating plastic bags they mistake for food, or they drown in fishing nets. Sea turtles come ashore to lay their eggs on the beach from which they themselves originally hatched from November to February, but female turtles don't commence this activity until they are 20 years old. Thus a drop in numbers today has irreversible consequences a generation later and it's estimated that breeding females already number in the hundreds or low thousands. Importing any sea turtle product is now prohibited in most developed countries, but protection is often inadequate in the South Pacific countries themselves. In Tahiti-Polynesia it's prohibited to capture sea turtles on land in November and at sea from June to January.

Geckos and skinks are small lizards often seen on the islands. The skink hunts insects by day; its tail breaks off if you catch it, but a new one quickly grows. The gecko is nocturnal and has no eyelids. Adhesive toe pads enable it to pass along vertical surfaces, and it changes color to avoid detection. Unlike the skink, which avoids humans, geckos often live in people's homes where they eat insects attracted by electric lights. Its loud ticking call may be a territorial warning to other geckos.

Tahiti-Polynesia has no land snakes and the sea snakes are shy and inoffensive. This, and the lack of leeches, poisonous plants, and dangerous wild animals, makes the South Pacific a paradise for hikers. Centipedes exist, but their bite, though painful, is not lethal. The main terrestrial hazards are dogs and mosquitoes.

LAND-BASED FAUNA

Island birdlife is more abundant than other land-based fauna, but still reflects the decline in variety from west to east. Of the 90 species of birds in Tahiti-Polynesia, 59 are found in the Society Islands, of which 33 are native.

The giant African snail (Achatina fulica). *Each individual has both male and female organs and can lay up to 500 eggs at a time. This scavenger is considered an agricultural pest and possible carrier of disease. Rats and coconut crabs help control their numbers.*

Among the seabirds are the white-tailed tropic birds, brown and black noddies, white and crested terns, petrels, and boobies. The *itatae* (white tern), often seen flying about with its mate far from land, lays a single egg in the fork of a tree without any nest. The baby terns can fly soon after hatching. Its call is a sharp ke-ke-yek-yek. The *oio* (black noddy) nests in colonies, preferably in palm trees, building a flat nest of dead leaves, sticks, and stems. It calls a deep cra-cra-cra. The hopping Indian mynah bird *(Acridotheres tristis)* with its yellow beak and feet was introduced from Indonesia at the turn of the century to control insects. Today these noisy, aggressive birds are ubiquitous feeding on fruit trees and forcing the native finches and blue-tinged doves out of their habitat.

The Polynesians brought with them chickens, dogs, pigs, and rats. Captain Cook introduced cattle, horses, and goats; Captain Wallis left behind cats. Whalers dropped more goats off in the Marquesas. Giant African snails *(Achatina fulica)* were brought to Tahiti from Hawaii in the 1960s by a local policeman fond of fancy French food. He tried to set up a snail farm with the result that some escaped, multiplied, and now crawl wild, destroying the vegetation. Dogs and roosters add to the sounds of the night.

(top) the beach near Club Med, Moorea (Don Pitcher)
(bottom) a peak on Moorea (Tahiti Tourisme)

(top) Mouaroa or "Shark's Tooth," Moorea (Paul Bohler)
(bottom) Papeete skyline with Mount Aorai, Tahiti (David Stanley)

the double-hulled sailing canoe, Hokule'a

HISTORY

THE POLYNESIANS

Discovery and Settlement

Three thousand five hundred years ago the early Polynesians set out from Southeast Asia on a migratory trek which would lead them to make the "many islands" of Polynesia their home. Great voyagers, they sailed their huge double-hulled canoes far and wide, steering with huge paddles and pandanus sails. They navigated by the sun, stars, currents, swells, winds, clouds, and birds. The first Polynesian islands settled were Tonga and Samoa; the oldest known dwelling site on Tongatapu dates from 1200 B.C. Around the time of Christ they pushed out into the eastern half of the Pacific from this primeval area remembered as Havaiki.

The eastern Polynesian islands, including those of Tahiti-Polynesia, were colonized at uncertain dates during the 1st millennium A.D. It's thought that about A.D. 300 the Polynesians reached the Marquesas from Samoa, and sometime around A.D. 500 they sailed on from the Marquesas to Hawaii and Easter Island. They were on the Society Islands by 800 and sailed from there to the Cooks and New Zealand around 1000, completing the occupation of the Polynesian triangle. These were planned voyages of colonization carrying all the plants and animals needed to continue their way of life.

To show how it was done, a group of Hawaiians led by American anthropologist Ben Finney sailed the recreated canoe *Hokule'a* from Hawaii to Tahiti and back in 1976 and 1980, without modern navigational instruments. Since then the *Hokule'a* has returned to Tahiti several times, most recently in March 1995 when master navigator Nainoa Thompson led a three-canoe flotilla from Hawaii to Tahiti by traditional means.

Early Culture

The Polynesians lived from fishing and agriculture, using tools made from stone, bone, shell, and wood. The men were responsible for planting, harvesting, fishing, cooking, and house and canoe building; the women tended the fields and animals, gathered food and fuel, prepared food, and made tapa clothes and household items. Both men and women worked together in family or community groups, not as individuals.

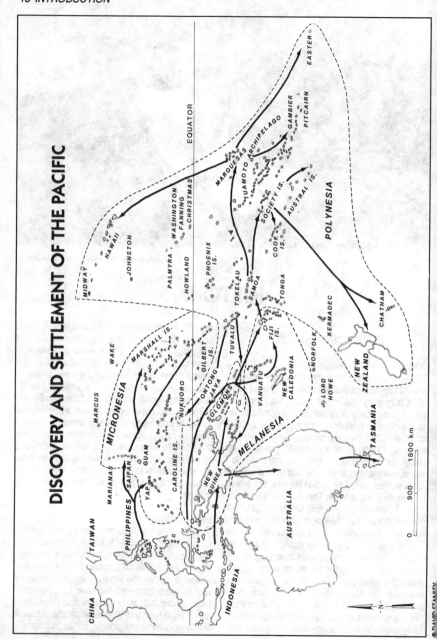

DISCOVERY AND SETTLEMENT OF THE PACIFIC

a chief mourner before a cadaver, 1773 (after William Hodges)

The Polynesians lost the art of pottery making during their long stay in Havaiki (possibly Samoa) and had to cook their food in underground ovens *(umu)*. It was sometimes *tapu* for men and women to eat together. Breadfruit, taro, yams, sweet potatoes, bananas, and coconuts were cultivated. Pigs, chickens, and dogs were also kept for food, but the surrounding sea yielded the most important source of protein.

Numerous taboos regulated Polynesian life, such as prohibitions against taking certain plants or fish that were intended for chiefly use. Land was collectively owned by families and tribes, and there were nobles and commoners. Though the land was worked collectively by commoners, the chiefly families controlled and distributed its produce by well-defined customs. Large numbers of people could be mobilized for public works or war.

Canoes were made of planks stitched together with sennit and caulked with gum from breadfruit trees. Clothing consisted of tapa (bark cloth). Both men and women wore belts of pandanus leaves or tapa when at work, and during leisure a skirt that reached to their knees. Ornaments were of feathers, whale or dolphin

teeth, and flowers. Both sexes were artfully tattooed using candlenut oil and soot.

For weapons there were clubs, spears, and slings. Archery was practiced only as a game to determine who could shoot farthest. Spear throwing, wrestling, boxing, kite flying, surfing, and canoe racing were popular sports. Polynesian music was made with nasal flutes and cylindrical sharkskin or hollow slit drums. Their dancing is still appreciated today.

The museums of the world possess many fine stone and wood tikis in human form from the Marquesas Islands, where the decorative sense was highly developed. Sculpture in the Australs was more naturalistic, and only here were female tikis common. The Tahitians showed less interest in the plastic arts but excelled in the social arts of poetry, oratory, theater, music, song, and dance. Life on the Tuamotus was a struggle for existence, and objects had utilitarian functions. Countless Polynesian cult objects were destroyed in the early 19th century by overzealous missionaries.

Prior to European contact three hereditary classes structured the Society Islands: high chiefs *(ari'i)*, lesser chiefs *(raatira)*, and commoners *(man-*

TAHITI-POLYNESIA CHRONOLOGY

A.D. 300: Polynesians reach the Marquesas

A.D. 800: Polynesians reach the Society Islands

1521: Magellan sights Pukapuka in the Tuamotus

1595: the Spaniard Mendaña contacts the Marquesas

1722: Dutchman Roggeveen sights Bora Bora

1767: Englishman Samuel Wallis contacts Tahiti

1768: Frenchman Bougainville visits Tahiti

1769: Captain Cook observes transit of Venus at Tahiti

1774: Spanish priests spend one year on Tahiti

1788: visit of Bligh's HMS *Bounty*

1797: arrival of the first Protestant missionaries

1803: Pomare II flees to Moorea

1812: Pomare's subjects convert to Protestantism

1827: 50-year reign of Queen Pomare IV begins

1834: French Catholic missionaries arrive at Mangareva

1836: French Catholic priests are expelled from Tahiti

1838: French gunboat demands compensation

1842: French protectorate is declared over Tahiti and Marquesas

1842: Herman Melville visits Tahiti-Polynesia

1843: founding of Papeete

1844: Mormon missionaries arrive on Tubuai, Austral Islands

1844-1847: Tahitian War of Independence

1847: Queen Pomare accepts French protectorate

1880: protectorate changes into a colony

1884: great fire burns most of Papeete

1887: France annexes the Leeward Islands

1888: Robert Louis Stevenson visits Tahiti

1891: Paul Gauguin arrives at Tahiti

1903: Paul Gauguin dies on Hiva Oa, Marquesas Islands

1914: German cruisers shell Papeete

1918: influenza epidemic kills 20% of population

1942: American military base is established on Bora Bora

1945: Tahitians become French citizens

1958: Pouvanaa a Oopa is arrested

1958: Tahiti-Polynesia becomes an overseas territory

1961: opening of Faa'a Airport

1962: French halt nuclear testing in Algeria

1963: French nuclear testing moves to Polynesia

1966: first atmospheric nuclear explosion in the Tuamotus

1974: nuclear testing moves underground

1977: Tahiti-Polynesia is granted partial internal autonomy

1984: internal autonomy increases slightly

1987: Université française du Pacifique is established

1992: President Mitterrand suspends nuclear testing

1995: President Chirac restarts nuclear testing

---

ahune). A small slave class *(titi)* also existed. The various *ari'i* tribes controlled wedge-shaped valleys, and their authority was balanced. None managed to gain permanent supremacy over the rest.

Two related forces governed Polynesian life: *mana* and *tapu. Mana* was a spiritual power of which the gods and high chiefs had the most and the commoners the least. In this rigid hierarchical system marriage or even physical contact between persons of unequal *mana* was forbidden. Children resulting from sexual relations between the classes were killed. Our word "taboo" originated from the Polynesian *tapu.* Early missionaries would often publicly violate the taboos and smash the images of the gods to show that their *mana* had vanished.

Religion centered around an open-air temple, called a *marae,* with a stone altar. Here priests prayed to the ancestors or gods and conducted all the significant ceremonies of Polynesian life. An individual's social position was determined by his or her family connections,

a tattooed Marquesan woman from Dumont d'Urville's Voyage au Sud Pole *(1846)*

Archaeology

The first archaeological survey of Tahiti-Polynesia was undertaken in 1925 by Prof. Kenneth P. Emory of Honolulu's Bernice P. Bishop Museum. Emory's successor, Prof. Yosihiko Sinoto of the same museum, has carried out extensive excavations and restorations in the area since 1960. In 1962, at a 9th-century graveyard on Maupiti's Motu Paeao, Emory and Sinoto uncovered artifacts perfectly matching those of the first New Zealand Maoris. A few years later, at Ua Huka in the Marquesas, Sinoto discovered a coastal village site dating from A.D. 300, the oldest yet found in Eastern Polynesia. Sinoto was responsible for the restoration of the Maeva *marae* on Huahine and many historical *marae* on Tahiti, Moorea, Raiatea, and Bora Bora. During construction of the Bali Hai Hôtel on Huahine in 1973-77 Sinoto's student diggers located 10 flat hand clubs of the *patu* model, previously thought to exist only in New Zealand, plus some planks of a 1,000-year-old sewn double canoe.

and the recitation of one's genealogy confirmed it. Human sacrifices took place on important occasions on a high chief's *marae*. Cannibalism was rife in the Marquesas, and was also practiced in the Tuamotus.

Members of the Raiatea-based Arioi Society traveled through the islands performing ritual copulation and religious rites. The fertility god Oro had descended on a rainbow to Bora Bora's Mount Pahia, where he found a beautiful *vahine*. Their child was the first Arioi. In their pursuit of absolute *free* love, the Arioi killed their own children and shared spouses.

But the Arioi were not the only practitioners of infanticide in Tahiti-Polynesia. The whole social structure could be threatened by a surplus of children among the chiefly class. Such children might demand arable land from commoners who supplied the chiefs with food and a struggle between too many potential heirs could create strife. Thus the *ari'i* often did away with unwanted infants after birth (rather than before birth as is the accepted practice today). The Arioi Society itself may have been a partial solution as unwanted *ari'i* children were assigned a benign role as Arioi with the assurance that they themselves would never produce any offspring.

EUROPEAN CONTACT

European Exploration

While the Polynesian history of the islands goes back at least 1,700 years, the European period only began in the 16th century when the Magellan expedition sailed past the Tuamotus and Mendaña visited the Marquesas. Quirós saw the Tuamotus in 1606, as did the Dutchmen Le Maire and Schouten in 1616 and Roggeveen in 1722. But it was not until 18 June 1767 that Capt. Samuel Wallis on the HMS *Dolphin* happened upon Tahiti. He and most of his contemporary explorers were in search of *terra australis incognita,* a mythical southern landmass thought to balance the northern hemisphere.

At first the Tahitians attacked the ship, but after experiencing European gunfire they decided to be friendly. Eager to trade, they loaded the Englishmen down with pigs, fowl, and fruit. Iron was in the highest demand, and Tahitian women lured the sailors to exchange nails for love. Consequently, to prevent the ship's timbers from being torn asunder for the nails, no man was allowed onshore except in parties strictly for food and water. Wallis sent ashore a landing party, which named Tahiti "King George III Island," turned some sod, and hoisted the Union Jack. A year later the French explorer Louis-Antoine de Bougainville arrived on the east coast, unaware of Wallis's discovery, and claimed Tahiti for the king of France.

Wallis and Bougainville only visited briefly, leaving it to Capt. James Cook to really describe Polynesia to Europeans. Cook visited "Otaheite" four times, in 1769, 1773, 1774, and 1777. His first three-month visit was to observe the transit of the planet Venus across the face of the sun. The second and third were in search of the southern continent, while the fourth was to locate a northwest passage between the Pacific and Atlantic oceans. Some of the finest artists and scientists of the day accompanied Captain Cook. Their explorations added the Leeward Islands, two Austral islands, and a dozen Tuamotu islands to European knowledge. On Tahiti Cook met a high priest from Raiatea named Tupaia, who had an astonishing knowledge of the Pacific and could name dozens of islands. He drew Cook a map that included the Cook Islands, the Marquesas, and perhaps also some Samoan islands!

In 1788 Tahiti was visited for five months by HMS *Bounty* commanded by Lt. William Bligh with orders to collect young breadfruit plants for transportation to the West Indies. However, the famous mutiny did not take place at Tahiti but in Tongan waters, and from there Bligh escaped by navigating an open boat 6,500 km to Dutch Timor. Thus in 1791, the HMS *Pandora* came to Tahiti in search of the *Bounty* mutineers, intending to take them to England for trial. They captured 14 survivors of the 16 who had elected to stay on Tahiti when Fletcher Christian and eight others left for Pitcairn. Although glamorized by Hollywood, the mutineers helped destroy traditional Tahitian society by acting as mercenaries for rival chiefs.

By the early 19th century, ruffian British and American whalers were fanning out over the Pacific. Other ships traded with the islanders for sandalwood, bêche-de-mer, and mother-of-pearl, as well as the usual supplies. They brought with them smallpox, measles, influenza, tuberculosis, scarlet fever, and venereal diseases, which devastated the unprepared Polynesians. Slave raids, alcohol, and European firearms did the rest.

Kings and Missionaries

In 1797 the ship *Duff* dropped off on Tahiti 18 English missionaries and their wives. By this time Pomare, chief of the area adjoining Matavai Bay, had become powerful through the use of European tools, firearms, and mercenaries. He welcomed the missionaries but would not be converted, and infanticide, sexual freedom, and human sacrifices continued. By 1800 all but five of the original 18 had left Tahiti disappointed.

In 1803 Pomare I died and his despotic son, Pomare II, attempted to conquer the entire island. After initial success he was forced to flee to Moorea in 1808. Missionary Henry Nott went with him, and in 1812 Pomare II turned to him for help in regaining his lost power. Though the missionaries refused to baptize Pomare II him-

Captain Cook and his officers sharing a meal with Tahitians

Omai, a native of Huahine, accompanied Captain Cook's second expedition to England in 1774 and immediately became the talk of London. For many Europeans he epitomized the "noble savage," but, to those who came to know him, he was a sophisticated man with a culture of his own.

self because of his heathen and drunken habits, his subjects on Moorea became nominal Christians. In 1815 this "Christian king" managed to regain Tahiti and overthrow paganism. The eager missionaries then enforced the Ten Commandments and dressed the Tahitian women in "Mother Hubbard" costumes—dresses that covered their bodies from head to toe. Henceforth singing anything but hymns was banned, dancing proscribed, and all customs that offended puritanical sensibilities wiped away. Morality police terrorized the confused Tahitians in an eternal crusade against sin. Even the wearing of flowers in the hair was prohibited.

In *Omoo* (1847) Herman Melville comments:

Doubtless, in thus denationalizing the Tahitians, as it were, the missionaries were prompted by a sincere desire for good; but the effect has been lamentable. Supplied with no amusements, in place of those forbidden, the Tahitians, who require more recreation than other people, have sunk into a listlessness, or indulge in sensualities, a hundred times more pernicious than all the games ever celebrated in the Temple of Tanee.

COLONIALISM

The Rape of Polynesia

Upon Pomare II's death from drink at age 40 in 1821, the crown passed to his infant son, Pomare III, but he passed away in 1827. At this junction the most remarkable Tahitian of the 19th century, Aimata, half-sister of Pomare II, became Queen Pomare IV. She was to rule Tahiti, Moorea, and part of the Austral and Tuamotu groups for half a century until her death in 1877, a barefoot Tahitian Queen Victoria. She allied herself closely with the London Missionary Society (LMS) and when two French-Catholic priests, Honoré Laval and François Caret, arrived on Tahiti in 1836 from their stronghold at Mangareva (Gambier Islands), she expelled them promptly.

This affront brought a French frigate to Papeete in 1838, demanding $2000 compensation and a salute to the French flag. Although the conditions were met, the queen and her chiefs wrote to England appealing for help, but none came. A second French gunboat returned and threatened to bombard Tahiti unless its missionaries were given free entry. Back in Mangareva, Laval pushed forward a grandiose building program, which wiped out 80% of the population of the Gambiers from overwork.

A French consul named Moerenhout was appointed to Queen Pomare in 1838. In September 1842, while the queen and George Pritchard, the English consul, were away, he tricked a few local chiefs into signing a petition asking to be brought under French "protection." This demand was immediately accepted by French Admiral Dupetit-Thouars, who was in league with Moerenhout, and on 9 September 1842 they forced Queen Pomare to accept a French protectorate. When the queen tried to maintain her power and kept her red-and-white royal flag, Dupetit-Thouars deposed the queen on 8 November 1843 and occupied her kingdom, an arbitrary act that was rejected by the French king who reestablished the protectorate in 1844. Queen

Pomare fled to Raiatea and Pritchard was deported to England in March 1844, bringing Britain and France to the brink of war. The Tahitians resisted for three years: old French forts and war memorials recall the struggle.

A French Protectorate

At the beginning of 1847, when Queen Pomare realized that no British assistance was forthcoming, she and her people reluctantly accepted the French protectorate. As a compromise, the British elicited a promise from the French not to annex the Leeward Islands, so Huahine, Raiatea, and Bora Bora remained independent. The French had taken possession of the Marquesas in 1842, even before imposing a protectorate on Tahiti. French missionaries then attempted to convert the Tahitians to Catholicism, but only in the Marquesas were they successful.

Queen Pomare tried to defend the interests of her people as best she could, but much of her nation was dying: between the 18th century and 1926 the population of the Marquesas fell from 80,000 to only 2,000. In April 1774 Captain Cook had tried to estimate the population of Tahiti by counting the number of men he saw in a fleet of war canoes and ascribing three members to each one's family. Cook's figure was 204,000, but according to Bengt Danielsson, the correct number at the time of discovery was about 150,000. By 1829 it had dropped to 8,568, and a low of 7,169 was reached in 1865. The name "Pomare" means "night cough," from *po*, night, plus *mare*, cough, because Pomare I's infant daughter died of tuberculosis in 1792.

Pomare V, the final, degenerate member of the line, was more interested in earthly pleasures than the traditions upheld by his mother. In 1880, with French interests at work on the Panama Canal, a smart colonial governor convinced him to sign away his kingdom for a 5000-franc-a-month pension. Thus, on 29 June 1880 the

Tomb of King Pomare V, Tahiti: *Pomare V's mother died in 1877 after reigning for 50 troubled years during which she was exhorted to accept a French protectorate over her Polynesian kingdom. A less heroic figure than his mother, King Pomare V (above, left) the fifth and last of his name to hold the throne, took over a luckless dynasty and also took to drink. He was particularly fond of Benedictine and although the distinctive symbol enshrined forever atop his pylon-shaped mausoleum at Arue appears to be a massive Benedictine bottle it is actually a Grecian vase. He died in 1891, an unhappy man.*

protectorate became the full French colony it is today, the "Etablissements français de l'Océánie." In 1957 the name was changed to "Polynésie Française."

The most earthshaking event between 1880 and 1960 was a visit by two German cruisers, the *Scharnhorst* and *Gneisenau,* which shelled Papeete on 22 September 1914. (Both were subsequently sunk by the British at the Battle of the Falkland Islands.) On 2 September 1940 the colony declared its support for the Free French, and the Americans arrived to establish a base on Bora Bora soon after Pearl Harbor. Polynesia remained cut off from occupied metropolitan France until the end of the war, although Tahitians served with the Pacific battalion in North Africa and Italy.

RECENT HISTORY

The early 1960s were momentous times for Polynesia. Within a few years, MGM filmed *Mutiny on the Bounty,* an international airport opened on Tahiti, and the French began testing their atomic bombs. After Algeria became independent in July 1962 the French decided to move their Sahara nuclear testing facilities to the Tuamotus. In 1963, when all local political parties protested the invasion of Polynesia by thousands of French troops and technicians sent to establish a nuclear testing center, Pres. Charles de Gaulle simply outlawed political parties. The French set off their first atmospheric nuclear explosion at Moruroa on 2 July 1966. In 1974, 44 bombs later, international protests forced the French to switch to underground tests, which were to continue until April 1992.

The spirit of the time is best summed up in the life of one man, Pouvanaa a Oopa, an outspoken WW I hero from Huahine. In 1949 he became the first Polynesian to occupy a seat in the French Chamber of Deputies. In 1957 he was elected vice-president of the Government Council. A dedicated proponent of independence, Pouvanaa was arrested in 1958 on trumped-up charges of arson, eventually sentenced to an eight-year prison term, and exiled by the French government. De Gaulle wanted Pouvanaa out of the way until French nuclear testing facilities could be established in Poly-

the Tahitian independence leader, Pouvanaa a Oopa (1895-1977)

nesia, and he was not freed until 1968. In 1971 he won the "French" Polynesian seat in the French Senate, a post he held until his death in early 1977. Tahitians refer to the man as *metua* (father), and his statue stands in front of Papeete's Territorial Assembly.

Pouvanaa's successors, John Teariki (now deceased) and Francis Sanford (since retired), were also defenders of Polynesian autonomy and opponents of nuclear testing. Their combined efforts convinced the French government to grant Polynesia a new statute with a slightly increased autonomy in 1977.

Analysis

Tahiti-Polynesia is part of a worldwide chain of French colonies including Kerguelen, Guyana, Martinique, Guadeloupe, Mayotte, New Caledonia, Wallis and Futuna, Reunion, and St. Pierre and Miquelon, under the DOM-TOM (Ministry of Overseas Departments and Territories). France spends 16 billion French francs a year to maintain this system, a clear indicator it's something totally different from colonial empires of the past, which were based on economic exploitation, not investment. A closer analogy is the American network of military bases around the world, which serve the same

the ceding of Matavai, Tahiti, to English missionaries in 1797

purpose—projecting power. What is at stake is French national prestige.

These conditions contradict what has happened elsewhere in the South Pacific. Over the past 20 years the British have voluntarily withdrawn from their Pacific colonies as French pretensions to global mid-sized nuclear power status grew stronger. This digging in has created the anachronism of a few highly visible bastions of white colonialism in the midst of a sea of English-speaking independent nations. When French officials summarily rejected all protests against their nuclear testing and suppression of independence movements, even going to the extreme of employing state terrorism to stop a protest vessel from leaving New Zealand, most Pacific islanders were outraged. Their subsequent boycotts of French goods and anti-French statements have only exacerbated the situation.

What must be accepted is that there's a place for France in the Pacific. It's no longer possible to turn the clock back to 1842 or 1767. In fact, in almost every Pacific micro-state the basis for complete self-reliance simply doesn't exist. In recent years France has come to realize that its interests in the Pacific are as well served by emphasizing social, cultural, and economic matters as by outright political and military domination. French universities have been established on Tahiti and New Caledonia, and economic/military aid to the smaller South Pacific countries stepped up. Space-age technology is being used to maintain this empire as never before.

Yet by continuing its uncontrolled immigration and military build-ups France risks an independence struggle with the Tahitians. This may well lead to increasing destabilization, plus continuing international condemnation and a black image in the region. By granting full internal self-government to its colonies, France would quickly be accepted as a good neighbor throughout the Pacific, as it was before 1963 when de Gaulle exported *la bombe.* (The commentary above was inspired in part by Jean Chesneaux's article "France in the Pacific: Global Approach or Respect for Regional Agendas?" in Vol. 18, No. 2, 1986, of the *Bulletin of Concerned Asian Scholars*).

GOVERNMENT

In 1885 an organic decree created the colonial system of government, which remained in effect until the proclamation of a new statute in 1958, making Tahiti-Polynesia an overseas territory. In 1977 the French granted the territory partial internal self-government, and Francis Sanford was elected premier of "autonomous" Polynesia. A new local-government statute, passed by the French parliament and promulgated on 6 September 1984, gave only slightly more powers to the Polynesians; the constitution of the Republic of France remains the supreme law of the land.

A Territorial Assembly elects the president of the government, who chooses 10 ministers. The Territorial Assembly is responsible for public works, sports, health, social services, and primary education. The 41 assembly members are elected from separate districts, with 22 seats from Tahiti/Moorea, eight from the Leeward Islands, five from the Tuamotus and Gambiers, three from the Australs, and three from the Marquesas. One vote in the Tuamotus has the weight of three on Tahiti, and many constituencies have been gerrymandered. French soldiers and civil servants can vote in local elections the day they arrive in the territory, and there are thousands of them, including many in the Tuamotus.

The territory is represented in Paris by two elected deputies, a senator, and a social and economic counselor. The French government, through its high commissioner, assisted by a

secretary-general of his choice, retains control over defense, foreign affairs, money, justice, immigration, the police, the civil service, foreign trade, TV and radio broadcasting, international communications, secondary education, and the municipal councils. As may be seen, the high commissioner has considerable power. He can also dissolve the Territorial Assembly, refer its decisions to an administrative tribunal, or take personal control of the territorial budget (as happened in 1992).

Tahiti-Polynesia is divided into 48 communes, each with an elected Municipal Council, which chooses a mayor from its ranks. These elected bodies, however, are controlled by appointed French civil servants, who run the five administrative subdivisions. The administrators of the Windward, Tuamotu-Gambier, and Austral subdivisions are based at Papeete, while the headquarters of the Leeward Islands administration is at Uturoa, and that of the Marquesas Islands is at Taiohae.

Politics

In 1982 the neo-Gaullist Tahoeraa Huiraatira (Popular Union) won the territorial elections, and the pronuclear, anti-independence mayor of Pirae, Gaston Flosse, became premier of the local government. In the 1986 territorial elections Flosse's party won a majority of assembly seats, but a year later Flosse resigned as president to devote his full time to the post of French secretary of state for the South Pacific. Flosse's reputation for fixing government contracts while in office earned him the title "Mr. Ten Percent" from the Paris newspaper *Libération*.

After rioting in Papeete and allegations of corruption, Tahoeraa deputy leader Alexandre Léontieff broke with Flosse in December 1987 and formed a coalition government with other Tahoeraa defectors and several smaller parties. Léontieff's 1987-91 administration was marked by financial mismanagement and political fence-sitting on the nuclear and independence issues, and the 17 March 1991 Territorial Assembly elections returned Flosse's Tahoeraa Huiraatira to power. Half of those voting for Flosse's party

pro-independence demonstrators at the High Commissioner's gate in Papeete

were French expatriates, civil servants, and military personnel.

The antinuclear, pro-independence Tavini Huiraatira No Te Ao Maohi (Polynesian Liberation Front), formed in 1978 by Faa'a mayor Oscar Temaru, doubled its assembly representation from two to four in the 1991 election. The *indépendentistes* are strongest in Papeete, weakest in the Tuamotus and Marquesas—areas heavily dependent on French aid.

ECONOMY

Government Spending

The inflow of people and money since the early 1960s has substituted consumerism for subsistence, and except for tourism and cultured pearls, the economy of Tahiti-Polynesia is now totally dominated by French government spending. Paris contributes very little to the territorial budget, but it finances the many departments and services under the direct control of the high commissioner, spending an average of US$300 million a year in the territory, two-thirds of it on the military. Much of the rest goes into salaries 1.84 times higher than those in France for 2,200 expatriate French civil servants.

Just a third of the population receives any direct benefit from French spending. The rest feel only the effects of inequalities and foreign interference. The nuclear testing program provoked an influx of 30,000 French settlers, plus a massive infusion of capital, which distorted the formerly self-supporting economy into one totally dependent on France.

In the early 1960s, many Polynesians left their homes for construction jobs with the *Centre d'Expérimentations du Pacifique* (CEP), the government, and the hotel chains. Now that the volume of this work is decreasing, most of them subsist in precarious circumstances on Tahiti, dependent on government spending. Until recently some 2,000 locals were employed by the testing program (compared to 10,000 in 1968). Though the testing was suspended in April 1992, the CEP is still headquartered at Pirae, just east of Papeete, with a major support base opposite the yacht club at Arue. (Just prior to his election to the French presidency in May 1995, Jacques Chirac announced that he intended to resume nuclear testing at the first opportunity, so these shameful activities may be in full swing again by the time you get there.)

Tahiti-Polynesia has the highest gross domestic product per capita in the South Pacific (A$19,745 in 1990). The suspension of nuclear testing in 1992 caused a recession as local workers were laid off and tax revenues on military imports suddenly dropped, so in 1993 the French government agreed to provide Tahiti-Polynesia with additional subsidies totaling

US$118 million a year over five years as part of a "Pacte de Progrès" development plan. A condition was that new revenue had to be raised locally, so the territorial government introduced an income tax of three percent on earnings over CFP150,000 a month where none had previously existed, plus new taxes on gasoline, wine, telecommunications, and unearned income.

Trade

Prior to the start of nuclear testing, trade was balanced. Only 29 years later, 1991 imports stood at A$1,117 million while exports amounted to only A$156 million, one of the highest disparities in the world. Much of the imbalance is consumed by the French administration itself, and a quarter of imports are related to military activities. Foreign currency spent by tourists on imported goods and services also helps explain the situation.

Half the imports come from France, which has imposed a series of self-favoring restrictions. Imports include food, fuel, building material, consumer goods, and automobiles. The main agricultural export from the outer islands is copra which is heavily subsidized by the government. The copra is crushed into coconut oil and animal feed at the Papeete mill, while cultured pearls from farms in the Tuamotus are the biggest export by far. Perfume and vanilla are also exported.

Indirect taxes, such as customs duties of 20-200% and licensing fees, have long accounted for half of territorial government revenue, and the price of many imported goods is more than doubled by taxation. There's also a flat 35% levy on businesses, which is simply passed along to consumers.

Law of the Sea

This law has changed the face of the Pacific. States traditionally exercised sovereignty over a three-mile belt of territorial sea along their shores; the high seas beyond these limits could be freely used by anyone. Then on 28 September 1945, Pres. Harry Truman declared U.S. sovereignty over the natural resources of the adjacent continental shelf. U.S. fishing boats soon became involved in an acrimonious dispute with several South American countries over their rich anchovy fishing grounds, and in 1952 Chile, Ecuador, and Peru declared a 200-nautical-mile Exclusive Economic Zone (EEZ) along their shores. In 1958 the United Nations convened a Conference on the Law of the Sea at Geneva, which accepted national control over shelves up to 200 meters deep. Agreement could not be reached on extended territorial sea limits.

National claims multiplied so much that in 1974 another U.N. conference was convened, leading to the signing of the Law of the Sea convention at Jamaica in 1982 by 159 states and other entities. This complex agreement— 200 pages, nine annexes, and 320 articles— extended national control over 40% of the world's oceans. The territorial sea was increased to 12 nautical miles and the continental shelf ambiguously defined as extending 200 nautical miles offshore. States were given full control over all resources, living or nonliving, within this belt. Fiji was the first country to ratify the convention and by November 1994 a total of 60 countries had signed up, allowing the treaty to come into effect for them.

Even before the Law of the Sea became international law, many aspects of it were accepted in practice. The EEZs mainly affect fisheries and seabed mineral exploitation; freedom of navigation within the zones is guaranteed. The Law of the Sea increased immensely the territory of independent oceanic states, giving them real political weight for the first time. For example, the land area of Tahiti-Polynesia comes to only 3,265 square km, while its EEZ

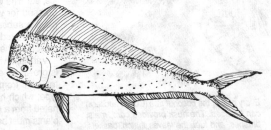

The dolphin fish (Coryphaena hippurus) or dorado is a large, fast-moving fish with a body of luminous purple, green, and gold colors that fade soon after death. Mahimahi (dolphin fish) is a favored food, but the fish has no relation to its namesake mammal dolphin.

LOUISE FOOTE

totals 5,030,000 square km! It's known that vast mineral deposits are scattered across this seabed, though the cost of extraction (estimated at US$1.5 billion) has prevented their exploitation to date.

In 1976 the French government passed legislation which gave it control of this zone, not only along France's coastal waters but also around all her overseas territories and departments. The National Marine Research Center and private firms have already drawn up plans to recover nickel, cobalt, manganese, and copper nodules from depths of over 4,000 meters. The French government has adamantly refused to give the Territorial Assembly any jurisdiction over this tremendous resource, an important indicator as to why they are determined to hold onto their colony at any price.

Agriculture

Labor recruiting for the nuclear testing program caused local agriculture to collapse in the mid-'60s. Between 1962 and 1988 the percentage of the workforce employed in agriculture dropped from 50% to 9%. Exports of coffee and vanilla had ceased completely by 1965 and coconut products dropped 40% despite massive subsi-

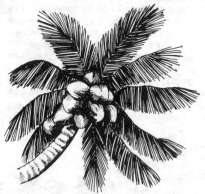

DIANA LASICH HARPER

Every part of the coconut tree (Cocos nucifera) can be used. The husk provides cord, mats, brushes, and fuel; the leaves thatch, baskets, and fans; and the trunk building material. Food and oil from the nuts are the greatest prize. A healthy tree will produce 50 nuts a year for over 60 years.

dies. Today about 80% of all food consumed locally is imported. Tahiti-Polynesia does manage, however, to cover three-quarters of its own fruit requirements, and most of the local pineapple and grapefruit crop goes to the fruit-juice factory on Moorea. In the 1880s-90s four million oranges a year were exported to Australia, New Zealand, and California. The industry was wiped out by a blight at the turn of the century, and now only a few trees grow wild.

Local vegetables supply half of local needs, while Tahitian coffee only covers 20% of consumption. Considerable livestock is kept in the Marquesas. Large areas have been planted in Caribbean pine to provide for future timber needs. Aquaculture, with tanks for freshwater shrimp, prawns, live bait, and green mussels, is being developed. Most industry is related to food processing (fruit-juice factory, brewery, soft drinks, etc.) or coconut products. It's rumored that marijuana *(pakalolo)* is now the leading cash crop, though you won't be aware of it.

The coconut tree has long been the mainstay of the outer islanders. A good tree gives nuts for 50 or 60 years (the 29-cm-wide metal bands around the trunk are for protection against rats). The green coconut provides food and drink, while the harder meat from more mature nuts is grated and squeezed to obtain coconut cream used as sauce and in cooking. The oldest nuts are cracked open and the meat dried in the sun to make copra. Schooners collect bags of copra, which they carry to a mill beside the interisland wharf at Papeete. Here the copra is pressed into coconut oil used in making vegetable oil, margarine, candles, soap, cosmetics, etc. The world price for copra has been depressed for years, so the government wisely pays a subsidy (more than twice the actual price) to producers to keep them gainfully employed on their home islands.

Vanilla, a vine belonging to the orchid family, is grown on small family plantations. Brought to Tahiti from Manila in 1848, the Tahitensis type, which has a worldwide reputation, originated from a mutation of Fragrans vanilla. The plants must be hand pollinated, then harvested between April and June. The pods are then put out to dry for a couple of months—an exceptionally time-consuming process generally entrusted to the Chinese. Between 1915 and 1933

Tahiti produced 50-150 tons of vanilla a year, peaking in 1949 at 200 tons. Production remained high until 1966, when a steady decline began due to the producers leaving for paid employment in Papeete related to nuclear testing. By 1990 production had fallen to only 39 metric tons, though the territorial government wants to get things going again.

Cultured Pearls

Tahiti-Polynesia's cultured-pearl industry, now second only to tourism as a money earner, originated in 1963 when an experimental farm was established on Hikueru atoll in the Tuamotus. Today cooperative and private pearl farms operate on 26 atolls in Tahiti-Polynesia, employing thousands of people. Pearl farming is ecologically benign, relieving pressure on natural stocks and creating a need to protect marine environments. Pollution from fertilizer runoff or sewage can make a lagoon unsuitable for pearl farming, which is why the farms are concentrated on lightly populated atolls where other forms of agriculture are scarcely practiced.

Unlike the Japanese cultured white pearl, the Polynesian black pearl is created only by the giant blacklipped oyster (Pinctada margaritifera), which thrives in the Tuamotu lagoons. Beginning in the 19th century the oysters were collected by Polynesian divers who could dive up to 40 meters. The shell was made into mother-of-pearl buttons; finding a pearl this way was pure chance. By the middle of this century overharvesting had depleted the slow-growing oyster beds and today live oysters are collected only to supply cultured-pearl farms. The shell is a mere byproduct, made into decorative items or exported. The strings of oysters must be monitored constantly and lowered or raised if there are variations in water temperature.

It takes around three years for a pearl to form in a seeded oyster. A spherical pearl is formed when a Mississippi River mussel graft is introduced inside the coat; the oyster only creates a hemispherical half pearl if the graft goes between the coat and the shell. Half pearls are much cheaper than real pearls and make outstanding rings and pendants. Some of the grafts used are surprisingly large and the layer of nacre around such pearls may be relatively thin, but only an X-ray can tell.

The cooperatives sell their production at an auction in Papeete organized by the chamber of commerce each October. The pearls are offered to bidders in lots of about 400 which can attract bids as high as US$170,000. Local jewelers vie with Japanese buyers at these events, with some 50,000 black pearls changing hands for about US$5 million. Private producers sell their pearls through independent dealers or plush retail outlets in Papeete. In 1991 black pearl exports were worth A$54 million, with 60% going to Japan. The next largest agricultural export, coconut oil, brought in only A$3.3 million that year.

The relative newness of this gemstone is reflected in wildly varying prices. A brilliant, perfectly round, smooth, and flawless pearl with a good depth of metallic green-gray/blue-gray color can sell for 100 times more than a similar pearl with only one or two defects. Unless you really know your pearls it's intelligent to stick to the cheaper, even "baroque" ones which, mounted in gold and platinum, still make exquisite jewelry. These pearls are now in fashion in Paris, so don't expect any bargains. Quality pearls cost US$1000 and up, but slightly flawed pearls are much cheaper (US$50 is average). Half the fun is in the shopping, so be in no hurry to decide. A reputable dealer will give you an invoice or certificate verifying the authenticity of your pearl.

Tourism

Two kinds of people visit Tahiti-Polynesia: package tourists on two-week trips from the States, who book all their accommodations in advance, stay at the best hotels, and travel interisland by air; and independent budget travelers (often young Europeans), who have more time, find a place to stay upon arrival, and travel by boat as much as possible. Tahiti, Moorea, Huahine, Raiatea, and Bora Bora are popular among visitors for their combination of beaches, mountain scenery, easy access, and the wealth of budget accommodations. The Society group is closely linked by sea and air, an island-hopper's playground.

Tourism only got underway with the opening of Faa'a Airport in 1961 and today Tahiti-Polynesia is second only to Fiji as a South Pacific tourist center, with 123,619 visitors in 1992, a third of them from the United States and another third from Europe. Yet tourism is far less de-

the cover of an official brochure promoting tourism as a source of income for Tahiti-Polynesia

veloped than in Hawaii. A single Waikiki hotel could have more rooms than the entire island of Tahiti; Hawaii gets more visitors in 10 days than Tahiti-Polynesia gets in a year. In Tahiti-Polynesia only one tourist is present for every 100 inhabitants at any given time, while overcrowded Hawaii has 11.

Distance and reports of high prices have kept Tahiti out of the American mass market, and high local labor costs have hampered development. Now tourism by high-budget Japanese (especially honeymooners) is being vigorously promoted and the number of European visitors is growing quickly. The US$200 million a year generated by tourism covers 18% of Tahiti-Polynesia's import bill and provides 4,000 jobs, but 80% of the things tourists buy are also imported.

Transnational corporations, either hotel chains, tour companies, or airlines, dominate the tourist industry. Top management of the big hotels is invariably French or foreign, as ownership rests with Japanese (Beachcomber Parkroyal, Hyatt Regency, Moana Beach, Bora Bora Lagoon, Kia Ora Village), French (Sofitel, Club Med), and American (Bali Hai) corporations. Carriers such as Air New Zealand and Qantas only promote Tahiti as a stopover on the way Down Under, limiting many tourists to a few nights in Papeete.

In September 1989 the Japanese corporation Electronic and Industrial Enterprises (EIE) purchased four major hotels, in 1990 a Tokyo company bought Rangiroa's Kia Ora Village, and in 1993 the Bora Bora Lagoon Resort opened, as the Japanese scramble to recycle their massive foreign-exchange surpluses. Many Polynesians are rather nervous about this Japanese-driven development, and in June 1991 voters on Moorea decided against a US$93.4 million Sheraton hotel and Arnold Palmer championship golf course Japanese investors had wanted to build on their island. In May 1990 the 200 traditional owners of Tupai, just north of Bora Bora, blocked the atoll's sale to a Japanese corporation that had intended to build a major resort there. On Tahiti, a 1993 protest occupation by 600 Tahitians halted construction of a 330-room Méridien Hôtel complex near the Museum of Tahiti in Punaauia. As a result, planned Méridien developments on Moorea, Bora Bora, and Rangiroa have been put on hold.

THE PEOPLE

The criteria used for defining the racial groups making up the 1988 population of 188,814 are so unsatisfactory that only an approximate breakdown can be made: 70% Polynesian, 12% European, 10% Polynesian/European, five percent Chinese, and three percent Polynesian/Chinese. All are French citizens. The 1988 population figures for the five administrative subdivisions are: Windward Islands 140,341, Leeward Islands 22,232, Austral Islands 6,509, Tuamotu/Gambier Islands 12,374, Marquesas Islands 7,358. About 70% of the total population lives on Tahiti (compared to only 25% before the nuclear-testing boom began in the 1960s) but a total of 65 far-flung islands are inhabited.

The indigenous people of Tahiti-Polynesia are the Maohi or Eastern Polynesians (as opposed to the Western Polynesians in Samoa and Tonga), and some local nationalists refer to their country as Maohinui. The word *colon* formerly applied to Frenchmen who arrived long before the bomb and made a living as planters

a Polynesian woman

or traders, and practically all of them married Polynesian women. Most of these *colons* have already passed away and their descendants are termed *demis,* or *afa.* The present Europeans are mostly recently arrived metropolitan French *(faranis).* Most *faranis* live in urban areas or are involved in the administration or military. Their numbers increased dramatically in the 1960s and 1970s.

Local Chinese *(tinito)* dominate the retail trade throughout the territory. In Papeete and Uturoa entire streets are lined with Chinese stores, and individual Chinese merchants are found on almost every island. During the American Civil War, when the supply of cotton to Europe was disrupted, Scotsman William Stewart decided to set up a cotton plantation on the south side of Tahiti. Unable to convince Tahitians to accept the heavy work, Stewart brought in a contingent of 1,010 Chinese laborers from Canton in 1865-66. When the war ended the enterprise went bankrupt, but many of the Chinese managed to stay on as market gardeners or shopkeepers.

In 1964 the French government decided to assimilate the Chinese by granting them citizenship, requiring that they adopt French-sounding names, and closing all Chinese schools. Despite this, the Chinese community has remained distinct. Most of the Tahiti Chinese used to be supporters of the Kuomintang regime in Taiwan and fierce anticommunists. But since France recognized mainland China in 1964 the Taiwanese consulate has been closed, and many local Chinese now visit their ancestral country.

From 1976 to 1983 some 18,000 people migrated to the territory, 77% of them from France and another 13% from New Caledonia. Nearly 1,000 new settlers a year continue to arrive. Some 40,000 Europeans are now present in the territory, plus 8,000 soldiers, policemen, and transient officials. Most Tahitians would like to see this immigration restricted, as it is in virtually every other Pacific state. Yet with the integration of the European Union, all 300 million E.U. citizens may soon gain the right to live in Polynesia. To protest this threatened "second invasion" (the first, related to nuclear testing, began in 1963), all local political parties boycotted the 1989 elections to the European Parliament.

There's an undercurrent of anti-French sentiment; English speakers are better liked by the Tahitians. Yet inevitably the newcomers get caught up in the Polynesian openness and friendliness—even the surliest Parisian. In fact, the Gallic charm you'll experience even in government offices is a delight. Tahiti-Polynesia really is a friendly place.

The New Class Structure

The creation of the Centre d'Expérimentations du Pacifique (CEP) in the early 1960s upset the economic and social equilibrium, drove up the cost of living, created artificial needs, and led to a migration toward Papeete. In 1962 46% of the labor force was engaged in fishing and agriculture. Since then there's been a massive shift to public and private services and about 80% of the working population of 58,000 are now employees. Of these, 40% work for the government, 40% in services, 11% in industry, and only eight percent in fishing and agriculture.

Civil servants in Tahiti-Polynesia get 84% higher salaries than their counterparts in France and pay only three percent income tax. There are generous expatriation benefits, and six months' paid leave is earned after three years. The minimum monthly wage in the territory is US$1500 in the public sector, but only US$850 in the private sector. Living standards in Tahiti-Polynesia may be far higher than in the surrounding insular countries due to the subsidies, yet this expansion of wealth has created inequalities; also, the number of unemployed or underemployed is increasing. The gap between an affluent foreign clique and the impoverished Tahitian mass has created an explosive situation.

In October 1987 the French high commissioner used riot police flown in from Paris to suppress a dockworkers' strike, leading to serious rioting in Papeete and US$50 million in damage. The mayor of Papeete, Jean Juventin, accused French officials of deliberately provoking the violence as a way of breaking the union, which handled cargo bound for the nuclear testing facilities. Most of those eventually convicted of looting were not strikers at all but unemployed Tahitian youths who took advantage of the disturbance to grab consumer goods. Fresh rioting in July 1991 forced the territorial government to cancel tax increases on gasoline, alcohol, and tobacco meant to cover a US$73.4 million budget deficit. The strikers said these levies placed an intolerable burden on Tahitian families and called for the imposition of income tax on salaries over US$3000 a month instead. In the end France agreed to pick up part of the deficit bill to restore calm.

An estimated 20,000 poor, unemployed, and marginalized Tahitians live in *bidonvilles* or slums on the outskirts of Papeete. In the valley shantytowns behind Papeete and Faa'a 10-15 Polynesians are crammed into each neat flower-decked plywood house. Many are children, as a government subsidy of US$50 per month per child encourages big families. Opportunities for young Tahitians with a taste for the consumer society are not adequate. Every year 3,000 young people turn 18 and begin competing for scarce jobs. The present social structure places *farani* officials at the top, followed by *demis* in the lower echelons of business and government, while *maohis* (indigenous people) work for wages or subsist at the bottom of the shredded social fabric.

Tahitian Life

For the French, lunch is the main meal of the day, followed by a siesta. Dinner may consist of leftovers from lunch. Tahitians traditionally eat their main meal of fish and native vegetables in the evening, when the day's work is over. People at home often take a shower before or after a meal and put flowers in their hair. If they're in a good mood a guitar or ukulele might appear.

Tahitians often observe with amusement or disdain the efforts of individuals to rise above the group. In a society where sharing and reciprocal generosity have traditionally been important qualities, the deliberate accumulation of personal wealth was always viewed as a vice. Now with the influx of government and tourist money, Tahitian life is changing, quickly in Papeete, more slowly in the outer islands. To prevent the Polynesians from being made paupers in their own country, foreigners other than French are not usually permitted to purchase land here and 85% of the land is still owned by the Polynesians. A new impoverished class is forming among those who have sold their ancestral lands to recent French immigrants.

The educational curriculum is entirely French. Children enter school at age three and for 12 years study the French language, literature, culture, history, and geography, but not much about Polynesia. The failure rate ranges from 40-60%, and most of the rest of the children are behind schedule. The best students are given scholarships to continue studying, while many of the dropouts become delinquents. About half the schools are privately run by the churches, but these must teach exactly the same curriculum or lose their subsidies. The whole aim is to transform the Polynesians into Pacific French. In 1987 the Université française du Pacifique (B.P. 4635, Papeete; tel. 42-16-80, fax 41-01-31) opened on Tahiti, specializing in law, humanities, social sciences, languages, and science.

Most Tahitians live along the coast because the interior is too rugged and possibly inhabited by *tupapau* (ghosts). Some people leave a light on all night in their home for the latter reason. A traditional Tahitian residence consists of several separate buildings: the *fare tutu* (kitchen), the *fare tamaa* (dining area), the *fare taoto* (bedrooms), plus bathing and sanitary outhouses. Often several generations live together, and young children are sent to live with their grandparents. Adoption is commonplace and family relationships complex. Young Tahitians generally go out as groups, rather than on individual "dates."

The lifestyle may be summed up in the words *aita e peapea* (no problem) and *fiu* (fed up, bored). About the only time the normally languid Tahitians go really wild is when they're dancing or behind the wheel of a car.

Sex

Since the days of Wallis and Bougainville, Tahitian women have had a reputation for promiscuity. Well, for better or worse, this is largely a thing of the past, if it ever existed at all. As a short-term visitor your liaisons with Tahitians are likely to remain polite. Westerners' obsession with the sexuality of Polynesians usually reflects their own frustrations, and the view that Tahitian morality is loose is rather ironic considering that Polynesians have always shared

a Polynesian vahine

ARCHIVES NATIONALES, SECTION OUTRE-MER, FRANCE

whatever they have, cared for their old and young, and refrained from ostracizing unwed mothers or attaching stigma to their offspring. The good Christian Tahitians of today are highly moral and compassionate.

Polynesia's *mahus* or third sex bear little of the stigma attached to female impersonators in the West. A young boy may adopt the female role by his own choice or that of his parents, performing female tasks at home and eventually finding a job usually performed by women, such as serving in a restaurant or hotel. Usually only one *mahu* exists in each village or community, proof that this type of individual serves a certain sociological function. George Mortimer of the British ship *Mercury* recorded an encounter with a *mahu* in 1789. Though Tahitians may poke fun at a *mahu*, they're fully accepted in society, seen teaching Sunday school, etc. Many, but not all, *mahus* are also homosexuals. Today, with money all-important, some transvestites have involved themselves in male prostitution and the term *raerae* has been coined for this category. Now there are even Miss Tane (Miss Male) beauty con-

TAHITI IN LITERATURE

Over the years the romance of legendary Tahiti has been elaborated by a succession of famous writers who came in search of Bougainville's Nouvelle Cythère or Rousseau's noble savage. Brought to the stage or silver screen, their stories entered the popular imagination alongside Gauguin's rich images. An enjoyable way to get a feel for the region is to read a couple of the books mentioned below before you come.

Herman Melville, author of the whaling classic *Moby Dick* (1851), deserted his New Bedford whaler at Nuku Hiva in 1842 and *Typee* (1846) describes his experiences there. An Australian whaling ship carried Melville on to Tahiti, but he joined a mutiny on board, which landed him in the Papeete *calabooza* (prison). His second Polynesian book, *Omoo* (1847), was a result. In both, Melville decries the ruin of Polynesian culture by Western influence.

Pierre Loti's *The Marriage of Loti* (1880) is a sentimental tale of the love of a young French midshipman for a Polynesian woman named Rarahu. Loti's naiveté is rather absurd, but his friendship with Queen Pomare IV and his fine imagery make the book worth reading. Loti's writings influenced Paul Gauguin to come to Tahiti.

In 1888-90 Robert Louis Stevenson, famous author of *Treasure Island* and *Kidnapped,* cruised the Pacific in his schooner, the *Casco.* His book *In the South Seas* describes his visits to the Marquesas and Tuamotus. Stevenson settled at Tautira on Tahiti Iti for a time, but eventually retired at Apia in Samoa which offered the author better mail service.

Jack London and his wife Charmian cruised the Pacific aboard their yacht, the *Snark,* in 1907-09.

A longtime admirer of Melville, London found only a wretched swamp at Taipivae in the Marquesas. His *South Sea Tales* (1911) was the first of the 10 books that he wrote on the Pacific. London's story "The House of Mapuhi," about a Jewish pearl buyer, earned him a costly lawsuit. London was a product of his time, and the modern reader is often shocked by his insensitive portrayal of the islanders.

In 1913-14 the youthful poet Rupert Brooke visited Tahiti, where he fell in love with Mamua, a woman from Mataiea whom he immortalized in his poem "Tiare Tahiti." Later Brooke fought in WW I and wrote five famous war sonnets. He died of blood poisoning on a French hospital ship in the Mediterranean in 1915.

W. Somerset Maugham toured Polynesia in 1916-17 to research his novel, *The Moon and Sixpence* (1919), a fictional life of Paul Gauguin. Of the six short stories in *The Trembling of a Leaf* (1921), "The Fall of Edward Barnard" contrasts the simple island life with the demands of the "real world." Maugham's *A Writer's Notebook* published in 1984, 19 years after his death, describes his travels in the Pacific. On Tahiti Maugham discovered not only material for his books but by chance located a glass door pane with a female figure painted by Gauguin himself, which he bought for 200 francs. In 1962 it sold at Sotheby's in London for $37,400.

American writers Charles Nordhoff and James Norman Hall came to Tahiti after WW I, married Tahitian women, and collaborated on 11 books. Their most famous was the *Bounty* trilogy (1934), which tells of Fletcher Christian's mutiny on the *Bounty,* the escape to Dutch Timor of Captain Bligh

tests! All this may be seen as the degradation of a phenomenon that has always been part of Polynesian life.

RELIGION

Though the old Polynesian religion died out in the early 19th century, the Tahitians are still a strongly religious people. Protestant missionaries arrived on Tahiti 39 years before the Catholics and 47 years before the Mormons, so over half of the Polynesians now belong to the Evangelical Church, which is strongest in the Austral and Leeward islands. Of the 34% of the total population who are Catholic, half are Polynesians from the Tuamotus and Marquesas, and the other half are French. Another six percent are Mormons. Seventh-Day Adventists and Jehovah's Witnesses are also represented, and some Chinese are Buddhists. It's not unusual to see two or three different churches in a village of 100 people. All the main denominations operate their own schools. Local ministers and priests are powerful figures in the outer-island communities. One vestige of the pre-Christian religion is a widespread belief in ghosts *(tupapau).*

Protestant church services are conducted mostly in Tahitian, Catholic services are in

and his crew in *Men Against the Sea,* and the mutineer's fate in *Pitcairn's Island.* Three generations of filmmakers have selected this saga as their way of presenting paradise.

Hall remained on Tahiti until his death in 1951 and his house at Arue still stands. His last book, *The Forgotten One,* is a collection of true stories about intellectuals and writers lost in the South Seas. Hall's account of the 28-year correspondence with his American friend Robert Dean Frisbie, who settled on Pukapuka in the Cook Islands, is touching.

James A. Michener joined the U.S. Navy in 1942 and ended up visiting around 50 South Sea islands, among them Bora Bora. His *Tales of the South Pacific* (1947) tells of the impact of WW II on the South Pacific and the Pacific's impact on those who served. It was later made into the long-running Broadway musical, *South Pacific.* Michener's *Return to Paradise* (1951) is a readable collection of essays and short stories.

Eugene Burdick is best known for his best-sellers *The Ugly American* (1958) and *Fail-Safe* (1962). Like Michener, Burdick served in the Pacific during WW II. His 1961 book *The Blue of Capricorn* is a collection of essays and short stories on the area.

Many of the classics mentioned above (or extracts from them) are available in cheap paperback editions in the series "Tales of the Pacific" from Mutual Publishing Company, 1127 11th Ave., Mezzanine B, Honolulu, HI 96816, U.S.A. (tel. 808/732-1709, fax 808/734-4094). Write for a complete list. See also "Resources" at the end of this book.

Robert Louis Stevenson

French. Sitting through one (one to two hours) is often worthwhile just to hear the singing and to observe the women's hats. Never wear a pareu to church—you'll be asked to leave. Young missionaries from the Church of Latter-day Saints (Mormons) continue to flock to Polynesia from the U.S. for two-year stays. They wear short-sleeved white shirts with ties and travel in pairs—you may spot a couple.

The most sinister religious development in recent years occurred on Faaite atoll in the Tuamotus in early September 1987. A pair of self-proclaimed fundamentalist crusaders from the "charismatic renewal movement" managed to instill such intense revivalist fervor in the villagers that six people were actually burned to death, some by their own children, to exorcise "devils" that threatened the island with disaster. A radio alert brought the mayor and a Catholic priest to the scene just in time to prevent another four "impure souls" from being sacrificed to the "healing" fire. In 1990 24 Faaite villagers were found guilty of the act, and ringleader François Mauati was sentenced to 14 years of imprisonment.

LANGUAGE

Tahitian and French are both official languages, but official documents and speeches as a rule are in French and are rarely translated. French is spoken throughout the territory, and visitors will sometimes have difficulty making themselves understood in English, although everyone involved in the tourist industry speaks English. It's useful to brush up on your high school French a little by checking out some French language records/tapes from your local public library before you arrive. The "Capsule French Vocabulary" at the end of this book may also help you get by. Large Chinese stores often have someone who speaks English, though members of the Chinese community use "Hakka" among themselves. Young Polynesians often become curious and friendly when they hear you speaking English.

Tahitian or Maohi is one of a family of Austronesian languages spoken from Madagascar through Indonesia, all the way to Easter Island and Hawaii. The related languages of Eastern

Robert Dodd's famous 1790 painting of Fletcher Christian aboard HMS Bounty bidding farewell to Capain Bligh and the loyal members of his crew.

Polynesia (Hawaiian, Tahitian, Tuamotuan, Mangarevan, Marquesan, Maori) are quite different from those of Western Polynesia (Samoan, Tongan). Today, as communications improve, the outer-island dialects are becoming mingled with the predominant Tahitian. Among the Polynesian languages the consonants did the changing rather than the vowels. The *k* and *l* in Hawaiian are generally rendered as a *t* and *r* in Tahitian.

Instead of attempting to speak French to the Tahitians—a foreign language for you both—turn to the Tahitian vocabulary at the end of this book and give it a try. Remember to pronounce each vowel separately, *a* as the *ah* in "far," *e* as the *ai* in "day," *i* as the *ee* in "see," *o* as the *oh* in "go," and *u* as the *oo* in "lulu"—the same as in Latin or Spanish. Written Tahitian has only eight consonants: *f, h, m, n, p, r, t, v.* Two consonants never follow one another, and all words end in a vowel. No silent letters exist in Tahitian, but there is a glottal stop, often marked with an apostrophe. A slight variation in pronunciation or vowel length can change the meaning of a word completely, so don't be surprised if your efforts produce some unexpected results!

Some of the many English words that have entered Tahitian through contact with early seamen include: *faraipani* (frying pan), *manua* (man of war), *matete* (market), *mati* (match), *moni* (money), *oniani* (onion), *painapo* (pineapple), *pani* (pan), *pata* (butter), *pipi* (peas), *poti* (boat), *taiete* (society), *tapitana* (captain), *tauera* (towel), and *tavana* (governor).

Writer Pierre Loti was impressed by the mystical vocabulary of Tahitian:

> *The sad, weird, mysterious utterances of nature: the scarcely articulate stirrings of fancy. . . . Faa-fano: the departure of the soul at death. Aa: happiness, earth, sky, paradise. Mahoi: essence or soul of God. Tapetape: the line where the sea grows deep. Tutai: red clouds on the horizon. Ari: depth, emptiness, a wave of the sea. Po: night, unknown dark world, Hell.*

CONDUCT AND CUSTOMS

The dress code in Tahiti-Polynesia is very casual—you can even go around barefoot. Cleanliness *is* important, however. Formal wear or jacket and tie are unnecessary (unless you're to be received by the high commissioner!). One exception is downtown Papeete, where scanty dress would be out of place. For clothing tips, see "What To Take," in the On the Road chapter.

People usually shake hands when meeting; visitors are expected to shake hands with everyone present. If a Polynesian man's hand is dirty he'll extend his wrist or elbow. Women kiss each other on the cheeks. When entering a private residence it's polite to remove your shoes. It's okay to show interest in the possessions of a host, but don't lavish too much praise on any single object or he/she may feel obligated to give it to you. It's rude to refuse food offered by a Tahitian, but don't eat everything on your plate just to be polite, as this will be a signal to your host that you want another helping. Often guests in a private home are expected to eat while the family watches.

All the beaches of Tahiti-Polynesia are public to one meter above the high-tide mark, although some watchdogs don't recognize this. Topless sunbathing is completely legal in Tahiti-Polynesia, though total nudity is only practiced on off-shore *motus* and floating pontoons.

Despite the apparent laissez-faire attitude promoted in the travel brochures and this book, female travelers should take care: there have been sexual assaults by Polynesian men on foreign women who seemed to project an image of promiscuity by sunbathing topless on a remote beach or even by traveling alone! Women should avoid staying in isolated tourist bungalows or camping outside organized campgrounds. We've also heard of cases of laundry being stolen from the line, hotel and car break-ins, park muggings, and even mass holdups at knifepoint, but luckily such things are still the exception here.

DIANA LASICH HARPER

a canoe race at Papeete

ON THE ROAD

Highlights

Tahiti-Polynesia abounds in things to see and do, including many in the "not to be missed" category. Papeete's colorful morning market and captivating waterfront welcome you to Polynesia. No visitor should miss the ferry ride to Moorea and the island's stunning Opunohu Valley, replete with splendid scenery, lush vegetation, and fascinating archaeological sites. Further afield, an even greater concentration of old Polynesian *marae* (temples) awaits visitors to Maeva on the enchanting island of Huahine. The natural wonders of Bora Bora have been applauded many times but neighboring Maupiti has more of the same, though its pleasures are far less known. Polynesia's most spectacular atoll may be Rangiroa, where the Avatoru and Tiputa passes offer exciting snorkel rides on the incoming tide.

Sports and Recreation

As elsewhere in the South Pacific, scuba diving is the most popular sport among visitors, and well-established dive shops exist on Tahiti, Moorea, Huahine, Raiatea, Bora Bora, Rangiroa, and Tikehau. Prices are highest on Bora Bora, so you may want to schedule your diving elsewhere. Instead, take one of the highly recommended boat trips (with shark feeding) on the Bora Bora lagoon. At Rangiroa, divers get to

float through the pass for their money. In these warm waters wetsuits are not required. Golfers will certainly want to complete the 18 holes at the International Golf Course Olivier Breaud on Tahiti, the territory's only major course. Horseback riding is available on Moorea, Huahine, and Raiatea, with the Huahine operation especially recommended. Virtually all of Tahiti-Polynesia's charter yacht operations are concentrated on Raiatea.

ENTERTAINMENT

The big hotels on Tahiti and Bora Bora offer exciting dance shows several nights a week. They're usually accompanied by a barbecue or traditional feast, but if the price asked for the meal is too steep, settle for a drink at the bar and enjoy the show (no cover charge). Many of the regular performances are listed in this book, but be sure to call the hotel to confirm the time and date as these do change to accommodate tour groups.

On Friday and Saturday nights discos crank up in most towns and these are good places to meet the locals. The nonhotel bar scene is limited mostly to Papeete. The drinking age in Tahiti-Polynesia is officially 18, but it's not strictly enforced.

Music and Dance

Though the missionaries banned dancing completely in the 1820s and the 19th-century French colonial administration only allowed performances that didn't disturb Victorian decorum, traditional Tahitian dancing experienced a revival in the 1950s with the formation of Madeleine Moua's Pupu Heiva dance troupe, followed in the 1960s by Coco Hotahota's Temaeva and Gilles Hollande's Ora Tahiti. These groups rediscovered the near-forgotten myths of old Polynesia and popularized them with exciting music, dance, song, and costumes. Now during major festivals several dozen troupes of 20-50 dancers and 6-10 musicians participate in thrilling competitions.

The Tahitian *tamure* or *'ori Tahiti* is a fast, provocative, erotic dance done by rapidly shifting the weight from one foot to the other. The rubber-legged men are almost acrobatic, though their movements tend to follow those of the women closely. The tossing, shell-decorated bast or fiber skirts *(mores)*, the pandanus wands in the hands, and the tall headdresses add to the drama.

Dances such as the *aparima*, *'ote'a*, and *hivinau* reenact Polynesian legends, and each movement tells part of a story. The *aparima* is a dance resembling the Hawaiian hula or Samoan siva executed mainly with the hands in a standing or sitting position. The hand movements repeat the story told in the accompanying song. The *'ote'a* is a theme dance executed to the accompaniment of drums with great precision and admirable timing by a group of men and/or women arrayed in two lines. The *ute* is a restrained dance based on ancient refrains.

Listen to the staccato beat of the *to'ere*, a slit rosewood-wood drum, each slightly different in size and pitch, hit with a stick. A split-bamboo drum *(ofe)* hit against the ground often provides a contrasting sound. The *pahu* is a more conventional bass drum made from a hollowed coconut tree trunk with a sharkskin cover. Another traditional Polynesian musical instrument is the bamboo nose flute *(vivo)*, though today guitars and ukuleles are more often seen. The ukulele was originally the *braguinha*, brought to Hawaii by Portuguese immigrants a century ago. Homemade ukuleles with the half-shells of coconuts as sound boxes emit pleasant tones, while those sporting empty tins give a more metallic sound.

Traditional Tahitian vocal music was limited to nonharmonious chants conveying oral history and customs, and the *himene* or "hymn" sung by large choirs today is based on these ancient chants. The spiritual quality of the *himene* can be electrifying, so for the musical experience of a lifetime, attend church any Sunday.

Stone Fishing

This traditional method of fishing is now practiced only on very special occasions in the Leeward Islands. Coconut fronds are tied end to end until a line half a km long is ready. Several dozen outrigger canoes form a semicircle. Advancing slowly together, men in the canoes beat the water with stones tied to ropes. The frightened fish are thus driven toward a beach. When the water is shallow enough, the men leap from their canoes, push the leaf line before them, yell, and beat the water with their hands. In this way the fish are literally forced ashore into an open bamboo fence, where they are caught. See "Tahaa" in the chapter on Raiatea and Tahaa for more information.

PUBLIC HOLIDAYS AND FESTIVALS

Public holidays in Tahiti-Polynesia include New Year's Day (1 January), Gospel Day (5 March), Good Friday and Easter Monday (March/April), Labor Day (1 May), Ascension Day (May), Whitsunday and Whitmonday (May/June), Bastille Day (14 July), Assumption Day (15 August), Internal Autonomy Day (29 June), All Saints' Day (1 November), Armistice Day (11 November), and Christmas Day (25 December). Ironically, Internal Autonomy Day actually commemorates 29 June 1880 when Tahiti-Polynesia became a full French colony, not 6 September 1984 when the territory achieved a small degree of internal autonomy. *Everything* will be closed on these holidays (and maybe also the days before and after—ask).

The big event of the year is the two-week-long **Heiva i Tahiti,** which runs from the end of June to Bastille Day (14 July). Formerly known as La Fête du Juillet or the Tiurai Festival (the Tahitian word *tiurai* comes from the English July), it brings

TAHITIAN DANCE MOVEMENTS

anuanua
rainbow

ao
day

here
to love

maeva
welcome

mana'o
to think

marama
moon

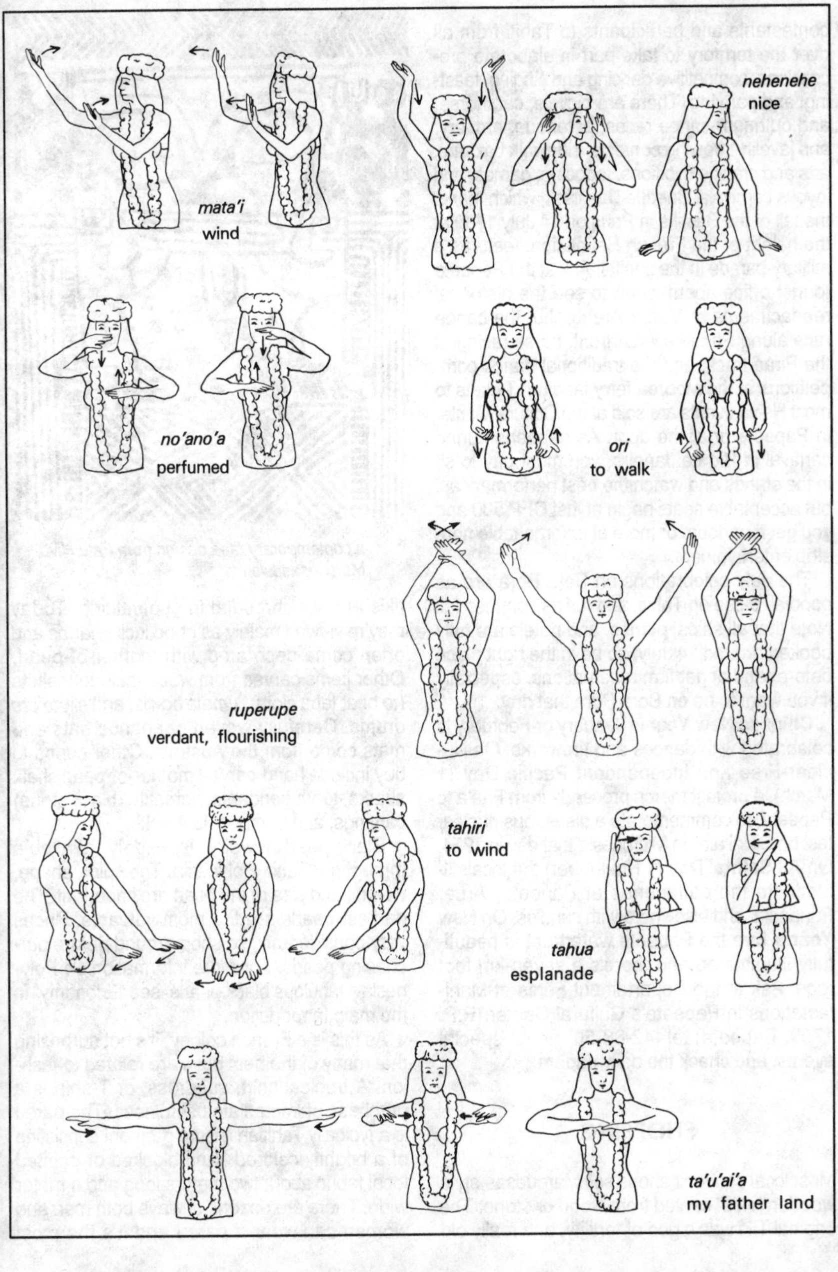

mata'i
wind

nehenehe
nice

no'ano'a
perfumed

ori
to walk

ruperupe
verdant, flourishing

tahiri
to wind

tahua
esplanade

ta'u'ai'a
my father land

LOUISE FOOTE

contestants and participants to Tahiti from all over the territory to take part in elaborate processions, competitive dancing and singing, feasting, and partying. There are bicycle, car, horse, and outrigger-canoe races, petanque, archery, and javelin-throwing contests, sidewalk bazaars, arts and crafts exhibitions, tattooing, games, and joyous carnivals. **Bastille Day** itself, which marks the fall of the Bastille in Paris on 14 July 1789 at the height of the French Revolution, features a military parade in the capital. Ask at the Papeete tourist office about when to see the historical reenactments at Marae Arahurahu, the canoe race along Papeete waterfront, horse racing at the Pirae track, and the traditional dance competitions at the Moorea ferry landing. Tickets to most Heiva events are sold at the Cultural Center in Papeete or at the door. As happens during carnival in Rio de Janeiro, you must pay to sit in the stands and watch the best performances, but acceptable seats begin at just CFP 500 and you get four hours or more of unforgettable nonstop entertainment.

The July celebrations on Bora Bora are as good as those on Tahiti, and not as commercial. Note that all ships, planes, and hotels are fully booked around 14 July, so be in the right place beforehand or get firm reservations, especially if you want to be on Bora Bora that day.

Chinese New Year in January or February is celebrated with dances and fireworks. On Nuclear-Free and Independent Pacific Day (1 March), a protest march proceeds from Faa'a to Papeete, to commemorate a disastrous nuclear test on Bikini atoll in Micronesia that day in 1954. On **All Saints' Day** (1 November) the locals illuminate the cemeteries at Papeete, Arue, Punaauia, and elsewhere with candles. On **New Year's Eve** the Papeete waterfront is beautifully illuminated and there's a seven-km foot race. Ask at the Departement Fêtes et Manifestations in Papeete's Cultural Center (B.P. 1709, Papeete; tel. 42-88-50) about special events, and check the daily papers.

SHOPPING

Most local souvenir shops sell Marquesas-style wooden "tikis" carved from wood or stone. The original Tiki was a god of fertility, and really old

a contemporary tapa design from Fatu Hiva, Marquesas Islands

tikis are still shrouded in superstition. Today they're viewed mainly as good luck charms and often come decorated with mother-of-pearl. Other items carved from wood include mallets (to beat tapa cloth), *umete* bowls, and slit *to'ere* drums. Carefully woven pandanus hats and mats come from the Australs. Other curios to buy include hand-carved mother-of-pearl shell, sharks'-tooth pendants, hematite (black stone) carvings, and bamboo fishhooks.

Black-pearl jewelry is widely available throughout Tahiti-Polynesia. The color, shape, weight, and size of the pearl are important. The darkest pearls are the most valuable. Prices vary considerably, so shop around before purchasing pearls. For more information on Polynesia's fabulous black pearls, see "Economy" in the main Introduction.

As this is a French colony, it's not surprising that many of the best buys are related to fashion. A tropical shirt, sundress, or T-shirt is a purchase of immediate usefulness. The pareu is a typically Tahitian leisure garment consisting of a brightly colored hand-blocked or painted local fabric about two meters long and a meter wide. There are dozens of ways both men and women can wear a pareu and it's the most common apparel for local women throughout the territory, including Papeete, so pick one up! Local cosmetics like Monoi Tiare Tahiti, a fragrant coconut-oil skin moisturizer, and coconut-oil soap will put you in form. Jasmine shampoo, cologne, and perfume are also made locally from the tiare Tahiti flower. Vanilla is used to flavor coffee.

As weaving was unknown in the old days, tapa cloth was made by women from the bark of the paper mulberry, breadfruit, and banyan trees. The boughs were soaked in a river for several days, the outer bark then stripped off and the inner bark separated from it. The softened inner bark was placed on a block of wood and beaten with a mallet. When the tapa was of a uniform thickness it was dried in the sun and dyed. Floral or geometric patterns were printed or painted on.

Early missionaries introduced the Tahitians to quilting, and two-layer patchwork *tifaifai* have now taken the place of tapa (bark cloth). Used as bed covers and pillows by tourists, *tifaifai* is still used by Tahitians to cloak newlyweds and to cover coffins. To be wrapped in a *tifaifai* is the highest honor. Each woman has individual quilt patterns that are her trademarks and bold floral designs are popular, with contrasting colors drawn from nature. A good *tifaifai* can take up to six months to complete and cost US$1000. The French artist Henri Matisse, who in 1930 spent several weeks at the now-demolished Stuart Hôtel on Papeete's boulevard Pomare, was so impressed by the Tahitian *tifaifai* that he applied the same technique and adopted many designs for his *"gouaches découpees."*

Those who have been thrilled by hypnotic Tahitian music and dance will want to take some Polynesian music home with them on cassette (CFP 2000) or compact disc (CFP 3000), available at hotels and souvenir shops throughout the islands. The largest local company producing these CDs is Editions Manuiti or Tamure Records (B.P. 755, Papeete; tel. 42-82-39, fax 43-27-24). Among the well-known local singers and musicians appearing on Manuiti are Bimbo, Charley Mauu, Guy Roche, Yves Roche, Emma Terangi, Andy Tupaia, and Henriette Winkler. Small Tahitian groups like the Moorea Lagon Kaina Boys, the Barefoot Boys, and Tamarii Punaruu, and large folkloric ensembles such as Maeva Tahiti, Tiare Tahiti, and Coco's Temaeva (often recorded at major festivals) are also well represented. Turn to the Resources chapter at the end of this book for specific CD listings.

Hustling and bargaining are not practiced in Tahiti-Polynesia: it's expensive for everyone. Haggling may even be considered insulting, so just pay the price asked or keep looking. Many local food prices are subsidized by the government. Avoid whopping markups and taxes; instead, purchase food and handicrafts from the producers themselves at markets or roadside stalls. Luckily, there's no sales tax in Tahiti!

ACCOMMODATIONS

With *Tahiti-Polynesia Handbook* in hand you're guaranteed a good, inexpensive place to stay on every island. Each and every hotel in the region is included herein, not just a selection. We don't solicit freebies from the hotel chains; our only income derives from the price you paid when you bought this book. So we don't mind telling you that, as usual, most of the luxury hotels are just not worth the exorbitant prices they charge. Many simply recreate Hawaii at twice the cost, offering far more luxury than you need. Even worse, they tend to isolate you in a French/American/Australian environment away from the South Pacific you came to experience. We list them here for comparison, and most are worth visiting as sightseeing attractions, watering holes, or sources of entertainment, but unless you're a millionaire sleep elsewhere.

One of the golden rules of independent travel is the more you spend, the less you experience. If you're on a budget, avoid prepaying hotel accommodations booked from home as you can always do better locally upon arrival. If, however, you really do intend to spend most of your time at a specific first-class hotel, you'll benefit from bulk rates by taking a package tour instead of paying the much higher "rack rate" the hotels charge individuals who just walk in off the street. Call Air New Zealand's toll-free number and ask them to mail you their *Hotpac* brochure, which lists deluxe hotel rooms on Tahiti, Moorea, Huahine, Bora Bora, Rangiroa, and other islands that can be booked on an individual basis at slightly reduced rates. Bear in mind, however, that on all the islands there are middle-level hotels that charge half what these top-end places ask, while providing adequate comfort. And if you really *can* afford US$250 a night and up, you'd do better chartering a skippered or bareboat yacht.

A wise government regulation prohibiting buildings higher than a coconut tree outside Papeete means that most of the hotels are low-rise or consist of small Tahitian *fares*. When picking a hotel, keep in mind that although a thatched bungalow is cooler and infinitely more attractive than a concrete box, it's also more likely to have insect problems. If in doubt check the window screens and carry mosquito coils and/or repellent. Hopefully there'll be a resident lizard or two to feed on the bugs. As the lagoon waters off the northwest corner of Tahiti become increasingly polluted with raw sewage, hotels like the Beachcomber and Maeva Beach fall back on their swimming pools. On all of the outer islands open to foreign tourists, the water is so clear it makes pools superfluous.

Hotel prices range from CFP 800 for a dormitory bed all the way up to CFP 58,000 single or double without meals, plus tax. Price wars often erupt between rival hotels, and at times you're charged less than the prices quoted herein! When things are really slow even the luxury

hotels sometimes discount their rooms. If your hotel can't provide running water, electricity, air-conditioning, or something similar because of a hurricane or otherwise, ask for a price reduction. You'll often get 10% off. The budget places often provide cooking facilities which allow you to save a lot on food. An eight percent room tax is added to the room rates at the hotels, but it doesn't apply to pensions and family-operated accommodations (the tax is used to finance tourism promotion). Many small hotels add a surcharge to your bill if you stay only one night and some charge a supplement during the high season (July, August, and at Christmas).

A room with cooking facilities can save you a lot on restaurant meals, and some moderately priced establishments have weekly rates. If you have to choose a meal plan, take only breakfast and dinner (Modified American Plan or half pension) and have fruit for lunch. As you check into your room, note the nearest fire exits. Don't automatically take the first room offered; if you're paying good money look at several, then choose. Single women intending to stay in isolated tourist bungalows should try to find someone with whom to share.

Low-Budget Accommodations

A tent saves the budget traveler a lot of money and proves very convenient to fall back on. The Polynesians usually don't mind if you camp, and quite a few French locals also have tents. Regular campgrounds exist on Tahiti, Moorea,

Club Bed at Fare, Huahine, is popular among budget travelers.

Raiatea, and Bora Bora, catering to the growing number of camper-tourists. On Huahine and Rangiroa it's possible to camp at certain small hotels (listed herein). On the outer islands camping should be no problem, but ask permission of the landowner, or pitch your tent well out of sight of the road. Ensure this same hospitality for the next traveler by not leaving a mess. Make sure your tent is water- and mosquito-proof and never pitch a tent directly below coconuts hanging from a tree or a precariously leaning trunk.

Dormitory or "bunkroom" accommodations are available on all of the main islands with communal cooking facilities usually provided. These are excellent if you're traveling alone and they're just the place to meet other travelers, although couples can usually get a double room for a price only slightly above two dorm beds. For the most part, the dormitories are safe and congenial for those who don't mind sacrificing their privacy to save money.

Be aware that some of the low-budget places included in this book are a lot more basic than what is sometimes referred to as "budget" accommodations in the States. The standards of cleanliness in the common bathrooms may be lower than you expected, the furnishings "early attic," the beds uncomfortable, linens and towels skimpy, housekeeping nonexistent, and window screens lacking. Luckily, good medium-priced accommodations are usually available for those of us unwilling to put up with spartan conditions, and we include all of them in this book too.

Paying Guests

A unique accommodations option worth looking into is the well-organized homestay program, in which you get a private room or bungalow with a local family. *Logement chez l'habitant* is available on all the outer islands, and even in Papeete itself; the tourist office supplies printed lists. Travel agents abroad won't book the cheaper hotels or lodgings with the inhabitants because no commissions are paid, so you must make reservations directly with the owners themselves by either mail or phone. Letters are usually not answered, so calling ahead from Papeete is best; things change fast and printed listings are often out of date. Most pensions don't accept credit cards, and English may not be spoken.

These private guesthouses can be hard to locate. There's usually no sign outside, and some don't cater to walk-in clients who show up unexpectedly. Also, the limited number of beds in each may all be taken. Sometimes you'll get airport transfers at no additional charge if you book ahead. Don't expect hot water in the bath or a lot of privacy. Often cooking facilities or meals are included (often seafood); the provision of blankets and towels may depend on the price. The family may loan you a bicycle and can be generally helpful in arranging tours, etc. It's a great way to meet the people while finding a place to stay.

In remote areas residents are often very hospitable and may offer to put you up. Try to find some tangible way to show your appreciation, such as paying for the groceries or giving a gift. It wouldn't hurt to offer cash payment if a stranger helps you when you're in a jam. Once you get home, don't forget to mail prints of any photos you've taken. If you do make friends on one island, ask them to write you a letter of introduction to their relatives on another.

FOOD AND DRINK

Restaurants are expensive, but you can bring the price way down by ordering only a single main dish. Fresh bread and cold water come with the meal. Avoid appetizers, alcohol, and desserts. No taxes or service charges are tacked on, and tipping is unnecessary. So it's really not as expensive as it looks! US$15 will usually see you through an excellent no-frills lunch of fried fish at a small French restaurant. The same thing in a hotel dining room will be about 50% more. Even the finest places are affordable if you order this way.

Most restaurants post their menu in the window. If not, have a look at it before sitting down. Check the main plates, as that's all you'll need to take. If the price is right, the ambiance is congenial, and local French are at the tables, sit right down. Sure, food at a snack bar would be half as much, but your Coke will be extra, and in the end it's smart to pay a little more to enjoy excellent cuisine once in a while. Steer clear of restaurants where you see a big plastic bottle of mineral water on every table, as this will add a couple of hundred francs to your bill. Also beware of set meals designed for tourists as these usually cost double the average entree. If you can't order a la carte walk back out the door.

Local restaurants offer French, Chinese, Vietnamese, Italian, and, of course, Tahitian dishes. The *nouvelle cuisine Tahitienne* is a combination of European and Asian recipes, with local seafoods and vegetables, plus the classic *maa Tahiti* (Tahitian food). The French are famous for their sauces, so try something exotic. Lunch is the main meal of the day in Tahiti-Polynesia, and many restaurants offer a *plat du jour* designed for regular customers. This is often displayed on a blackboard near the entrance and is usually good value. Most restaurants stop serving lunch at 1400, dinner at 2200. Don't expect snappy service: what's the rush, anyway?

If it's all too expensive, groceries are a good alternative. There are lots of nice places to picnic, and at CFP 35 a loaf, that crisp French white bread is incredibly cheap and good.

French baguettes are subsidized by the government, unlike that awful sliced white bread in a plastic package which is CFP 240 a loaf! Cheap red wines like Selection Faragui are imported from France in bulk and bottled locally in plastic bottles. Add a nice piece of French cheese to the above and you're ready for a budget traveler's banquet. *Casse-croûtes,* big healthy sandwiches made with those long French baguettes, are CFP 250.

There's also Martinique rum and Hinano beer (CFP 130 in grocery stores), brewed locally by Heineken. Remember the CFP 60 deposit on Hinano beer bottles, which makes beer cheap to buy cold and carry out. Moorea's famous Rotui fruit drinks are sold in tall liter containers in a variety of types. The best is perhaps *pamplemousse* (grapefruit), produced from local Moorea fruit, but the pineapple juice is also outstanding. At about CFP 210 a carton, they're excellent value.

If you're going to the outer islands, take as many edibles with you as possible; it's always

underwater attractions of Tahiti-Polynesia (photos courtesy Tahiti Tourisme)

(top left) lighthouse, Point Venus, Tahiti (David Stanley); (top right) church at Pueu, Tahiti Iti (David Stanley); (bottom) a house on Moorea (Phil Esmonde)

more expensive there. Keep in mind that virtually every food plant you see growing on the islands is cultivated by someone. Even fishing floats or seashells washed up on a beach, or fish in the lagoon near someone's home, may be considered private property.

Tahitian Food

If you can spare the cash, attend a Tahitian *tamaaraa* (feast) at a big hotel and try some Polynesian dishes roasted in an *ahimaa* (underground oven). Basalt stones are preheated with a wood fire in a meter-deep pit, then covered with leaves. Each type of food is wrapped separately in banana leaves to retain its own flavor and lowered in. The oven is covered with more banana leaves, wet sacking, and sand, and left one to three hours to bake: suckling pig, mahimahi, taro, *umara* (sweet potato), *uru* (breadfruit), and *fafa,* a spinachlike cooked vegetable made from taro tops.

Also sample the gamy flavor of *fei,* the red cooking banana that flourishes in Tahiti's uninhabited interior. The Tahitian chestnut tree *(mape)* grows near streams and the delicious cooked nuts can often be purchased at markets. *Miti hue* is a coconut-milk sauce fermented with the juice of river shrimp. Traditionally *maa Tahiti* is eaten with the fingers.

Poisson cru (ia ota), small pieces of raw bonito (skipjack) or yellowfin marinated with lime juice and soaked in coconut milk, is enjoyable, as is *fafaru* ("smelly fish"), prepared by marinating pieces of fish in seawater in an airtight coconut-shell container. As with the durian, although the smell is repugnant, the first bite can be addicting. Other typical Tahitian plates are chicken and pork casserole with *fafa,* pork and cabbage casserole *(pua'a chou),* and kid cooked in ginger.

Poe is a sweet pudding made of starch flour flavored with either banana, vanilla, papaya, taro, or pumpkin and topped with salted coconut-milk sauce. Many varieties of this treat are made throughout Polynesia. *Faraoa ipo* is Tuamotu coconut bread. The local coffee is flavored with vanilla bean and served with sugar and coconut cream.

Taro is an elephant-eared plant cultivated in freshwater swamps. The sweet potato (*umara*) is a vegetable of South American ori-

gin—varying explanations of how it reached Oceania still provoke controversy. Papaya (pawpaw) is nourishing: a third of a cup contains as much vitamin C as 18 apples. To ripen a green papaya overnight, puncture it a few times with a knife. Don't overeat papaya—unless you *need* an effective laxative. Atoll dwellers especially rely on the coconut for food. The tree reaches maturity in eight years, then produces about 50 nuts a year for 60 years. Many islanders eat raw shellfish and fish, but know what you're doing before you join them—their stomachs may be stronger than yours. It's safer to eat well-cooked food, and to peel your own fruit.

Breadfruit

The breadfruit *(uru)* is the plant most often associated with the South Pacific. The theme of a man turning himself into such a tree to save his family during famine often recurs in Polynesian legends. Ancient voyagers brought breadfruit shoots or seeds from Southeast Asia. When baked in an underground oven or roasted over flames, the now-seedless Polynesian variety resembles bread. Joseph Banks, botanist on Captain Cook's first voyage, wrote:

> *If a man should in the course of his lifetime plant 10 trees, which if well done might take the labor of an hour or thereabouts, he would completely fulfill his duty to his own as well as future generations.*

breadfruit (Artcarpus altilis)

LOUISE FOOTE

The French naturalist Sonnerat transplanted breadfruit to Reunion in the Indian Ocean as early as 1772, but it's Capt. William Bligh who shall always be remembered when the plant is mentioned. In 1787 Bligh set out to collect young shoots in Tahiti for transfer to the West Indies, where they were to be planted to feed slaves. On the way back, his crew mutinied in Tongan waters and cast off both breadfruit and Bligh. The indomitable captain managed to reach Dutch Timor in a rowboat and in 1792 returned to Tahiti with another ship to complete his task.

The breadfruit *(Artocarpus altilis)*, a tall tree with broad green leaves, provides shade as well as food. A well-watered tree can produce as many as 1,000 pale green breadfruits a year. Robert Lee Eskridge described a breadfruit thus:

Its outer rind or skin, very hard, is covered with a golf-ball-like surface of small irregular pits or tiny hollows. An inner rind about a half-inch thick surrounds the fruit itself, which when baked tastes not unlike a doughy potato. Perhaps fresh bread, rolled up until it becomes a semi-firm mass, best describes the breadfruit when cooked.

The starchy, easily digested fruit is rich in vitamin B. When consumed with a protein such as fish or meat it serves as an energy food. The Polynesians learned to preserve breadfruit by pounding it into a paste, which was kept in leaf-lined pits to ferment into *mahi*. Like the coconut, the breadfruit tree itself had many uses, including the provision of wood for outrigger canoes.

SERVICES AND INFORMATION

VISAS AND OFFICIALDOM

Everyone needs a passport. French citizens are admitted freely for an unlimited stay, and citizens of the European Union (E.U.) countries, Norway, and Switzerland, get three months without a visa. Citizens of the United States, Canada, New Zealand, and Japan can obtain a one-month "visa" free upon arrival at Papeete (no different than any other passport stamp). Most others (Australians included) must apply to a French diplomatic mission for a three-month visa (US$50), but it's usually issued without delay. Make sure the words "French Polynesia" are endorsed on the visa, otherwise you could have problems.

Extensions of stay are possible after you arrive, but they cost CFP 3000 and you'll have to go to the post office to buy a stamp. You'll also need to show "sufficient funds," and your ticket to leave Tahiti-Polynesia, and provide one photo. North Americans are limited to three months total; it's better to ask for a three-month stay upon arrival, making this formality unnecessary.

Tahiti-Polynesia requires a ticket to leave of everyone (including nonresident French citizens). If you arrive without one, you'll be refused entry or required to post a cash bond equivalent to the value of a ticket back to your home country. If you're on an open-ended holiday, you can easily get around this requirement by purchasing a refundable Air New Zealand ticket back to the U.S. or wherever before leaving home. If you catch a boat headed to Fiji (for example), simply have the airline reissue the ticket so it's a ticket to leave your next destination—and on you go.

Yacht Entry

The main port of entry for cruising yachts is Papeete. Upon application to the local gendarme, entry may also be allowed at Moorea, Huahine, Raiatea, Bora Bora, Rurutu, Tubuai, Raivavae, Rangiroa, Nuku Hiva, Hiva Oa, or Ua Pou. The gendarmes are usually friendly and courteous, if you are. Boats arriving from Tonga, Fiji, and the Samoas must be fumigated.

Anyone arriving by yacht without an onward ticket must post a bond at a local bank equivalent to the airfare back to their country of origin. In Taiohae the bond is US$1200 pp, but in Papeete it's only US$600 (for Americans). This is refundable upon departure at any branch of the same bank, less a three percent adminis-

---

FRENCH CONSULATES-GENERAL

Here are a few French consulates-general:

Australia: St. Martin's Tower, 31 Market St., Sydney, NSW 2000 (tel. 61-2/261-5779); 492 St. Kilda Rd., Melbourne, Victoria 3004 (tel. 61-3/9820-0921); 6 Perth Ave., Yarralumla, Canberra, ACT 2600 (tel. 61-6/270-5111)

Canada: French consulates-general are found in Edmonton, Halifax, Moncton, Montreal, Ottawa, Quebec, Toronto, and Vancouver.

Chile: Ave. Condell 65, Providencia, Santiago de Chile (tel. 56-2/225-1030)

Fiji: Dominion House, Thomson St., Private Mail Bag, Suva (tel. 679/300-991)

Hawaii: 2 Waterfront Plaza, 500 Ala Moana Blvd., Honolulu, HI 96813 (tel. 808/599-4458)

Japan: 11-44, 4 Chome, Minami Azabu, Minato-Ku, Tokyo 106 (tel. 81-3/5420-8800); Ohbayashi Bldg., 24th Floor, 4-33, Kitahama-Higashi, Chuo-Ku, Osaka 540 (tel. 81-6/946-6181)

Hong Kong: Admiralty Center Tower 2, 26th Floor, 18 Harcourt Rd., G.P.O. Box 13, Hong Kong (tel. 852-5/294351)

New Zealand: 1 Willeston St., Box 1695, Wellington (tel. 64-4/472-0200)

Singapore: 5 Gallop Rd., Singapore 1025 (tel. 65/466-4866)

U.S.A.: French consulates-general exist in Atlanta, Boston, Chicago, Houston, Los Angeles, Miami, New Orleans, New York, Puerto Rico, San Francisco, and Washington. Get the address of the one nearest you by dialing the toll-free number of Air France.

trative fee. Make sure the receipt shows the currency in which the original deposit was made and get an assurance that it will be refunded in kind. To reclaim the bond you'll also need a letter from Immigration verifying that you've officially checked out. If any individual on the yacht doesn't have the bond money, the captain is responsible. Once the bond is posted, a "temporary" three-month visa (CFP 3000) is issued, which means you have three months to get to Papeete where an additional three months (another CFP 3000) may be granted. Actually, the rules are not hard-and-fast, and everyone has a different experience. Crew changes should be made at Papeete.

After clearing Customs in Papeete, outbound yachts may spend the duration of their period of stay cruising the outer islands. Make sure every island where you *might* stop is listed on your clearance. The officials want all transient boats out of the country by 31 October, the onset of the hurricane season. Yachts staying longer than one year are charged full Customs duty on the vessel.

TAHITI - POLYNÉSIE FRANÇAISE
CARTE DÉBARQUEMENT - EMBARQUEMENT/*Disembarkation - Embarkation card*

IMPORTANT Veuillez remplir ce document avec soin. Toutes les copies doivent être lisibles. Please print clearly. All copies must be legible.	Nom/*Surname (En caractères d'imprimerie/Block letters)*
	Nom de jeune fille/*Maiden name*
	Prénom/*Given name*

| Sexe/*Sex* (Cochez/*Tick*) | ☐ Masculin/*Male* | ☐ Féminin/*Female* |

Date de naissance
Date of birth   Quantième/*Day*   Mois/*Month*   Année/*Year*

Lieu de naissance
Place of birth

Nationalité
Nationality

Profession
Occupation

Domicile permanent
Permanent address   Rue/*Street*

Ville/*City*   Département/*State*   Pays/*Country*

Port d'embarquement
Port of embarkation   Vol n°
Flight

Port de débarquement après la Polynésie Frse
Port of disembarkation after French Polynesia

Adresse ou hôtel(s) en Polynésie Frse
Address or hotel(s) in French Polynesia

Durée de séjour en Polynésie Frse ...... jours   ☐ Transit (moins de 24 h)
Length of stay in French Polynesia ...... days   (less than 24 h)

Je suis   ☐ Visiteur   ☐ Résident temporaire de P.F   ☐ Résident permanent de P.F
I am   ☐ Visitor   ☐ Temporary resident of F.P   ☐ Permanent resident of F.P

Passeport N°
Passport N°

N° 144196

MONEY

The French Pacific franc or *Cour de Franc Pacifique* (CFP) is legal tender in both Tahiti-Polynesia and New Caledonia. There are beautifully colored big banknotes of CFP 500, 1000, 5000, and 10,000, coins of CFP 1, 2, 5, 10, 20, 50, and 100.

The origin of this currency is interesting. During WW II the French franc (FF) had been devalued to less than a third its prewar value, while prices remained stable in the Pacific. When the French colonies reestablished contact with metropolitan France after wartime separation, a new currency was needed to avoid economic chaos. Thus the CFP was created in 1945 at the rate of 2.4 FF to one CFP. Over the next few years the French franc was further devalued three times and each time the CFP was revalued against it, lowering the French franc to 5.50 to one CFP by 1949. At the same time 100 old FF became one new FF, thus 5.5 new FF equaled 100 old CFP, a relationship which has been maintained ever since. Until 1967 the Banque de l'Indochine was responsible for issuing and circulating the Pacific franc, a function now carried out by the French government.

The CFP is fixed at one French franc (FF) to 18.18 Pacific francs, so you can determine how many CFP you'll get for your dollar or pound by finding out how many FF you get, then multiplying by 18.18. Or to put it another way, 5.5 FF equals CFP 100, so divide the number of FF you get by 5.5 and multiply by 100. A rough way to convert CFP into U.S. dollars is simply to divide by 100, so CFP 1000 is US$10, etc. The exact rate is published weekly in the "World Value of the Dollar" column in the Monday issue of the *Wall Street Journal*.

All banks levy a stiff commission on foreign currency transactions. The Banque Socredo and Banque de Tahiti both deduct CFP 350 commission, the Banque de Polynésie CFP 400, and the Westpac Bank CFP 450. Traveler's checks bring a rate of exchange about 1.5% higher than cash, but a passport is required for identification (photocopy sometimes accepted). The best currency to have with you by far is French francs in cash or traveler's checks as these are converted back and forth at the fixed

EXCHANGE RATES

(approximate figures for orientation only)

One French Franc = 18.18 Pacific Francs
One U.S. Dollar = 89 Pacific Francs
One Canadian Dollar = 66 Pacific Francs
One Australian Dollar = 68 Pacific Francs
One New Zealand Dollar = 54 Pacific Francs
One Pound Sterling = 142 Pacific Francs
One Swiss Franc = 79 Pacific Francs
One German Mark = 65 Pacific Francs
One Dutch Guilder = 58 Pacific Francs
100 Japanese Yen = 106 Pacific Francs

rate of CFP 18.18 to one FF without any commission charge. If you're from the States, you might also bring a few U.S. dollars in small bills to cover emergency expenses.

The **American Express** representative on Tahiti is Tahiti Tours (B.P. 627, Papeete, tel. 54-02-50) at 15 rue Jeanne d'Arc near the Vaima Center in Papeete. If your American Express traveler's checks are stolen contact this office or call Australia tel. 61-2/886-0688 collect to report the loss and find out about a refund. They'll also cancel lost credit cards if stolen with the checks. Of course, they'll need to know the numbers!

Credit cards are accepted in many places, but Pacific francs in cash are easier to use at restaurants, shops, etc. To avoid wasting time hassling at banks for cash advances, it's best to bring enough traveler's checks to cover all your out-of-pocket expenses and then some. If you do wish to use a credit card at a restaurant, ask first. Visa and MasterCard credit cards are universally accepted in the Society Islands, but American Express is not.

On some outer islands credit cards, traveler's checks, and foreign banknotes won't be accepted, so it's essential to change enough money before leaving Papeete. Apart from Tahiti, there are banks on Bora Bora, Huahine, Hiva Oa, Moorea, Nuku Hiva, Raiatea, Rangiroa, Rurutu, Tahaa, Tubuai, and Ua Pou. All of these islands have Banque Socredo branches, and the Banque de Tahiti (38% of which is owned by the Bank of Hawaii) is represented on six of

them. Bora Bora, Moorea, and Raiatea each have four different banks. If you're headed for any island other than these, take along enough CFP in cash to see you through.

Although Tahiti is easily the most expensive corner of the South Pacific, it also has the lowest inflation rate in the region (never over three percent between 1986 and 1990, compared to 10 percent in many neighboring countries). In 1991 the retail price index rose only 0.1%. Fortunately facilities for budget travelers are now highly developed throughout the Society Islands, often with cooking facilities which allow you to save a lot on meals. Cheap transportation is available by interisland boat and local *truck,* and bicycles can be hired in many places. What you need the most of to see Tahiti-Polynesia on a low budget is time, and the wisdom to avoid trying to see and do too much. There are countless organized tours and activities designed to separate you from your money, but none are really essential and the beautiful scenery, spectacular beaches, challenging hikes, and exotic atmosphere are free. Bargaining is not common in Tahiti-Polynesia, and no one will try to cheat you. There's **no tipping,** and they *mean* it.

POST AND TELECOMMUNICATIONS

Post

The 34 regular post offices and 58 authorized agencies throughout Tahiti-Polynesia are open weekdays 0700-1500. Main branches sell ready-made padded envelopes and boxes. Parcels with an aggregate length, width, and height of over 90 cm or weighing more than 20 kg cannot be mailed. Rolls (posters, calendars, etc.) longer than 90 cm are also not accepted. Letters cannot weigh over two kg Registration *(recommandation)* and insurance *(envois avec valeur déclarée)* are possible. Always use airmail *(poste aérienne)* when posting a letter; surface mail takes months to arrive. Postcards can still take up to two weeks to reach the United States.

To pick up poste restante (general delivery) mail, you must show your passport and pay CFP 40 per piece. If you're going to an outer island and are worried about your letters being returned to sender after 30 days (at Nuku Hiva after 15 days), pay CFP 1500 per month for a *garde de courrier,* which obliges the post office to hold all letters for at least two months. If one of your letters has "please hold" marked on it, the local postmaster may decide to hold all your mail for two months, but you'll have to pay the CFP 1500 to collect it. Packages may be returned after one month in any case. For a flat fee of CFP 1600 you can have your mail forwarded for one year. Ask for an *"Ordre de Réexpédition Temporaire."*

In this book all post office box numbers are rendered B.P. *(Boîte Postale).* Since there are usually no street addresses, always include the B.P. when writing to a local address, plus the name of the commune or village and the island. The postal authorities recognize "French Polynesia" as the official name of this country, and it's best to add "South Pacific Ocean" to that for good measure. Tahiti-Polynesia issues its own colorful postage stamps—available at local post offices. They make excellent souvenirs.

Telecommunications

Local telephone calls are CFP 50, and the pay phones usually work! A flashing light means you're about to be cut off, so have another coin ready. All calls within a single island are considered local calls, except on Tahiti, which is divided into two zones. Long-distance calls are best placed at post offices, which also handle fax *(télécopier)* services. Calls made from hotel rooms are charged double or triple. Collect calls overseas are possible to Canada, the U.S., Australia, and New Zealand (but not to the U.K.): dial 19 and say you want a *conversation payable a l'arrive.* For information (in French), dial 12; to get the operator, dial 19.

Anyone planning on making a lot of calls should pick up a telephone card *(télécarte),* sold at all post offices. They're valid for both local and overseas calls, and are available in denominations of 30 units (CFP 1000), 60 units

(CFP 2000), and 150 units (CFP 5000). It's cheaper than paying cash and you don't get hit with three-minute minimum charges for operator-assisted calls (CFP 1824 to the U.S.). North American AT&T telephone credit cards can be used in Tahiti-Polynesia.

To dial overseas direct from Tahiti, listen for the dial tone, then push 00 (Tahiti's international access code). When you hear another dial tone, press the country code of your party (Canada and the U.S. are both 1), the city or area code, and the number. The procedure is clearly explained in notices in English in the phone booths.

With a card, the cost per minute is CFP 250 to Australia and New Zealand, CFP 375 to Hawaii, CFP 490 to the U.S., CFP 576 to Britain, and CFP 600 to Canada. That's still very expensive, so wait to call from another country if you can. If you're calling North America, it's cheaper to quickly leave your number and have your party call you back. Otherwise fax them your hotel's phone and fax numbers. If you want to talk to someone periodically, leave your hotel telephone and fax numbers (provided in this book) and travel dates with friends, family, and associates so they can try to get hold of you. To call Tahiti-Polynesia direct from the U.S., you must dial 011-689 and the six-digit telephone number. International access codes do vary, so always check in the front of your local telephone book. If you need to consult the Tahiti-Polynesia phone book, ask to see the *annuaire* at any post office.

Throughout this book we've tried to supply the local telephone numbers you'll need. Any tourist-oriented business is sure to have someone handy who speaks English, so don't hesitate to call ahead. You'll get current information, be able to check prices and perhaps make a reservation, and often save yourself a lot of time and worry.

Tahiti-Polynesia's telephone code is 689.

BUSINESS HOURS AND TIME

Businesses open early in Tahiti-Polynesia and often close for a two-hour siesta at midday. Normal office hours are weekdays 0730-1130/1330-1630. Many shops keep the same schedule but remain open until 1730 and Saturday 0730-

1200. A few shops remain open at lunchtime and small convenience stores are often open Saturday afternoon until 1800 and Sunday 0600-0800. Banking hours are variable, either 0800-1530 or 0800-1100/1400-1700 weekdays. A few banks in Papeete open Saturday mornings (check the sign on the door).

Tahiti-Polynesia operates on the same time as Hawaii, 10 hours behind Greenwich Mean Time or two hours behind California (except May to September, when it's three hours). The Marquesas are 30 minutes behind the rest of Tahiti-Polynesia. Tahiti-Polynesia is east of the international date line, so the day is the same as that of the Cook Islands, Hawaii, and the U.S., but a day behind Fiji, New Zealand, and Australia.

To avoid confusion, all clock times in this book follow the 24-hour airline timetable system, i.e., 0100 is 1 a.m., 1300 is 1 p.m., 2330 is 11:30 p.m. From noon to midnight, merely add 12 onto regular time to derive airline time. Timings between midnight and 1:00 a.m. are expressed by the figures 0001 to 0059.

WEIGHTS AND MEASURES

The metric system is used throughout Tahiti-Polynesia. Study the conversion table in the back of this handbook if you're not used to thinking metric. Most distances herein are quoted in kilometers and they become easy to comprehend when you know than one km is the distance a normal person walks in 10 minutes. A meter is slightly more than a yard and a liter is just over a quart.

North is at the top of all maps in this handbook. When using official topographical maps you can determine the scale by taking the representative fraction (RF) and dividing by 100. This will give the number of meters represented by one cm. For example, a map with an RF of 1:10,000 would represent 100 meters for every centimeter on the map.

Electricity

The electric voltage is 220 volts AC, 60 cycles. If you're taking along an American 110-volt AC razor or other appliance you'll need a converter. Some hotels with their own generators operate on 110 volts, 60 cycles, however, so be sure to ask before plugging in. Most electrical outlets have two round holes, so an adaptor may also be necessary. Also keep this situation in mind if you buy any duty-free appliances.

MEDIA

There are two French-owned morning papers, *La Dépêche de Tahiti* (B.P. 50, Papeete; tel. 42-43-43) and *Les Nouvelles de Tahiti* (B.P. 1757, Papeete; tel. 43-44-45). *La Dépêche* is the larger, with more international news, but both papers provide the daily exchange rate. In 1989 the previously locally owned *Les Nouvelles* was purchased by French publishing magnate Robert Hersant, who also owns *La Dépêche*.

The free weekly *Tahiti Beach Press* (B.P. 887, Papeete; tel. 42-68-50), edited by Al Prince, was called the *Tahiti Sun Press* from 1980 till the end of 1990, when the paper was forced to drop all news coverage unrelated to tourism due to economic pressure from the big hotel chains and government tourism officials. The present "sanitized" newspaper is still well worth perusing to find out which local companies are interested in your business; just don't expect to find Al's excellent articles on social or political conditions in Tahiti-Polynesia in it anymore.

The French government attempts to control what happens in the territory through the state-owned TV and radio. Television was introduced to Tahiti in the mid-1960s and Radio France Outre-Mer (RFO) broadcasts on two channels in French and (occasionally) Tahitian. Nine private radio stations also operate and it's fun to listen to the Tahitian-language stations which play more local music than the French stations. The Tahitian call-in shows with messages to families on outer islands are a delightful slice of real life. Pro-independence Radio Te Reo o Tefana (tel. 81-97-97) broadcasts from Faa'a on Tahiti.

The best local guidebook is *Tahiti, Circle Island Tour Guide* by Bengt Danielsson. Bengt and his wife, Marie-Thérèse, have also written a

TAHITI TOURISME OFFICES

Tahiti Tourisme, B.P. 65, Papeete, Tahiti (fax 689/43-66-19)

Tahiti Tourisme, 300 North Continental Blvd., Suite 180, El Segundo, CA 90245, U.S.A. (fax 310/414-8490)

Tahiti Tourisme, Level 1, Southpac Tower, 45 Queen St., Auckland, New Zealand (fax 64-9/373-2415)

Tahiti Tourisme, 620 St. Kilda Rd., Suite 301, Melbourne 3004, Victoria, Australia (fax 61-3/9521-3867)

PT Aviamas Megabuana, Chase Plaza, Jalan Jend, Sudirman kav 21, Jakarta 12910, Indonesia (fax 62-21/570-3439)

Pacific Leisure, 11 Craig Rd., Tangjong Pagar, Singapore 0208, Singapore (fax 65/221-1747)

Tahiti Tourisme, 2-5, 2-6 Angkasa Raya Building, Jalan Ampang, 50450 Kuala Lumpur, Malaysia (fax 60-3/242-1129)

Pacific Leisure, Tung Ming Building, Suite 902, 40 Des Voeux Rd., Central, Hong Kong (tel. 852/525-3290)

Travelswift Ltd., 98 Nanking East Rd., Section 2, 5th Floor, Taipei 10048, Taiwan (fax 886-2/263-7425)

Korea Leisure, 250-503 Olympic Apt., Bangee-dong Soongpa-ku, Seoul 138-150, South Korea (fax 82-2/448-5645)

Tahiti Tourisme, Sankyo Building (No. 20) Room 802, 3-11-5 Iidabashi, Chiyoda-Ku, Tokyo 102, Japan (fax 81-3/3265-0581)

Oficina de Turismo de Tahiti, Casilla 16057, Santiago 9, Chile (fax 56-2/251-2826)

Office du Tourisme de Tahiti, 28 Boulevard Saint-Germain, 75005 Paris, France (fax 33-1/4325-4165)

Fremdenverkehrsbüro von Tahiti, Haingasse 22, D-61348 Bad Homburg v.d.H, Germany (fax 49-6172/690458)

---

superb account of the French nuclear testing program entitled *Poisoned Reign* (Australia, Penguin Books, 1986). Other books on Tahiti-Polynesia are described in the Resources chapter at the back of this volume.

INFORMATION

Tahiti-Polynesia has one of the best-equipped tourist offices in the South Pacific, Tahiti Tourisme (B.P. 65, Papeete; tel. 50-57-00, fax 43-66-19). A list of their overseas offices is above. Within Tahiti-Polynesia the same organization calls itself Tahiti Animation and operates tourist information offices on Tahiti, Moorea, Huahine, Raiatea, Bora Bora, and Hiva Oa. These offices can provide free brochures and answer questions, but they're not travel agencies, so you must make your own hotel and transportation bookings. Ask for their current information sheets on the islands you intend to visit.

HEALTH

For a tropical location, Tahiti-Polynesia has very few pest or insect problems. Malaria is nonexistent. Yellow-fever vaccinations are required if you've been in an infected area (such as the Amazon basin) within the previous six days (infants under the age of one are excused). Cholera vaccinations are not really effective but may be required if there was an outbreak in your last destination (unlikely). Tetanus-diphtheria, polio, and typhoid boosters are not required, but are always a good idea if you're going to out-of-the-way places. Filariasis (elephantiasis) and leprosy are the endemic diseases of Polynesia, but there's little chance of visitors contracting these.

The sale of travel insurance is big business in the U.S., but the value of the policies themselves is often questionable. If your regular group health insurance also covers you while you're traveling abroad it's probably enough (and most travel insurance is worthless unless you have some other form of insurance). If you do opt for the security of travel insurance, insist on a policy that also covers theft or loss of luggage and emergency medical evacuations. If you'll be involved in any "dangerous activities," such as scuba diving or surfing, read the fine print to make sure your policy is valid.

Most of the products in local pharmacies are imported from France, although some U.S. brands are available at twice U.S. prices. If you're not particular about the kind of medicine you take, go to any large Chinese general store and ask the owner to recommend a good Chinese patent medicine for what ails you. The price will be a third what the European medicines or herbs cost and they're often just as effective or better. Antibiotics should only be used to treat serious wounds, and only after medical advice.

The sea and air are clear and usually pollution-free. The humidity nourishes the skin and the local fruit is brimming with vitamins. If you take a few precautions, you'll never have a sick day. The information provided below is intended to make you knowledgeable, not fearful.

Acclimatizing

Don't go from winter weather into the steaming tropics without a rest before and after. Minimize jet lag by setting your watch to local time at your destination as soon as you board the flight. Westbound flights into the South Pacific from North America or Europe are less jolting since you follow the sun and your body gets a few hours of extra sleep. On the way home you're moving against the sun and the hours of sleep your body loses cause jet lag. Airplane cabins have low humidity, so drink lots of juice or water instead of carbonated drinks and don't overeat in-flight. It's also best to forgo coffee, as it will only keep you awake, and alcohol helps dehydrate you. Scuba diving on departure day can give you a severe case of the bends.

If you start feeling seasick onboard ship, stare at the horizon, which is always steady, and stop thinking about it. Anti-motion-sickness pills are useful to have along.

Frequently the feeling of thirst is false and only due to mucous membrane dryness. Gargling or taking two or three gulps of warm water should be enough. Other means to keep moisture in the body are to have a hot drink like tea or black coffee, or any kind of slightly salted or sour drink in small quantities. Salt in fresh lime juice is remarkably refreshing.

The tap water is safe to drink in the main towns, but ask first elsewhere. If in doubt, boil it or use purification pills. Tap water that is uncomfortably hot to touch is usually safe. Allow it to cool in a clean container. If the tap water is contaminated, the local ice will be too. Avoid brushing your teeth with water unfit to drink, and wash or peel fruit and vegetables if you can. Cooked food is less subject to contamination than raw.

Sunburn

The Tahitian name for us white folks, *papa'a,* means literally "sunburned skin." Though you may think a tan will make you *look* healthier and more attractive, it's very damaging to the skin, which becomes dry, rigid, and prematurely old and wrinkled, especially on the face. And

Monoi Tiare Tahiti is a scented coconut oil used to replenish natural skin oils lost to the effects of the tropical sun and seas.

a burn from the sun greatly increases your risk of getting skin cancer. Begin with short exposures to the sun, perhaps half an hour at a time, followed by an equal time in the shade. Drink plenty of liquids to keep your pores open and avoid the sun from 1000 to 1400. Clouds and beach umbrellas will not protect you fully. Wear a T-shirt while snorkeling to protect your back. Sunbathing is the main cause of cataracts to the eyes, so wear sunglasses and a wide-brimmed hat and beware of reflected sunlight.

Use a sunscreen lotion containing PABA rather than oil (don't forget your nose, lips, forehead, neck, hands, and feet). Sunscreens protect you from ultraviolet rays (a leading cause of cancer), while oils magnify the sun's effect. A 29- or 30-factor sunscreen such as Presun 29 or Sundown 30 will provide adequate protection. Apply the lotion *before* going to the beach to avoid being burned on the way, and reapply periodically to replace sunscreen washed away by perspiration. After sunbathing take a tepid shower rather than a hot one, which would wash away your natural skin oils. Stay moist and use a vitamin E evening cream to preserve the youth of your skin. Calamine ointment soothes skin already burned, as does coconut oil. Pharmacists recommend Solarcaine to soothe burned

skin. Rinsing off with a vinegar solution reduces peeling, and aspirin relieves some of the pain and irritation. Vitamin A and calcium counteract overdoses of vitamin D received from the sun. The fairer your skin, the more essential it is to take care.

As earth's ozone layer is deleted due to the commercial use of chlorofluorocarbons (CFCs) and other factors, the need to protect oneself from ultraviolet radiation is becoming more urgent. In 1990 the U.S. Centers for Disease Control in Atlanta reported that deaths from skin cancer increased 26% between 1973 and 1985. Previously the cancers didn't develop until age 50 or 60, but now much younger people are affected.

Ailments

Cuts and scratches infect easily in the tropics and take a long time to heal. Prevent infection from coral cuts by washing wounds with soap and fresh water, then rubbing in vinegar or alcohol (whiskey will do)—painful but effective. Tahitians usually dab coral cuts with lime juice. All cuts turn septic quickly in the tropics, so try to keep them clean and covered.

For bites, burns, and cuts, an antiseptic such as Solarcaine speeds healing and helps prevent infection. Pure aloe vera is good for sunburn, scratches, and even coral cuts. Bites by *nono* flies itch for days and can become infected. Not everyone is affected by insect bites in the same way. Some people are practically immune to insects, while traveling companions experiencing exactly the same conditions are soon covered with bites. You'll soon know which type you are. Locally produced *monoi* oil helps keep *nonos* (bugs) away.

Prickly heat, an intensely irritating rash, is caused by wearing heavy clothing that is inappropriate for the climate. When the glands are blocked and the sweat is unable to evaporate, the skin becomes soggy and small red blisters appear. Synthetic fabrics like nylon are especially bad in this regard. Take a cold shower, apply calamine lotion, dust with talcum powder, and take off those clothes! Until things improve, avoid alcohol, tea, coffee, and any physical activity that makes you sweat. If you're sweating profusely, increase your intake of salt slightly to avoid fatigue, but not without concurrently drinking more water.

Use antidiarrheal medications sparingly. Rather than take drugs to plug yourself up, drink plenty of unsweetened liquids like green coconut or fresh fruit juice to help flush yourself out. Egg yolk mixed with nutmeg helps diarrhea, or have a rice and tea day. Avoid dairy products. Most cases of diarrhea are self-limiting and require only simple replacement of fluids and salts lost in diarrheal stools. If the diarrhea is persistent or you experience high fever, drowsiness, or blood in the stool, stop traveling, rest, and consider attending a clinic. For constipation eat pineapple or any peeled fruit.

Dengue fever is a mosquito-transmitted disease endemic to the South Pacific. Signs are headaches, sore throat, pain in the joints, fever, chills, nausea, and rash. It can last anywhere from five to 15 days; although you can relieve the symptoms somewhat, the only real cure is to stay in bed, drink lots of water, take aspirin for the headaches, and wait it out. It's painful, but dengue fever usually only kills infants. No vaccine exists, so just avoid getting bitten.

Toxic Fish

Over 400 species of tropical reef fish, including wrasses, snappers, groupers, barracudas, jacks, moray eels, surgeonfish, and shellfish,

are known to cause seafood poisoning (ciguatera). There's no way to tell if a fish will cause ciguatera: a species can be poisonous on one side of the island, but not on the other.

Over a decade ago scientists on Tahiti determined that a one-celled dinoflagellate called *Gambierdiscus toxicus* was the cause. Normally these microalgae are found only in the ocean depths, but when a reef is disturbed by natural or human causes they can multiply dramatically in a lagoon. The dinoflagellates are consumed by tiny herbivorous fish and the toxin passes up through the food chain to larger fish where it becomes concentrated in the head and guts. The toxins have no effect on the fish that feed on them.

Tahiti-Polynesia's 700-800 cases of ciguatera a year are more than in the rest of the South Pacific combined, leading to suspicions that the French nuclear testing program is responsible. Ciguatera didn't exist on Hao atoll in the Tuamotus until military dredging for a 3,500-meter runway began in 1965. By mid-1968 43% of the population had been affected. Between 1971 and 1980 over 30% of the population of Mangareva near the Moruroa nuclear test site suffered from seafood poisoning.

The symptoms (tingling, prickling, itching, nausea, vomiting, erratic heartbeat, joint and muscle pains) usually subside in a few days. Induce vomiting and take castor oil as a laxative if you're unlucky. Symptoms can recur for up to a year, and victims may become allergic to all seafoods. In the Marshall Islands, a drug called Mannitol has been effective in treating ciguatera, but as yet little is known about it. Avoid biointoxication by cleaning fish as soon as they're caught, discarding the head and organs, and taking special care with oversized fish. Whether the fish is consumed cooked or raw has no bearing on this problem. Local residents often know from experience which species may be eaten.

AIDS

In 1981 scientists in France and the United States first recognized the Acquired Immune Deficiency Syndrome (AIDS), which was later discovered to be caused by a virus called the Human Immuno-deficiency Virus (HIV). HIV breaks down the body's immunity to infections, leading to full-blown AIDS. The virus can lie hidden in the body for many years without producing any obvious symptoms or before developing into the AIDS disease.

HIV lives in blood cells and is present in the sexual fluids of humans. It's difficult to catch and is spread mostly through sexual intercourse, by needle or syringe sharing among intravenous drug users, in blood transfusions, and during pregnancy and birth (if the mother is infected). Using another person's razor blade or having your body pierced or tattooed are also risky, but the HIV virus cannot be transmitted by shaking hands, kissing, cuddling, fondling, sneezing, cooking food, or sharing eating or drinking utensils. You cannot be infected by saliva, sweat, tears, urine, or feces; toilet seats, telephones, swimming pools, or mosquito bites do not cause AIDS. Ostracizing a known AIDS victim is not only immoral but it is also absurd.

Most blood banks now screen their products for HIV and you can protect yourself against dirty needles by only allowing an injection if you see the syringe taken out of a fresh unopened pack. The simplest safeguard during sex is the proper use of a condom. Unroll the condom onto the erect penis; while withdrawing after ejaculation, hold onto the condom as you come out. Never try to recycle a condom, and pack a supply with you as it's a nuisance trying to buy them locally.

HIV is spread more often through anal than vaginal sex because the lining of the rectum is much weaker than that of the vagina and ordinary condoms sometimes tear when used in anal sex. If you have anal sex, only use extra-strong condoms and special water-based lubricants since oil, Vaseline, and cream weaken the rubber. During oral sex you must make sure you don't get any semen or menstrual blood in your mouth. A woman runs 10 times the risk of catching AIDS from a man than the other way around, and the threat is always greater when another sexually transmitted disease (STD) is present.

The very existence of AIDS calls for a basic change in human behavior. No vaccine or drug exists which can prevent or cure AIDS, and because the virus mutates frequently, no remedy may ever be totally effective. Other STDs such as syphilis, gonorrhea, chlamydia, hepatitis B, and herpes are far more common than AIDS and can lead to serious complications such as infertility, but at least they can usually be cured.

The euphoria of travel can make it easier to fall in love or have sex with a stranger, so travelers must be informed of these dangers. As a tourist you should always practice safe sex to prevent AIDS and other STDs. You never know who is infected or even if you yourself have become infected. It's important to bring the subject up *before* you start to make love. Make a joke out of it by pulling out a condom and asking your new partner, "Say, do you know what this is?" Far from being unromantic or embarrassing, you'll both feel more relaxed with the subject off your minds and it's much better than worrying afterwards if you might have been infected. The golden rule is safe sex or no sex.

By mid-1994 an estimated 16 million people worldwide were HIV carriers, and hundreds of thousands had died of AIDS. Statistics released by the South Pacific Commission in February 1995 acknowledge 611 HIV infections and 220 cases of AIDS in the Pacific islands. Most affected were Tahiti-Polynesia (HIV 144, AIDS 43), New Caledonia (HIV 115, AIDS 37), Papua New Guinea (HIV 236, AIDS 87), and Guam (HIV 64, AIDS 24). In Tahiti-Polynesia and New Caledonia over two-thirds of those affected are males, but in Papua New Guinea men and women are affected in equal numbers. Although these figures are negligible compared to the 401,789 confirmed AIDS cases in the U.S., the real number could be 50 times higher and other STDs have already reached epidemic proportions in the islands. Thus it's essential that everyone does their utmost to combat this killer disease.

An HIV infection can be detected through a blood test because the antibodies created by the body to fight off the virus can be seen under a microscope. It takes at least three weeks for the antibodies to be produced and in some cases as long as six months before they can be picked up during a screening test. If you think you may have run a risk you should discuss the appropriateness of a test with your doctor. It's always better to know if you are infected so as to be able to avoid infecting others, to obtain early treatment of symptoms, and to make realistic plans. If you know someone with AIDS you should give them all the support you can (there's no danger in such contact unless blood is present).

WHAT TO TAKE

Packing

Assemble everything you simply must take and cannot live without—then cut the pile in half. If you're still left with more than will fit into a medium-size suitcase or backpack, continue eliminating. You have to be tough on yourself and just limit what you take. Now put it all into your bag. If the total (bag and contents) weighs over 16 kg, you'll sacrifice much of your mobility. If you can keep it down to 10 kg, you're traveling *light*. Categorize, separate, and pack all your things into plastic bags or stuff sacks for convenience and protection from moisture. In addition to your principal bag, you'll want a day pack or flight bag. When checking in for flights, carry anything that cannot be replaced in your hand luggage.

Your Luggage

A soft medium-sized backpack with a lightweight internal frame is best. Big external-frame packs are fine for mountain climbing but get caught in airport conveyor belts and are very inconvenient on public transport. The best packs have a zippered compartment in back where you can tuck in the straps and hip belt before turning your pack over to an airline or bus. This type of pack has the flexibility of allowing you to simply walk when motorized transport is unavailable or unacceptable, and with the straps zipped in it looks like a regular suitcase, should you wish to go upmarket for a while.

Make sure your pack carries the weight on your hips, has a cushion for spine support, and doesn't pull backwards. The pack should strap snugly to your body but also allow ventilation to your back. It should be made of a water-resistant material such as nylon and have a Fastex buckle.

Look for a pack with double, two-way zipper compartments and pockets you can lock with miniature padlocks. They might not *stop* a thief, but they will be a deterrent to the casual pilferer. A 60-cm length of lightweight chain and another padlock will allow you to fasten your pack to something. Keep valuables locked in your bag, out of sight, as even upmarket hotel rooms aren't 100% safe.

Camping Equipment and Clothing

A small nylon tent guarantees you a place to sleep every night, but it *must* be mosquito- and waterproof. Get one with a tent fly, then waterproof both tent and fly with a can of waterproofing spray. You'll seldom need a sleeping bag in the tropics, so that's one item you can easily cut. A youth hostel sleeping sheet is ideal—all YHA handbooks give instructions on how to make your own, or buy one at your local hostel. You don't really need to carry a bulky foam pad, as the ground is seldom cold.

For clothes take loose-fitting cotton washables, light in color and weight. Synthetic fabrics are hot and sticky, and most of the things you wear at home are too heavy for the tropics—be prepared for the humidity. The dress is casual, with slacks and a sports shirt okay for men even at dinner parties. Local women often wear long colorful dresses in the evening, but shorts are okay in daytime. If in doubt, bring the minimum with you and buy tropical garb upon arrival. Stick to clothes you can rinse in your room sink. The pareu (pronounced "par-RAY-o") is a bright two-

Go native in a Tahitian pareu. Throw one corner over your right shoulder, then pass the other under your left arm and pull tight. Tie the ends and you're dressed.

DIANA LASICH HARPER

meter piece of cloth both men and women wrap about themselves as an all-purpose garment. Any Tahitian can show you how to wear it.

Neutral gray eyeglasses protect your eyes from the sun and give the least color distortion. Take an extra pair (if you have them). Take comfortable shoes that have been broken in. Running shoes and rubber thongs (flip-flops) are very handy for day use but will bar you from nightspots with strict dress codes. Scuba divers' rubber booties are lightweight and perfect for both crossing rivers and reefwalking, though an old pair of sneakers may be just as good. Below we've provided a few checklists to help you assemble your gear. The listed items combined weigh well over 16 kg, so eliminate what doesn't suit you:

pack with internal frame
day pack or airline bag
nylon tent and fly
tent-patching tape
mosquito net
sleeping sheet
sun hat
essential clothing only
bathing suit
sturdy walking shoes
rubber thongs
rubber booties
mask and snorkel

Accessories

Bring some reading material, as good books in English can be expensive or hard to find in these islands. A clip-on book light with extra batteries allows campers to read at night. Serious scuba divers bring their own regulator and buoyancy-control device, and perhaps a wetsuit for protection against coral. A mask and snorkel are essential equipment—you'll be missing half of Polynesia's beauty without them.

camera and 10 rolls of film
compass
pocket flashlight
extra batteries
candle
pocket alarm calculator
pocket watch
sunglasses
padlock and lightweight chain

collapsible umbrella
string for a clothesline
powdered laundry soap
universal sink plug
minitowel
silicon glue
sewing kit
miniscissors
nail clippers
fishing line for sewing gear
plastic cup and plate
can and bottle opener
corkscrew
penknife
spoon
water bottle
matches
tea bags

Toiletries and Medical Kit

Since everyone has his/her own medical requirements and brand names vary from country to country, there's no point going into detail here. Note, however, that even the basics (such as aspirin) are unavailable on some outer islands, so be prepared. Bring medicated powder for prickly heat rash. Charcoal tablets are useful for diarrhea and poisoning (they absorb the irritants). Bring an adequate supply of any personal medications, plus your prescriptions (in generic terminology).

High humidity causes curly hair to swell and bush, straight hair to droop. If it's curly have it cut short or keep it long in a ponytail or bun. A good cut is essential with straight hair. Water-based makeup is best, as the heat and humidity cause oil glands to work overtime. High quality locally made shampoo, body oils, and insect repellent are sold in all the islands, and the bottles are conveniently smaller than those sold in Western countries. See "Health," above, for more ideas.

wax earplugs
soap in plastic container
soft toothbrush
toothpaste
roll-on deodorant
shampoo
comb and brush
skin creams
makeup

tampons or napkins
white toilet paper
multiple vitamins and minerals
Cutter's insect repellent
PABA sunscreen
Chap Stick
a motion-sickness remedy
contraceptives
iodine
water-purification pills
delousing powder
a diarrhea remedy
Tiger Balm
a cold remedy
Alka-Seltzer
aspirin
antihistamine
antifungal
Calmitol ointment
antibiotic ointment
painkiller
antiseptic cream
disinfectant
simple dressings
plastic bandages
prescription medicines

Money and Documents

All post offices have passport applications. Carry your valuables in a money belt worn around your waist or neck under your clothing; most camping stores have these. Make several photocopies of the information page of your passport, personal identification, driver's license, scuba certification card, credit cards, airline tickets, receipts for purchase of traveler's checks, etc.— you should be able to get them all on one page. A brief medical history with your blood type, allergies, chronic or special health problems, eyeglass and medical prescriptions, etc., might also come in handy. Put these inside plastic bags to protect them from moisture, then carry the lists in different places, and leave one at home.

passport
vaccination certificates
airline tickets
scuba certification card
driver's license
traveler's checks
some U.S. cash

photocopies of documents
money belt
address book
notebook
envelopes
extra ballpoints

FILM AND PHOTOGRAPHY

Look at the ads in photographic magazines for the best deals on mail-order cameras and film, or buy at a discount shop in any large city. Run a roll of film through your camera to be sure it's in good working order; clean the lens with lens-cleaning tissue and check the batteries. Remove the batteries from your camera when storing it at home for long periods. Register valuable cameras or electronic equipment with Customs before you leave home so there won't be any argument over where you bought the items when you return; or at least carry the original bill of sale.

The type of camera you choose could depend on the way you travel. If you'll be staying mostly in one place, a heavy single-lens reflex (SLR) camera with spare lenses and other equipment won't trouble you. If you'll be moving around a lot for a considerable length of time, a 35-mm automatic compact camera may be better. The compacts are mostly useful for close-up shots; landscapes will seem spread out and far away. A wide-angle lens gives excellent depth of field, but hold the camera upright to avoid converging verticals. A polarizing filter prevents reflections from glass windows.

Take double the amount of film and mailers you think you'll need: in Tahiti-Polynesia camera film costs over double what you'd pay in the U.S., and even then you never know if it's been spoiled by an airport X-ray on the way there. Take full advantage of your 10-roll duty-free allowance. In the U.S. film can be purchased at big discounts through mail-order companies, which advertise in photography magazines. Choose 36-exposure film over 24-exposure to save on the number of rolls you have to carry. Whenever purchasing film in the islands, take care to check the expiration date.

Films are rated by their speed and sensitivity to light, using ISO numbers from 25 to 1600. The higher the number, the greater the film's sensitivity to light. Slower films with lower ISOs (like 100-200) produce sharp images in bright sunlight. Faster films with higher ISOs (like 400) stop action and work well in low-light situations, such as in dark rainforests or at sunset. If you have a manual SLR you can avoid overexposure at midday by reducing the exposure half a stop. From 1000 to 1600 the light is often too bright to take good photos, and panoramas usually come out best early or late in the day.

Wayne J. Andrews of Eastman Kodak offers the following suggestions for enhanced photography. Keep your photos simple with one main subject and an uncomplicated background. Get as close to your subjects as you can and lower or raise the camera to their level. Include people in the foreground of scenic shots to add interest and perspective. Outdoors a flash can fill in unflattering facial shadows caused by high sun or backlit conditions. Most of all, be creative. Look for interesting details and compose the photo before you push the trigger. Instead of taking a head-on photo of a group of people, step to one side and ask them to face you. The angle improves the photo. Photograph subjects coming toward you rather than passing by. Ask permission before photographing people. If you're asked for money (rare) you can always walk away—give your subjects the same choice.

When packing, protect your camera against vibration. Checked baggage is scanned by powerful airport X-ray monitors, so carry both camera and film aboard the plane in a clear plastic bag and ask security for a visual inspection. Some airports will refuse to do this, however. Otherwise, use a lead-laminated pouch. The old high-dose X-ray units are the worst, but even low-dose inspection units can ruin fast film (400 ASA and above). Beware of the cumulative effect of X-ray machines.

Keep your camera in a plastic bag during rain and while traveling in motorized canoes, etc. In the tropics the humidity can cause film to stick to itself; silica-gel crystals in the bag will protect film from humidity and mold growth. Protect camera and film from direct sunlight and load the film in the shade. When loading, check that the takeup spool revolves. Never leave camera or film in a hot place like a car floor, glove compartment, or trunk.

GETTING THERE

Preparations

Your plane ticket will be your biggest single expense, so spend some time considering the possibilities. Start by calling the airlines directly at their toll-free 800 numbers to get current information on fares. In the U.S., the ones to call are Air France (tel. 800/237-2747), Air New Zealand (tel. 800/262-1234), AOM French Airlines (tel. 800/553-3477 or 800/892-9136), Corsair (tel. 800/677-0720), Hawaiian Airlines (tel. 800/367-5320), Lan Chile Airlines (tel. 800/735-5526), and Qantas Airways (tel. 800/227-4500), all with flights to Tahiti. Sometimes Canada and the various parts of the U.S. have different toll-free numbers, so if the number given above doesn't work, dial 800 information at (800) 555-1212 (all 800 numbers are free). In Canada, Air New Zealand's toll-free number is (800) 663-5494.

Call all of these carriers and say you want the *lowest possible fare*. Ask about fare seasons and restrictions. If you're not happy with the answers you get, call the same number later and try again. Many different agents take calls on these lines, and some are more knowledgeable than others. The numbers are busy during business hours, so call at night or on the weekend. *Be persistent.*

Travel Agents

Use your local travel agent but be aware that any agent worth his/her commission will probably want to sell you a package tour, and it's a fact that some vacation packages actually cost less than regular roundtrip air fare! If they'll let you extend your stay to give you some time to yourself this could be a good deal, especially with the hotel thrown in for "free." But check the restrictions.

Pick your agent carefully as many are pitifully ignorant about Tahiti. Many don't want to hear about discounts, cheap flights, or alternative routes. With alarming frequency, they give wrong or misleading information in an offhand manner. Ask an airline to suggest a travel agent. They won't *recommend* any, but they will give you the names of a few in your area that specialize in Pacific travel. Agencies belonging to the American Society of Travel Agents (ASTA), the Alliance of Canadian Travel Associations (ACTA), or the Association of British Travel Agents must conform to a strict code of ethics. A travel agent's commission is paid by the airline, so you've got nothing to lose.

Even if you decide to take advantage of the convenience of an agent, do call the airlines yourself beforehand so you'll know if you're getting a good deal. Airline tickets are often refundable only in the place of purchase, so ask about this before you invest in a ticket you may not use. There can be tremendous variations in what different passengers on the same flight have paid for their tickets. Allow yourself time to shop around; a few hours spent on the phone, asking questions, could save you hundreds of dollars.

One of the most knowledgeable Canadian travel agents for South Pacific tickets is the **Adventure Centre** (25 Bellair St., Toronto, Ontario M5R 3L3; tel. 800/267-3347), with offices in Calgary, Edmonton, Toronto, and Vancouver. Also try Travel Cuts with offices throughout Canada (check the phone book). Their Toronto office (187 College St., 2nd Floor, Toronto, Ontario M5T 1P7, Canada; tel. 416/979-2406, fax 416/979-8167) has a special South Pacific department. Similar tickets are sold through travel agents in the U.S. by the **Adventure Center** (1311 63rd St., Suite 200, Emeryville, CA 94608, U.S.A.; tel. 800/227-8747). (The Emeryville office doesn't accept direct consumer sales but ask your travel agent to check with them.)

Discover Wholesale Travel (2192 Dupont Dr., Suite 105, Irvine, CA 92715, U.S.A.; tel. 800/576-7770 in California, tel. 800/759-7330 elsewhere in the U.S., fax 714/833-1176) is one of the few large tour operators willing to sell discounted air tickets alone directly to the public. President Mary Anne Cook claims everyone on her staff has 10 years experience selling Tahiti and "most importantly, we all love the area!"

Onward Tickets

Tahiti-Polynesia requires an onward ticket as a condition for entry. If you're planning a long trip including locally arranged sea travel to another country, this can be a nuisance. One way to satisfy the ticket-to-leave requirement is to purchase a full-fare one-way economy ticket out of the area from Air New Zealand (valid one year). As you're about to depart for the next country on your route, have the airline reissue the ticket, so it's a ticket to leave from there. Otherwise buy a ticket across the Pacific with stops in all the countries you'll visit, then use it *only* to satisfy immigration. When you finally complete your trip return the ticket to the issuing office for a full refund. Keep in mind that the sort of deals and discount air fares available elsewhere are not available in the South Pacific. Have your *real* means of departure planned.

AIR SERVICES

In 1990 France's state-owned national airline, **Air France,** bought out privately owned UTA French Airlines to become *the* international carrier to the French colonies in the South Pacific. In October 1992 Air France discontinued direct flights from San Francisco to Tahiti, but they still fly nonstop between Tokyo and Papeete once a week.

Both Air France and **AOM French Airlines** (9841 Airport Blvd., Suite 1120, Los Angeles, CA 90045, U.S.A.; tel. 310/338-9613, fax 310/645-1947) fly three times a week from Paris to Papeete via Los Angeles. AOM (Air Outre-Mer), owned by the French bank Crédit Lyonnais, has a policy of consistently setting their fares slightly below those of Air France while offering comparable service. AOM also flies from Paris to Nouméa via Bangkok, and round-the-world tickets Paris-Los Angeles-Papeete-Nouméa-Bangkok-Paris begin as low as 13,475 French francs.

The charter airline **Corsair,** owned by the French tour operator Nouvelles Frontières (APS, Inc., 5757 West Century Blvd., Suite 660, Los Angeles, CA 90045-6407, U.S.A.), also has weekly scheduled Paris-Los Angeles-Papeete flights. Corsair prices its tickets differently than the other carriers: you pay according to the season in which each leg is actually flown, whereas all of the other airlines base their fares on the season when the journey begins. Thus while Corsair may be cheaper, it's also more complicated, and requires more careful planning. The seating on Corsair planes is reported to be rather cramped.

Both **Air New Zealand** and **Qantas Airways** have flights from Los Angeles to Papeete twice a week, with connections to/from many points in North America and Western Europe. Both carriers continue southwest to Auckland, with one of the Air New Zealand flights calling at Rarotonga on the way. Qantas carries on to Sydney and Melbourne. **Hawaiian Airlines** offers weekly nonstop service to Papeete from Honolulu with connections from Las Vegas, Los Angeles, San Francisco, and Seattle.

An interesting way to arrive is on the weekly **Air Calédonie International** flight from Nouméa to Papeete via Wallis Island. This flight is combined with Air France's service to/from Sydney via Nouméa.

Lan Chile Airlines runs their Boeing 767 service from Santiago to Tahiti via Easter Island twice a week. In conjunction with Air New Zealand, Lan Chile offers several "Circle Pacific" fares, including Los Angeles-Papeete-Easter Island-Santiago-Miami (US$1694) and Los Angeles-Santiago-Easter Island-Papeete-Los Angeles (US$1828), both valid one year.

From North America

Air France, Air New Zealand, AOM French Airlines, Corsair, and Qantas Airways are the major carriers serving Tahiti out of Los Angeles. See "French Charter Flights" below for information on some of these. Unfortunately there are no direct flights from Canada to Tahiti and all passengers must change planes at Los Angeles, although there are immediate connections from **Canadian Airlines International** flights.

Fares from Los Angeles to Tahiti on **Air New Zealand** vary slightly according to season: the high season is from July to mid-August and in the middle of December; the rest of the year is low season. Their 14-day advance-purchase "Economy APEX" fare to Tahiti is US$838/995 low/high with a maximum stay of one month and a 35 percent cancellation fee. If you book on shorter notice the fare is almost 50 percent higher. "Add-on" fares to Los Angeles from cities all across North America are available.

Many people think of Tahiti as somewhere far away on the other side of the globe but it's only 7.5 hours from Los Angeles. Or to put it another way, Tahiti is only 2.5 hours farther from Los Angeles than Hawaii, yet a world apart. Most flights arrive at Papeete in the middle of the night. The Air New Zealand schedules are especially inconvenient as Tahiti is only a stopover and flight times are planned so the aircraft arrive in Auckland in the morning. Air New Zealand flights back to Los Angeles depart Papeete well after midnight, costing you another night's sleep.

From New Zealand

Unrestricted low air fares to Tahiti are surprisingly hard to come by in New Zealand. Some tickets have advance purchase requirements, so start shopping well ahead. Ask around at a number of different travel agencies for special unadvertised or under-the-counter fares. Fares to Tahiti

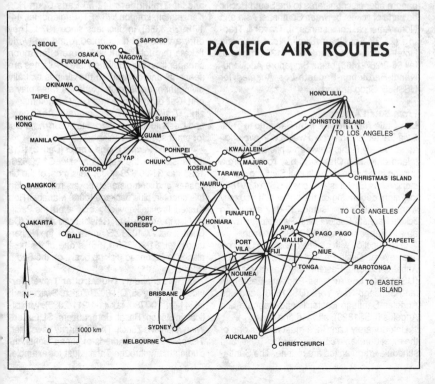

PACIFIC AIR ROUTES

often allow a stop in the Cook Islands, but it's hard to get a seat on these fully booked planes.

Air New Zealand offers reduced excursion fares from Auckland to Tahiti-Polynesia with a minimum stay of seven days and a maximum stay of 45 days. It's actually cheaper to buy a package tour with airfare, accommodations, and transfers all included, but these are usually limited to seven nights on one island and you're stuck in a boring touristic environment.

From Australia and Southeast Asia

To help subsidize Qantas Airways, the Australian government keeps airfares out of Australia as high as they can; they also require foreign carriers to set high fares. The airlines sometimes offer specials during the off months, so see a travel agent. For information on slightly reduced fares available from STA Travel, see "Student Fares," below.

Bucket shops in Bangkok, Penang, and Singapore offer discount fares to the South Pacific as parts of tickets between Southeast Asia and North America. For instance, **J. Travel & Trading** (21/33 Soi Ngam Dupli, Near Malaysia Hotel, Rama 4 Rd., Bangkok 10120, Thailand; fax 66-2/287-1468) offers Singapore-Auckland-Nandi-Rarotonga-Papeete-Los Angeles for US$965. Shop around.

From South America

Lan Chile Airlines flies from Santiago to Tahiti via Easter Island twice a week, with two additional weekly flights between Chile and Easter Island only. Lan Chile's 30-day roundtrip excursion fare between Tahiti and Santiago, with a stopover on Easter Island, costs US$1433/1809 low/high, depending on the season. If you only want to visit Easter Island, 30-day excursion tickets Papeete-Easter Island-Papeete are available in Papeete for US$819/998 low/high.

In conjunction with other airlines, Lan Chile offers several "Circle-Pacific" fares, including Los Angeles-Papeete-Easter Island-Santiago-Miami (US$1694), Los Angeles-Papeete-Easter Island-Santiago-New York (US$1828), and Los Angeles-Santiago-Easter Island-Papeete-Los Angeles (US$1828), all valid one year.

Unfortunately Lan Chile must rate as one of the most unreliable carriers flying to Tahiti, and schedule irregularities are routine. The Santiago-Easter Island portion of their Tahiti service is often heavily booked, so try to reserve far in advance, though this can be hard to do.

From Europe

Air New Zealand offers nonstop flights London-Los Angeles three times a week, Frankfurt-Los Angeles twice a week, with connections in L.A. to Tahiti. Air France, AOM French Airlines, and Corsair fly directly to Tahiti from Paris via Los Angeles.

Air New Zealand reservations numbers around Europe are tel. 32-3/202-1355 (Belgium), tel. 33/0590-7712 (France), tel. 49-1/3081-7778 (Germany), tel. 39/1678-76126 (Italy), tel. 41/0800-2527 (Luxemburg), tel. 31-060/221016 (Netherlands), tel. 34-900/993241 (Spain), tel. 020/910-150 (Sweden), tel. 41/155-7778 (Switzerland), and tel. 44-181/741-2299 (United Kingdom). Call them up and ask about their Coral Routes fares.

The British specialist in South Pacific itineraries is **Trailfinders** (42-50 Earls Court Rd., Kensington, London W8 6FT, England; tel. 44-171/938-3366), in business since 1970. They offer a variety of discounted round-the-world tickets through Tahiti which are often much cheaper than the published fares. All rates are seasonal and depend on the airlines actually giving them deals, plus exchange rates play a part. Call or write for a free copy of their magazine, *Trailfinder,* which appears in April, July, and December. Also check the ads in *Time Out* for other such companies.

In Holland **Pacific Island Travel** (Dam 3, 1012 JS Amsterdam, the Netherlands; tel. 31-20/626-1325, fax 31-20/623-0008) sells most of the air passes and long-distance tickets mentioned in this chapter, plus package tours. Manager Rob Kusters is quite knowledgeable about the Pacific. Also in Amsterdam, **Reisbureau Amber** (Da Costastraat 77, 1053 ZG Amsterdam, the Netherlands; tel. 31-20/685-1155) is one of the best places in Europe to pick up books on the South Pacific.

In Switzerland try **Globetrotter Travel Service** (Rennweg 35, CH-8023 Zürich, Switzerland; tel. 41-1/211-7780, fax 41-1/211-2035), with offices in Baden, Basel, Bern, Luzern, St. Gallen, Winterthur, and Zürich. Their quarterly newsletter, *Ticket-Info,* lists hundreds of cheap flights, including many through Tahiti. Just for example,

Frankfurt-Los Angeles-Tahiti-Rarotonga-Fiji-Auckland-Los Angeles-Frankfurt costs 2350 Swiss francs from Globetrotter (2100 Swiss francs for those under 30 years). Most Europeans, however, go right around the world, and according to Globetrotter a favorite routing is Zürich-Rome-Bangkok-Singapore-Bali-Sydney-Auckland-Fiji-Tahiti-Los Angeles-Frankfurt which costs 2500 Swiss francs. Highly recommended.

Bucket shops in Germany sell a "Pacific Airpass" on Air New Zealand from Frankfurt to the South Pacific for around DM 2500 low season, DM 3000 high season. You may stop at a choice of any six of Tahiti, Rarotonga, Fiji, Auckland, Tonga, Apia, and Honolulu, and the ticket is valid six months. All flights must be booked prior to leaving Europe and there's a US$50 charge to change the dates once the ticket has been issued. One agency selling such tickets is **Walther-Weltreisen** (Hirschberger Strasse 30, D-53119 Bonn, Germany; tel. 49-228/661-239, fax 49-228/661-181).

French Charter Flights
Nouvelles Frontières Inc. (87 boulevard de Grenelle, Paris Cedex 75015, France; tel. 33-1/4141-5858) handles weekly charter flights from Paris and Los Angeles to Papeete and Nouméa on the French charter company **Corsair**. Fares to Papeete are broken down into four seasons, beginning at US$725/1150 single/return from Paris or US$475/780 from Los Angeles in the low season (mid-September to mid-June), and going up to US$1150/1850 from Paris or US$700/1150 from Los Angeles in the peak season. Penalties must be paid to change your flight dates, and in Papeete changes of date can only be made 15 days in advance. Refunds (minus a US$75 penalty) are only possible if the agency manages to resell your ticket, but you're forbidden to sell your own ticket to a third party. Corsair reserves the right to alter flight times up to 48 hours without compensation, but if you miss your flight you lose your money. Still, if you're sure when you'll be traveling, these prices are a couple of hundred

dollars lower than anything offered by the scheduled airlines.

Nouvelles Frontières has 200 offices in France and 40 others around the world, including these: 12 East 33rd St., 11th Floor, New York, NY 10016, U.S.A. (tel. 212/779-0600); APS, Inc., 5757 West Century Blvd., Suite 660, Los Angeles, CA 90045-6407, U.S.A. (tel. 310/670-7302; fax 310/338-0708); and 11 Blenheim St., London W1, England (tel. 44-171/629-7772).

Student Fares
If you're a student, recent graduate, or teacher, you can sometimes benefit from lower student fares by booking through a student travel office. There are two rival organizations of this kind: Council Travel Services, with offices in college towns across the U.S., and a sister organization in Canada known as Travel Cuts; and STA Travel (Student Travel Australia), formerly called the Student Travel Network in the U.S. Both organizations require you to pay a nominal fee for an official student card, and to get the cheapest fares you have to prove you're really a student. Slightly higher fares on the same routes are available to nonstudents, so it's always worth checking them out.

STA Travel has been flying students across the Pacific for years. They offer special airfares for students and young people under 26 years with minimal restrictions. One-way tickets run about half the roundtrip price and cheaper fares are available for shorter stays. Call their toll-free number (800) 777-0112 for the latest information.

Slightly different student fares are available from **Council Travel Services,** a division of the nonprofit Council on International Educational Exchange (CIEE). Both they and **Travel Cuts** in Canada are much stricter about making sure you're a "real" student: you must first obtain the widely recognized International Student Identity Card (US$16) to get a ticket at the student rate. Some fares are limited to students and youths under 26 years of age, but part-time students and teachers also qualify. Seasonal pricing applies,

so plan ahead. Get hold of a copy of their free *Student Travel Catalog,* which, although mostly oriented toward travel to Europe, contains useful information for students. Circle-Pacific and round-the-world routings are also available from Council Travel Services and there are special connecting flights to Los Angeles from other U.S. points.

STA TRAVEL OFFICES

STA Travel, 297 Newbury St., Boston, MA 02115, U.S.A. (tel. 617/266-6014)

STA Travel, 7202 Melrose Ave., Los Angeles, CA 90046, U.S.A. (tel. 213/934-8722)

STA Travel, 10 Downing St. (6th Ave. and Bleecker), New York, NY 10014, U.S.A. (tel. 212/477-7166, fax 212/477-7348)

STA Travel, 3730 Walnut St., Philadelphia, PA 19104, U.S.A. (tel. 215/382-2928)

STA Travel, 51 Grant Ave., San Francisco, CA 94108, U.S.A. (tel. 415/391-8407)

STA Travel, 120 Broadway #108, Santa Monica, CA 90401, U.S.A. (tel. 310/394-5126, fax 310/394-8640)

STA Travel, 2401 Pennsylvania Ave. #G, Washington, DC 20037, U.S.A. (tel. 202/887-0912)

STA Travel, 222 Faraday St., Carlton, Melbourne 3053, Australia (tel. 61-3/9349-2411, fax 61-3/9347-8070)

STA Travel, 1st Floor, 732 Harris St., Ultimo, Sydney, NSW 2007 (tel. 61-2/212-1255)

STA Travel, 10 High St., Auckland, New Zealand (tel. 09/366-6673, fax 64-9/309-9723)

STA Travel, #02-17 Orchard Parade Hotel, 1 Tanglin Rd., Singapore 1024 (tel. 65/734-5681, fax 65/737-2591)

STA Travel, Wall Street Tower, Suite 1405, 33 Surawong Rd. Bangrak, Bangkok 10500, Thailand (tel. 66-2/233-2582)

SRID Reisen, Bockenheimer Landstrasse 133, D-60325 Frankfurt, Germany (tel. 49-69/703-035, fax 49-69/777-014)

STA Travel, Priory House, 6 Wright's Lane, London W8 6TA, England (tel. 44-171/937-9962)

COUNCIL TRAVEL OFFICES

2000 Guadalupe St., Austin, TX 78705, U.S.A. (tel. 512/472-4931)

2486 Channing Way, Berkeley, CA 94704, U.S.A. (tel. 510/848-8604)

729 Boylston St., Suite 201, Boston, MA 02116, U.S.A. (tel. 617/266-1926)

1153 N. Dearborn St., 2nd Floor, Chicago, IL 60610, U.S.A. (tel. 312/951-0585)

1138 13th St., Boulder, CO 80302, U.S.A. (tel. 303/447-8101)

1093 Broxton Ave., Suite 220, Los Angeles, CA 90024, U.S.A. (tel. 310/208-3551)

One Datran Center, Suite 320, 9100 South Dadeland Blvd., Miami, FL 33156, U.S.A. (tel. 305/670-9261)

205 East 42nd St., New York, NY 10017-5706, U.S.A. (tel. 212/661-1450)

715 S.W. Morrison, Suite 600, Portland, OR 97205, U.S.A. (tel. 503/228-1900)

953 Garnet Ave., San Diego, CA 92109, U.S.A. (tel. 619/270-6401)

919 Irving St., Suite 102, San Francisco, CA 94122, U.S.A. (tel. 415/566-6222, fax 415/566-6730)

1314 N.E. 43rd St., Suite 210, Seattle, WA 98105, U.S.A. (tel. 206/632-2448)

Travel Cuts, 187 College St., Toronto, Ont. M5T 1P7, Canada (tel. 416/979-2406, fax 416/979-8167)

110D Killiney Rd., Tah Wah Building, Singapore 0923 (tel. 65/7387-066)

108/12-13 Kosan Rd., Banglumpoo, Bangkok 10200, Thailand (tel. 66-2/282-7705)

Council Travel, Sanno Grand Building, Room 102, 14-2 Nagata-cho 2-chome, Chiyoda-ku, Tokyo 100, Japan (tel. 81-3/3581-5517)

Council Travel, 18 Graf Adolph Strasse, D-40212 Düsseldorf 1, Germany (tel. 49-211/329-088, fax 49-211/327-469)

22 rue des Pyramides, 75001 Paris, France (tel. 33-1/4455-5565)

Council Travel, 28A Poland St., near Oxford Circus, London W1V 3DB, England (tel. 44-171/437-7767)

Important Note

Airfares, rules, and regulations tend to fluctuate a lot, so some of the above may have changed. This is only a guide; we've included precise fares to give you a rough idea how much things might cost. Your travel agent will know best what's available at the time you're ready to travel, but if you're not satisfied with his/her advice, keep shopping around. The biggest step is deciding to go—once you're over that the rest is easy!

PROBLEMS

When planning your trip allow a minimum two-hour stopover between connecting flights at U.S. airports, although with airport delays on the increase even this may not be enough. In the islands allow at least a day between flights. In some airports flights are not called over the public address system, so keep your eyes open. Whenever traveling, always have a paperback or two, some toiletries, and a change of underwear in your hand luggage.

If your international flight is canceled due to a mechanical problem with the aircraft, the airline will cover your hotel bill and meals. If they reschedule the flight on short notice for reasons of their own or you're bumped off an overbooked flight, they should also pay. They may not feel obligated to pay, however, if the delay is due to weather conditions, a strike by another company, national emergencies, etc., although the best airlines still pick up the tab in these cases. (The above doesn't apply to domestic flights within Tahiti-Polynesia itself.)

It's an established practice among airlines to provide light refreshments to passengers delayed two hours after the scheduled departure time and a meal after four hours. Don't expect to get this on some remote Polynesian island, but politely request it if you're at a gateway airport. If you are unexpectedly forced to spend the night somewhere, the airline may give you a form offering to telephone a friend or relative to inform them of the delay. Don't trust them to do this, however. Call your party yourself if you want to be sure they get the message. (Air New Zealand is notorious for not conveying messages of this kind.)

Overbooking

To compensate for no-shows, most international airlines overbook their flights. To avoid being bumped, ask for your seat assignment when booking, check in early, and go to the departure area well before flight time. Of course, if you *are* bumped by a reputable airline at a major airport you'll be regaled with free meals and lodging, and sometimes even free flight vouchers (don't expect anything like this from Air Tahiti).

Whenever you break your journey for more than 72 hours, always reconfirm your onward reservations and check your seat assignment at the same time. Get the name of the person who takes your reconfirmation so they cannot later deny it. Failure to reconfirm could result in the cancellation of your complete remaining itinerary. This could also happen if you miss a flight for any reason. If you want special vegetarian or kosher food in-flight, request it when buying your ticket, booking, and reconfirming.

When you try to reconfirm your Air New Zealand flight the agent will probably tell you that this formality is no longer required. Theoretically this may be true, but unless you request your seat assignment in advance, either at an Air New Zealand office or over the phone, you could be "bumped" from a full flight, reservation or no reservation. Air New Zealand's ticket cover bears this surprising message:

> *. . . no guarantee of a seat is indicated by the terms "reservation," "booking," "O.K." status, or the times associated therewith.*

They do admit in the same notice that confirmed passengers denied seats may be eligible for compensation, so if you're not in a hurry, a night or two at an upmarket hotel with all meals courtesy of Air New Zealand may not be a hardship. Your best bet if you don't want to get "bumped" is to request seat assignments for your entire itinerary before you leave home, or at least at the first Air New Zealand office you pass during your travels. Any good travel agent selling tickets on Air New Zealand should know enough to automatically request your seat assignments as they make your bookings. Check Air New Zealand's reconfirmation policy at one of their offices as it could change.

Baggage

International airlines allow economy-class passengers either 20 kilos of baggage or two pieces not over 32 kilos each (ask which applies to you). Under the piece system, neither bag must have a combined length, width, and height of over 158 cm (62 inches) and the two pieces together must not exceed 272 cm (107 inches). On most long-haul tickets to/from North America or Europe, the piece system applies to all sectors, but check this with the airline. The frequent flier programs of some major airlines allow participants to carry up to 10 kilos of excess baggage free of charge. Air Tahiti restricts you to 10 kilos unless you buy your ticket abroad, so it's better to pack according to the lowest common denominator.

Bicycles, folding kayaks, and surfboards can usually be checked as baggage (sometimes for an additional US$50 charge), but windsurfers may have to be shipped airfreight. If you do travel with a windsurfer, be sure to call it a surfboard at check-in.

Tag your bag with name, address, and phone number inside and out. Stow anything that could conceivably be considered a weapon (scissors, penknife, toy gun, Mace, etc.) in your checked luggage. Incidentally, it can be considered a criminal offense to make jokes about bombings or hijackings in airports or aboard aircraft.

One reason for lost baggage is that some people fail to remove used baggage tags after they claim their luggage. Get into the habit of tearing off old baggage tags, unless you want your luggage to travel in the opposite direction! As you're checking in, look to see if the three-letter city codes on your baggage tag receipt and boarding pass are the same.

If your baggage is damaged or doesn't arrive at your destination, inform the airline officials *immediately* and have them fill out a written report, otherwise future claims for compensation will be compromised. Airlines usually reimburse out-of-pocket expenses if your baggage is lost or delayed over 24 hours. The amount varies from US$25-50. Your chances of getting it are better if you're polite but firm. Keep receipts for any money you're forced to spend to replace missing articles.

Claims for lost luggage can take weeks to process. Keep in touch with the airline to show your concern and hang onto your baggage tag until the matter is resolved. If you feel you did not receive the attention you deserved, write the airline an objective letter outlining the case. Get the names of the employees you're dealing with so you can mention them in the letter. Of course, don't expect any pocket money or compensation on a remote outer island. Report the loss, then wait till you get back to the airline's main office. Whatever happens, avoid getting angry. The people you're dealing with don't want the problem any more than you do.

ORGANIZED TOURS

Packaged Holidays

While this book is written for independent travelers rather than package tourists, reduced group airfares and hotel rates make some tours worth considering. For two people with limited time and a desire to stay at a first-class hotel, this may be the cheapest way to go. The "wholesalers" who put these packages together get their rooms at rates far lower than individuals pay. Special-interest tours are popular among sportspeople who want to be sure they'll get to participate in the various activities they enjoy. The main drawback to the tours is that you're on a fixed itinerary among other tourists, out of touch with local life. Singles pay a healthy supplement. Some of the companies mentioned below do not accept consumer inquiries and require you to work through a travel agent.

Specialists in tours (and all travel arrangements) to Tahiti-Polynesia include **Manuia Tours** (74 New Montgomery St., San Francisco, CA 94105, U.S.A.; tel. 415/495-4500, fax 415/495-2000), **Tahiti Vacations** (9841 Airport Blvd., Suite 1124, Los Angeles, CA 90045, U.S.A.; tel. 800/553-3477), **Tahiti Nui's Island Dreams** (Box 9170, Seattle, WA 98109, U.S.A.; tel. 800/359-4359), **Islands In The Sun** (2381 Rosecrans Ave. #325, El Segundo, CA 90245-4913, U.S.A.; tel. 800/828-6877), **Island Vacations** (2042 Business Center Dr., Irvine, CA 92715, U.S.A.; tel. 800/745-8545), and **Discover Wholesale Travel** (2192 Dupont Dr., Suite 105, Irvine, CA 92715, U.S.A.; tel. 800/576-7770 in California, tel. 800/759-7330 elsewhere in the U.S., fax 714/833-1176). One-week packages to Moorea or Huahine can begin as low as US$699 pp double occupancy including airfare from Los Angeles, transfers, and accommodations, so check all of these companies for specials like this before booking a tour. **Sunmakers** (Box 9170, Seattle, WA 98109, U.S.A.) books customized itineraries in Tahiti-Polynesia.

Club Méditerranée (40 W. 57th St., New York, NY 10019, U.S.A.; tel. 800/CLUB-MED, fax 212/315-5392) offers one-week packages to their resort villages on Bora Bora and Moorea. Package prices include room (double occupancy), food, land and water sports, evening entertainment, and transfers, but airfare and bicycle rentals are extra. Due to all the activities Club Med's a good choice for single travelers; families with small children should look elsewhere. Book a couple of months in advance, especially if you want to travel in July, August, or December. For more information on *le Club,* see the Bora Bora and Moorea entries in this handbook.

Qantas Holidays (141 Walker St., North Sydney, NSW 2060, Australia; tel. 61-2/957-0781) and **Hideaway Holidays** (994 Victoria Rd., West Ryde, NSW 2114, Australia; tel. 61-2/807-4222, fax 61-2/808-2260) offer a variety of standard package tours to Tahiti which combine accommodations with cheap group airfares. In Europe, package tours to Tahiti-Polynesia are most easily booked through Nouvelles Frontières offices.

Scuba Tours

Tahiti-Polynesia is one of the world's prime scuba locales, and most islands have good facilities for divers. Although it's not difficult to do it on your own, if you have limited time and want to get in as much diving as possible, you should consider joining an organized scuba tour. To stay in business, dive travel specialists are forced to charge prices similar to what you'd pay if you just walked in off the street, and the convenience of having all your arrangements made for you by a company able to pull weight with island suppliers is often worth it. Request the brochures of the companies listed below, and before booking, find out exactly where you'll be staying and ask if daily transfers and meals are provided. Of course, diver certification is mandatory.

The largest American wholesalers putting together scuba tours to Polynesia are **Tropical Adventures Travel** (111 2nd Ave. N., Seattle,

WA 98109, U.S.A.; tel. 800/247-3483, fax 206/441-5431), **See & Sea Travel Service** (50 Francisco St., Suite 205, San Francisco, CA 94133, U.S.A.; tel. 800/DIV-XPRT, fax 415/434-3409), **Adventure Express** (650 5th St. #505, San Francisco, CA 94107, U.S.A. (tel. 800/443-0799, fax 415/442-0289), and **Sea Safaris** (3770 Highland Ave., Suite 102, Manhattan Beach, CA 90266, U.S.A.; tel. 800/821-6670, fax 310/545-1672). For example, Sea Safaris has five-night packages to Rangiroa's Kia Ora Village at US$1500 per diver. Also check Ocean Voyages mentioned under "Yacht Tours and Charters" below for live-aboard scuba diving from chartered yachts.

One of the leading experts on scuba diving around Tahiti-Polynesia is marine biologist and dive instructor Richard Johnson, director of **Paradise Dive Travel** (B.P. 6008, Faa'a, Tahiti; tel./fax 689/41-08-54). Dick sells "prepaid diving vouchers" for customized scuba diving at Tahiti, Moorea, Huahine, Raiatea, Bora Bora, Rangiroa, and Manihi at discounts of 5-20 percent. Write or fax for his free leaflet, *Why Dive Tahiti?,* which outlines the advantages and disadvantages of each island in refreshingly straightforward language. Dick's U.S. agent is Islands In The Sun (tel. 800/828-6877).

Alternatively, you can make your own arrangements directly with island dive shops. Information about these operators is included under the heading "Sports and Recreation" in the destinations chapters of this book.

Bicycle Tours

About the only North American company offering tours especially designed for cyclists is **Journeys Beyond** (Box 7511, Jackson, WY 83001, U.S.A.; tel. 307/733-9615). Three times a year there are 10-day cycle tours of the Leeward Islands of Tahiti-Polynesia (US$2620, double occupancy). Interisland travel between the four islands visited is by chartered yacht. Prices include food, a shared cabin on the yacht, and bicycles, but airfare is extra. This trip offers an excellent combination of sailing and cycling.

Surfing Tours

The largest operator of surfing tours to the South Pacific is **The Surf Travel Company** (Box 446, Cronulla, NSW 2230, Australia; tel. 61-2/527-

4722, fax 61-2/527-4522). At Raiatea/Huahine they offer surfing from a chartered Beneteau yacht at A$1699 pp for seven nights, including accommodations, meals, transfers (but not airfare). Their groups are never bigger than 12. "Luxury yacht, beautiful tropical islands, grinding clean surf—say no more." In New Zealand book through Mark Thompson (7 Danbury Dr., Torbay, Auckland; tel./fax 64-9/473-8388).

Yacht Tours and Charters

If you were planning on spending a substantial amount to stay at a luxury resort, consider chartering a yacht instead! Divided up among the members of your party, the per-person charter price will be about the same, but you'll experience much more of Polynesia's beauty on a boat than you would staying in a hotel room. All charterers visit remote islands accessible only by small boat and thus receive special insights into island life unspoiled by normal tourist trappings. Of course, activities such as sailing, snorkeling, and general exploring by sea and land are included in the price.

Yacht charters are available either "bareboat" (for those with the skill to sail on their own) or "crewed" (in which case charterers pay a daily fee for a skipper plus his/her provisions).

One of the finest companies arranging such charters is **Ocean Voyages Inc.** (1709 Bridgeway, Sausalito, CA 94965, U.S.A.; tel. 415/332-4681, fax 415/332-7460). Unlike their competitors, Ocean Voyages organizes "shareboat" charters in which singles and couples book a single cabin on a chartered yacht. Ask about shareboat yacht cruises on fixed one- and two-week itineraries, usually between Huahine and Bora Bora. Individuals are welcome and there are about 10 departures a year from April to November. Scuba diving is possible at extra cost on some boats (ask). This is perfect if you're alone or in a party of two and can't afford to charter an entire bareboat yacht. The groups are limited to a maximum of 15 participants, often less.

Other outstanding Ocean Voyages offerings include the annual voyages from Tahiti to Pitcairn, and local cruises on the 15-meter sailing catamaran *Fai Manu* captained by Louis Corneglio. They've also developed one-week catamaran cruises especially designed for individual scuba divers to the remote islands of the Tuamotus (US$2350) and Marquesas (US$2150 pp)—the *crème de la crème* of Polynesian dive experiences. These prices are all-inclusive, covering everything but air transportation and liquor. All trips should be booked and paid for at least 60 days in advance. Ocean Voyages caters to a very select, professional clientele, and their crews are carefully chosen. Over 35% of the participants are repeaters—the best recommendation there is.

The Moorings (4th Floor, 19345 U.S. 19 North, Clearwater, FL 34624, U.S.A.; tel. 800/535-7289) offers bareboat and crewed yacht charters from their base at Raiatea. Prices range from US$2800 a week for a four-berth boat to US$10,780 weekly for a six-berth air-conditioned yacht. Prices are for the entire boat, but extras are airfare, food (US$32 pp daily), skipper (US$140 daily, if required), and cook (US$120, if desired). They check you out to make sure you're really capable of handling their vessels. Other obligatory extras are security insurance (US$18 a day), cancellation insurance (US$60 pp), and three percent local tax. Charter rates are higher during the April-October high season. All charters are from noon to noon. Their New Zealand office is **Moorings Rainbow Yacht Charters** (Box 8327, Symonds St., Auckland, New Zealand; tel. 64-9/377-4840, fax 64-9/377-4820). In Europe contact **Adventure Holidays** (Box 920113, 90266 Nürnberg, Germany; fax 49-911/979-9588).

For more information on this and other yacht charter companies, see "Sports and Recreation" under "Raiatea" in the chapter on Raiatea and Tahaa.

The Moorings' Raiatea competitor, ATM Yacht Charters, is represented by **Tahiti Vacations** (9841 Airport Blvd., Suite 1124, Los Angeles, CA 90045, U.S.A.; tel. 800/553-3477), so call to compare prices.

A few private brokers arranging bareboat or crewed yacht charters at Raiatea are **Sun Yacht Charters** (Box 737, Camden, ME 04843, U.S.A.; tel. 800/772-3500, fax 207/236-3972), **Charter World Pty. Ltd.** (579 Hampton St., Hampton, Melbourne 3188, Australia; tel. 61-3/9521-0033, fax 61-3/9521-0081), **Sail Connections Ltd.** (Freepost 4545, Box 3234, Auckland, New Zealand; tel. 64-9/358-0556, fax 64-9/358-4341), and **Yachting Partners International** (28/29 Richmond Place, Brighton, BN2 2NA, East Sussex, England; tel. 44-1273/571722, fax 44-1273/571720). As they don't own their boats (as the Moorings does), they'll be more inclined to fit you to the particular boat that suits your individual needs.

Luxury Cruises out of Papeete

Windstar Cruises (300 Elliott Ave. W, Seattle, WA 98119, U.S.A.; tel. 206/281-3535, fax 206/286-3229) offers cruises around the Society Islands year-round in their gigantic, four-masted *Wind Song*. Participants join the boat at Papeete on a Saturday. The pp price for one of 74 double, classless cabins for an eight-day cruise varies according to season: US$2695 (low), US$2795 (base), US$2895 (peak), plus US$125 port charges. Single occupancy is 50% more, and airfare to Tahiti is extra. Bookings can be made through **Tahiti Vacations** (9841 Airport Blvd., Suite 1124, Los Angeles, CA 90045, U.S.A.; tel. 800/553-3477, fax 310/337-1126).

Although the 134-meter-long, 62-meter-high Bahamas-registered *Wind Song* could hardly be classed as a yacht, it is a step up from the impersonal pretension of a love boat. One of three identical high-tech vessels that also ply the Mediterranean and Caribbean, the *Wind Song's* sails are fully computer-controlled, saving on both fuel and crew. Though the ship can heel up to six degrees, ballast tanks and stabilizers ensure a smooth ride and nights are often spent in port, so you don't have to struggle to get to sleep on a rolling ship. The Windstar fleet, commissioned at Le Havre, France, during 1986-88, deserves credit for experimenting with an alternative energy source (the wind!).

Very similar but bigger, and with five masts instead of four, is the 188-meter, US$125-million *Club Med 2* which moved here from New Caledonia in 1995. Four-night cruises from Papeete to Moorea, Huahine, and Bora Bora begin at US$1150, plus US$80 port charges. A three-day cruise from Bora Bora to Rangiroa and back to Papeete begins at US$850, plus US$60. The complete seven-night Saturday-to-Saturday circuit begins at US$1980, plus US$140. These can be combined with stays at the Club Med villages on Moorea and Bora Bora. The 392 passengers enjoy many luxuries, and like the *Wind Song*, the *Club Med 2* is environmentally correct: computerized sails, ozone-friendly high-grade fuel, proper waste disposal, and vegetarian food (upon request). Information is available from **Club Méditerranée** (40 W. 57th St., New York, NY 10019, U.S.A.; tel. 800/4-LE-SHIP, fax 212/315-5392) or at the Club Med office in the Vaima Center, Papeete.

Several times a year **Saga Holidays** (222 Berkeley St., Boston, MA 02116, U.S.A.; tel. 800/343-0273, fax 617/375-5950) offers luxury cruises from Los Angeles or Honolulu to Tahiti via Christmas Island aboard Princess Cruises' vessels.

BY SAILING YACHT

Getting Aboard

Hitch rides to Tahiti on private yachts from California, New Zealand, and Australia, or around the yachting triangle Papeete-Suva-Honolulu. At home, scrutinize the classified listings of yachts seeking crews, yachts to be delivered, etc., in magazines like *Yachting, Cruising World,* and *Sail*. You can even advertise yourself for about US$25. Check the bulletin boards at yacht clubs. The **Seven Seas Cruising Association** (1525 South Andrews Ave., Suite 217, Fort Lauderdale, FL 33316, U.S.A.; tel. 305/463-2431, fax 305/463-7183) is in touch with yachties all around the Pacific, and the classified section "Crew Exchange" in their monthly *Commodores' Bulletin* (US$53 a year) contains ads from captains in search of crew.

Cruising yachts are recognizable by their foreign flags, wind-vane steering gear, sturdy appearance, and laundry hung out to dry. Put up notices on yacht club and marine bulletin boards, and meet people in bars. When a boat is hauled out, you can find work scraping and repainting the bottom, varnishing, and doing minor repairs. It's much easier, however, to crew on yachts already in the islands. In Tahiti, for example, after a month on the open sea, some of the original crew may have flown home or onward, opening a place for you.

If you've never crewed before, it's better to try for a short passage the first time. Once at sea on the way to Tahiti, there's no way they'll turn around to take a seasick crew member back to Hawaii. Good captains evaluate crew on personality and attitude more than experience, so don't lie. Be honest and open when interviewing with a skipper—a deception will soon become apparent. It's also good to know what a captain's *really* like before you commit yourself to an isolated month with her/him. Once you're on a boat and part of the yachtie community, things are easy. (P.S. from veteran yachtie Peter Moree: "We do need more ladies out here—adventurous types naturally.")

Time of Year

The weather and seasons play a deciding role in any South Pacific trip by sailboat and you'll have to pull out of many beautiful places, or be unable to stop there, because of bad weather. The best season for rides in the South Pacific is May to October; sometimes you'll even have to turn one down. Around August or September start looking for a ride from the South Pacific to Hawaii or New Zealand.

Be aware of the hurricane season: November to March in the South Pacific, July to December in the northwest Pacific (near Guam), and June to October in the area between Mexico and Hawaii. Few yachts will be cruising these areas at these times. Most South Pacific cruisers will have left for hurricane-free New Zealand by October.

Also, know which way the winds are blowing; the prevailing trade winds in the tropics are from the northeast north of the equator, from the southeast south of the equator. North of the Tropic of Cancer and south of the Tropic of Capricorn the winds are out of the west. Due to the action of prevailing southeast trade winds boat trips are smoother from east to west than west to east throughout the South Pacific, so that's the way to go.

Yachting Routes

The South Pacific is good for sailing; there's not too much traffic and no piracy like you'd find in the Mediterranean or in Indonesian waters. The common yachting route across the Pacific utilizes the northeast and southeast trades: from California to Tahiti via the Marquesas or Hawaii, then Rarotonga, Tonga, Fiji, and New Zealand. In the other direction, you'll sail on the westerlies from New Zealand to a point south of the Australs, then north on the trades to Tahiti.

Some 300 yachts leave the U.S. West Coast for Tahiti every year, almost always crewed by couples or men only. Most stay in the South Seas about a year before returning to North America, while a few continue around the world. About 60-80 cross the Indian Ocean every year (look for rides from Sydney in May, Cairns or Darwin from June to August, Bali from August to October, Singapore from October to December); around 700 yachts sail from Europe to the Caribbean (from Gibraltar and Gran Canaria from October to December)

Cruising yachts average about 150 km a day, so it takes about a month to get from the West Coast to Hawaii, then another month from Hawaii to Papeete. To enjoy the best weather conditions many yachts clear the Panama Canal or depart California in February to arrive in the Marquesas in March. Many yachts stay on for the *Heiva i Tahiti* festival, which ends on 14 July, at which time they sail west to Tonga or Fiji, where you'll find them in July and August. In mid-September the yachting season culminates with a race by about 40 boats from Fiji's Malololailai Island to Vanuatu (it's very easy to hitch a ride at this time). By late October the bulk of the yachting community is sailing south via New Caledonia to New Zealand or Australia to spend the southern summer there.

A law enacted in New Zealand in February 1995 requires foreign yachts departing New Zealand to obtain a "Certificate of Inspection" from the New Zealand Yachting Federation prior to customs clearance. Before heading into a situation where thousands of dollars may have to be spent upgrading safety standards on their boats, yachties should query others who have left New Zealand recently about the impact of this law.

Life Aboard

To crew on a yacht you must be willing to wash and iron clothes, cook, steer, keep watch at night, and help with engine work. Other jobs might include changing and resetting sails, cleaning the boat, scraping the bottom, pulling up the anchor, climbing the main mast to watch for reefs, etc. Do more than is expected of you. A safety harness must be worn in rough weather. As a guest in someone else's home you'll want to wash your dishes promptly after use and put them, and all other gear, back where you found them. Tampons must not be thrown in the toilet bowl. Smoking is usually prohibited as a safety hazard.

You'll be a lot more useful if you know how to use a sextant—the U.S. Coast Guard Auxiliary holds periodic courses in its use. Also learn how to tie knots like the clove hitch, rolling hitch, sheet bend, double sheet bend, reef knot, square knot, figure eight, and bowline. Check your local library for books on sailing or write away for the comprehensive free catalog of nautical books available from International Marine/TAB Books, Blue Ridge Summit, PA 17294-0840, U.S.A.

Anybody who wants to get on well under sail must be flexible and tolerant, both physically and emotionally. Expense-sharing crew members pay US$50 a week or more per person. After 30 days you'll be happy to hit land for a freshwater shower. Give adequate notice when you're ready to leave the boat, but *do* disembark when your journey's up. Boat people have few enough opportunities for privacy as it is. If you've had a good trip, ask the captain to write you a letter of recommendation; it'll help you hitch another ride.

Food for Thought

When you consider the big investment, depreciation, cost of maintenance, operating expenses, and considerable risk (most cruising yachts are not insured), travel by sailing yacht is quite a luxury. The huge cost can be surmised from charter fees (US$500 a day and up for a 10-meter yacht). International law makes a clear distinction between passengers and crew. Crew members paying only for their own food, cooking gas, and part of the diesel are very different from charterers who do nothing and pay full costs. The crew is there to help in operating the boat, adding safety, but like passengers, they're very much under the control of the captain. Crew has no say in where the yacht will go.

The skipper is personally responsible for crew coming into foreign ports: he is entitled to hold their passports and to see that they have onward tickets and sufficient funds for further traveling. Otherwise the skipper might have to pay their hotel bills and even return airfares to the crew's country of origin. Crew may be asked to pay a share of third-party liability insurance. Possession of dope can result in seizure of the yacht. Because of such considerations, skippers often hesitate to accept crew. Crew members should remember that at no cost to themselves they can learn a bit of sailing and see places nearly inaccessible by other means.

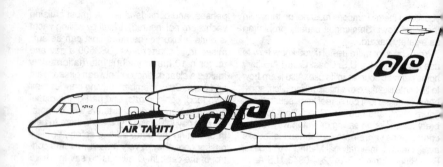

GETTING AROUND

BY AIR

The domestic carrier, **Air Tahiti** (B.P. 314, Papeete; tel. 86-42-42, fax 86-40-69), flies to 35 airstrips in every corner of Tahiti-Polynesia, with important hubs at Papeete (Windward Islands), Bora Bora (Leeward Islands), Rangiroa (western Tuamotus), Hao (eastern Tuamotus), and Nuku Hiva (Marquesas). Their fleet consists of two ATR 72 66-seat aircraft, four 46-seat ATR 42s, and one 19-seat Dornier 228. The Italian-made ATRs are economical in fuel consumption and maintenance requirements, and perform well under island conditions.

Air Tahiti doesn't allow stopovers on their tickets, so if you're flying roundtrip from Tahiti to Bora Bora and want to stop at Raiatea on the way out and Huahine on the way back, you'll have to purchase four separate tickets (total CFP 29,800). Ask about their "Pass Bleu" which allows you to visit these islands plus Moorea for CFP 20,000 (certain restrictions apply).

No student discounts are available, but persons under 25 and over 60 can get discounts of up to 50% on certain flights by paying CFP 1000 for a discount card *(carte de réduction)*. Family reduction cards (CFP 2000) provide a 50% reduction for the parents and 75% off for children 16 and under. Identification and one photo are required.

Slightly better than point-to-point fares are the Air Tahiti **Air Passes.** These are valid 28 days, but only one stopover can be made on each is-

land included in the package. For example, you can go Papeete-Moorea-Huahine-Raiatea-Bora Bora-Papeete for CFP 30,500. Otherwise pay CFP 45,500 for Papeete-Moorea-Huahine-Raiatea-Bora Bora-Rangiroa-Manihi-Papeete. This compares with an individual ticket price of CFP 33,200 to do the first circuit, CFP 67,500 for the second, which makes an air pass good value if you want to get to Rangiroa and Manihi as well as Bora Bora, but hardly worth considering if you're only going as far as Bora Bora. Air Passes which include the Austral Islands are CFP 50,500 (compared to CFP 78,800 on an individual basis); with the Tuamotu and Marquesas islands they're CFP 87,000 (compared to CFP 113,200). All flights must be booked in advance but date changes are possible. Tahiti Tourisme and Air France offices around the world act as Air Tahiti agents, so inquire at any of them about Air Passes. The passes are nonrefundable once travel has begun.

Air Tahiti tickets are refundable at the place of purchase, but you must cancel your reservations at least two hours before flight time to avoid a CFP 1000 penalty. Do this in person and have your flight coupon amended as no-shows are charged CFP 2000 to make a new reservation. It's not necessary to reconfirm confirmed reservations for flights between Tahiti, Moorea, Huahine, Raiatea, Bora Bora, Rangiroa, and Manihi, but elsewhere it's essential to reconfirm. Beware of planes leaving 20 minutes early.

The main Air Tahiti office in Papeete is upstairs in Fare Tony, the commercial center off

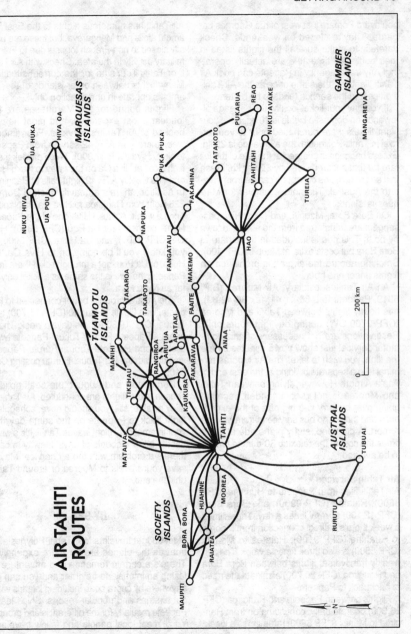

AIR TAHITI ROUTES

MARQUESAS ISLANDS

GAMBIER ISLANDS

TUAMOTU ISLANDS

SOCIETY ISLANDS

AUSTRAL ISLANDS

UA HUKA
HIVA OA
UA POU
NUKU HIVA
NAPUKA
PUKA PUKA
PUKARUA
REAO
NUKUTAVAKE
MANGAREVA
TATAKOTO
FAKAHINA
VAHITAHI
TUREIA
FANGATAU
HAO
MAKEMO
TAKAROA
TAKAPOTO
MANIHI
FAAITE
ARUTUA
APATAKI
RANGIROA
ANAA
TIKEHAU
FAKARAVA
KAUKURA
MATAIVA
TAHITI
TUBUAI
RURUTU
MAUPITI
BORA BORA
HUAHINE
MOOREA
RAIATEA

0   200 km

N

boulevard Pomare just west of rue Georges Lagarde. They're closed on weekends. Check carefully to make sure all the flights listed in their published timetable are actually operating! Any travel agency in Papeete can book Air Tahiti flights for the same price as the Air Tahiti office and the service tends to be better.

If you buy your ticket locally, the baggage allowance on domestic flights is 10 kg, but if your flight tickets were purchased prior to your arrival in Tahiti-Polynesia, the allowance is 20 kg. Excess baggage is charged at the rate of the full fare for that sector divided by 80 per kg. Fresh fruit and vegetables cannot be carried from Tahiti to the Austral, Tuamotu, Gambier, or Marquesas islands.

On Bora Bora, Maupiti, and Nuku Hiva passengers are transferred from the airport to town by boat. This ride is included in the airfare at Bora Bora but costs extra at Maupiti (CFP 400). Smoking aboard the aircraft is prohibited on flights under one hour.

An Air Tahiti subsidiary, **Air Moorea** (B.P. 6019, Papeete; tel. 86-41-41, fax 86-42-69), has hourly flights between Tahiti and Moorea (CFP 2700 OW) during daylight hours only. Reservations are not necessary on this commuter service: just show up 15 minutes before the flight you wish to take. The Air Moorea terminal is in a separate building at the east end of Faa'a Airport. However, flying between Tahiti and Moorea is not recommended because going over by ferry is a big part of the experience and there's no bus service to/from Moorea Airport. A cramped, stuffy plane ride at three times the cost of the relaxing 30-minute ferry is to be avoided.

Air Tahiti Services
Air Tahiti flies from Papeete to Huahine (CFP 8600), Raiatea (CFP 9900), and Bora Bora (CFP 12,100) several times a day. Three times a week there's a direct connection from Moorea to Huahine (CFP 9100); Raiatea to Maupiti (CFP 5500) is also three times a week. The two weekly transversal flights between Bora Bora and Rangiroa (CFP 20,700) eliminate the need to backtrack to Papeete.

Flights between Papeete and Rangiroa (CFP 13,300) operate daily, continuing on from Rangiroa to Manihi (CFP 8600) three times a week.

Air Tahiti has numerous flights to the East Tuamotu atolls and Mangareva, but these are usually closed to non-French tourists due to French military activity in the area. Check with Air Tahiti or Tahiti Tourisme for the current situation. Many flights between outer islands of the Tuamotus operate in one direction only.

Flights bound for the Marquesas are the longest, most expensive, and most heavily booked of Air Tahiti's services. Four times a week there's an ATR 42 service from Papeete to Nuku Hiva (CFP 37,800). Twice a week these flights call at Hiva Oa on their way to Nuku Hiva, and one weekly ATR 42 flight calls at Rangiroa. In addition, there's a heavily booked Dornier 228 flight from Rangiroa to Hiva Oa via Napuka once a week. At Nuku Hiva one of the Papeete flights connects for Ua Pou (CFP 5000), Hiva Oa (CFP 8600), and Ua Huka (CFP 5000). If you know you'll be going on to Hiva Oa, Ua Huka, or Ua Pou, get a through ticket there from Papeete; the fare is the same as a ticket only as far as Nuku Hiva.

The Austral group is better connected to Papeete, with flights to Rurutu (CFP 17,700) and Tubuai (CFP 19,800) three days a week. These operate Papeete-Rurutu-Tubuai-Papeete twice a week and Papeete-Tubuai-Rurutu-Papeete weekly, with the leg Tubuai-Rurutu costing CFP 8100.

During July and August, the peak holiday season, extra flights are scheduled. Air Tahiti is fairly reliable; still, you should never schedule a flight back to Papeete on the same day that your international flight leaves Tahiti. It's always best to allow a couple of days' leeway in case there's a problem with the air service. Maybe save your travels to Moorea or around Tahiti until the end.

BY SEA

Most budget travelers tour Tahiti-Polynesia by boat as the planes are far more expensive. There's a certain romance and adventure to taking an interisland freighter and you can go anywhere by copra boat, including islands without airstrips and popular resorts. Ships leave Papeete regularly for the different island groups. You'll meet local people and fellow travelers,

(top left) boy with baguettes, Moorea (Robert Leger); (top right) children, Maupiti (David Stanley); (bottom left) Papeete market, Tahiti (Robert Leger); (bottom right) kids at a general store, Moorea (Robert Leger)

(top) *Raromatai Ferry* at Bora Bora (David Stanley); (bottom left) unloading at Vairaatea, Tuamotus (Anselm Zänkert); (bottom right) maintenance, *Raromatai Ferry* (David Stanley)

and receive a gentle introduction to the island of your choice. Problems about overweight baggage, tight reservations, and airport transport are eliminated, and travel by ferry or passenger-carrying freighter is four times cheaper than the plane. Seasickness, cockroaches, diesel fumes, and the heavy scent of copra are all part of the experience.

Below you'll find specific information on the main interisland boats. The tourist office in Papeete also has lists. Prices and schedules have been fairly stable over the past few years, and new services are being added all the time. Lots of visitors travel this way to Moorea and Bora Bora, so don't feel intimidated if you've never done it before.

For the cheapest ride and the most local color, travel deck class. There's usually an awning in case of rain, and you'll be surrounded by Tahitians, but don't count on getting a lot of sleep if you go this way—probably no problem for one night, right? Lay your mat pointed to one side of the boat because if you lie parallel to the length of the boat you'll roll from side to side. Don't step over other peoples' mats, but if you must, first remove your shoes and excuse yourself. Otherwise take a cabin, which you'll share with three or four other passengers, still cheaper than an airplane seat. Food is only included on really long trips (ask), but snacks may be sold on board. On a long trip you're better off taking all your own food than buying a meal plan.

For any boat trip farther than Moorea check the schedule and pick up tickets the day before at the company office listed below. If you're headed for a remote island outside the Societies or want cabin class, visit the office as far in advance as possible. Except on the *Aranui*, it's not possible (nor recommended) to book your passage before arriving on Tahiti. If you really want to go, there'll be something leaving around the date you want. On an outer island, be wary when someone, even a member of the crew, tells you the departure time of a ship: they're as apt to leave early as late.

Boat trips are always smoother northwest-bound than southeast-bound because you go with the prevailing winds. Take this into consideration if you plan to fly one way, in which case it would be better to come back by air. *Bon voyage.*

Ferry to Moorea

There are two types of ferries to Moorea: two fast 320-passenger catamarans carrying walk-on commuters only (30 minutes), and two large car ferries with a capacity for 400 foot-passengers and 80 vehicles (one hour). Departure times are posted at the ferry landing on the Papeete waterfront (punctual) and reservations are not required: you buy your ticket just before you board. Stroll around the open upper deck and enjoy the scenic one-hour crossing. The crossing can be rather rough on a stormy day, so if you're prone to seasickness, try to cross in good weather.

The high-speed catamarans *Aremiti II* (B.P. 9254, Papeete; tel. 42-88-88, fax 42-06-15) and *Tamahine Moorea II* (tel. 43-76-50) make five trips a day between Tahiti and Moorea at CFP 800 pp. Unlike the airport catamaran at Bora Bora where you're forced to stay in a stuffy enclosed room, on the Moorea cats you're allowed to sit outside on the roof, which makes them fun and well worth taking one way.

The two car ferries, both named *Tamarii Moorea* (B.P. 3917, Papeete; tel. 43-76-50, fax 42-10-49), shuttle five or six times a day between Papeete and Vaiare Wharf on Moorea (CFP 700 OW, students and children under 13 CFP 350, car CFP 2000, scooter CFP 500, bicycle CFP 200).

Le truck meets all ferries on the Moorea side and will take you anywhere on that island for CFP 200. Just don't be too slow getting on or it could be full.

Cargo Ships to the Leeward Islands

You have a variety of choices if you're headed for the Leeward Islands. The cargo ship MV *Taporo VI* departs Papeete's Motu Uta wharf every Monday, Wednesday, and Friday after-

LEEWARD ISLANDS FERRY SCHEDULES

MV *Ono-Ono* (450 passengers)
MV *Raromatai Ferry* (550 passengers, 50 cars)

	NORTHBOUND				PORTS		SOUTHBOUND				
A	C	E	G	I	OF CALL		B	D	F	H	J
0900	1630		1800	1630	dep. Papeete arr.		1815	2015		2100	0530
1215	1945		0230	0030	arr. Huahine dep.		1500	1700		1300	2030
1230	2000	1130	0330	0100	dep. Huahine arr.		1445	1645	1115	1230	2000
1330	2100	1230	0530	0330	arr. Raiatea dep.		1345	1545	1015	1030	1800
1345	2115	1330	0800	0400	dep. Raiatea arr.		1330	1530	1000	1000	1730
			0845	0430	arr. Tahaa dep.					0915	1645
			0930	0500	dep. Tahaa arr.					0900	1630
1515	2245	1500	1130	0700	arr. Bora Bora dep.		1200	1400	0830	0700	1430

A—*Ono Ono* departs Papeete Monday and Wednesday
B—*Ono Ono* departs Bora Bora Tuesday and Thursday
C—*Ono Ono* departs Papeete Friday
D—*Ono Ono* departs Bora Bora Sunday
E—*Ono Ono* departs Huahine Saturday
F—*Ono Ono* departs Bora Bora Saturday
G—*Raromatai Ferry* departs Papeete Tuesday
H—*Raromatai Ferry* departs Bora Bora Thursday
I—*Raromatai Ferry* departs Papeete Friday
J—*Raromatai Ferry* departs Bora Bora Sunday

Schedules may change during holidays or otherwise.

noon around 1600. *Taporo VI* calls at Huahine at 0200, Raiatea at 0530, and Tahaa at 0700, reaching Bora Bora at 1000 Tuesday, Thursday, and Saturday. It departs Bora Bora for Papeete once again Tuesday, Thursday, and Saturday at 1130, calling at Raiatea at 1500 and Huahine at 1730, reaching Papeete early Wednesday, Friday, and Sunday morning (you can stay on board till dawn).

Northbound the MV *Vaeanu* leaves Papeete Monday, Wednesday, and Friday at 1700; southbound it leaves Bora Bora Tuesday at noon, Thursday at 0830, and Sunday at 0930. On both ships, the timings are more civilized if you go direct from Papeete to Bora Bora, then work your way back via Raiatea and Huahine. However, travelers on extremely low budgets who don't mind discomfort can save on accommodations by visiting Huahine and Raiatea first and sleeping on the dock those nights. There's a good shelter for this purpose at Huahine.

Although the ships do make an effort to stick to their timetables, the times are approximate—ask at the company offices. Expect variations if there's a public holiday that week and beware of voyages marked "carburant" on the schedules because when fuel *(combustible)* is being carried, only cabin passengers are allowed aboard (this often happens on the Wednesday departures from Papeete). Northbound you won't get much sleep due to noise and commotion during the early-morning stops. No mattresses or bedding are provided for deck passengers. In Papeete board the ship two hours prior to departure to be sure of a reasonable place on deck to sleep (mark your place with a beach mat). If you've got some time to kill before your ship leaves Papeete, have a look around the coconut-oil mill next to the wharf.

On *Taporo VI* the deck fare from Papeete to any of the Leeward Islands is CFP 1656. However, they only accept 12 deck passengers (who sleep in a large open container on the rear deck), so it's important to book ahead at the **Compagnie Française Maritime de Tahiti** (B.P. 368, Papeete; tel. 42-63-93, fax 42-06-17) in Fare Ute (open weekdays 0730-1100/1330-1700, Saturday 0730-1100). The two four-bed cabins are CFP 20,000 each. If you're only traveling between the islands of Huahine, Raiatea, Tahaa, and Bora Bora, the interisland deck fares are under CFP 1000 each trip. If you jump off for a quick look around while the ship is in port, you may be asked to buy another ticket when you reboard. A bicycle is about CFP 600 extra. No meals are included, so take food and water with you.

The *Vaeanu* carries a much larger number of deck and cabin passengers and you can usually buy a ticket at their office (B.P. 9062, Motu Uta; tel. 41-25-35, fax 41-24-34) facing the wharf at Motu Uta a few hours prior to departure (except on holidays). Do buy your ticket before boarding, however, as there can be problems for non-Tahitians trying to pay once the ship is underway. In the Leeward Islands buy a ticket from the agent on the wharf as soon as the boat arrives.

The Compagnie Française Maritime de Tahiti also runs a supply ship from Papeete to Maiao occasionally, so ask. (The CFMT itself has a place in local history, having been founded around 1890 by Sir James Donald, who had the contract to supply limes to the British Pacific fleet. At the turn of the century Donald's schooner, the *Tiare Taporo,* was the fastest in Polynesia, and the CFMT is still the Lloyd's of London agent.)

Ferry to the Leeward Islands
The **Compagnie Maritime des Îles Sous-Le-Vent** (B.P. 50712, Pirae; tel. 43-19-88, fax 43-19-99), with an office in a red-and-white kiosk at the Moorea ferry wharf in Papeete, handles the car-carrying, 400-passenger *Raromatai Ferry* which departs Papeete to Huahine, Raiatea, Tahaa, and Bora Bora on Tuesday and Friday afternoons. This ship uses a landing behind the tourist office in downtown Papeete, not the wharf at Motu Uta where *Taporo VI* and the *Vaeanu* dock. Tickets for walk-on passengers are usually available just prior to departure. Prices from Papeete to Bora Bora are CFP 3800 for a seat

in the salon, CFP 6000 in a four-berth cabin, CFP 10,000 for a car, CFP 500 for a bicycle. A double "cruise cabin" is CFP 17,000 for two people. There are discounts for students and those 18 and under.

The *Raromatai Ferry* salon is a spacious sitting room with aircraft-style Pullman seats, but French TV shows blast at you nonstop and the powerful air-conditioning means you freeze at night unless you have a sleeping bag. The *Raromatai Ferry* rolls a lot in rough weather. Between the Leeward Islands the *Raromatai Ferry* is a good deal (CFP 1000 salon interisland) for these daylight crossings (southbound), with an excellent open promenade deck on top.

Jet Cruiser to the Leeward Islands
The big news in sea travel from Papeete to Huahine, Raiatea, and Bora Bora is the high-speed monohull *Ono-Ono* (Société Polynésienne d'Investissement Maritime, B.P. 16, Papeete; tel. 45-35-35, fax 43-83-45) which began service in 1994. This Australian-built, 48-meter jet boat carries 450 passengers at speeds of up to 35 knots, cutting traveling times from Papeete to Huahine to just three hours (CFP 4300), to Raiatea 4.5 hours (CFP 4800), and to Bora Bora six hours (CFP 5800). Children under 12 years of age get half price on tickets to/from Papeete.

The *Ono-Ono* departs Papeete's Moorea ferry wharf Monday and Wednesday at 0900, Friday at 1630, departing Bora Bora for the return trip on Tuesday and Thursday at 1200, Sunday at 1400. On Saturday there's an shorter interisland run within the Leeward Islands only (about CFP 1600 a hop). Tickets should be purchased in advance (for insurance purposes, the booking agent will need to know the middle name and age of each passenger). Seating is 10 or 12 abreast on two enclosed decks. Though twice as expensive as the cargo boats or ferry, it's half the price of going by air and certainly makes getting around these enchanting islands a lot easier.

Government Ships to Maupiti and Beyond

The government supply ship *Meherio III* leaves Papeete for Maupiti about twice a month via Raiatea, usually on a Wednesday. Tickets to Maupiti are available from the **Direction de l'Equipment** (weekdays 0730-1500; B.P. 85, Papeete; tel. 42-44-92, fax 42-13-41) at Motu Uta, costing CFP 1374 from Papeete or CFP 1035 from Raiatea. This office also sells tickets on government boats to the Tuamotus and Marquesas, and only deck passage is available.

Ships to the Austral Islands

The **Service de Navigacion des Australes** (B.P. 1890, Papeete; tel. 43-15-88, fax 42-06-09), at the Motu Uta interisland wharf on the west side of the copra sheds in Papeete, runs the *Tuhaa Pae II* to the Austral Islands twice a month: CFP 31,518 cabin, CFP 18,010 deck for the 10-day RT. No meals are included, but food can be ordered at CFP 2300 pp a day extra (take your own). Some of the cabins are below the waterline and very hot. The rear deck has a diesely romantic feel, for a day or two. For sanitary reasons the seats have been removed from the ship's toilets (squat). The *Tuhaa Pae II* calls at Rimatara, Rurutu, Tubuai, Raivavae, and very occasionally Rapa Iti. Maria Atoll is visited annually. Their schedule changes at a moment's notice, so actually being able to go with them is pure luck.

Ships to the Tuamotus and Gambiers

The 26-meter motor vessel *Dory* (B.P. 9274, Papeete; tel./fax 42-88-88) leaves every Monday at 1300 from the Moorea ferry wharf in Papeete for Tikehau (Tuesday 0600), Rangiroa (Tuesday 1200), Arutua (Wednesday 0600), and Kaukura (Wednesday 1400), arriving back in Papeete Thursday at 0800 (CFP 3000 OW). This routing means it takes only 23 hours to go from Papeete to Rangiroa but 44 hours to return. There are no cabins and meals are not included. The *Dory* visits the islands to pick up fish and deliver frozen bread, chicken, and ice cream. The same company runs the *Cobia II* to the Tuamotus, departing

Monday at 1200 for Kaukura (Tuesday 0800), Arutua (Tuesday 1300), Apataki (Tuesday 1630), Aratika (Wednesday 0700), and Toau (Wednesday 1330), returning to Papeete Friday at 1000 (also CFP 3000 OW). Foreign visitors use these boats regularly, so they're probably your best bet.

The *Kauaroa Nui* (B.P. 9266, Papeete; tel./fax 41-07-11), with an office next to the *Vaeanu* office at the Motu Uta interisland wharf, has three departures a month for the middle Tuamotus (Fakarava, Faaite, Raraka, Katiu, and Makemo), leaving Thursday afternoons. Roundtrip fares are CFP 10,200 deck, CFP 17,000 in a basic four-bed cabin; no meals are included.

The 48-meter cargo boat *Manava II* (B.P. 1816, Papeete; tel. 43-83-84, fax 42-25-53) runs to the northern Tuamotus (Rangiroa, Tikehau, Mataiva, Ahe, Manihi, Takaroa, Takapoto, Aratika, Kauehi, Fakarava, Toau, Apataki, Arutua, and Kaukura) once or twice a month. There are no cabins: the deck passage to Rangiroa is CFP 3000.

Many smaller copra boats, such as the *Kura Ora, Rairoa Nui, Ruahatu*, and *Saint Xavier Maris Stella*, also service the Tuamotu and Gambier groups. Ask around the large workshops west of Papeete's Motu Uta interisland wharf. The *Saint Xavier Maris Stella* (B.P. 11366, Papeete; tel. 42-23-58) charges CFP 25,000 including meals for a one-week trip Tahiti-Mataiva-Tikehau-Rangiroa-Ahe-Manihi-Takaroa-Kauehi-Fakarava-Tahiti. Some of the ships serving the forbidden military zone in the Tuamotus won't accept non-French tourists as passengers, and others accept only men due to a lack of facilities for women.

Ships to the Marquesas

The 57-meter cargo ship *Taporo V* departs Papeete Thursday at 1400 every two weeks for Tahuata, Hiva Oa, Nuku Hiva, and Ua Pou, charging CFP 17,000 deck or CFP 24,000 cabin OW from Papeete to Hiva Oa. It takes 3.5 days on the open sea to reach the first Marquesan island, so you should certainly try for a cabin. Otherwise you can do the whole eight-day RT for CFP 36,000 deck or CFP 50,000 cabin, but only three to eight hours are spent at each port. Food is included but it's marginal, so take extras and bring your own bowl. Meals are served at 0600, 1100, and 1800. No pillows or towels are supplied in the cabins and the shower is only open three hours a day. The agent is **Compagnie Française Maritime de Tahiti** (B.P. 368, Papeete; tel. 42-63-93, fax 42-06-17) at Fare Ute.

The *Tamarii Tuamotu II* departs every five weeks to the Marquesas with only deck passage available (no cabins). This ship runs from Papeete direct to the Marquesas, but visits several of the Tuamotu atolls on the way back. It calls at every inhabited bay in the Marquesas (this alone takes 12 days). Check at their city office (Vonken et Cie., B.P. 2606, Papeete; tel. 42-95-07), corner of rue des Remparts and Ave. du Prince Hinoi. Since the *Tamarii Tuamotu II* calls at certain restricted islands in the Tuamotus, a permit from the Subdivision Administrative des Tuamotu-Gambier in Papeete may be required (see "Permission" under "Getting There" in the Tuamotu Islands chapter for more information).

The *Aranui*, a passenger-carrying freighter, cruises 15 times a year between Papeete and the Marquesas. The ship calls at most of the inhabited Marquesas Islands, plus a couple of the Tuamotus. The routing might be Papeete-Takapoto-Ua Pou-Nuku Hiva-Hiva Oa-Fatu Hiva-Hiva Oa-Ua Huka-Nuku Hiva-Ua Pou-Rangiroa-Papeete. A vigorous daily program with fairly strenuous but optional hikes is included in the tour price. The only docks in the Marquesas are at Taiohae, Vaipaee, Hakahau, and Atuona; elsewhere everyone goes ashore in whale boats, a potential problem for elderly passengers. Still, the *Aranui* is fine for the adventuresome visitor who wants to see a lot in a short time.

This modern freighter had its inaugural sailing in 1990, replacing a smaller German-built boat that had served the Marquesas since 1981. It's clean and pleasant compared to the other schooners, but far more expensive. A hundred passengers are accommodated in 30 a/c cabins or given mattresses on the bridge deck. Deck passage for a 15-day, eight-island cruise to the

Tuamotus and Marquesas costs CFP 153,800 RT; the cheapest cabin is CFP 280,500 RT (double occupancy), all meals included. An additional US$75 port tax is charged. Single occupancy costs 50% more. Cheaper one-way deck fares on the *Aranui* for local residents are not available to tourists. In any case, deck passage can be hot, noisy, and tiring on such a long trip.

Despite the fares charged, don't expect cruise ship comforts on the *Aranui*. Accommodations are spartan (but adequate), and meals are served in two shifts due to lack of space in the dining area. Aside from three classes of cabins (the cheaper ones are cramped), there's a large covered area where the deck passengers sleep. The roster of American/French/German passengers is congenial.

The *Aranui*'s Papeete office (**Compagnie Polynésienne de Transport Maritime,** B.P. 220, Papeete; tel. 42-62-40, fax 43-48-89) is at the interisland wharf at Motu Uta. In the U.S. advance bookings should be made through the CPTM office at 595 Market St., Suite 2880, San Francisco, CA 94105, U.S.A. (tel. 415/541-0677, fax 415/541-0766). One Australian reader wrote: "The trip is fantastic and I hope to do it again soon." (The *Aranui* recently costarred with Warren Beatty and Annette Bening in the Warner Brothers film *Love Affair*.)

LOCAL TRANSPORT

By Bus

Polynesia's folkloric *le truck* provides an entertaining unscheduled passenger service on Tahiti and some outer islands. Passengers sit on long wooden benches in back and there's no problem with luggage. Fares are fairly low and often posted on the side of the vehicle. You pay through the window on the right side of the cab. Drivers are generally friendly and will stop to

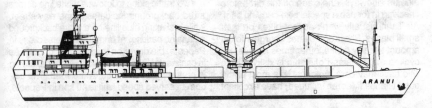

pick you up anywhere if you wave—they're all privately owned, so there's no way they'd miss a fare! On Tahiti the larger *trucks* leave Papeete for the outlying districts periodically throughout the day until 1700; they continue running to Faa'a Airport and the Maeva Beach Hôtel until around 2200. On Huahine and Raiatea service is usually limited to a trip into the main town in the morning and a return to the villages in the afternoon. On Moorea and Bora Bora they meet the boats from Papeete.

By Bicycle

Cycling in Polynesia? Sure, why not? It's cheap, convenient, healthy, quick, environmentally sound, safe, and above all, *fun*. You'll be able to go where and when you please, stop easily and often to meet people and take photos, save money on taxi fares—really *see* the countries. Cycling every day can be fatiguing, however, so it's best to have bicycle-touring experience beforehand. Most roads are flat along the coast, but be careful on coral roads, especially inclines: if you slip and fall you could hurt yourself badly. On the high islands interior roads tend to be very steep. Never ride your bike through mud.

A sturdy, single-speed mountain bike with wide wheels, safety chain, and good brakes might be best. Thick tires and a plastic liner between tube and tire will reduce punctures. Know how to fix your own bike. Take along a good repair kit (pump, puncture kit, freewheel tool, spare spokes, cables, chain links, assorted nuts and bolts, etc.) and a repair manual; bicycle shops are poor to nonexistent in the islands. Don't try riding with a backpack: sturdy, waterproof panniers (bike bags) are required; you'll also want a good lock. Refuse to lend your bike to *anyone*.

Many international airlines will carry a bicycle as checked luggage, either free, at the standard overweight charge, or for a flat US$50 fee. Take off the pedals and panniers, turn the handlebars sideways, and clean off the dirt before checking in (or use a special bike-carrying bag). Air Tahiti usually won't accept bikes on their small planes. Boats sometimes charge a token amount to carry a bike; other times it's free. Bicycling on the island of Tahiti is risky due to wild devil-may-care motorists, but most of the outer islands (Moorea included) have excellent uncrowded roads. It's best to use *le truck* on Tahiti, though a bike will come in real handy on the other islands where *le truck* is rare. The distances are just made for cycling!

Car Rentals

Car rentals are available at most of the airports served by Air Tahiti, but they ain't cheap. On Tahiti there's sometimes a mileage charge, whereas on Moorea, Huahine, Raiatea, and Bora Bora all rentals come with unlimited mileage. Public liability insurance is included by law, but collision damage waiver (CDW) insurance is extra. If you can get a small group together, consider renting a minibus for a do-it-yourself island tour. Unless you have a major credit card you'll have to put down a cash deposit on the car. Your home driver's license will be accepted, although you must have had your driver's license for at least a year. Visitors under the age of 25 are usually refused service unless they show a major credit card, and those under 21 cannot rent a car at all. Rental scooters are usually available. On Tahiti a strictly enforced local regulation requires you to wear a helmet *(casque)* at all times (CFP 5000 fine).

One major hassle with renting cars on the outer islands is that they usually give you a car with the fuel tank only a quarter full, so immediately after renting you must go to a gas station and tank up. Try to avoid putting in more gas than you can use by calculating how many km you might drive, then dividing that by 10 for the number of liters of gasoline you might use. Don't put in over CFP 2000 (about 20 liters) in any case or you'll be giving a nice gift to the rental agency (which, of course, is their hope in giving you a car that's not full). Gas stations are usually only in the main towns and open only during business hours on weekdays, plus perhaps a couple of hours on weekend mornings. Expect to pay around CFP 100 a liter for gas (which works out to just under US$4 per American gallon).

Two traffic signs to know: a white line across a red background indicates a one-way street, while a slanting blue line on a white background means no parking. At unmarked intersections in Papeete, the driver on the right has priority. As in continental Europe and North America, driving is on the right-hand side of the road. The seldom-observed speed limit is 40 kph in Papeete,

60 kph around the island. Drive with extreme care in congested areas—traffic accidents are frequent.

Others

Taxis are a rip-off throughout Tahiti-Polynesia and are best avoided. If you must, always verify the fare before getting in. The hitching is still fairly good in Polynesia, although local residents along the north side of Moorea are getting tired of it. Hitching around Tahiti is only a matter of time.

By Ocean Kayak

Ocean kayaking is experiencing a boom in Hawaii, but Tahiti-Polynesia is still largely virgin territory. Virtually every island has a sheltered lagoon ready-made for the excitement of kayak touring, but this effortless new transportation mode hasn't yet arrived, so you can be a real independent 20th-century explorer! Many airlines accept folding kayaks as checked baggage at no charge.

Companies like **Long Beach Water Sports** (730 E. 4th St., Long Beach, CA 90802, U.S.A.; tel. 310/432-0187, fax 310/436-6812) sell inflatable one- or two-person sea kayaks for around US$1800, fully equipped. If you're new to the game, LBWS runs four-hour introductory sea kayaking classes (US$55) every Saturday and all-day intermediate classes (US$70) monthly—a must for L.A. residents. They also rent kayaks by the day or week. Write for a free copy of their newsletter, *Paddle Strokes*.

For a better introduction to ocean kayaking than is possible here, check at your local public library for *Sea Kayaking, A Manual for Long-Distance Touring* by John Dowd (Seattle: University of Washington Press, 1981), *Derek C. Hutchinson's Guide to Sea Kayaking* (Seattle: Basic Search Press, 1985), or something similar. Noted author Paul Theroux toured the entire South Pacific by kayak, and his experiences are recounted in *The Happy Isles of Oceania: Paddling the Pacific* (London: Hamish Hamilton, 1992).

By Canoe

If you get off the beaten track, it's more than likely that a local friend will offer to take you out in his/her canoe. Never attempt to take a dugout canoe through even light surf: you'll be swamped. Don't try to pull or lift a canoe by its outrigger: it will break. Drag the canoe by holding the solid main body. A bailer is *essential* equipment.

INTERNATIONAL AIRPORT

Faa'a Airport (PPT), 5.5 km southwest of Papeete, handles around 32,000 domestic, 2,300 international, and 1,000 military flights a year. The runway was created in 1959-61, using material dredged from the lagoon or trucked in from the Punaruu Valley. A taxi into town is CFP 1000 (CFP 1200 on Sunday), double that after 2000. *Le truck* up on the main highway will take you to the same place for only CFP 140 (CFP 200 at night) and starts running around 0530.

Many flights to Tahiti arrive in the middle of the night, but you can stretch out on the benches inside the terminal. Representatives of the low-budget hostels are often on hand looking for prospective guests off the international flights, so ask the tourist information counter if there's anyone around from the place you've picked and, if there is, you'll probably get a free ride. If it's already early morning, you may be allowed to occupy your room for the balance of the night at no additional charge, provided you agree to stay at least two nights.

The Westpac Bank (tel. 82-44-24) in the terminal opens weekdays 0745-1530, and one hour before and after the arrival and departure of all international flights. They give the same rate as the banks in town and take the usual CFP 450 commission on all currencies other than French francs. The post office in the airport is open weekdays 0500-0900 and 1830-2230, weekends 0600-1000. Public toilets are located near the domestic check-in counter and upstairs from the bank.

The airport luggage-storage counter is open 0700-1700 and two hours before and after international departures. They charge CFP 180 per day for a small bag, CFP 360 for a large bag, CFP 600 for surfboards, etc. If they're closed when you arrive, ask at the nearby bar.

You can spend your leftover Pacific francs at the duty-free shops in the departure lounge, but don't expect any bargains. The Fare Hei, just outside the terminal, sells shell and flower leis for presentation to arriving or departing passengers.

All passengers arriving from Samoa or Fiji must have their baggage fumigated upon arrival, a process which takes about two hours (don't laugh if you're told this is to prevent the introduction of the "rhinoceros" into Polynesia—they mean the rhinoceros *beetle*.) Fresh fruits, vegetables, and flowers are prohibited from entry. There's no airport tax.

One nice touch is the welcoming committee Tahiti Tourisme sends out to meet every incoming international flight. As pareu-clad musicians strum their guitars or ukuleles, a smiling *vahine* puts a white *tiare Tahiti* blossom behind your ear. There's no catch; it's their way of saying *maeva*.

LOUISE FOOTE

SOCIETY ISLANDS
The Windward Islands
Tahiti, Moorea, Tetiaroa

King Pomare II of Tahiti
(reigned 1803-1821)

Parau na te Varua ino (Words of the Devil); *Paul Gauguin; National Gallery of Art, Washington; gift of the W. Averell Harriman Foundation in memory of Marie N. Harriman*

TAHITI

Tahiti, largest of the Societies, is an island of legend and song lying in the eye of Polynesia. Though only one of 118, this lush island of around 135,000 inhabitants is paradise itself to most people. Here you'll find an exciting city, big hotels, restaurants, nightclubs, things to see and do, valleys, mountains, reefs, trails, and history, plus transportation to everywhere. Since the days of Wallis, Bougainville, Cook, and Bligh, Tahiti has been the eastern gateway to the South Pacific.

In 1891 Paul Gauguin (goh-GANN) arrived at Papeete after a 63-day sea voyage from France. He immediately felt that Papeete "was Europe—the Europe which I had thought to shake off . . . it was the Tahiti of former times which I loved. That of the present filled me with horror." So Gauguin left the town and rented a native-style bamboo hut in Mataiea on the south coast, where he found happiness in the company of a 14-year-old Tahitian *vahine* whose "face flooded the interior of our hut and the landscape round about with joy and light." Somerset Maugham's *The Moon and Sixpence* is a fictional tale of Gauguin's life on the island.

Legends created by the early explorers, amplified in Jean-Jacques Rousseau's "noble savage" and taken up by the travel industry, make it difficult to write objectively about Tahiti. Though the Lafayette Nightclub is gone from Arue and Quinn's Tahitian Hut no longer graces Papeete's waterfront, Tahiti remains a delightful, enchanting place. In the late afternoon, as Tahitian crews practice canoe racing in the lagoon and Moorea gains a pink hue, the romance resurfaces. If you steer clear of the traffic jams and congestion in commercial Papeete and avoid the tourist ghettos west of the city, you can get a taste of the magic Gauguin encountered. But in fact, it's only on the outer islands of Polynesia, away from the motorists and the military complexes, that the full flavor lingers.

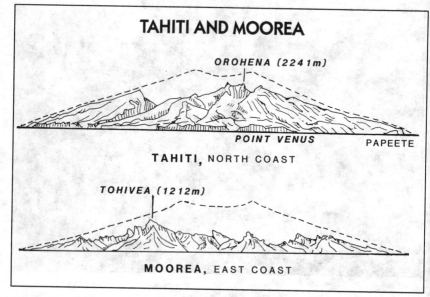

TAHITI AND MOOREA

OROHENA (2241m)

POINT VENUS   PAPEETE

TAHITI, NORTH COAST

TOHIVEA (1212m)

MOOREA, EAST COAST

The Land

The island of Tahiti accounts for almost a quarter of the land area of Tahiti-Polynesia. Like Hawaii's Maui, Tahiti was formed by two ancient volcanoes joined at the isthmus of Taravao. The rounded, verdant summits of Orohena (2,241 meters) and Aorai (2,066 meters) rise in the center of Tahiti Nui and deep valleys radiate in all directions from these central peaks. Steep slopes drop abruptly from the high plateaus to coastal plains. The northeast coast is rugged and rocky, without a barrier reef, and thus exposed to intense, pounding surf; villages lie on a narrow strip between mountains and ocean. The south coast is broad and gentle with large gardens and coconut groves; a barrier reef shields it from the sea's fury.

Tahiti Iti (also called Taiarapu) is a peninsula with no road around it. Mount Rooniu (1,323 meters) is its heart. The populations of big *(nui)* and small *(iti)* Tahiti are concentrated in Papeete and along the coast; the interior of both Tahitis is almost uninhabited. Contrary to the popular stereotype, mostly brown/black beaches of volcanic sand fringe this turtle-shaped island. To find the white/golden sands of the travel brochures, you must cross over to Moorea.

Environmental Concerns

Nonstop development over the past 35 years has had a heavy impact on the crowded 40-km coastal strip around Papeete. Aside from high-profile traffic congestion, the lagoon off northwestern Tahiti has been seriously affected by the quarrying of coral building materials from the seabed (halted in 1987), soil erosion resulting from construction work on adjacent hillsides, and inadequate treatment of sewage and solid wastes.

Half of the coastline between Punaauia and Arue is now artificial or reclaimed, and mud carried into the lagoon from unprotected terraces at building sites has increased turbidity, suffocating coral growth and causing flooding. A 1993 case study released by the South Pacific Regional Environment Program reports heavy metal concentrations on the lagoon floor up to 12 times higher than normal with especially high contamination in the port area. The SPREP study warns that "faecal pollution rules out swimming from most of the beaches within Papeete urban area, because of the lack of a coherent, integrated waste water collection and treatment system, and because effluent is still often disposed of straight into the lagoon."

The city's six official solid waste dumps are not only ugly, but they create a stench due to the lack of sorting and frequent fires. Recently a large amount was spent on a methane-producing incinerator in the heavily populated Tipaerui Valley above the Hôtel Matavai, but this sparked heated protests from local residents who felt endangered by emissions and in early 1994 part of the plant was closed. According to the SPREP study, Papeete's "water is piped from many open, above-ground catchments that have uneven degrees of protection and control, and is often untreated and not potable." Even in paradise, progress has a price which we as consumers must pay in the end.

Orientation

Almost everyone arrives at Faa'a International Airport five km west of Papeete, the capital and main tourist center of Tahiti-Polynesia. East of Papeete are Pirae, Arue, and Mahina, with a smattering of hotels and things to see, while south of Faa'a lie the commuter communities Punaauia, Paea, and Papara. On the narrow neck of Tahiti is Taravao, a refueling stop on your 117-km way around Tahiti Nui. Tahiti Iti is a backwater, with dead-end roads on both sides. Boulevard Pomare curves around Papeete's harbor to the tourist office near the market—that's where to begin. Moorea is clearly visible to the northwest.

PAPEETE

Papeete (pa-pay-EH-tay) means "Water Basket." The most likely explanation for this name is that islanders originally used calabashes enclosed in baskets to fetch water at a spring behind the present Territorial Assembly. In the 1820s whalers began frequenting its port, which offered better shelter than Matavai Bay. It became the seat of government when young Queen Pomare settled here in 1827. The French governors who "protected" the island from 1842 also used Papeete as their headquarters.

Today Papeete is the political, cultural, economic, and communications hub of Tahiti-Polynesia. Some 69,000 persons live in this cosmopolitan city and its satellite towns, Faa'a, Pirae, and Arue—over half the people on the island. "Greater Papeete" extends for 32 km from Paea to Mahina. In addition, some 4,000 French soldiers are stationed here, mostly hardened foreign legionnaires and police. The French Navy maintains facilities in the harbor area to support its bases in the Tuamotus.

Since the opening of Faa'a International Airport in 1961 Papeete has blossomed with new hotels, expensive restaurants, bars with wild dancing, radio towers, skyscrapers, and electric

Papeete as it looked around the turn of the century

rock bands pulsing their jet-age beat. Where a nail or red feather may once have satisfied a Tahitian, VCRs and Renaults are now in demand. Over 50,000 registered vehicles jam Tahiti's 200 km of roads. Noisy automobiles, motorcycles, and mopeds clog Papeete's downtown and roar along the boulevards buffeting pedestrians with pollution and noise. Crossing the street you can literally take your life in your hands.

Yet along the waterfront the yachts of many countries rock luxuriously in their Mediterranean moorings (anchor out and stern lines ashore). Many of the boats are permanent homes for expatriate French working in the city. "Bonitiers" moored opposite the Vaima Center fish for *auhopu* (bonito) for the local market. You should not really "tour" Papeete, just wander about without any set goal. Visit the highly specialized French boutiques, Chinese stores trying to sell everything, and Tahitians clustered in the market. Avoid the capital on weekends when life washes out into the countryside; on Sunday afternoons it's a ghost town. Explore Papeete, but make it your starting point—not a final destination.

Orientation
Thanks to airline schedules you'll probably arrive at the crack of dawn. Change money at the airport bank or use a couple of US$1 bills to take *le truck* to Papeete market. The helpful

DIANA LASICH HARPER

tourist office on the waterfront opens early, as do the banks nearby. You'll probably want a hotel in town for the first couple of nights to attend to "business": reconfirm your flights, check out the boats or planes, then take off for the outer islands.

A trip around the island will fill a day if you're waiting for connections, and Papeete itself can be fun. Fare Ute, north of French naval headquarters, was reclaimed with material dredged from the harbor in 1963. West across a bridge, past more military muscle, is Motu Uta, where you can jump aboard a passenger-carrying freighter. The high-speed boats and all of the Moorea ferries leave from the landing behind the tourist office downtown. For a day at the beach take a *truck* to Point Venus (see below).

SIGHTS

Papeete
Begin your visit at teeming **Papeete market** where you'll see Tahitians selling fish, fruit, root crops, and breadfruit; Chinese gardeners with their tomatoes, lettuce, and other vegetables; and French or Chinese offering meat and bakery products. The colorful throng is especially picturesque 1600-1700 when the fishmongers spring to life. Fish and vegetables are sold downstairs on the main floor, handicrafts and pareus upstairs on the balcony. The biggest market of the week begins around 0500 Sunday morning and is over by 0730.

The streets to the north of the market are lined with two-story Chinese stores built after the great fire of 1884. The US$14.5-million **Town Hall** on rue Paul Gauguin was inaugurated in 1990 on the site of a smaller colonial building demolished to make way. The architect designed the three-story building to resemble the palace of Queen Pomare that once stood on Place Tarahoi near the present post office.

Notre Dame Catholic Cathedral (1875) is on rue du Général de Gaulle, 1.5 blocks southeast of the market. Notice the Polynesian faces and the melange of Tahitian and Roman dress on the striking series of paintings of the crucifixion inside. Diagonally across the street is the **Vaima Center,** Papeete's finest window-shopping venue.

Farther down on rue de Gaulle is Place Tarahoi. The **Territorial Assembly** on the left occupies the site of the former royal palace, demolished in 1966. The adjacent residence of the French high commissioner is private, but the assembly building and its lovely gardens are worth a brief visit. In front of the entrance gate is a monument to **Pouvanaa a Oopa** (1895-1977), a Tahitian WW I hero who struggled all his life for the independence of his country (see "Recent History" under "History" in the Introduction to this book). The plaque on the monument says nothing about Pouvanaa's fight for independence and against the bomb!

Beside the post office across the busy avenue from Place Tarahoi is **Bougainville Park.** A monument to Bougainville himself, who sailed around the world in 1766-69, is flanked by two old naval guns. One, stamped "Fried Krupp 1899," is from Count Felix von Luckner's famous raider *Seeadler,* which ended up on the Maupihaa reef in 1917; the other is off the French gunboat *Zélée,* sunk in Papeete harbor by German cruisers in 1914.

Much of the bureaucracy works along Ave. Bruat just west, a gracious tree-lined French provincial avenue. You may observe French justice in action at the **Palais de Justice** (weekdays 0800-1100/1400-1600). The public gallery is up the stairway and straight ahead. Farther up Ave. Bruat, beyond the War Memorial, are the colonial-style French army barracks, **Quartier Broche.**

Back on the waterfront just before the Protestant church is the **Tahiti Perles Center** (B.P. 850, Papeete; tel. 50-53-10). A black pearl museum (weekdays 0800-1200/1400-1730, Saturday 0900-1200; admission free) and aquarium are the main attractions, but look around the showroom where the famous black pearls are sold. A 20-minute video presentation shown on request explains how cultured black pearls are "farmed" in the Gambier Islands.

Next to the pearl museum is Paofai, the headquarters of the **Evangelical Church** in Tahiti-Polynesia, with a church (rebuilt 1980), public cafeteria, girls' hostel, and health clinic. This church is descended from the London Missionary Society; the British consulate occupied the hostel site from 1837 to 1958. George Pritchard (see "History" in the main Introduction had his office here.

Continue west along the bay past the outrigger racing canoes to the "neo-Polynesian" **Cultural Center** (1973), which houses a public library, notice boards, and auditoriums set among pleasant grounds. This complex is run by the Office Territorial d'Action Culturelle (OTAC), which organizes the annual Heiva Festival and many other events. The municipal swimming pool is beyond (go upstairs to the snack bar for a view). Return to the center of town along the waterfront.

Another walk takes you east from downtown to the Catholic **Archbishop's Palace** (1869), a lonely remnant of the Papeete that Gauguin saw. To get there, take the road behind the Catholic Cathedral, keep straight, and ask for the *archevêché catholique.* Without doubt, this is the finest extant piece of colonial architecture in a territory of fast-disappearing historic buildings. The park grounds planted in citrus and the modern open-air church nearby (to the right) also merit a look.

Fautaua Valley

If you'd like to make a short trip out of the city, go to the Hôtel de Ville and take a Mamao-Titioro *truck* to the **Bain Loti,** three km up the Fautaua Valley from the Mormon Temple. A bust of writer Pierre Loti marks the spot where he had the love affair described in *The Marriage of Loti,* but the area has been spoiled by tasteless construction.

A dirt road continues three km further up the Fautaua Valley but because it's part of a water catchment, private cars are prohibited, so you must walk. From the end of the road, a trail straight ahead leads directly to **Fautaua Falls** (30 minutes) with several river crossings. Back a bit on the left, just before the end of the road, is a wooden footbridge across the river. Here begins a steep one-hour trail up to a 19th-century French fort at the top of the falls. The fort controlled the main trail into Tahiti's interior and it's still an excellent hiking area. There's an occasional CFP 500 pp charge to go up the valley and officially you're supposed to go on a weekday. Go early and make a day of it.

Back on Ave. Georges Clemenceau near the Mormon Temple is the impressive **Kanti Chinese Temple,** built in 1986.

East of Papeete

Arue (pronounced a-roo-AY) and Point Venus can be done easily as a half-day side trip from

*Matavai Bay, Tahiti,
as it appeared in the
early 19th century*

Papeete by *le truck* (12 km each way). Begin by taking a Mahina *truck* from near the tourist office to the **tomb of King Pomare V** at PK 4.7 Arue, five km outside the city. The mausoleum was built in 1879 for Queen Pomare IV, but her remains were subsequently removed to make room for her son, Pomare V, who died of drink in 1891 (Paul Gauguin witnessed the funeral). A century earlier, on 13 February 1791, his grandfather, Pomare II, then nine, was made first king of Tahiti on the great *marae* that once stood on this spot. Pomare II became the first Christian convert and built a 215-meter-long version of King Solomon's Temple here, but nothing remains of either temple.

At PK 5.4, Arue, next to the École Maternelle Ahutoru, stand the tombs of Pomare I, II, III, and IV in the **Cimetière Pomare.** This lesser-known site is not signposted, but a building across the street is marked Artisanat. A board next to the cemetery clearly identifies the many Pomare graves here.

The **Hyatt Regency Hôtel** (PK 8.1) on One Tree Hill, a couple of km east of the Pomare graves, was built in 1968 on a spectacular series of terraces down the hillside to conform to a local regulation that no building should be more than two-thirds the height of a coconut tree. There's a superb view of Point Venus, Tahiti, and Moorea from the Governor's Bench on the knoll just beyond the hotel entrance. In Matavai Bay below the Hyatt Regency, Capt. Samuel Wallis anchored in 1767, after having "discovered" Tahiti. There's good swimming off the black beach below the hotel.

Catch another *truck* or walk on to **Point Venus** (PK 10). Captain Cook camped on this point between the river and the lagoon during his visit to observe the transit of the planet Venus across the sun on 3 June 1769. Captain Bligh also occupied Point Venus for two months in 1788 while collecting breadfruit shoots for transportation to the West Indies. On 5 March 1797, the first members of the London Missionary Society landed here, as a monument recalls. From Tahiti, Protestantism spread throughout Polynesia and as far as Vanuatu.

Today there's a park on the point, with a 25-meter-high lighthouse (1867) among the palms and ironwood trees. The view of Tahiti across

Captain James Cook (1728-1779) as painted at the Cape of Good Hope by John Webber, 1776

Matavai Bay is superb, and twin-humped Oro-hena, highest peak on the island, is in view (you can't see it from Papeete itself). Topless sun-bathing is common on the wide dark sands along the bay and you can see pareus being made in the handicraft center in the park. Week-days, Point Venus is a peaceful place, the per-fect choice if you'd like to get away from the rat race in Papeete and spend some time at the beach (weekends it gets crowded).

AROUND THE ISLAND

A 117-km Route de Ceinture (Belt Road) runs right around Tahiti Nui, the larger part of this hourglass-shaped island. Construction began in the 1820s as a form of punishment. For ori-entation you'll see red-and-white kilometer stones, called PK *(point kilométrique)*, along the inland side of the road. These are num-bered in each direction from the Catholic cathe-dral in Papeete, meeting at Taravao.

Go clockwise to get over the most difficult stretch first; also, you'll be riding on the inside lane of traffic and less likely to go off a cliff in case of an accident (an average of 55 people a year are killed and 700 injured in accidents on this island). Southern Tahiti is much quieter than the northwest, whereas from Paea to Mahina it's even hard to slow down as tailgating mo-torists roar behind you.

If you're a bit adventurous it's quite possible to do a circle-island tour on *le truck,* provided you get an early start and go clockwise with no stop until Taravao. Ask for the Tautira *truck,* but if it looks like they won't be going for quite a while, take any *truck* headed for Papenoo and wait there. Once at Taravao, walk across the peninsula (15 minutes) and look for another *truck* coming from Teahupoo to take you back to Papeete along the south coast. If you get stuck, it's comforting to know that hitchhiking *(l'autostop)* is fairly easy and relatively safe on Tahiti. The local people are very receptive to foreign visitors, so you'll improve your chances if it's obvious you're not French. For instance, try using a destination sign (never used by lo-cals). There's lots of traffic along the straight south coast highway all day and it's almost cer-tain you'll get a ride eventually. For more infor-mation on *le truck,* see "Getting Around" under "Practicalties".

However you travel around Tahiti, it's cus-tomary to smile and wave to the Tahitians you see (outside Papeete). And if you want an ex-cellent second resource, pick up Bengt Danielsson's *Tahiti, Circle Island Tour Guide* at a Papeete bookstore before you set out.

The Northeast Coast

The coast is very rugged all along the north-east side of the island. The **leper colony** at Orofara (PK 13.2) was founded in 1914. Pre-viously the colony was on Reao atoll in the Tu-amotus, but this proved too remote to service. Some 50 patients are housed at Orofara today.

Surfers ride the waves at Chinaman's Bay, Papenoo (PK 16). The bridge over the broad **Papenoo River** (PK 17.1) allows a view up the largest valley on Tahiti.

At the **Arahoho Blowhole** (PK 22), jets of water shoot up through holes in the lava rock beside the highway at high tide. Just a little be-

the "buffoon" of the leper colony, Tahiti

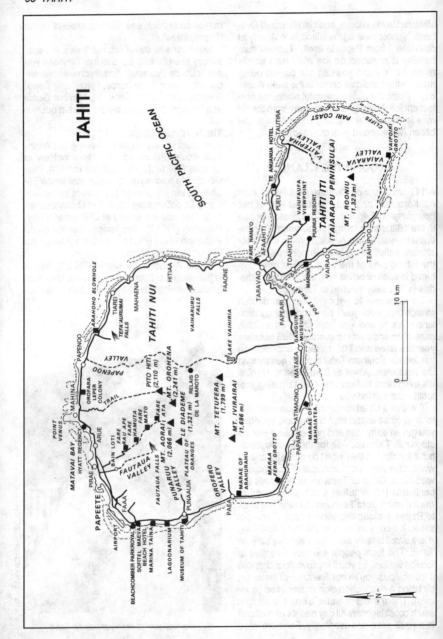

TAHITI

SOUTH PACIFIC OCEAN

10 km

TAUTIRA

TE ANUANUA HOTEL

VAITEPIHA
VALLEY

VAIARAVA
VALLEY

CLIFFS

VAIPOHI
GROTTO

PARI COAST

PUEU

VAUFAUFA
VIEWPOINT

FARE NANAO

AFAAHITI

PUUNUI RESORT

TAHITI ITI
(TAIARAPU PENINSULA)

TOAHOTU

MT. ROONIU
(1,323 m)

FAARUMAI
FALLS

MAHAENA

TIAREI

TERA AURUMAI
FALLS

ARAHOHO BLOWHOLE

HITIAA

TAHITI NUI

VAIHARURU
FALLS

TEAHUPOO

VAIRAO

MARINA

TARAVAO

PORT PHAETON

PAPEARI

GAUGUIN
MUSEUM

PAPENOO

OROFARA LEPER COLONY

MAHINA

POINT
VENUS

MATAVAI BAY

HYATT REGENCY

PIRAE

ARUE

PAPEETE

FAAA

PAPENOO
VALLEY

PITO HITI
(2,110 m)

FARE
MATO

FARE
HAMUTA

FARE
ATA

FARE
RAPAE

MT. OROHENA
(2,241 m)

MT. AORAI
(2,066 m)

BAIN LOTI

FAUTAUA
VALLEY

FAUTAUA FALLS

PINARUU
VALLEY

PLATEAU OF
LE DIADEME
(1,321 m)

ORANGES

PLATEAU
OF
LE MAROTO

RELAIS
DE LA MAROTO

LAKE VAIHIRIA

MT. TETUFERA
(1,799 m)

MT. IVIRAIRAI
(1,696 m)

OROFERO
VALLEY

PAEA

MARAE OF
ARAHURAHU

PUNAAUIA

ATIMAONO

MATAIEA

MARAE OF
MAHAIATEA

PAPARA

MARAE
FERN GROTTO

AIRPORT

BEACHCOMBER PARKROYAL

SOFITEL MAEVA
BEACH HOTEL

MARINA TAINA

LAGOONARIUM

MUSEUM OF TAHITI

N

yond it, a road to the right leads one km up to the three **Tefa'aurumai Waterfalls** (admission free), also known as the Faarumai Falls. Vaimahuta Falls is accessible on foot in five minutes along the easy path to the right across the bridge. The 30-minute trail to the left leads to two more waterfalls, Haamaremare iti and Haamaremare rahi, but it's more difficult and even impassible if the river is high. The farthest falls has a pool deep enough for swimming. Bring insect repellent and beware of theft if you park a rental car at these falls.

At **Mahaena** (PK 32.5) is the battleground where 441 well-armed French troops defeated a dug-in Tahitian force twice their size on 17 April 1844 in the last fixed confrontation of the French-Tahitian War. The Tahitians carried on a guerrilla campaign another two years until the French captured their main mountain stronghold.

The French ships *La Boudeuse* and *L'Étoile,* carrying explorer Louis-Antoine de Bougainville, anchored by the southernmost of two islets off **Hitiaa** (PK 37.6) on 6 April 1768. Unaware that an Englishman had visited Tahiti a year before, Bougainville christened the island "New Cythera," after the Greek isle where love goddess Aphrodite rose from the sea. A plaque near the bridge recalls the event. The clever Tahitians recognized a member of Bougainville's crew as a woman disguised as a man and an embarrassed Jeanne Baret entered history as the first woman to sail around the world.

From the bridge over the Faatautia River at PK 41.8 **Vaiharuru Falls** are visible in the dis-

tance. The American filmmaker John Huston intended to make a movie of Herman Melville's *Typee* here in 1957 but when Huston's other Melville film, *Moby Dick,* became a box-office flop, the idea was dropped.

Tahiti Iti

At Taravao (PK 53), on the strategic isthmus joining the two Tahitis where the PKs meet, is an **old fort** built by the French in 1844 to cut off the Tahitians who had retreated to Tahiti Iti after the battle mentioned above. Germans were interned here during WW II and the fort is still in use today by the 1st Company of the Régiment d'Infanterie de Marine du Pacifique.

The small assortment of grocery stores, banks, post office, gasoline stations, and restaurants at Taravao make it a good place to break your trip around the island; however, accommodations in this area are inadequate. A good place for lunch is **Snack Guilloux** (closed Monday; tel. 57-12-91), a hundred meters down the road to Tautira from the Westpac Bank in Taravao. It's a regular restaurant, not a snack bar as the name implies. If you have your own transportation, three roads are explorable on rugged Tahiti Iti. If you're hitching or traveling by *truck,* choose the Tautira route.

An excellent 18-km highway runs east from Taravao to **Tautira,** where two Spanish priests from Peru attempted to establish a Catholic mission in 1774; it lasted for only one year. Scottish author Robert Louis Stevenson stayed at Tautira for two months in 1888 and called it "the most beautiful spot, and its people the most amiable, I have ever found." The road peters out a few km beyond Tautira. Obstructions by landowners and high cliffs make it impractical to try hiking around the Pari Coast to Teahupoo. Intrepid sea kayakers have been known to paddle the 30 km around, although there's a wild four-km stretch not protected by reefs.

The unoccupied beach at the mouth of the **Vaitepiha River** near Tautira is a potential campsite. A dirt road runs two km up the right bank of the river, where you could find more secluded places to camp. If you're keen, hike beyond the end of the road for a look at this majestic, unoccupied valley and a swim in the river. In the dry season rugged backpackers could hike south across the peninsula to the

Captain Louis-Antoine de Bougainville

Vaiarava Valley and Teahupoo in two days, but a guide is definitely necessary. The ruins of at least three old *marae* are at the junction of the Vaitia and Vaitepiha rivers a couple of hours inland, and it's reported tikis are hidden in there.

Another paved nine-km road runs straight up the Taravao Plateau from just before the hospital in Taravao. If you have a car or scooter and only time to take in one of Tahiti Iti's three roads, this one should be your choice. At the 600-meter level on top is the **Vaiufaufa Viewpoint,** with a breathtaking view of both Tahitis. No one lives up here: in good weather it would be possible to pitch a tent on the grassy hill above the reservoir at the end of the road (or sleep in your car if it's cold and raining). The herds of cows grazing peacefully among the grassy meadows give this upland an almost Swiss air. A rough side road near the viewpoint cuts down to join the Tautira road.

The third road on Tahiti Iti runs 18 km along the south coast to **Teahupoo.** Seven km east of Taravao is a **marina** with an artificial white-sand beach (PK 7). American pulp Western writer Zane Grey had his fishing camp near here in the 1930s. Just east of the marina is a natural white-sand public beach where you'll see fishermen spearing by torchlight on the opposite reef in the evening. In the afternoon it's a great picnic spot. Tahiti's best surfing is possible out there in the pass, but you'll need a boat.

The Teahupoo road ends abruptly at a river crossed by a narrow footbridge. There's an excellent mountain view from this bridge, but walk east along the beach to capture one of the only remaining glimpses of outer-island Polynesian lifestyle remaining on Tahiti. After a couple of km the going becomes difficult due to yelping dogs, seawalls built into the lagoon, fences, fallen trees, and *tapu* signs. Beyond is the onetime domain of "nature men" who tried to escape civilization by living alone with nature over half a century ago.

Three hours on foot from the end of the road is **Vaipoiri Grotto,** a large water-filled cave best reached by boat. Try hiring a motorized canoe or hitch a ride with someone at the end of the road. Beyond this the high cliffs of Te Pari terminate all foot traffic along the shore; the only way to pass is by boat. All the land east of

Teahupoo is well fenced off, so finding a campsite would involve getting someone's permission. It's probably easier to look elsewhere.

Gauguin Museum

Port Phaeton on the southwest side of the Taravao Isthmus is an excellent harbor. Timeless oral traditions tell that the first Polynesians to reach Tahiti settled at Papeari (PK 52—measured now from the west). In precontact times the chiefly family of this district was among the most prestigious on the island.

The Gauguin Museum (B.P. 7029, Taravao; tel. 57-10-58; open daily 0900-1700, CFP 450 admission) is at PK 51.7 in Papeari District. The museum, opened in 1965, tells the painter's tormented life story and shows the present locations of his works throughout the world. Strangely, Gauguin's Tahitian mistresses get little attention in the museum. A couple of his minor woodcarvings and prints are exhibited (but no Gauguin paintings). Most of the photos are numbered and you may be able to borrow a catalog.

Teha'amana, who lived with Gauguin at Mataiea from 1892 to 1893, was Gauguin's great love and is mentioned often in Noa Noa.

Ex-Paris stockbroker Paul Gauguin arrived at Papeete in 1891 at age 43 in search of the roots of "primitive" art. He lived at Mataiea with his 14-year-old mistress Teha'amana for a year and a half, joyfully painting. In 1893 he returned to France with 66 paintings and about a dozen woodcarvings, which were to establish his reputation. Unfortunately, his exhibition flopped and Gauguin returned to Tahiti a second time, infected with VD and poor, settling at Punaauia. After a failed suicide he recovered somewhat and in 1901 a Paris art dealer named Vollard signed a contract with Gauguin assuring him a monthly payment of 350 francs and a purchase price of 250 francs per picture. His financial problems alleviated, the painter left for Hiva Oa, Marquesas Islands, to find an environment uncontaminated by Western influences. During the last two years of his life at Atuona Gauguin's eccentricities put him on the wrong side of the ecclesiastical and official hierarchies. He died in 1903 at age 53, a near outcast among his countrymen in the islands, yet today a Papeete street and school are named after him!

The two-meterish, two-ton stone tiki on the museum grounds is said to be imbued with a sacred *tapu* spell. Tahitians believe this tiki, carved on the island of Raivavae hundreds of years ago, still lives. The three Tahitians who moved the statue here from Papeete in 1965 all died mysterious deaths within a few weeks. A curse is still said to befall all who touch the tiki.

A **botanical garden** rich in exotic species is part of the Gauguin Museum complex (CFP 400 additional admission). This 137-hectare garden was created in 1919-21 by the American botanist Harrison Smith (1872-1947), who introduced over 200 new species to the island, among them the sweet grapefruit (pomelo), mangosteen, rambutan, and durian. Actually, if you have to choose between the garden or the museum (due to the high admission fees), it's probably better to see the garden and give the superficial museum a miss.

The attractive **Gauguin Museum Restaurant** (tel. 57-13-80), a km west of the museum, hosts circle-island tour groups for lunch, and you can join them for CFP 2100 for the buffet (daily noon-1430). Even if you're not hungry, it's still worth a stop to see the fish swimming in the enclosure around the wharf and to take in the view.

At PK 49 is the **Jardin Vaipahi** with a lovely waterfall minutes from the road (admission free).

Lake Vaihiria

The unmarked road to Lake Vaihiria begins at PK 47.6 between a housing settlement and a Mormon church (Église de Jesus-Christ des Saints Des Derniers Jours), just before the bridge over the Vairaharaha River as you travel west. The rough track leads 12 km up to Lake Vaihiria, Tahiti's only lake, following the Vaihiria River which has been harnessed for hydroelectricity. Two km up the road you'll encounter a white hydro substation and the first of a series of Piste Privee signs advising motorists that the road is closed to nonresidents, though open to pedestrians. This regulation is not enforced, and in dry weather a rental car could continue another five km to a dam and the lower power station, provided the chain across the road isn't locked.

A km beyond is an archaeological site with restored *marae*. Three km beyond this (11 km from the main road) is a second dam and an upper (larger) power station. Beyond this point only a 4WD vehicle could proceed, passing prominent Danger signs, another km up a steep concrete track to Lake Vaihiria itself.

Sheer cliffs and spectacular waterfalls squeeze in around the spring-fed lake, and the shore would make a fine campsite (though overrun by mosquitoes). Native floppy-eared eels known as *puhi taria,* up to 1.8 meters long, live in these cold waters. With its luxuriant vegetation this rain-drenched 473-meter-high spot is one of the most evocative on the island. The track proceeds up and through a 200-meter tunnel and over to the Papenoo Valley, a four-hour trip by 4WD jeep or two days on foot. You must wade through the rivers about 20 times.

The easiest way to do this trip is seated in a chauffeur-driven 4WD jeep booked through **Tahiti Mer et Loisirs** (B.P. 3488, Papeete; tel. 43-97-99, fax 43-33-68), in a houseboat on the Papeete waterfront opposite the post office. It's CFP 9500 pp including lunch and drinks (four-person minimum participation).

The 24-room **Relais de la Maroto** (B.P. 20687, Papeete; tel. 41-48-60 or 58-26-12, fax 57-90-30) is a cluster of large concrete buildings at the junction of the Vaituoru and Vainavenave rivers in the upper Papenoo Valley. The

Tahiti's Mahaiatea Marae as illustrated in James Wilson's A Missionary Voyage *(London, 1779): this 11-step pyramid was once the largest pagan temple on the island.*

accommodations here are upmarket at CFP 6000 pp, plus CFP 4500 extra for breakfast and dinner in the sharp modern restaurant. The only access is by 4WD, helicopter, or foot. Local French often come here for the weekend. If you can afford it, the Relais provides a good base for exploring the many waterfalls and archaeological remains in this area.

The South Coast

Tahiti-Polynesia's only golf course, the **International Golf Course Olivier Breaud** (B.P. 12008, Papara; tel. 57-40-32) at PK 41, Atimaono, stretches up to the mountainside on the site of Terre Eugenie, a cotton and sugar plantation established by Scotsman William Stewart at the time of the U.S. Civil War (1863). Many of today's Tahitian Chinese are descended from Chinese laborers imported to do the work, and a novel by A. T'Serstevens, *The Great Plantation,* was set here. The present 6,355-meter, 18-hole course (run by Tahiti Tourisme) was laid out in 1970 with a par 72 for men, par 73 for women. If you'd like to do a round the green fees are CFP 3000, and clubs and cart rent for another CFP 2500 (open daily 0800-1700). The Tahiti Open in June or July attracts professionals from around the Pacific. The golf course restaurant is said to be good.

Behind the golf course is the **Parc d'Atimaono,** a favorite hiking area. A road closed to cars which begins next to the golf course park-

ing lot leads several km up into this area, though you may be charged CFP 500 as a "day visitor" to the golf course.

The **Marae of Mahaiatea** (PK 39.2) at Papara was once the most hallowed temple on Tahiti. Captain Cook's botanist Joseph Banks wrote, "It is almost beyond belief that Indians could raise so large a structure without the assistance of iron tools." Less than a century later planter William Stewart raided the *marae* for building materials, and storms did the rest. Today it's only a rough heap of stones, but still worth visiting for its aura and setting. You could swim and snorkel off the beach next to the *marae,* but watch the currents. The unmarked turnoff to the *marae* is a hundred meters west of Beach Burger, then straight down to the beach.

Surfers take the waves at Papara Beach (PK 38), one of the best sites on Tahiti. By the church at **Papara** (PK 36) is the grave of Dorence Atwater (1845-1910), U.S. consul to Tahiti from 1871 to 1888. Atwater's claim to fame dates back to the American Civil War, when he recorded the names of 13,000 dead Union prisoners at Andersonville Prison, Georgia, from lists the Confederates had been withholding. Himself a Union prisoner, Atwater escaped with his list in March 1865. When you consider how the present U.S. government continues to use troops allegedly missing in Indochina as pawns in its dealings with Vietnam, the political value of Atwater's contribution to the Union officials of his day is clear. Atwater's tombstone provides details. Across the street from the church is a Centre Artisanal selling handicrafts, and a Sea Shell Museum.

Maraa Fern Grotto (PK 28.5) is by the road just across the Paea border. An optical illusion, the grotto at first appears small but is quite deep and some Tahitians believe *varua ino* (evil spirits) lurk in the shadowy depths. Others say that if you follow an underground river back from the grotto you'll emerge at a wonderful valley in the spirit world. Paul Gauguin wrote of a swim he took across the small lake in the cave; you're also welcome to jump in the blue-gray water. You can fill your water bottle with fresh mineral water from eight spouts next to the parking lot.

On the mountain side of the road at PK 26.5 is the small **Ava Tea Distillery** (B.P. 10398, Paea; tel. 53-32-43) which can be visited daily 0900-1200/1400-1700.

The Southwest Coast
The **Marae Arahurahu** at PK 22.5, Paea, is up the road from Magasin Laut—take care, the sign faces Papeete, so it's not visible if you're traveling clockwise. This temple, lying in a tranquil, verdant spot under high cliffs, is perhaps Tahiti's only remaining pagan mystery. The ancient open altars built from thousands of cut

stones were completely restored in 1954 (open daily, admission free). Historical pageants (CFP 1500 admission) recreating pagan rites are performed here during the July festivities.

For some hiking, Paea's **Orofero Valley** is recommended and camping might be possible up beyond the end of the road (six km). From the main highway take the first road inland south of the large Catholic church by the Vaiatu River at PK 21.5 (look for the sign reading Prefabriques Piccolini). You can drive a car three km up. When you get to the *tapu* sign, park, cross the river, and continue up the other side on foot. A jeep track runs another three km up the valley (half-hour walk), through half a dozen river crossings (wear rubber booties or zories). At the end of the road a tall waterfall is to the left and the trail continues ahead. Orofero is one of the few Tahitian valleys free of trash!

The West Coast
On Fishermen's Point, Punaauia, is the **Museum of Tahiti and the Islands** (B.P. 6272, Faa'a; tel. 58-22-09; open Tuesday to Sunday 0930-1700; admission CFP 500). Located in a large, modern complex on the lagoon, about a km down a narrow road from PK 15.1, this worthwhile museum has four halls devoted to the natural environment, the origins of the Polynesians, Polynesian culture, and the history of Polynesia. What isn't covered is the history of France's nuclear

This photo, taken by Bengt Danielsson in the 1950s and published in his book Gauguin in the South Seas, *shows Emile Marae a Tai, son of Gauguin and his vahine, Pau'ura a Tai. The resemblance is striking.*

testing program in Polynesia and how the Polynesians feel about it. Outside is a huge double-hulled canoe and Captain Cook's anchor from Tautira. Most of the captions are in French, Tahitian, and English (photography allowed).

When the waves are right, you can sit on the seawall behind the museum and watch the Tahitian surfers bob and ride, with the outline of Moorea beyond. On your way back to the main highway from the museum, look up to the top of the hill at an **old fort** used by the French to subjugate the Tahitians in the 1840s. The crown-shaped pinnacles of **Le Diadème** (1,321 meters) are also visible from this road.

If you want to see pollution on a massive scale, follow the route up the once-beautiful **Punaruu Valley** behind the Punaauia industrial zone (PK 14.8). You can drive a normal car five km up a valley incredibly trashed out with garbage dumps all the way. At the end of the valley is a water catchment and, although the way leads on to the fantastic Plateau of Oranges, entry is forbidden. Tahitian enterprises dump their refuse in valleys all around the island, but this has got to be the ugliest! Here paradise ends.

From 1896 to 1901 Gauguin had his studio at PK 12.6 Punaauia, but nothing remains of it; his *Two Tahitian Women* was painted here. The **Lagoonarium** (B.P. 2381, Papeete; tel. 43-62-90), below the lagoon behind Captain Bligh Restaurant at PK 11.4, Punaauia, provides a vision of the underwater marinelife of Polynesia safely behind glass. The big tank full of black-tip sharks is a feature. Entry is CFP 500 pp, open daily, half price for restaurant customers, and CFP 300 for children under 12. The shark feeding takes place around noon.

Punaauia and Paea are Tahiti's "Gold Coast," with old colonial homes hidden behind trees along the lagoonside and *nouveau riche* villas dotting the hillside above. At PK 8, Outumaoro, is the turnoff for the RDO bypass to Papeete, Tahiti's only superhighway! Follow the "Université" signs from here up to the ultramodern campus of the **French University of the Pacific** with its fantastic hilltop view of Moorea and excellent library (tel. 45-01-65).

On the old airport road just north are Tahiti's biggest hotels: the **Sofitel Maeva Beach** (PK 7.5) and **Beachcomber Parkroyal** (PK 7), each worth a stop—though their beaches are polluted. From the point where the Beachcomber Parkroyal is today, the souls of deceased Tahitians once leapt on their journey to the spirit world. A sunset behind Moorea's jagged peaks, across the Sea of the Moon from either of these hotels, is a spectacular finale to a circle-island tour. As you reenter Papeete, **Uranie Cemetery** (PK 1.5) is on your right.

The west coast of Tahiti can also be visited as a day-trip from Papeete; start by taking a *truck* to the Fern Grotto at Paea, then work your way back. *Trucks* back to Papeete from the vicinity of the Maeva Beach Hôtel run late into the night, but the last one from the Museum of Tahiti is around 1630.

MOUNTAIN CLIMBING

Tahiti's finest climb is to the summit of **Aorai** (2,066 meters), third-highest peak on the island. A beaten 10-km track all the way to the top makes a guide unnecessary but food, water, flashlight, and long pants *are* required, plus a sleeping bag and sweater if you plan to spend the night up there. At last report the refuges at Fare Mato (1,400 meters) and Fare Ata (1,800 meters) were in good shape with drinking water available and splendid sunset views.

The trailhead is at Fare Rau Ape (600 meters) near **Le Belvédère** (tel. 42-73-44), an overpriced tourist restaurant seven km up a rough, potholed road from Pirae. The restaurant offers a free *truck* from Papeete at 1130 and 1700 for those willing to spend CFP 4200 on a mediocre meal, the easiest way to get there. Parking near the restaurant is limited. Taxis want CFP 5000 for the trip and few people live up there, so hitching would be a case of finding tourists headed for the restaurant and weekends are best for this. A large signboard outside the restaurant maps out the hike.

Just above the restaurant is the French Army's Centre d'Instruction de Montagne, where you must sign the register. From Fare Rau Ape to the summit takes seven hours: 1.5 hours to Hamuta, another two to Fare Mato (good view of Le Diadème, not visible from Papeete), then 2.5 to Fare Ata, where most hikers spend the first night in order to cover the last 40 minutes to the summit the following morning.

You'll get this unobstructed view of Le Diadème from the Mt. Aorai Trail.

The view from Aorai is magnificent, with Papeete and many of the empty interior valleys in full view. To the north is Tetiaroa atoll, while Moorea's jagged outline fills the west. Even on a cloudy day the massive green hulk of neighboring Orohena (2,241 meters) often towers above the clouds like Mt. Olympus. A bonus is the chance to see some of the original native vegetation of Tahiti, which survives better at high altitudes and in isolated gullies. In good weather Aorai is exhausting but superb; in the rain it's a disaster.

When the author of this book climbed Aorai some years ago, the trip could be done by anyone in reasonable physical shape. Later we heard that the trail had deteriorated, with sheer slopes and slippery, crumbling ridges to be negotiated. In the past we've asked readers to write in with current information on Aorai, and we're grateful to Charlie Appleton of Nottingham, England, for sending us this report:

The trail has been restored and is now well maintained. The chalets at Fare Mato and Fare Ata were in excellent order, the former sitting on a recently reconstructed platform. They'll sleep 12-15 without difficulty, though only the hut at Fare Ata has drinking water. Just above Fare Mato cables have been fixed along the section of trail with the steepest drops on both sides, allowing some fairly inexperienced hikers I met to traverse it with confidence. Very few people do the climb, and if you go in the middle of the week you can expect to have the mountain to yourself. It might be worth mentioning that the compelling reason for spending the night on top (apart from sunset and sunrise) is that those who make the roundtrip in a day are likely to find that by the time they near the summit the mountain will have put on its midday hat of clouds, limiting their views.

More recently, Will Paine of Maidstone, England, sent us this:

Thanks to clear weather, Aorai was one of the most satisfying "officially endorsed" hikes I've ever done. It's not for the fainthearted, but otherwise thoroughly recommended. The dangerous part is from 1,400 meters onwards and constant awareness is necessary on the knife-edge ridges (walking roped together is an idea). Some early sections have cables for hanging on, but the irons are shaky as they've only been installed "after the fact," as it were.

Neighboring **Orohena** is seldom climbed, since the way involves considerable risks. The route up Orohena begins at the office of the

Sheriff de Mahina, opposite the military laboratories. Follow the road five km straight up through Mahinarama subdivision. At about 600 meters elevation, where the paved road becomes a dirt track, there's a chain across the road. Park here and hike up the track past two large water tanks. A jeep track built into the slope in 1975 follows the contour six km up the Tuauru River valley to the **Thousand Springs** at 900 meters elevation. Anyone at Mahinarama will be able to direct you to the "Route des Mille Sources." The actual Orohena trail begins at the Thousand Springs and climbs steeply to Pito iti where hikers spend the night before ascending Orohena the following morning. To climb Orohena a guide is most certainly required, but anyone can do the Thousand Springs hike of their own, enjoying good views of the rounded peaks of Orohena to the left and Aorai's long ridge to the right. There's nothing special to see at the Thousand Springs, so turn back whenever you like.

Guides

These and other hikes on Tahiti are led on weekends and holidays by **Pierre Florentin** (B.P. 5323, Pirae; tel./fax 43-72-01), a professional mountain guide with 20 years of experience. Pierre charges a fixed rate of CFP 16,000 a day for groups of up to eight persons maximum—well worth considering if there are a few of you. The trips offered include climbs up Orohena (three days) and Aorai (two days), the hike across Tahiti Iti (two days), and day-trips to Fautaua Falls, Papenoo Falls, Mt. Marau, a lava tube, etc. Pierre also organizes hang gliding from Mt. Marau. Transport to the trailheads is included, but backpacks and tents are extra (if required), and participants must bring their own food. Pierre's services are highly recommended for small groups of serious hikers/climbers concerned about both safety and success.

Another professional guide, **Angélien Zéna** (B.P. 7426, Taravao; tel. 57-22-67), specializes in hikes around the Pari Coast at the east end of Tahiti Iti, the "Circuit Vert." Angélien's three-day trip costs CFP 110,000 for up to 10 persons, meals and transport from/to Taravao included. Time off is allowed for swimming and fishing. A boat from Vairao to Vaipoiri Grotto is used on the two-day hikes, and day-trips can

also be arranged. Even if there are only a few of you, it's worth calling both Pierre and Angélien to learn if they have any trips scheduled that you might join.

The **Club Te Fenua O Te Mau Mato** (Pierre Wrobel, B.P. 9304, Papeete; tel. 43-04-64) organizes weekend hikes on Tahiti and Moorea several times a month. Also call the president of the **Tahitian Alpine Club,** Marc Allain (B.P. 11553, Mahina; tel. 48-10-59).

SPORTS AND RECREATION

For information on the International Golf Course Olivier Breaud at Atimaono, see "The South Coast" under "Around the Island," above.

Tahiti Plongée (B.P. 2192, Papeete; tel. 41-00-62, fax 42-26-06), also known as "Club Corail Sub," offers scuba diving several times daily from its base at the Hôtel Te Puna Bel Air, Punaauia. The charge is CFP 3800 per dive all-inclusive, or CFP 18,000 for a five-dive card, CFP 28,000 for 10 dives. You can ocean dive Tuesday to Sunday at 0800 and on Wednesday and Saturdayat 1400; lagoon diving is daily at 1000 and weekdays at 1400 (no diving on Monday).

Divemaster Henri Pouliquen was one of the first to teach scuba diving to children. The youngest person Henri has taken down was aged two years, six months—the oldest was a woman of 72 on her first dive. Since 1979 Tahiti Plongée has arranged over 10,000 dives with children, certainly a unique accomplishment. Handicapped diving is also a specialty. Most diving is on the Punaauia reef. Other favorite scuba locales include a scuttled Pan Am Catalina PBY seaplane near the airport, its upper wing 12 meters down; and a schooner wreck, 10 meters down, about 45 meters from the breakwater at the entrance to the harbor.

Tahiti Aquatique (B.P. 6008, Faa'a; tel. 42-80-42, fax 41-08-54) beside the wharf at the Maeva Beach Hôtel also offers professional scuba-diving services. Their prices are higher than those of Tahiti Plongée (CFP 5000 for scuba diving). For CFP 700 pp RT they'll shuttle you out to their offshore sunbathing pontoon anchored above a snorkeling locale (no lifeguard or shade). Rental of mask, snorkel, and fins is extra. Underwater photography equipment and PADI certification courses are available. This company is run by American marine biologist Dick Johnson who came to Tahiti to research a book on sharks, and never left.

Scuba diving can also be arranged with Pascal Le Cointre at the **Yacht Club of Tahiti** (B.P. 1456, Papeete; tel. 42-23-55, fax 42-37-07) at PK 4, Arue. Outings are offered daily at 0900 and 1400 except Sunday afternoon and Monday, with reduced rates for five-dive packages. They also do certification courses.

If you want to set out on your own, **Nauti-Sport** (B.P. 62, Papeete; tel. 42-09-94, fax 42-17-75) sells every type of scuba gear and also rents tanks (CFP 2500). They sometimes offer

scuba trips at very competitive prices and have information on diving all around Polynesia. For serious divers, this is an excellent place to come for information.

Deep-sea fishing can be arranged by **Tahiti Mer et Loisirs** (B.P. 3488, Papeete; tel. 43-97-99, fax 43-33-68), in a houseboat on the Papeete waterfront opposite the post office. Their charter boats begin at CFP 60,000 a day (0800-1600) and up to six anglers can go for that. Bring your own snacks and drinks.

Papeete's **municipal swimming pool** (tel. 42-89-24) is open to the public Tuesday to Friday 1145-1600, Saturday and Sunday 0730-1700 (CFP 350). Most evenings after 1800 **soccer** is practiced in the sports field opposite the municipal swimming pool.

PRACTICALITIES

ACCOMMODATIONS

Almost all of the places to stay are in the congested Punaauia-to-Mahina strip engulfing Faa'a International Airport and Papeete. Representatives of the various hotels often meet incoming flights, and most provide free transport to their establishments. If not, call them up and ask. The hotels below are listed clockwise in each category, beginning in Punaauia.

Budget Accommodations
Near the Airport
Chez Armelle (B.P. 13291, Punaauia; tel. 58-42-43, fax 58-42-81) at PK 15.5 in Punaauia (almost opposite a large Mobil service station), has 10 rooms at CFP 3500/6000 single/double including breakfast. Some of the rooms have private bath, and communal cooking facilities are provided. Dinner is available at CFP 1000 pp. It's right on the beach (though the rooms are not), but this place caters more to people planning long stays: you get seven nights for the price of five and one month is CFP 100,000 double.

In a pinch, **Chez Sorensen** (Joséphine Dahl, tel. 82-63-30), directly across the street from the airport terminal (the second house on the left up the hill beside Blanchisserie Pressing Mea Ma), has three rooms with bath at CFP 3500/6000 single/double, breakfast included. Communal cooking facilities are available, but the location is noisy due to the nearby industrial laundry and airport.

The **Heitiare Inn** (B.P. 6830, Papeete; tel. 83-33-52 or 82-77-53) at PK 4.3, Faa'a, a km east of the airport, has six rooms at CFP 3500/4500 single/double with shared bath, CFP 5000/5500 with a/c, and CFP 6000 double with a/c and private bath. Communal cooking facilities are provided. The snack bar at the inn is inexpensive and you'll meet the locals here, but otherwise it's overpriced for what it is and the location isn't great.

Budget Accommodations in Papeete
Chez Myrna (Myrna Dahmeyer, B.P. 790, Papeete; tel. 42-64-11), Chemin vicinal de Tipaerui 106, half a km up the road from the Hôtel

Matavai, offers two shared-bath rooms at CFP 3500/4500 single/double with breakfast (minimum stay two nights). Dinner is CFP 1000 pp extra. Myrna's husband, Walter, is a German expat who has been on Tahiti for 30 years.

The **Hôtel Shogun** (Bruno Gato, B.P. 2880, Papeete; tel. 43-13-93), 10 rue du Commandant Destremeau, Papeete, has seven a/c rooms facing the noisy road at CFP 6000 single or double, or CFP 6500 single or double on the back side. A monthly rate of CFP 90,000 double is available.

The **Hôtel Mahina Tea** (B.P. 17, Papeete; tel. 42-00-97), up rue Sainte-Amélie from Ave. Bruat, is about the only regular budget hotel in the city. The 16 rooms with private bath are CFP 3800 single or double (CFP 3500 with a single bed), discounted 15% if you stay three or more nights. There are also six small studios with cooking facilities at CFP 90,000 a month double. Dishes are not provided, electricity is extra, and the availability of hot water is irregular. The Mahina Tea could be cleaner, friendlier, and quieter—at night, the rooster noise here can be annoying. This place has been around for many years.

Women can stay at the five-story **Foyer de Jeunes Filles de Paofai** (B.P. 1719, Papeete; tel. 42-87-80) near the Protestant church on boulevard Pomare. This Evangelical Church-operated women's residence provides 125 beds in rooms of two, three, four, or six beds at CFP 2000 a day, CFP 30,000 a month, breakfast included. There's a 2200 curfew daily, except Wednesday, Friday, and Saturday when it's midnight. This hostel is officially open to travelers in July and August only (although you can always try other months—they may have beds available). The bulk of the guests are outer-island Polynesian women aged 16-23, so it's a good opportunity for female travelers to meet local women.

Many backpackers head straight for **Hostel Teamo** (Kay Teriierooiterai, B.P. 2407, Papeete; tel. 42-47-26, fax 43-56-95), 8 rue du pont Neuf, Quartier Mission, a characterful century-old house in an attractive neighborhood near the Archbishop's Palace, just a short walk east of downtown. To get there from the market walk straight inland on rue François Cardella. It's a lit-

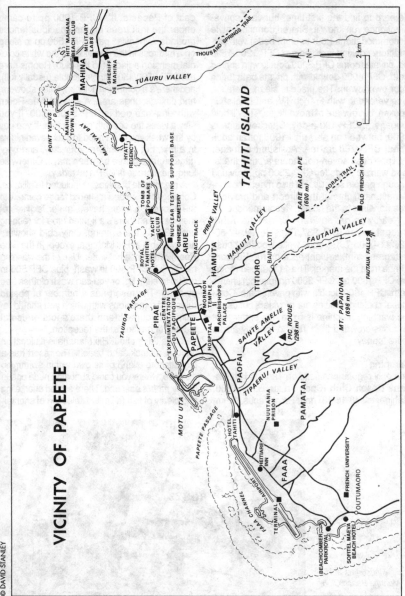

VICINITY OF PAPEETE

© DAVID STANLEY

TAHITI ISLAND

2 km

-N-

THOUSAND SPRINGS TRAIL

Hiti Mahana Beach Club

Military Labs

MAHINA

Sheriff de Mahina

TUAURU VALLEY

Mahina Town Hall

POINT VENUS

MATAVAI BAY

Hyatt Regency

Tomb of Pomare V

Nuclear Testing Support Base

Chinese Cemetery

ARUE

Racetrack

PIRAE VALLEY

FARE RAU APE (600 m)

AORAI TRAIL

Old French Fort

Royal Tahitien Hotel

Yacht Club

TAUNOA PASSAGE

PIRAE

HAMUTA

HAMUTA VALLEY

FAUTAUA VALLEY

FAUTAUA FALLS

Centre d'Expérimentation du Pacifique

Mormon Temple

PAPEETE

Hospital

Archbishops Palace

TITIORO

BAIN LOTI

SAINTE AMELIE VALLEY

PIC ROUGE (298 m)

MT. PAPAIONA (696 m)

PAOFAI

PAPEETE PASSAGE

MOTU UTA

TIPAERUI VALLEY

PAMATAI

Nuutania Prison

Hotel Tahiti

FAAA CHANNEL

FAAA AIRPORT

Heitiare Inn

TERMINAL

FAAA

FRENCH UNIVERSITY

OUTUMAORO

BEACHCOMBER PARKROYAL

SOFITEL MAEVA BEACH HOTEL

tle hard to find the first time, but very convenient once you know it. Shared dormitory-style accommodations (four to eight beds) with satisfactory cooking facilities are CFP 1200-1500 pp, private rooms CFP 3000 double with shared bath, CFP 4000 double with private bath (bring your own towel). The place is clean, there's a nice verandah with French TV, and English is spoken, but beware of mosquitoes. They'll hold luggage at CFP 100 a day. Checkout time is 1000, but you can stay until 1900 for an additional CFP 700 pp fee. Assistant manager Philippe does seven-hour tours around the island with 10 stops for CFP 2500 pp, provided enough people sign up. He also meets most international flights at the airport and provides free transfers to the hostel. Recommended.

Nearby on rue du Frère Alain is the **Tahiti Budget Lodge** (B.P. 237, Papeete; tel. 42-66-82, fax 43-06-79), a quiet white wooden house with green trim, straight back on rue Edouard Ahnne from the market. The 11 four-bed rooms are CFP 1800 pp, CFP 3800 double with shared bath, CFP 4800 double with private bath. Communal cooking facilities are provided, but use of the washing machine is extra. It's better kept and less crowded than Teamo for only a little more money.

Camping

The only regular campsite on Tahiti is **Hiti Mahana Beach Club** (Coco Pautu, B.P. 11580, Mahina; tel. 48-16-13) near Point Venus, 12 km east of Papeete. It's CFP 1000 pp to camp under the fruit trees on the spacious fenced grounds. Otherwise pay CFP 1500 pp to sleep on a mattress in the dormitory of the white colonial mansion adjacent to the club. Rooms here run CFP 3500/4500 single/double (usually full), and there's a communal kitchen, toilet, showers, and dining/lounge area. A special Blue Room with king-size bed is CFP 5000/6000. If you stay a week the seventh night is free. If you pay by the week you don't need to stay seven nights in a row, but can split up your stay, and baggage storage is free between stays. Otherwise luggage storage is CFP 100 a day.

A reasonable breakfast is included in all rates. Cooking facilities and a shared fridge come with the above. Campers have simpler facilities of their own, and there's a lighted area for reading until 2200 in the evening. Only cold showers are available at Hiti Mahana, except in the Blue Room, which has hot water. Use of the washing machine is CFP 500 to wash, plus CFP 500 to dry up to eight kg, or you can wash clothes free by hand. The resort has a number of posted rules and regulations with which you should familiarize yourself, and there's lots of useful tourist information at the reception.

A nice thing about Hiti Mahana is its location right on a black-sand beach. The resort has a tiny offshore island of its own within swimming distance, where you could sunbathe nude or surf off the *motu's* east end. There's good snorkeling and plenty of fish (a limited selection of snorkel-

windsurfers at Hiti Mahana Beach Club, Tahiti

the black volcanic sands of Tahiti

ing gear is loaned free). Windsurfers churn the waters, especially on windy weekends. Cold beer and rum punch are on tap daily and happy hour runs 1700-1900 (except Monday), but the resort snack bar is only open weekends. Video films are shown on rai`ny days at 2030. On Sunday the resort offers excursions to Tefa'aurumai Falls in the back of a pickup truck (CFP 500 pp) and on Tuesday there's a circle-island tour (CFP 2500). They also act as an agent for Pacificar, renting cars and bicycles (though they're often all taken). Hiti Mahana is also a good place to begin a circle-island tour (clockwise).

To get to Hiti Mahana at PK 10.5, Mahina, take the Mahina *truck* (CFP 160, no service after 1715) from near the Papeete tourist office. If you ask, the driver will often bring you directly to the campsite. You pass the Point Venus turnoff, cross a bridge, then turn left at a school and follow the road straight to the beach (one km). The Hiti Mahana *truck* is often at the airport in search of arriving clients, even in the middle of the night, so ask (transfers free). The office is closed 1200-1500.

Upmarket Hotels near the Airport

The French-owned **Sofitel Maeva Beach** (B.P. 6008, Faa'a; tel. 42-80-42, tel. 43-84-70) at PK 7.5, Punaauia, built by UTA French Airlines in the late 1960s, is the least expensive of the three big international hotels on Tahiti (the oth-

ers are the Beachcomber Parkroyal and the Hyatt Regency). The 224 a/c rooms in this pyra-midal high-rise cost CFP 18,400 single or dou-ble garden view, CFP 21,200 single or double lagoon view, CFP 24,500 single or double panoramic view (children under 12 free). The seven-story Maeva Beach faces a man-made white beach. With pollution on the increase in the adjacent lagoon, most swimmers stick to the hotel pool, however.

The **Hôtel Te Puna Bel Air** (B.P. 6634, Faa'a; tel. 42-09-00, fax 41-31-84) at PK 7.2, Punaauia, also known as the Belair Hôtel, is one of the few large hotels owned and operated by a Tahitian family. The way in is rather con-fusing: around the corner and down a side road to an unmarked entrance opposite the scuba diving office. Rates are CFP 8000/9000/11,500 single/double/triple for the 24 garden bunga-lows and 48 standard rooms. The beach is poor, and watch out for eels if you decide to swim in their lovely pond.

The **Tahiti Country Club** (B.P. 13019, Punaauia; tel. 42-60-40, fax 41-09-28) is up on the hillside above the Te Puna Bel Air. The 40 a/c rooms with TV in a neat two-story building are CFP 11,000 single, CFP 13,000 double or triple (children under 12 free), plus CFP 3800 pp extra for breakfast and dinner (if desired). Prices have almost doubled here in recent years. Swimming pool, volleyball, and tennis courts are

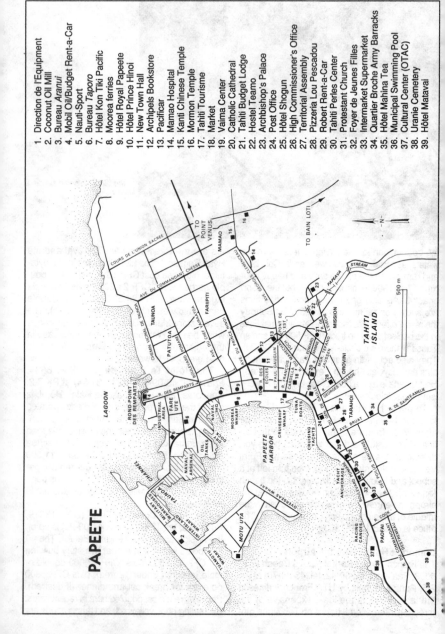

1. Direction de l'Equipment
2. Coconut Oil Mill
3. Bureau *Aranui*
4. Mobil Oil/Budget Rent-a-Car
5. Nauti-Sport
6. Bureau *Taporo*
7. Hôtel Kon Tiki Pacific
8. Moorea ferries
9. Hôtel Royal Papeete
10. Hôtel Prince Hinoi
11. New Town Hall
12. Archipels Bookstore
13. Pacificar
14. Mamao Hospital
15. Kanti Chinese Temple
16. Mormon Temple
17. Tahiti Tourisme
18. Market
19. Vaima Center
20. Catholic Cathedral
21. Tahiti Budget Lodge
22. Hostel Teamo
23. Archbishop's Palace
24. Post Office
25. Hôtel Shogun
26. High Commissioner's Office
27. Territorial Assembly
28. Pizzeria Lou Pescadou
29. Robert Rent-a-Car
30. Tahiti Perles Center
31. Protestant Church
32. Foyer de Jeunes Filles
33. Intermarket Supermarket
34. Quartier Broche Army Barracks
35. Hôtel Mahina Tea
36. Municipal Swimming Pool
37. Cultural Center (OTAC)
38. Uranie Cemetery
39. Hôtel Matavai

PAPEETE

(top left) vanilla stalk (David Stanley); (top right) black noddy (Tahiti Tourisme);
(bottom left) view of Mt. Duff from Aukena, Gambier Islands (Anselm Zänkert);
(bottom right) view of Rikitea from Mt. Duff, Gambier Islands (Anselm Zänkert)

(top) Ahu O Mahine, Moorea (David Stanley);
(bottom) Marae Arahurahu, Tahiti (Tahiti Tourisme, Tini Colombel)

on the premises (free). The hike up to this hotel from the main road is also quite a workout! One reader wrote in complaining about bugs in the rooms and poor food in the hotel restaurant.

The **Tahiti Beachcomber Parkroyal** (B.P. 6014, Faa'a; tel. 86-51-10, fax 86-51-30), PK 7 Faa'a, a former TraveLodge (1974), was purchased by the Japanese corporation EIE in September 1989 for US$35 million. It's the first place west of the airport, and a smart international hotel. The 212 rooms in the main building begin at CFP 22,000/26,000/31,000 single/double/triple; for one of the 15 overwater bungalows add 50% again. Children and teens (to age 16) sharing the room with their parents stay for free. A breakfast and dinner meal plan is CFP 5800 pp extra. Tahitian dancing and crafts demonstrations are regular features. The hotel pool is reserved for guests and the beach is artificial, but the attendants in the water-sports kiosk on the beach will gladly ferry you out to the nudist pontoons anchored mid-lagoon for CFP 700 RT. Every afternoon at 1645 there's a 1.5-hour sunset cruise along the coast from the Beachcomber Parkroyal (CFP 2000 including one drink).

The tastefully decorated **Hôtel Tahiti** (B.P. 416, Papeete; tel. 82-95-50, fax 81-31-51), at PK 2.6 between Papeete and the airport, is the most charming of the higher-priced hotels, with a gracious South Seas atmosphere. There are 86 spacious a/c rooms with bath beginning at CFP 8000/9000 single/double, and 18 thatched lagoonfront bungalows with fan at CFP 12,000 single or double, CFP 14,000 triple—good value for Tahiti. This colonial-style hotel opened in 1960 with a freshwater pool, overwater restaurant (great salads), bar, etc., plus a lovely lagoonside setting on the grounds of what was the residence of Princess Pomare, daughter of the last king of Tahiti. It's very easy to jump on *le truck* to downtown, yet the hotel a world away when you tire of the hustle and bustle of Papeete. We recommend this place as your best choice in the middle-to-upper price range.

Upmarket Hotels in Papeete

The 138-room **Hôtel Matavai** (B.P. 32, Papeete; tel. 42-67-67, fax 42-36-90) has little going for it at CFP 12,000/16,000/208,000 single/double/triple with bath, TV, and two double beds. You can almost tell this four-floor concrete edifice was once a Holiday Inn, but it is the closest luxury hotel to the center. Tennis and squash courts are on the premises.

Business travelers often stay at the high-rise **Hôtel Prince Hinoi** (B.P. 4545, Papeete; tel. 42-32-77, fax 42-33-66), Ave. du Prince Hinoi at boulevard Pomare, formerly known as the Hôtel Ibis Papeete. The 72 small a/c rooms are CFP 9500/11,200 double/triple, plus CFP 3600 for breakfast and dinner (if desired).

The **Hôtel Le Mandarin** (B.P. 302, Papeete; tel. 42-16-33, fax 42-16-32), 51 rue Colette, is a clean, modern hotel with an Asian flair. Unfortunately, the 37 rooms are somewhat overpriced at CFP 12,000/13,500/15,500 single/double/triple (children under 12 free).

The elegant old **Hôtel Royal Papeete** (B.P. 919, Papeete; tel. 42-01-29, fax 43-79-09), downtown on boulevard Pomare opposite the Moorea ferry landing, has 78 rooms beginning at CFP 8900/10,600/12,100 single/double/triple. The Royal Papeete should be your choice if you don't mind spending a fair bit of money to stay right in the heart of Papeete's nightlife quarter. The hotel's two lively nightclubs downstairs offer free admission to guests. Just make sure you don't get a room directly above the clubs unless you enjoy being rocked to sleep by a disco beat.

Hôtel Kon Tiki Pacific (B.P. 111, Papeete; tel. 43-72-82, fax 42-11-66) is the cheapest high-rise hotel in the city center. The 44 spacious rooms begin at CFP 8000/9500/11,500 single/double/triple. Don't accept one of the noisy rooms near the elevator, which are always offered first. This hotel is popular with French military personnel and secret agents in transit. Immerse yourself in the intrigue (and get an eyeful of Papeete) by having a meal in the 7th-floor restaurant (closed Sunday).

Upmarket Hotels East of Papeete

The **Royal Tahitien Hôtel** (B.P. 5001, Papeete; tel. 42-81-13, fax 41-05-35), at PK 3.5, directly behind the Mairie de Pirae, is a peaceful two-story building with 40 rooms facing beautifully kept grounds on a black-sand beach. The windsurfing offshore is good. For CFP 15,000 single or double, CFP 18,000 triple, you may just find the Tahiti you imagined here. Breakfast and dinner served on the terrace overlooking the lagoon are CFP 4400 pp extra.

The **Hyatt Regency Tahiti** (B.P. 14700, Arue; tel. 48-11-22, fax 48-25-44) at PK 8, Mahina, takes the award for charging the highest prices on the island. The 190 spacious rooms begin at CFP 27,000 single or double, CFP 32,000 triple (children under 18 free). Happy hour at the hotel bar is 1730-1830. Formerly known as the Tahara'a Hôtel, the Hyatt was built by Pan American Airways in 1968 and purchased for US$30 million in September 1989 by the Japanese group Electronic and Industrial Enterprises, which also has big investments in Fiji. Built on a hillside overlooking Matavai Bay, this is one of the few hotels in the world where you take an elevator *down* to your room. The views from the balconies are superb and a black-sand beach is at the foot of the hill. The Hyatt provides a shuttle service to and from Papeete for guests.

Accommodations near Taravao

The only reasonably inexpensive place to stay on the far side of the island is **Fare Nana'o** (B.P. 7193, Taravao; tel. 57-18-14, fax 57-76-10), operated by sculptor Jean-Claude Michel and his wife Monique. It's on the lagoon side in a colorful compound overflowing with vegetation and fragments of sculpture, very near the PK 52 marker a km north of the old French fort at Taravao. The seven thatched bungalows vary in price, from CFP 5000 double for the treehouse (you climb up a pole), CFP 5500 double for an overwater *fare* on stilts (you must wade through the lagoon), CFP 6000 double for one of the three units with cooking facilities, to CFP 7500 double for the only room with private bath. A third person is CFP 500 at all of these, and the weekly discount is 10%. Although unique and wonderful, Fare Nana'o is not for everyone: the walls are constructed of tree trunks and branches left partially open, there's no hot water, flashlights are required to reach the shared toilet and shower at night, and you may be visited in the night by crabs, spiders, lizards, and a marauding cat. This Robinson Crusoe-style place has had TV exposure in Los Angeles, so advance reservations are necessary, especially on weekends. Recommended.

At the four-unit **Te Anuanua Hôtel** (B.P. 1553, Papeete; tel. 57-12-54, fax 45-14-39), just west of the church in Pueu at PK 10, Tahiti Iti, the garden bungalows are CFP 8000 single,

double, or triple. Lagoonfront bungalows are CFP 1000 more. Check the rooms before checking in, as some lack window screens, fans, or functioning plumbing. A nice seafood restaurant faces the lagoon, making the Te Anuanua worth a stop as you travel around the island, and every Sunday at noon there's a buffet of authentic Tahitian food (CFP 3800 pp). This hotel doesn't have a beach, but the water off their wharf is crystal clear and inviting to jump in.

A more distant choice would be the **Puunui Resort** (B.P. 7016, Taravao; tel. 57-19-20, fax 57-27-43), four km up a steep paved road off the Teahupoo road, seven km from Taravao. You'll have to rent a car if you stay here. At CFP 12,000 for one of the 54 four-bed bungalows or CFP 18,000 for each of the 23 six-bed villas, the Puunui is overpriced unless you're in a small group. A breakfast and dinner meal plan is CFP 4000 pp extra, though the units have kitchenettes. They do offer horseback riding (tel. 57-19-20 for reservations 48 hours in advance), so it may be worth dropping by for a ride and the view. Roundtrip airport transfers are CFP 4500 pp. Be sure to call ahead to check availability if you wish to stay here.

FOOD

Food Trailers

In the early evening take a stroll along the Papeete waterfront near the Moorea ferry landing, past the dozens of gaily lit vans known as *les roulettes* which form a colorful night market. Here you'll find everything from couscous, pizza, and *brouchettes* (shish kebab) to steak with real *pommes frites*. As the city lights wink gently across the harbor, sailors promenade with their *vahines,* adding a touch of romance and glamour. The food and atmosphere are excellent, but even if you're not dining, it's a scene not to miss. No alcohol is available.

Self-Service Cafeterias

Poly-Self Restaurant (tel. 43-75-32), 8 rue Gauguin behind the Banque de Polynésie, dispenses filling Chinese-style lunches at about CFP 800. It's unpretentious but a little overpriced.

The **Foyer de Jeunes Filles de Paofai** (tel. 42-87-80) opposite the Protestant church has a

The food trucks along the Papeete waterfront are about the best places in the city to eat.

good modern self-service cafeteria open for lunch 1130-1300 (closed Saturday and Sunday). Alcohol is not available here.

Snack Bars

To sample the local cuisine, check out the eateries on rue Cardella right beside the market. Try *maa tinito,* a melange of red beans, pork, macaroni, and vegetables on rice (CFP 750). A large Hinano beer is CFP 350.

Snack Roger, 3 rue Jaussen next to the Catholic cathedral, offers good plate lunches, *plats du jour,* cheap salads, real espresso coffee, and ice cream. It's a good place to catch your breath, so locate it early in your visit!

The *plat du jour* at **Big Burger** (tel. 43-01-98), beside Aline, is often big value (CFP 1400), and it's not fast food as the name implies (closed Sunday).

Salvani's Café (tel. 45-17-45) below Hôtel Shogun serves reasonably priced meals in a bright, attractive locale.

Inexpensive grilled meat and fish dishes are the specialty at **Snack Paofai** (tel. 42-95-76) near Clinique Paofai (daily 1730-2130). A complete meal here will run CFP 700 if you dine on their airy terrace or CFP 100 less if you take the food away. On Thursday they prepare a special couscous dish.

If you're catching the interisland boats *Vaeanu* or *Taporo* from Motu Uta, check out the **Restaurant Motu Uta** behind the *Vaeanu* office near the wharf. Lunch is good—especially with big

bottles of cold beer. Indulge before you embark (if they're open). There's also a public water tap here where you can fill your canteen for the journey.

Those staying at Hôtel Tahiti will want to know about **Snack Nu'utere Faa'a,** on the left opposite the Mobil station, 300 meters up the road to the airport. The friendly Tahitian owners will welcome you warmly and feed you delicious local fare.

Asian Restaurants

Many Chinese restaurants in Papeete specialize in chicken and Hinano beer, but none are special bargains. The most popular is the **Waikiki Restaurant** (open daily 1100-1300/1800-2100, closed Sunday lunch; tel. 42-95-27), rue Leboucher 20, near the market. At **Te Hoa Restaurant** (closed Sunday; tel. 43-99-27), 30 rue du Maréchal Foch behind the market, the furnishings aren't as neat, but the portions are bigger and the prices slightly lower than at Waikiki.

Papeete's finest Cantonese restaurant is **Le Mandarin** (tel. 42-99-03), 26 rue des Écoles. Their specialty is Chinese fondue.

Restaurant La Saigonnaise (closed Sunday; tel. 42-05-35) on Ave. du Prince Hinoi has moderately expensive Vietnamese food. Saigonese soup makes a good lunch.

Italian Restaurants

For a taste of the Mediterranean, **La Pizzeria** (closed Sunday and holidays; tel. 42-98-30), on boulevard Pomare near the Tahiti Pearl Center, prepares real pizza in a brick oven. The prices are reasonable for the waterfront location—they're all spelled out on a big blackboard menu.

Pizzeria Lou Pescadou (open daily 1130-1400/1830-2230; tel. 43-74-26) on rue Anne-Marie Javouhey behind the cathedral is friendly, unpretentious, breezy, and inexpensive. Their pizza pescatore makes a good lunch, and a big pitcher of ice water is included in the price. Owner Mario Vitulli may be from Marseille, but you won't complain about his spaghetti—a huge meal for about CFP 700. Drinks are on the house while you wait for a table. The service is lively, and French, and Lou Pescadou is very popular among local French, a high recommendation.

A block toward the mountains on rue Georges Lagarde is **Pizzeria Caesario** with a home delivery service at tel. 42-21-21. More good pizza is baked at **Don Camillo** (tel. 42-80-96), 14 rue des Écoles, next to the Piano Bar.

Other Restaurants

Papeete's most famous restaurant is **Acajou** (closed Sunday; tel. 42-87-58), corner of rue Georges Lagarde and boulevard Pomare near the Vaima Center. House specialties include slices of mahimahi *au gratin,* coconut-curry shrimp, and filet mignon with mustard sauce. The plates are individually prepared, so allow some time.

A cheaper branch of Acajou (open Monday to Saturday 0400-1700, Sunday 0300-1100; tel. 43-19-22) is at 7 rue Cardella by the market, half a block from the tourist office. The coffee with fresh buttered bread offered here makes an excellent breakfast or mid-morning snack.

For a change of pace have lunch at the restaurant of the **Lycée Hôtelier** (tel. 45-23-71), a bit east of Pirae Municipal Market (open October to June from Tuesday to Friday noon-1400, except during the Christmas holidays). The food is prepared and served by students.

Cafés

Le Retro (tel. 42-40-01) on the boulevard Pomare side of the Vaima Center is *the* place to sit and sip a drink while watching the passing parade. The atmosphere here is really Côte d'Azur.

The Papeete equivalent of a Hard Rock Café is **Morrison's Café** (tel. 42-78-61), upstairs in the Vaima Center, which offers a full bar, a short pub menu (not cheap), and a swimming pool. Here MTV-deprived local youths mix with island-hopping yachties on an airy terrace with a view of Tahiti (weekdays 1100-0100, Saturday 1600-0100).

On boulevard Pomare across the park from the Moorea ferry landing is a row of sidewalk cafés frequented by French servicemen, happy hookers, gays, and assorted groupies. Some establishments even have a happy hour. This is a good place to sit and take in the local color of every shade and hue.

When the heat gets to you, **Pâtisserie La Marquisienne** (tel. 42-83-52), 29 rue Colette, offers coffee and pastries in a/c comfort. It's popular among French expats.

Groceries

The supermarket in the **Fare Tony Commercial Center** next to the Vaima Center in central Papeete is open weekdays 0730-1830, Saturday 0730-1800. **Intermarket** is a large supermarket on rue du Commandant Destremeau (open Monday to Friday 0730-1845, Saturday 0730-1200/1500-1830, Sunday 0730-1130). Get whole barbecued chickens and chow mein in the deli section.

At PK 8 Punuuai, just south of the junction of the autoroute to Papeete, is the **Centre Commercial Moana Nui**, Tahiti's first enclosed shopping mall, with a large adjoining supermarket, **Continent**. A barbecued chicken from the deli section in the supermarket makes for a good meal, and there's also a snack bar in the mall.

ENTERTAINMENT AND EVENTS

Five Papeete cinemas show B-grade films dubbed into French (admission CFP 700). The Concorde is in the Vaima Center; Hollywood I and II are on rue Lagarde beside the Vaima Center; Liberty Cinema is on rue du Maréchal Foch near the market; and the Mamao Palace is near Mamao Hospital.

Ask for the monthly program of activities at the departement Fêtes et Manifestations in the **Cultural Center** (B.P. 1709, Papeete; tel. 42-88-50) at Te Fare Tahiti Nui on the waterfront.

Nightlife

Papeete after dark is not just for the tourists! Lots of little bars crowding the streets around rue des Écoles are full of locals. The places with live music or a show generally impose a CFP 1000 cover charge, which includes one drink. Nothing much gets going before 2200 and by 0100 everything is very informal for the last hour before closing.

The **Piano Bar** (tel. 42-88-24), beside Hôtel Prince Hinoi on rue des Écoles, is the most notorious of Papeete's *mahu* (transvestite) discos; **Le Lido Nightclub** (tel. 42-95-84) next door offers unisex striptease. **Le Club 5** nearby features female stripping. Young French servicemen are in their element in these places.

Café des Sports on the corner across the street from the Piano Bar has beer on tap and usually no cover. More locals than tourists patronize this pleasant, inexpensive establishment, where a good Tahitian band plays on weekends.

Another local drinking place is the **Royal Kikiriri** (no cover; tel. 43-58-64), rue Colette 66, where you can get a beer without paying a cover.

French soldiers and sailors out of uniform patronize the bars along boulevard Pomare opposite the Moorea ferry landing, such as **La Cave** (tel. 42-01-29) inside the Hôtel Royal Papeete (entry through the lobby), which has live Tahitian music for dancing on Friday and Saturday 2200-0300 (CFP 1500 cover charge, free for Royal Papeete guests). **Le Tamure Hut** (tel. 42-01-29), also at the Royal Papeete, is one of the few downtown Papeete clubs that caters for visitors. Through the music and decor they've attempted to recapture the nightlife milieu of a decade or more ago, before Quinn's Tahitian Hut closed in 1973. It's open Friday 1600-0300, Saturday 2100-0300, and Sunday 1600-2200. There's no cover charge for guests of the Royal Papeete, otherwise it's CFP 1500 (includes one drink).

The **Tiki d'Or Bar Américain** (no cover; tel. 42-07-37), 26 rue Georges Lagarde near the Vaima Center, gets lively around happy hour. You'll locate it by the ukuleles and impromptu singing.

The **Pitate Bar,** on the corner of Ave. Bruat beside the Air France office, is loud and dark, but there's often Tahitian-style music you can dance to and lots of local atmosphere. Check out the Pitate on Sunday afternoon.

Discos

Papeete's top disco is **Galaxy Night-Club Discotheque** (tel. 43-15-36) on rue Jaussen directly back from the Catholic cathedral (open Wednesday to Saturday 2200-0300). There's no cover charge on Wednesday and Thursday; otherwise it's CFP 1500 on Friday and Saturday, but they often let foreign tourists in free. Galaxy mostly caters to people in their teens and twenties, and smart dress is required. A slightly older crowd patronizes the **New Orleans Jazz Club** (tel. 43-15-36) next door which is open the same hours.

Le Rolls Club Discotheque (tel. 43-41-42) in the Vaima Center (opposite Big Burger) is open Wednesday to Saturday, with *karaoke* singing 2100-2300 and disco dancing 2300-0300. Friday and Sunday they're also open 1600-2100.

a Tahitian dancer at a Papeete hotel

TAHITI TOURISME

Cultural Shows for Visitors

A Tahitian dance show takes place in the Bougainville Restaurant, downstairs at the **Maeva Beach Hôtel** (tel. 42-80-42), Friday and Saturday at 2000. If you're not interested in having dinner, a drink at the Bar Moorea by the pool will put you in position to see the action (no cover charge). Sunday this hotel puts on a full Tahitian feast at 1200, complete with earth oven *(ahimaa)* and show (CFP 4900).

The **Beachcomber Parkroyal Hôtel** (tel. 86-51-10) presents one of the best Tahitian dance shows on the island; attend for the price of a drink at the bar near the pool (no cover charge). Tahiti's top dance troupe, Coco's Temaeva, often performs here (check). The dancers' starting time tends to vary (officially Wednesday, Friday, Saturday, and Sunday at 2000), so arrive early and be prepared to wait. For something special try the barbecue (on Wednesday) and the Tahitian feast (on Sunday)—CFP4500 each. The seafood dinner show on Friday is CFP 5950.

At the **Hyatt Regency** (tel. 48-11-22) the Tahitian dancing is Friday and Saturday at 2015.

Sometimes there's Tahitian dancing in the **Captain Bligh Restaurant** (tel. 43-62-90) at the Punaauia Lagoonarium on Friday and Saturday nights at 2100 (call ahead to check).

SHOPPING

Normal shopping hours in Papeete are weekdays 0730-1130/1330-1730, Saturday 0730-1200. Papeete's largest shopping complex is the **Vaima Center,** where numerous shops sell black pearls, designer clothes, souvenirs, books, etc. It's certainly worth a look; then branch out into the surrounding streets. **Galerie Winkler** (tel. 42-81-77), 17 rue Jeanne d'Arc beside American Express, sells contemporary paintings of Polynesia.

For reproductions of authentic Marquesan woodcarvings, have a look in **Manuia Curios** on the east side of the cathedral. Also try **Manuia Junior,** corner of rues Albert Leboucher and des Écoles opposite the Café des Sports. Upstairs in the market is another good place to buy handicrafts, or just a pareu.

Don't overlook the local fashions. **Marie Ah You** on the waterfront between the Vaima Center and the tourist office sells very chic island clothing—at prices to match.

Magasin Côte d'Azur, rue Paul Gauguin 26, has cheap pareus; several other shops along this street also flog inexpensive tropical garb.

Surfers can visit **Shop Tahiti Surf and Skate,** 10 rue Édouard Ahnne near the market, sells boards, plus all attendant gear. **Caroline** at 41 rue Colette, and **Waikiki Beach** at 9 rue Jeanne d'Arc, also have surfing gear.

Photo Lux (tel. 42-84-31) on rue du Maréchal Foch near the market has some of the cheapest color print film you'll find and they repair Minolta cameras.

The **Philatelic Bureau** (tel. 41-43-35) at the main post office sells the stamps and first-day covers of all the French Pacific territories. Some are quite beautiful and inexpensive.

a Marquesan wood carving

SERVICES

Banks

The Banque de Tahiti in the Vaima Center (weekdays 0800-1145/1330-1630, Saturday 0800-1130) charges CFP 350 commission to change traveler's checks. The Banque Socredo also deducts CFP 350, but the Banque de Polynésie and Westpac Bank are a bit more expensive. There's no commission at all if you're changing French francs, and the buying and selling rates are identical! Several banks around town have automatic tellers where you can get cash advances on credit cards.

Post and Telecommunications

The main post office is on boulevard Pomare across from the yacht anchorage. Aerograms and large mailing envelopes/boxes are sold at the counters up the escalators (closes at 1500). Pick up poste restante (general delivery) mail at window No. 15 downstairs (CFP 40 per piece). The post office is also the place to make a long-distance telephone call, but there's a CFP 1824 three-minute minimum for an operator-assisted call to the States. It's cheaper to use a telephone card for such calls.

Around Tahiti, small branch post offices with public telephones are found in Arue, Faa'a Airport, Mahina, Mataiea, Paea, Papara, Papeari, Pirae, Punaauia, and Taravao.

If you have an American Express card you can have your mail sent c/o Tahiti Tours, B.P. 627, Papeete. Their office (tel. 54-02-50) is at 15 rue Jeanne d'Arc next to the Vaima Center.

Immigration Office

If you arrived by air, visa extensions are handled by the **Police de l'Air et des Frontières** (open weekdays 0800-1200/1400-1700; B.P. 6362, Faa'a; tel. 82-67-99) at the airport (up the stairs beside the snack bar). Yachties are handled by the immigration office next to a small Banque Socredo branch on the waterfront behind Tahiti Tourisme in the center of town (Monday to Thursday 0730-1100/1330-1530, Friday 0730-1100/1330-1500; tel. 42-40-74). Be patient and courteous with the officials if you want good service.

For those uninitiated into the French administrative system, the **police station** (in emergencies tel. 17) opposite the War Memorial on Ave. Bruat deals with Papeete matters, while the gendarmerie (tel. 46-73-73) at the head of Ave. Bruat is concerned with the rest of the island. The locally recruited Papeete police wear blue uniforms, while the paramilitary French-import gendarmes are dressed in khaki.

Consulates

The honorary consul of Australia is Brian Banston (B.P. 1695, Papeete; tel. 43-88-38) at the Qantas office in the Vaima Center. The honorary consul of New Zealand is Richard Hall (B.P. 73, Papeete; tel. 43-88-29). The honorary British consul is Robert Withers (B.P. 1064, Papeete, tel. 42-84-57) at Avis Rent-a-Car, 35 rue Charles Viénot. The honorary consul of Germany is Claude-Eliane Weinmann (B.P. 452, Papeete; tel. 42-99-94), rue Tihoni Te Faatau off Ave. du Prince Hinoi in Afareru on the far east side of the city. Other countries with honorary consuls at Papeete are Austria, Belgium, Chile, Denmark, Finland, Holland, Italy, Monaco, Norway, South Korea, Sweden, and Switzerland. There's no U.S. diplomatic post in Tahiti-Polynesia. All visa applications and requests for replacement of lost passports must be sent to Suva, Fiji, where the paperwork can take up to five weeks. Canada and Japan are also *not* represented.

Laundromats

Central Pressing, 72 rue Albert Leboucher (the street behind the Royal Papeete Hôtel), offers a special service to visitors: for CFP 600 they'll wash, dry, and fold one kg of laundry.

Laverie Gauguin Pressing Lavomatic, rue Gauguin 64 (weekdays 0630-1730, Saturday 0630-1200), charges CFP 600 to wash six kg, another CFP 600 to dry, and CFP 100 for soap.

Public Toilets

Public toilets are found next to the immigration office near the small Banque Socredo behind Tahiti Tourisme, at the bus stop opposite Hôtel Le Mandarin beside the Hôtel de Ville, and on the waterfront opposite Air France. The ones near immigration are the most likely to be open regularly, so locate them early in your stay.

Yachting Facilities

Yachts pay CFP 900 a day to moor Mediterranean-style (stern-to, bow anchor out) along the quay on boulevard Pomare. For half the price you can anchor farther west along the boulevard. A one-time entry fee and optional daily electricity hookup are charged. The port captain, Customs, and Immigration are all in the building next to Banque Socredo behind Tahiti Tourisme. Visiting boats can also use one of the anchor buoys at the **Yacht Club of Tahiti** (B.P. 1456, Papeete; tel. 42-78-03) at PK 4, Arue, for a monthly charge.

INFORMATION

Tahiti Tourisme (B.P. 65, Papeete; tel. 50-57-00) at Fare Manihini, a neo-Polynesian building on the waterfront not far from the market, can answer questions and supply maps. They have detailed "small hotel" accommodations lists for all the outer islands. Ask here about special events and boats to the outer islands. They're open weekdays 0730-1700, Saturday 0800-1200.

The **Institute Territorial de la Statistique** (B.P. 395, Papeete; tel. 43-71-96), 2nd floor, Bloc Donald (behind Voyagence Tahiti, opposite the Vaima Center), puts out a quarterly *Statistical Bulletin*.

Bookstores and Maps

You'll find Papeete's best selection of English books at **Libraire Archipels** (B.P. 20676, Papeete; tel. 42-47-30), 68 rue des Remparts. Archipels is about the only place you can find books and guides to the Pacific.

Vaima Libraire (B.P. 2399, Papeete; tel. 45-57-44), in the Vaima Center, and **Polygraph** (B.P. 707, Papeete; tel. 42-80-47), 12 Ave. Bruat, are Papeete's largest French bookstores. **Libraire Le Petit Prince** (B.P. 13080, Papeete; tel. 43-26-24) in the Centre Commercial Moana Nui, Punaauia, is also good.

La Boutique Klima (B.P. 31, Papeete; tel. 42-00-63), behind the cathedral, sells old topographical maps, nautical charts, and many interesting books on Polynesia.

Newer topographical maps (CFP 1500) of some islands are available from the **Service de l'Aménagement** (B.P. 866, Papeete), 4th floor, Administrative Building, 11 rue du Commandant Destremeau.

For the best selection of French nautical charts, visit **Ouvrages Cartes et Instruments** in the white Marine Nationale building next to the Air France office on the waterfront (open Monday, Tuesday, Thursday, and Friday 1330-1600).

There's a **newsstand** with magazines in English in front of the Vaima Center by the taxi stand on boulevard Pomare.

Public Library

A public library (open Monday to Thursday 0800-1700, Friday 0800-1600; tel. 42-88-50) is located in the Cultural Center. To take books out you must buy an annual card for CFP 4000.

Travel Agencies

One of Papeete's most reliable regular travel agencies is **Tahiti Tours** (B.P. 627, Papeete; tel. 54-02-50), 15 rue Jeanne d'Arc next to the Vaima Center. **Tahiti Nui Travel** (B.P. 718, Papeete; tel. 42-68-03, fax 43-53-00) in the Vaima Center often has cheap package tours to Easter Island.

Yacht cruises around the Society Islands, Tuamotus, and Marquesas can be arranged by **Tahiti Mer et Loisirs** (B.P. 3488, Papeete; tel. 43-97-99, fax 43-33-68), in a houseboat on the Papeete waterfront opposite the post office. For example, a seven-night cruise around the Marquesas from Nuku Hiva will run CFP 180,000 pp.

Airline Offices

Reconfirm your international flight at your airline's Papeete office. Most of the airline offices are in the Vaima Center: Air New Zealand (tel. 43-01-70), Hawaiian Airlines (tel. 42-15-00), Lan Chile (tel. 42-64-55), and Qantas (tel. 43-06-65). AOM French Airlines (tel. 43-25-25) is at 90 rue des Remparts; Corsair (tel. 42-28-28) is at 9 rue Jaussen next to the Catholic cathedral. Air France (tel. 43-63-33), which also represents Air Calédonie International, is on boulevard Pomare near Ave. Bruat.

HEALTH

Mamao Hospital is always crowded with locals awaiting free treatment, so you're better off attending a private clinic. The **Clinique Paofai** (B.P. 545, Papeete; tel. 43-02-02) on boulevard

Pomare accepts outpatients weekdays 0700-1900, Saturday 0700-1200, emergencies anytime. The facilities and attention are excellent, but be prepared for fees of around CFP 2900. The **Clinique Cardella** (tel. 42-81-90) on rue Anne-Marie Javouhey is also open day and night.

Dr. Vincent Joncker and Dr. J.-M. P. Rosenstein, in the building above the pharmacy opposite the Catholic cathedral, operate a **Cabinet Médical** (tel. 43-10-43) where you'll pay around CFP 3000 for a consultation during business hours. Otherwise, their **S.O.S. Médecins** (tel. 42-34-56) are on call 24 hours a day, but home visits begin at CFP 6000.

To call an ambulance dial 15.

GETTING AROUND

For information on air and sea services from Tahiti to other Polynesian islands, see "Getting Around" in the main Introduction.

Le Truck

You can go almost anywhere on Tahiti by *les trucks,* converted cargo vehicles with long benches in back. *Trucks* marked Outumaoro run from Papeete to Faa'a International Airport and the Maeva Beach Hôtel every few minutes during the day, with sporadic service after dark until 2000 daily, then again in the morning from 0500 on. On Sundays long-distance *trucks* run only in the very early morning and evening; weekdays the last trip to Mahina, Paea, and points beyond is around 1700.

Trucks don't run right around the island. Although a couple go as far as Tautira and Teahupoo on Tahiti Iti, you could have difficulty getting a *truck* back to Papeete from those remote villages in the afternoon. To go around the island by *truck,* start early and travel clockwise. Get out at Taravao and walk down to the Gauguin Museum (three km). With lots of traffic along the south coast, it'll be easy to hitch a ride back this way, though the last Papeete-bound *truck* leaves around 1300. Luckily, so far, hitching is usually no problem.

Trucks to Arue, Mahina, and Papenoo leave from boulevard Pomare across the street from Tahiti Tourisme. Those to the airport, Outumaoro, Punaauia, Paea, and Papara are found on rue du Maréchal Foch near the market. Local services to Motu Uta, Mission, Mamao, Titioro, and Tipaeriu depart from rue Colette near the Hôtel de Ville.

Destinations and fares are posted on the side of the vehicle: CFP 140 to Punaauia, CFP 160 to Mahina, CFP 170 to Paea, CFP 200 to Papara, CFP 240 to Mataiea or Papeari, CFP 300 to Taravao, CFP 350 to Teahupoo or Tautira. After dark all *truck* fares increase. Outside Papeete you don't have to be at a stop: *trucks* stop anywhere if you wave. Luggage rides for free.

Taxis

Taxis in Papeete are expensive, and it's important not to get in unless there's a meter that works or you've agreed to a flat fare beforehand. Expect to pay at least CFP 800 for a trip within Papeete, CFP 1000 to the airport, or CFP 1500 to the Hyatt Regency or Maeva Beach. Fares are 25% more on Sunday and holidays; 2000-0600 daily they're 50% higher. The taxis also charge extra for luggage at these times. Taxi stands are found at the Vaima Center (tel. 42-33-60), the market (tel. 43-19-62), the Hôtel de Ville, and the airport (tel. 43-30-07). If you feel cheated by a taxi driver, take down the license number and complain to the tourist office.

Car Rentals

To rent a car you must be 21 (or 18 with Pacificar, 25 with Avis) and have held a driver's license for at least a year. Check the car as carefully as they check you and comment on dents, scratches, flat tires, etc. All the car rental agencies include third-party public liability insurance in the basic price, but collision damage waiver (CDW) varies from CFP 700 to CFP 1300 extra per day. Most agencies charge the client for damage to the tires, insurance or no insurance, and Tahiti insurance isn't valid if you take the car across to Moorea. On Tahiti the car comes full of gas, and you'll see Mobil and Total gas stations all around the island.

If you want to whiz the island and pack in as many side trips as you can in one day, an unlimited-mileage rental is for you, and with four people sharing it's not a bad deal. You should only consider renting on a per-km basis if you plan to keep the car for at least three days and intend to use it only for short hops. Most agencies impose a 50-km daily minimum on their per-km rentals to prevent you from traveling *too* slowly; most rentals are for a minimum of 24 hours. Many car rental companies have kiosks inside Faa'a Airport, and most offer clients a free pickup and drop-off service to the hotels and airport.

The best rates are usually offered by **Pacificar** (B.P. 1121, Papeete; tel. 41-93-93, fax 42-19-11), 56 rue des Remparts at pont de l'Est, at the east end of rue Paul Gauguin. They also have a counter in the large wooden building facing the Moorea ferry wharf and a desk at the airport. Their smallest car is CFP 1500 a day, plus CFP 28 a km, plus CFP 800 insurance. They also offer a flat three-day rental price of CFP 12,000, mileage and insurance included (additional days CFP 4000). They're open 24 hours a day—if the main office is closed, the guard in the parking lot can give you a car.

Budget (B.P. 306, Papeete; tel. 43-80-79, fax 45-01-01), in the flashy Mobil Oil Australia building north of downtown, charges CFP 6600 a day with unlimited mileage plus CFP 1100 insurance. With their weekend rate you pay only two days' rental to keep the car from Friday to Monday, but you're charged three days' insurance.

Avis (B.P. 1683, Papeete; tel. 42-96-49, 41-08-47), 35 rue Charles Viénot, offers cars with unlimited mileage from CFP 7400 (minimum two-day rental) and their insurance charges are also among the highest (CFP 1300). They're expensive because most of their business is through desks at the big hotels.

Hertz (tel. 42-04-71, fax 42-48-62), at Paradise Tours, on Vicinal de Tipaerui opposite Hôtel Matavai, is also overpriced (from CFP 2500 a day, plus CFP 35 a km, or CFP 7300 with unlimited mileage). Their CDW insurance is CFP 1300.

A good place to try for a per-km rental is **Robert Rent-a-Car** (B.P. 1047, Papeete; tel. 42-97-20, fax 42-63-00), rue du Commandant Destremeau (from CFP 1200 daily, plus CFP 35 a km, plus CFP 700 insurance).

More expensive is **Garage Daniel** (B.P. 1445, Papeete; tel. 82-30-04), at PK 5.5 across the highway from the airport terminal. They charge CFP 1600 a day, plus CFP 33 a km, plus CFP 1000 insurance, or CFP 14,000 for three days with unlimited mileage.

Scooter and Cycle Rentals

Pacificar (tel. 41-93-93) on pont de l'Est rents one-person motor scooters at CFP 1000 a day, plus CFP 23 a km (50-km daily minimum). Compulsory helmets are provided, but no insurance is available for the scooters. They will let you take the scooter to Moorea (ferry charges are CFP 1000 return), but an authorization must be obtained from Pacificar in advance. They'll warn you that if you have any problems with the scooter while on Moorea, it's up to you to get it back to Tahiti. (On Moorea scooters are more expensive at CFP 3000 a day with unlimited kilometers.)

Cycles Evasion (tel. 45-11-82), boulevard Pomare 483 (directly behind the Moana Iti Restaurant), rents quality mountain bikes at CFP 1000 daily (CFP 20,000 deposit). The fast and furious traffic on Tahiti's main highways makes cycling dangerous and/or unpleasant, but you might consider getting a bicycle here to take over to Moorea. They're open weekdays 0830-1200/1400-1700, Saturday 0800-1200.

Garage Bambou (B.P. 5592, Papeete; tel. 42-80-09), on Ave. Georges Clemenceau near the Chinese temple, sells new bicycles from CFP 24,000 and does repairs.

Local Tours

Twice a day William Leeteg of **Adventure Eagle Tours** (B.P. 6719, Faa'a; tel. 41-37-63) takes visitors on four-hour trips to the top of Mt. Marau (1,372 meters) by 4WD vehicle for CFP 5000 pp. A visit to Vaimahuta Falls is included, but the tour is canceled on rainy days. There's also a full-day tour around the island at CFP 3800 (admissions and lunch not included). William speaks good English and can arrange special guided tours for groups of up to seven.

Patrice Bordes of **Tahiti Safari Expedition** (B.P. 14445, Arue; tel. 42-14-15, evenings only) offers 4WD jeep tours to Mt. Marau, the Papenoo Valley, and Lake Vaihiria.

GETTING AWAY

The **Air Tahiti** booking office (tel. 42-24-44) is upstairs in Fare Tony, the building behind Acajou off boulevard Pomare. **Air Moorea** (tel. 86-41-41) is at Faa'a International Airport. Interisland services by air and sea are covered in "Getting Around" in the main Introduction.

The ferries to Moorea depart from the landing just behind the tourist office downtown. The

Raromatai Ferry and *Ono-Ono* to the Leeward Islands also leave from there, as do cruise ships and a few other small boats. All other interisland ships, including the cargo vessels *Taporo VI* and *Vaeanu,* leave from the Tuamotu wharf or Quai des Caboteurs in Motu Uta, across the

harbor from downtown Papeete. You can catch a *truck* directly to Motu Uta from the Hôtel de Ville. The ticket offices of some of the vessels are in Fare Ute just north of downtown, while others are at Motu Uta (addresses given in "Getting Around" in the main Introduction.

OTHER WINDWARD ISLANDS

Mehetia is an uninhabited high island (435 meters) about 100 km east of Tahiti. It's less than two km across, with no lagoon, and landing is difficult. Fishermen from the south coast of Tahiti visit occasionally.

Maiao, or Tapuaemanu, 70 km southwest of Moorea, is a low coral island with an elongated, 154-meter-high hill at the center. On each side of this hill is a large greenish blue lake. Around Maiao is a barrier reef with a pass on the south side accessible only to small boats. Some 250 people live on 8.3-square-km Maiao, all Polynesians. Europeans and Chinese are not allowed to reside on the island as a result of problems with an Englishman, Eric Trower, who attempted to gain control of Maiao for phosphate mining in the 1930s.

There are no tourist accommodations on Maiao and an invitation from a resident is required to stay. There's no airstrip. For information on the monthly supply ship from Papeete, contact the **Compagnie Française Maritime de Tahiti** (B.P. 368, Papeete; tel. 42-63-93) at

Fare Ute. A roundtrip voyage on this ship would give you at least a glimpse of Maiao.

TETIAROA

Tetiaroa, 42 km north of Tahiti, is a low coral atoll with a turquoise lagoon and 13 deep-green coconut-covered islets totaling 490 hectares. Only small boats can enter the lagoon. Tahuna Iti has been designated a seabird refuge (fenced off), the lagoon a marine reserve. On three-km-long Rimatuu islet may be seen the remains of Polynesian *marae* and giant *tuu* trees.

The former Tahitian royal retreat was, in 1904, given by the Pomare family to a British dentist named Walter Williams to pay their bills. Dr. Williams, who was also the British consul from 1923 to 1935, had a daughter who sold Tetiaroa to actor Marlon Brando in 1962. Brando came to Tahiti in 1960 to play Fletcher Christian in the MGM film *Mutiny on the* Bounty and ended up marrying his leading lady, Tarita Teriipaia. She and her family still run the small tourist resort on Motu Onetahi. Tarita and Marlon had two children, son Teihotu, born in 1965, and daughter Cheyenne, born in 1970.

The gunshot death of Dag Drollet, Cheyenne's ex-boyfriend and father of her son Tuki, at the Brando residence in Los Angeles in 1990 resulted in a 10-year prison sentence for Cheyenne's half-brother, Christian Brando, on a plea bargain. On Easter Sunday 1995 Cheyenne committed suicide and was buried next to Dag in the Drollet family crypt on Tahiti. These tragedies continue to haunt the Brando family, and the resort on Tetiaroa has been seriously neglected as a result. Marlon is seldom present on Tetiaroa these days, and when he is the atoll is closed to tourists.

MAIAO

TEPUATAU POINT

-N-

LAKE ROTO ITI

▲ (154 m)

VAVATUNU POINT

PAPAROA POINT

LAKE ROTO RAHI

LAGOON

AUPARIRUA POINT

0   1 km

APOOTOO PASS

Getting There

A reservation office (B.P. 2418, Papeete; tel. 82-63-03, fax 85-00-51) in the Air Moorea terminal at Faa'a International Airport arranges visits by air to Tetiaroa. A seven-hour day-trip including airfare, bird island tour, and lunch is CFP 22,500 pp. If you arrange this trip through your hotel, their commission will boot the price up a bit. To spend the night in a rustic bungalow at the **Tetiaroa Village Hôtel** you'll pay CFP 35,000/64,000 single/double for a one-night package, or CFP 40,000/74,000 for a two-night

package including air ticket, bungalow, meals, and excursion. But to be frank, this hotel is in need of major renovations and you'll be shocked to see traces of past glory slowly being eaten away by termites. So—though the price may suggest it—don't expect anything resembling a luxury resort, and come prepared to rough it.

Less expensive visits to Tetiaroa can be arranged at **Tahiti Mer et Loisirs** (B.P. 3488, Papeete; tel. 43-97-99, fax 43-33-68), in a houseboat on the Papeete waterfront opposite the post office. Their yacht cruises to the atoll are CFP 16,000 pp for one day (CFP 9500 without lunch or drinks), CFP 26,400 pp for two days, including snorkeling gear, trips ashore, and all meals. Longer stays are possible at CFP 10,000 pp for each additional day, all-inclusive. (In mid-1995 Marlon Brando won a lawsuit to prohibit "floating hotels" in the Tetiaroa lagoon, so overnight trips many now only be possible for those staying at the Tetiaroa Village Hôtel.)

Other yachts moored near Mer et Loisirs offer day-trips to Tetiaroa for as little as CFP 7000 (meals not included), but they don't depart according to any set schedule, so you just have to look around and ask. On all boat trips to Tetiaroa, be aware that up to three hours will be spent traveling each way and on a day-trip you'll only have about four hours on the atoll. The boat trip tends to be rough and many people throw up their fancy lunch on the way back to Papeete.

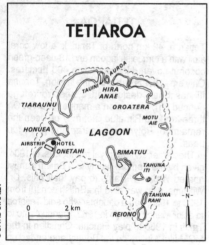

TETIAROA

TAUINI
TAUROA
HIRA
ANAE
TIARAUNU
OROATERA
MOTU
AIE
HONUEA
LAGOON
AIRSTRIP
HOTEL
ONETAHI
RIMATUU
TAHUNA
ITI
TAHUNA
RAHI
REIONO

0   2 km

-N-

© DAVID STANLEY

MOOREA
INTRODUCTION

Moorea, Tahiti's heart-shaped sister island, is clearly visible across the Sea of the Moon, just 16 km northwest of Papeete. This enticing island offers the white-sand beaches rare on Tahiti, plus long, deep bays, lush volcanic peaks, and a broad blue-green lagoon. Dino de Laurentiis filmed *The Bounty* here in 1983. Much more than Tahiti, Moorea is the laid-back South Sea isle of the travel brochures. And while Bora Bora has a reputation as Polynesia's most beautiful island, easily accessible Moorea seems to merit the distinction more.

With a population of just 9,000, Moorea lives a quiet, relaxed lifestyle; coconut, pineapple, and vanilla plantations alternate with pleasant resorts and the vegetation-draped dwellings of the inhabitants. Tourism is concentrated along the north coast around Paopao and Club Med; most of the locals live in the south. The accommodations are good and plentiful, while

weekly and monthly apartment rentals make even extended stays possible. Don't try to see it as a day-trip from Tahiti: this is a place to relax!

The Land
This triangular island is actually the surviving south rim of a volcano once 3,000 meters high. Moorea is twice as old as its Windward partner, Tahiti, and weathering is noticeably advanced. The two spectacular bays cutting into the north coast flank Mt. Rotui (899 meters), once Moorea's core. The crescent of jagged peaks facing these long northern bays is scenically superb.

Shark-tooth-shaped Mouaroa (880 meters) is a visual triumph, but Mt. Tohivea (1,207 meters) is higher. Polynesian chiefs were once buried in caves along the cliffs. Moorea's peaks protect the north and northwest coasts from the rain-bearing southeast trades; the drier climate and scenic beauty explain the profusion of hotels along this side of the island. Moorea is surrounded by a coral ring with several passes into the lagoon. Three *motus* enhance the lagoon, one off Afareaitu and two off Club Med.

Moorea's interior valley slopes are unusually rich, with large fruit and vegetable plantations and human habitation. At one time or another, coconuts, sugarcane, cotton, vanilla, coffee, rice, and pineapples have all been grown in the rich soil of Moorea's plantations. Stock farming and fishing are other occupations. Vegetables like taro, cucumbers, pumpkins, and lettuce, and fruit such as bananas, oranges, grapefruit, papaya, star apples, rambutans, avocados, tomatoes, mangos, limes, tangerines, and breadfruit make Moorea a veritable Garden of Eden.

History

Legend claims that Aimeho (or "Eimeo," as Captain Cook spelled it) was formed from the second dorsal fin of the fish that became Tahiti. The present name, Moorea, means "offshoot." A hole right through the summit of Mt. Mouaputa (830 meters) is said to have been made by the spear of the demigod Pai, who tossed it across from Tahiti to prevent Mt. Rotui (899 meters) from being carried off to Raiatea by Hiro, the god of thieves.

Captain Samuel Wallis was the European discoverer of the Windward Islands in 1767. After leaving Tahiti, he passed along the north coast of Moorea without landing. He named it Duke of York's Island. The first European visitors were botanist Joseph Banks, Lieutenant Gore, the surgeon William Monkhouse, Herman Sporing, and half a dozen sailors sent over by Captain Cook on 1 June 1769 to ob-

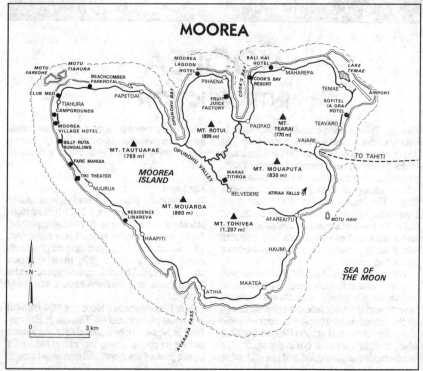

MOOREA

In June 1769 a party led by Captain Cook's botanist Joseph Banks became the first Europeans to land on Moorea. This fictitious engraving by a contemporary London artist shows "Mr. Banks receiving a Visit from the King of Duke of York's Island."

serve the transit of Venus. (The main observatory was, of course, on Point Venus, but the transit was also observed by officers on Moorea and on a small islet off the east coast of Tahiti.) The telescope was set up on the small Motu Irioa, halfway between Club Med and Opunohu Bay, and the observation was duly made on 3 June. Banks landed several times on the north coast at Papetoai. The party returned to Tahiti on 4 June. Captain Cook anchored in Opunohu Bay for one week in 1777, but he never visited the bay that today bears his name! His visit was uncharacteristically brutal, as he smashed the islanders' canoes and burned their homes when they refused to return a stolen goat.

In 1792 Pomare I conquered Moorea using arms obtained from the *Bounty* mutineers. Moorea had long been a traditional place of refuge for defeated Tahitian warriors, thus in 1808 Pomare II fled into exile here with a party of English missionaries after his bid to bring all Tahiti under his control failed. Moorea has a special place in the history of Christianity: here in 1812 the missionaries finally managed to convert Pomare II after 15 years of trying. On 14 February 1815, Patii, high priest of Oro, publicly accepted Protestantism and burned the old heathen idols at Papetoai, where the octagonal church is today. Shortly afterward the whole population followed Patii's example. The *marae* of Moorea were then abandoned and the Opunohu Valley depopulated. The first Tahitian translation of part of the Bible was printed on Moorea in 1817. From this island Protestantism spread throughout the South Pacific.

After Pomare II finally managed to reconquer Tahiti in 1815 with missionary help (the main reason for his "conversion"), Moorea again became a backwater. American novelist Herman Melville visited Moorea in 1842 and worked with other beachcombers on a sweet-potato farm in Maatea. His book *Omoo* contains a marvelous description of his tour of the island. Cotton and coconut plantations were created on Moorea in the 19th century, followed by vanilla and coffee in the 20th, but only with the advent of the travel industry has Moorea become more than a beautiful backdrop for Tahiti.

Orientation

If you arrive by ferry you'll get off at Vaiare, four km south of Temae Airport. Your hotel may be at Maharepa (Hôtel Bali Hai), Paopao (Bali Hai Club, Motel Albert), Pihaena (Moorea Lagoon Hôtel), or Tiahura (Club Med, the campgrounds, Moorea Village Hôtel), all on the north coast. The Paopao hotels enjoy better scenery, but the beach is far superior at Tiahura.

The PKs (kilometer stones) on Moorea are measured in both directions from PK 0 at the access road to Temae Airport. They're numbered up to PK 35 along the north coast via Club Med and up to PK 24 along the south coast via Afareaitu, meeting at Haapiti halfway around the island. Our circle-island tour and the accommodations and restaurant listings below begin at Vaiare Wharf and go counterclockwise around the island in each category.

SIGHTS

Northeast Moorea

You'll probably arrive on Moorea at **Vaiare Wharf,** which is officially PK 4 on the 59-km road around the island. To the north is the **Sofitel la Ora** (PK 1.5), Moorea's most sophisticated resort. If you have your own transport, stop here for a look around and to see the colorful fish swimming below the la Ora's wharf. It's also enjoyable to walk north along the beach from this hotel or even to go snorkeling. At PK 1 on the main road, high above the la Ora, is a fine **lookout** over the deep passage, romantically named the Sea of the Moon, between Tahiti and Moorea.

One of the few good public beaches on Moorea is at **Temae,** about a km down a gravel road to the right a bit before you reach the airport access road. Watch out for black spiny sea urchins here. There's good snorkeling opposite Lilishop Boutique at **Maharepa** (look for the gaudy pareus hanging outside).

Around Cook's Bay

On the grounds of the American-owned **Hôtel Bali Hai** at PK 5 are historic replicas of anchors lost by captains Bougainville and Cook in the 18th century. Just past the Bali Hai on the mountain side of the road is the "White House," the stately mansion of a former vanilla plantation, now used as a pareu salesroom.

At the entrance to Cook's Bay (PK 7) is the **Galerie Aad Van der Heyde** (tel. 56-14-22), as much a museum as a gallery. Aad's paintings hang outside in the flower-filled courtyard; inside are his black-pearl jewelry, a large collection of Marquesan sculpture, and artifacts from around the Pacific.

Paopao boasts a gendarmerie, pharmacy, three banks, gas station, municipal market, hotels, and restaurants. At the **Moorea Pearl Center** (admission free; tel. 56-13-13), opposite Club Bali Hai in Paopao (PK 8.5), are exquisite black pearls and more Polynesian woodcarvings.

A rough dirt road up to the Belvédère begins just west of the bridge at Paopao (PK 9) and it's nice to hike up it past the pineapple plantations. On the west side of Cook's Bay a km, farther along the north-coast highway, is a **Catholic church** (PK 10); an interesting altar painting with Polynesian angels was done by the Swedish artist Peter Heyman in 1948.

It's possible to visit the Distillerie de Moorea **fruit-juice factory** (B.P. 23, Moorea; tel. 56-11-33, fax 56-21-52), up off the main road at PK 12, Monday to Thursday 0800-1130. Monday to Wednesday they'll show you the pineapple processing; Thursday is grapefruit or papaya day.

an old photo of
Mouaroa across
Cook's Bay, Moorea

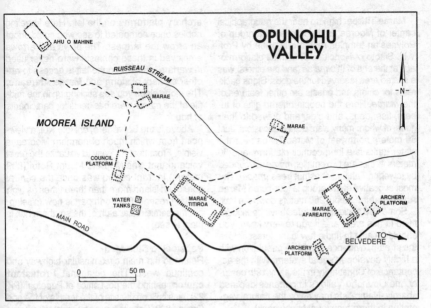

OPUNOHU VALLEY

MOOREA ISLAND

AHU O MAHINE

RUISSEAU STREAM

MARAE

MARAE

COUNCIL PLATFORM

WATER TANKS

MARAE TITIROA

MAIN ROAD

ARCHERY PLATFORM

MARAE AFAREAITO

ARCHERY PLATFORM

TO BELVEDERE

0   50 m

-N-

Aside from the excellent papaya, grapefruit, and pineapple juices made from local fruits, the factory produces apple, orange, and passion fruit juices from imported concentrate, with no preservatives added. They also make 40-proof brandies (carambola or "star fruit," ginger, grapefruit, mango, orange, and pineapple flavors) and 25-proof liqueurs (coconut, ginger, and pineapple varieties). These are sold to the public at the Accueil counter and if they think you might buy a bottle, they'll invite you to sample the brews.

Opunohu Bay to le Belvédère
The **Moorea Lagoon Hôtel** at PK 14 is the only large hotel between Paopao and Tiahura. An overgrown trail up **Mt. Rotui** begins opposite the "Faimano Village" accommodations nearby. Ask a local to point out the way. Reader Greg Sawyer of Lafayette, Indiana, sent us this:

The trail up Mt. Rotui is quite strenuous but you're rewarded with billion-dollar views. It should be attempted in fair weather only, as it follows a razorback ridge quite narrow in places. In the rain it would be dangerous. Start very early

and allow most of a day to really enjoy the trail and views (though fit people could push it through in four to five hours return). Mt. Rotui is Moorea's second-highest peak, and lies alone between the two bays on the north shore. There's little shade and no water but there are a couple of fixed ropes near the top at a couple of short steep pitches. Take care. The trail is not maintained but it's easy to follow once found. Just get to and stay on the ridgeline.

Shrimp are bred in large basins at the head of Opunohu Bay (PK 18). A paved road up the pineapple-filled **Opunohu Valley** to the Belvédère begins here: 1.5 km to the connecting road from Cook's Bay, another two km to Marae Titiroa, then one more steep km up to the lookout. On the way, you'll pass Moorea's agricultural high school. This worthy institution, with students from all the islands of Tahiti-Polynesia, has hundreds of hectares planted in pineapples, vanilla, coffee, fruit trees, decorative flowers, and native vegetables.

Marae Titiroa, high up near the geographical center of Moorea, is the largest of a group of Polynesian temples restored in 1969 by Prof. Y.H. Sinoto of Honolulu. The small platform or *ahu* at the end of this *marae* (and the others) was a sacred area reserved for the gods. Stone backrests for chiefs and priests are other features of the *marae*. Here the people offered gifts of tubers, fish, dogs, and pigs, and prayed to their gods, of whom many were deified ancestors. Just 50 meters northwest of Marae Titiroa near the water tanks is a long council platform, and 50 meters farther are two smaller *marae* surrounded by towering Tahitian chestnut trees *(mape)*. The most evocative of the group is four-tiered **Marae Ahu o Mahine,** about 250 meters down the trail.

Some 500 ancient structures have been identified in this area, and if you're very keen, you should be able to find a few in the forest across the stream, evidence of a large population with a highly developed social system. With the acceptance of Christianity in the early 19th century, the Opunohu Valley's importance declined sharply. Naturalists may enjoy the natural vegetation in there (you must bushwhack).

Continue up the main road from Marae Titiroa about 200 meters and watch for some stone

Moorea's Rotui rises above a country road.

archery platforms on the left. Here kneeling nobles once competed to see who could shoot an arrow the farthest. The bows and arrows employed in these contests were never used in warfare. Just up on the left is access to another archery platform and **Marae Afareaito.** The stone slabs you see sticking up in the middle of the *marae* were backrests for participants of honor.

Above is the **Belvédère,** or Roto Nui, a viewpoint from which much of northern Moorea is visible. From here it's easy to visualize the great volcano that was Moorea. Mount Rotui (899 meters) in front of you was once the central core of an island more than three times as high as the present. The north part is now missing, but the semicircular arch of the southern half is plain to see.

Papetoai to Club Med
Return to the main circuminsular highway and continue west. The octagonal **Protestant church,** behind the post office at Papetoai (PK 22), was built on the site of the temple of the god Oro in 1822. Despite having been rebuilt several times, the church is known as "the oldest European building still in use in the South Pacific."

As the road begins to curve around the northwest corner of Moorea, you pass a number of large resort hotels, including the **Beachcomber Parkroyal** (PK 24), **Club Med** (PK 26), and the **Moorea Village Hôtel** (PK 27); only Club Med forbids you to walk through their grounds to the beach. It's possible to snorkel out to Tarahu and Tiahuru *motus* from this beach; recreation people at the Beachcomber Parkroyal and Moorea Beach Hôtel could also ferry you over. Try feeding bread to the fish. There's excellent reef break surfing here, too. In **Le Petit Village** shopping mall, across the street from Club Med, are a tourist information kiosk, bank, grocery store, snack bar, gas station, and many tourist shops.

Southern Moorea
The south coast of Moorea is much quieter than the north. You'll drive for kilometers through the open coconut plantations past several unspoiled villages and scenic vistas. At PK 31 is **Tiki Theater,** described below under "Entertainment." You could stop for a excellent upmarket lunch (1200-1400) or a drink at **Résidence Linareva**

(PK 34) (see below). At PK 35/24, Haapiti, the kilometer numbering begins its descent to Temae Airport. The twin-towered **Église de la Sainte Famille** (1891) at Haapiti was once the head church of the Catholic mission on the island.

Tiny Motu Hahi lies just off **Afareaitu** (PK 9), the administrative center of Moorea. The London Missionary Society originally had its Academy of the South Seas here. On 30 June 1817, at the missionary printing works at Afareaitu, King Pomare II ceremonially printed the first page of the first book ever published on a South Pacific island, a Tahitian translation of the Gospel of St. Luke. Before the press was moved to Huahine a year later, over 9,000 books totaling more than half a million pages were printed at Afareaitu!

Hike an hour up the **Afareaitu Valley** from the old Protestant church (1912) to a high waterfall, which cascades down a sheer cliff into a pool. You can drive a car two-thirds of the way up the valley. Park at the point where a normal car would have problems and hike up the road to the right. When this road begins to climb steeply, look for a well-beaten footpath on the right which will take you directly to the falls. You'll need a bit of intuition to find the unmarked way on your own.

The access road to a different waterfall, **Atiraa Falls**, is a little beyond the hospital at Afareaitu. Admission to this one is CFP 200 pp, but at least the way is clearly marked. It's a 30-minute walk from the parking area.

Across the Island

An excellent day hike involves taking a morning *truck* to Vaiare Wharf, then hiking over the mountains to Paopao. From there you can catch another *truck* back to your accommodation, or try hitching. The shaded three-hour trail, partly marked by red, white, and green paint dabbed on tree and rock, does take perseverance, however, as Tahiti Tourisme hasn't done any trail maintenance in years. After rains the trail can be muddy and there are a few very steep ascents and descents.

Take the road inland beside Snack Chez Meno, about 50 meters south of the first bridge south of the Vaiare ferry wharf. As you follow the dirt road up the valley, you'll take two forks to the right, then you'll pass some houses and continue straight up along a small stream. Just before the end of the overgrown jeep track, look for a trail up the hill to the left. All of the locals know about this trail and if you say "Paopao?" to them in a questioning way, they'll point you in the right direction.

When you reach the divide, go a short distance south along the ridge past some barbed wire to a super viewpoint over the pineapple plantations behind Paopao. On a clear day the rounded double peak of Orohena, Tahiti's highest, is visible, plus the whole interior of Moorea. This rigorous hike is also worth doing simply to see a good cross section of the vegetation. Don't miss it, but do take water and wear sturdy shoes.

SPORTS AND RECREATION

The waters of northern Moorea are the realm of **M.U.S.T. Plongée Scuba Diving,** or Moorea Underwater Scuba-diving Tahiti (B.P. 336, Moorea; tel. 56-17-32, fax 56-29-18), on the dock behind the Cook's Bay Resort Hotel. They offer diving daily (except Monday) at 0900 and 1400 for CFP 5000 for one dive, CFP 22,500 for five dives. Divemaster Philippe Molle, author of a well-known French book on scuba diving, knows 20 different spots in and outside the reef. Philippe's slogan is: "Diving with M.U.S.T. is a must!"

Bernard and Collette Begliomini's **Bathy's Club** (B.P. 1019, Papetoai; tel. 56-21-07), at the Beachcomber Parkroyal, offers scuba diving for CFP 5000, plus PADI certification courses. Both the M.U.S.T. and Bathy's Club dive shops specialize in underwater fish, eel, and shark feeding. Sometimes the swarm of fish becomes so thick the guide is lost from sight, yet as the resident shark scatters the mass of fish to steal the bait, the divemaster is seen again patting *le requin* as it passes!

Marc Quattrini's **Scubapiti** (B.P. 1002, Moorea; tel. 56-20-38, tel. 56-29-25), at Résidence Les Tipaniers, offers scuba diving daily at 0900 and 1430 (CFP 4000). Rather than put on a show, Marc keeps things natural on his cave dives, canyon dives, and drift dives.

The "Activities Nautiques" kiosk on the wharf at the **Beachcomber Parkroyal** (tel. 56-19-19) has a one-hour glass-bottom boat ride (CFP 1200 pp), which leaves at 1000 and 1400. A two-hour lagoon cruise is CFP 2600. For more excitement hire a lagoon Jet Ski at CFP 6500 for half an hour, CFP 10,000 for one hour; or try your hand at parasailing.

For horseback riding try **Rupe-Rupe Ranch** (tel. 56-17-93), on the mountain side just south of the Hôtel Hibiscus. To take one of their 12 horses along the beach for an hour is CFP 2000. Group rides commence at 0830, 1400, and 1600, but it's best to call ahead. **Tiahura Ranch** (tel. 56-28-55) across the highway offers more of the same.

PRACTICALITIES

ACCOMMODATIONS

Camping

One of the nicest campgrounds in the South Pacific is **Backpackers' Beach Club** (tel. 56-15-18), beside the Hôtel Hibiscus, just south of Club Med (PK 26). Also known as "Chez Nelson et Josiane" and "Tumoana Village," it's beautifully set in a coconut grove right on the beach. The camping charge is CFP 700 pp, with toilets, showers, refrigerator, and good communal cooking facilities provided. No tents are for rent, but the 10 two-bed "dormitory" rooms go for CFP 1000 pp (CFP 1200 for one night). The five beach cabins with shared bath are CFP 2200 single or double (CFP 2500 for one night); four larger *fares* near the office are CFP 2500 single or double (CFP 3000 for one night). They also have three larger bungalows with kitchen and private bath at CFP 6000 double. For CFP 300 pp (minimum of seven) they'll ferry you across to a *motu* for snorkeling. Josiane is a little eccentric and can be rather reserved at first, but she has a heart of gold. The place is clean, quiet, breezy, spacious, and well equipped, but unfortunately, however, there have been reports of theft here, so don't leave valuables unattended or within reach of an open window at night.

A second, smaller campground (CFP 500 pp) is just a little south of Backpackers' Beach Club, near the Moorea Village Hôtel. **Backpackers' Paradise** (tel. 56-14-47), also known as "Moorea Camping" and "Chez Viri et Claude," faces the same white-sand beach and has nine four-bed dorms at CFP 800 pp (CFP 1000 for one night), plus another nine double rooms in a long building at CFP 2000 single or double (CFP 2500 for one night). The five beachfront bungalows with fridge are CFP 4000 single or double. Communal kitchen and washing facilities are provided and they'll loan you snorkeling gear and perhaps even a canoe. Bus trips around the island are CFP 1000 pp if at least six people sign up and they can also take you to a *motu*. Several readers wrote in recommending this place. Both campgrounds are simple, but great for young low-budget travelers and other adventurers. A large grocery store (with cold beer) is between the two camping grounds.

Budget Accommodations

Motel Albert (Albert Haring, tel./fax 56-12-76), up on the hill opposite Club Bali Hai at Paopao (PK 8.5), catches splendid views across Cook's Bay. The eight older units with double beds are CFP 3000 single or double, CFP 4000 triple (two-night minimum stay). The 10 larger houses, accommodating up to four persons each, are CFP 6000. Monthly rates are CFP 70,000 double. Each unit has cooking facilities, and several stores are nearby. Despite an oversupply of mosquitoes and undersupply of hot water, it's excellent value and often full (try to make reservations).

The three bungalows behind **Boutique Dina** (Dina Dhieux, tel. 56-10-39) at Pihaena, a km east of the Moorea Lagoon Hôtel, are CFP 4500 triple, CFP 5000 for up to five; subtract CFP 500 a day for the weekly rate. Cooking facilities are provided and the bathroom is communal. It's easy to drive past this place, so watch for the pareu display.

Several small places near the Moorea Lagoon Hôtel (PK 14) rent more expensive bungalows. **Chez Nani** (Maeva Bougues, B.P. 117, Papeete; tel. 56-19-99) on the west side of the hotel has three thatched bungalows with kitchenettes for CFP 7000 single or double. The signposted **Faimano Village** (Hinano Feidel, B.P. 1676, Papeete; tel. 56-10-20, fax 56-36-47) next to Chez Nani has six bungalows with cooking facilities at CFP 10,500 for up to six persons with private bath, CFP 7500/8000 double/triple with shared bath (two-night minimum stay). **Chez Francine** (Francine Lumen, tel. 56-13-24), 400 meters farther west (no sign), has a two-room house at CFP 6000 double with kitchenette or CFP 5000 double without. There's no grocery store near the Moorea Lagoon—the nearest is by the bridge in Paopao.

Hôtel Résidence Tiahura (William Estall, B.P. 1068, Papetoai; tel. 56-15-45, fax 56-37-67), at PK 25 Tiahura on the mountain side just east of Club Med, is a five-minute walk from the beach. One of the six bungalows without kitchenette is CFP 4500 single or double, one of the six with kitchenette CFP 5500 double. All units have fridge and private bath. It's friendly but has an abandoned feel.

Billy Ruta Bungalows (tel. 56-12-54) is right on the beach at PK 28, Tiahura. The 12 thatched A-frame bungalows begin at CFP 4000 double without kitchenette, CFP 5000 double with kitchenette. There's disco dancing here on Friday and Saturday nights from 2230. Billy drives the local school and church *truck* and is a very friendly guy.

Fare Mato Tea (Ronald Cabral, B.P. 1111, Papetoai; tel. 56-14-36), on the beach just south of Billy Ruta (PK 29), is okay if you're in a group: CFP 8000 for four, CFP 10,000 for six (minimum stay two nights). All eight large thatched bungalows on the spacious grounds have full cooking facilities and private bath.

At the south end of the west coast strip (PK 30) is **Fare Manuia** (Jeanne Salmon, tel. 56-26-17) with five thatched bungalows with cooking facilities at CFP 7000 for up to four people, CFP 8500 for up to six people.

Chez Pauline (Pauline Teariki, tel. 56-11-26) at PK 9, Afareaitu, is between the two stores near the church (no sign). The seven rooms with double beds and shared bath in this lovely old colonial house run CFP 2500 single or double, CFP 4000 triple. A picturesque restaurant (closed Sunday), with Pauline's tikis on display, rounds out this establishment, which would have great atmosphere if it weren't for the eccentric manner of the proprietors. Dinner here is around CFP 2000 (fish and Tahitian vegetables).

Medium-Priced Accommodations

The locally owned **Cook's Bay Resort Hotel** (B.P. 30, Paopao; tel. 56-10-50, fax 56-29-18) is by the highway at the entrance to Cook's Bay. You can't miss this mock-colonial edifice constructed in 1985, with its false-front Waikiki feel (even the manager is Hawaiian). The 76 rooms begin at CFP 8400 single or double, 9900 triple with fan, though the rates seem to fluctuate according to what the market will bear, so you might call ahead to find out if they have a special going. Though it isn't on the beach, you can swim off the pier in front of the restaurant and there's a swimming pool. Moorea's top dive shop is on the premises and all the usual resort activities are available. A sunset cruise aboard the *Fat Cat* is offered every other afternoon at 1630 (CFP 500).

Right next door to the Cook's Bay Resort (and under the same ownership) is the **Kaveka Beach Club** (B.P. 13, Temae, Moorea; tel. 56-18-30), at PK 7.5, Paopao. The 24 thatched bungalows run CFP 9500/11,000/12,000 single/double/triple plus tax; the breakfast and dinner meal plan is CFP 3200 pp extra.

The **Moorea Lagoon Hôtel** (B.P. 11, Moorea; tel. 56-37-32, fax 56-26-25) at PK 14, Pihaena, is CFP 11,000/12,000/15,000 single/double/triple for one of the 40 thatched garden bungalows (beach bungalows 50% more). A small gambling casino is on the premises (Tuesday to Saturday 2000-0100; passport required). This hotel, along with the Te Puna Bel Air Hôtel on Tahiti, is owned by the local Rey family. The beach is fine—have fun if your tour company drops you here.

The **Moorea Beach Club** (B.P. 1017, Papetoai; tel. 56-15-48, fax 56-25-70), formerly the Climate de France, is the first hotel on the white sandy shores of the Tiahura tourist strip. The 40 a/c rooms with fridge begin at CFP 10,400 single, CFP 11,800 double or triple, plus CFP 3800 pp extra for breakfast and dinner (if

profile of Moorea

desired). The more expensive bungalows have cooking facilities. The less expensive units are on two floors, so you will have someone above or below. Outrigger canoes, tennis, snorkeling, and fishing gear are free.

Résidence Les Tipaniers (B.P. 1002, Moorea; tel. 56-12-67, fax 56-29-25) is cramped around the reception, but better as you approach the beach. The 22 rooms are CFP 7800/10,000/11,500 single/double/triple, while the 11 thatched bungalows with kitchen are a few thousand francs extra. They'll shuttle you over to a *motu* for snorkeling free. This hotel and its Italian restaurant have a good reputation, and there's a resident divemaster.

The **Hôtel Hibiscus** (B.P. 1009, Papetoai; tel. 56-12-20, fax 56-20-69), beside Club Med (PK 26), offers 29 thatched garden bungalows beneath the coconut palms at CFP 10,000 for up to two adults and two children (CFP 12,000 with kitchenette). There's a two-night minimum stay and weekly rates are available. Late-night party noise from Club Med can be a nuisance.

The 48-unit **Moorea Village Noa Noa** (B.P. 1008, Moorea; tel. 56-10-02, fax 56-22-11), also called "Fare Gendron," at PK 27 has fan-cooled thatched bungalows for CFP 7000/8000 single/double, or CFP 10,500 for up to four people. For a kitchen in your unit add CFP 3500 to the price (all units have fridges). To be on the beach is another CFP 25000. The breakfast and dinner plan is CFP 3500 pp. Saturday at 1900 there's a barbecue; the Tahitian feast with Polynesian dancing is Sunday at 1230. There are lots of free activities, such as the canoe trip to the *motu,* outrigger canoes, tennis, snorkeling, swimming pool, bicycles, etc. This place is somewhat of a hangout for local Tahitians and the management leaves a lot to be desired.

Résidence Linareva (B.P. 1, Haapiti; tel. 56-15-35, fax 56-25-25) sits amid splendid mountain scenery at PK 34 on the wild side of the island. Prices begin at CFP 7200/8200/9800 single/double/triple, with 20% weekly discounts. Each of the seven units is unique, but there are no cooking facilities. Linareva's floating seafood restaurant, the *Tamarii Moorea I,* is an old ferryboat that once plied between Moorea and Tahiti. Colorful reef fish swim around the dock.

Upmarket Accommodations

The easy going **Sofitel la Ora** (B. P. 28, Temae; tel. 56-12-90, fax 56-12-91), at PK 1.5 between Vaiare and the airport, is *the* place if you want luxury and don't give a damn about the price. The 80 deluxe thatched bungalows begin at CFP 21,100 single or double (children under 12 free). Breakfast and dinner are CFP 4800 pp extra together. Unfortunately, the service deteriorates when large groups are present. On the shore is a restaurant with its own open-air aquarium (free), and the adjacent beach is one of the best on the island, with a splendid view of Tahiti.

The 63-room **Hôtel Bali Hai** (B.P. 26, Moorea; tel. 56-13-59, fax 56-19-22) at PK 5, Maharepa, caters mainly to American tour groups staying three, four, or seven nights. The cheapest rooms are CFP 9500/14,000/16,000 single/double/triple (children under 12 free), bungalows 50% more and up. For breakfast and dinner add CFP 3900 pp extra. Rides on the Bali Hai's new thatched catamaran *Liki Tiki* are free for guests. The Bali Hai was founded by the so-called Bali Hai Boys, Hugh, Jay, and Muk. The happy-go-lucky tale of this gang of three's arrival on Moorea in 1959 is posted in the lobby, if you're interested.

Club Bali Hai (B.P. 8, Temae; tel. 56-16-25, fax 56-13-27) at PK 8.5, Paopao, has 20 rooms in the main two-story building at CFP 9000 single or double, CFP 10,500 triple, and 19 beachfront or overwater bungalows at CFP 17,500 or 23,500 double. Only the bungalows include cooking facilities, but all rooms have a spectacular view of Cook's Bay. Many units have been sold to affluent Americans on a time-share basis, with each owner getting two weeks a year at the Club. It's homey, clean, and not at all pretentious. Enjoy half-price drinks during happy hour at the lagoonside bar Tuesday and Friday 1800-1900. We've heard Club Bali Hai welcomes visiting yachties warmly.

The 150-room **Moorea Beachcomber Parkroyal** (B.P. 1019, Papetoai; tel. 56-19-19, fax 56-18-88) at PK 24, takes the cake as the most expensive hotel on Moorea. Rooms in the main building start at CFP 24,000/26,000/31,000 single/double/triple—much too much. For an overwater bungalow, tack on an additional 50%. The Beachcomber Parkroyal, built in 1987, was purchased for US$13.5 million in 1989 by Japanese interests that have since spent further millions of dollars upgrading the place.

Club Méditerranée (B.P. 1010, Moorea; tel. 56-17-51, fax 56-19-51) at PK 26 has 350 simple fan-cooled bungalows. You can reserve one by paying CFP 14,000 pp a day (double occupancy) at the Club Med office in the Vaima Center, Papeete (B.P. 575, Papeete; tel. 42-96-99). The price includes breakfast, lunch, and dinner, and a wide range of regimented activities (including one scuba dive a day), but no airport transfers. Unlimited beer and wine come with lunch and dinner, but other drinks are expensive and laundry charges will knock your socks off! The full PADI scuba diving center here is for guests only. Sunbathing in the raw is permitted on the small *motu* just offshore. Club Med's for you if nonstop activity is a high priority, otherwise all the canned entertainment can be to the detriment of peace at night, and occasional helicopter landings beside the restaurant often interrupt afternoon naps. Clocks inside the village are set ahead to give guests an extra hour in the sun. Club Med's G.O.s *(gentils organisateurs)* tend to resist the unusual or nonroutine (such as requesting a specific room), so try to "go with the flow" (i.e., conform). It's not a "swinging singles club" anymore, but rather a haven for couples where singles can also be found. No visitors are allowed.

FOOD

Aside from the hotel restaurants, table hoppers are catered for by a mixed bag of eateries along the east side of Cook's Bay. **Le Cocotier Restaurant** (closed Sunday; tel. 56-12-10) at PK 4, Maharepa, offers a number of reasonably priced fish dishes on a blackboard menu at the entrance.

The upscale **Restaurant Chez Michel et Jackie** (tel. 56-11-08), at PK 5, on the main road just east of the Hôtel Bali Hai, features French cooking and big two-person pizzas (from CFP 1850).

Le Pécheur Restaurant (tel. 56-36-12), also at Maharepa, near the pharmacy at the east entrance to Cook's Bay, has an excellent reputation for its seafood dishes which begin around

a charming Polynesian woman

ARCHIVES NATIONALES, SECTION OUTRE-MER, FRANCE

CFP 1500. If you lack transport, they'll come and pick you up. The overwater **Fisherman's Wharf Restaurant** at the Kaveka Beach Club also serves excellent seafood.

Snack Te Honu Iti (closed Tuesday; tel. 56-19-84), at PK 9 near the municipal market at the head of Cook's Bay, lists a good selection of dishes on their blackboard, such as hamburgers, tuna burgers, and a *plat du jour,* all of which you consume on their airy terrace. The papaya, coconut, and banana milkshakes are served warm! A food *truck* parks in front of the market at Paopao in the evening.

The restaurant at **Club Bali Hai** (tel. 56-16-25) at Paopao is surprisingly reasonable, so wander in and peruse the posted menu. The snack bar down by the dock serves a wicked hot dog! Happy hour at the bar is 1830-1930 (half-price drinks).

Alfredo's Restaurante Italiano, on the inland side of the road by Cook's Bay, a few hundred meters south of Club Bali Hai, has some of the island's best pizza and pasta, plus a few fish and meat dishes.

Restaurant Fare Manava (closed Wednesday; tel. 56-14-24), also known as "Chez Monique et Conny," at the inland end of Paopao Bay, has a pleasant dining room overlooking Cook's Bay. Prices are reasonable (superb mahimahi steamed with ginger at CFP 1400) and there's excellent Chinese food too. It's probably Moorea's best restaurant for the money.

Near Club Med
Tropical Iceberg (tel. 56-29-53) in Le Petit Village shopping mall opposite Club Med has ice cream sundaes (CFP 650), and it's also a good place for breakfast with bacon and eggs for CFP 350 (served 0900-1100 only). **Le Dauphin Restaurant,** attached to Tropical Iceberg, has pizza from CFP 950 and fish dishes from CFP 1600 (Tuesday to Sunday 1130-1430/1830-2130). Good reports.

Better pizza, reasonable fish dishes, and ocean views are available at beachfront **Caesario Pizzeria** (closed Monday) at the Hôtel Hibiscus. **Pâtisserie Le Sylesie II** (tel. 56-20-45) is next door.

Groceries
If you've got access to cooking facilities, there are lots of grocery stores spread all around Moorea. The largest and cheapest is **Toa Moorea,** a km south of the Vaiare ferry wharf (Monday to Saturday 0800-2000, Sunday 0700-1300).

Don't make a special trip to the **municipal market** at Paopao, however, as all you're likely to find there is some sliced fish and a few pineapples, limes, papaya, and grapefruit. Fresh produce is much harder to obtain on Moorea than it is on Tahiti, so buy things when you see them and plan your grocery shopping carefully. Ask the stores what time the bread arrives, then be there promptly. The hybrid lime-grapefruit being developed on Moorea has a thick green skin and a really unique taste.

ENTERTAINMENT

Moorea's top nonhotel disco with live music is **Le Tabou** (tel. 45-02-62), directly across the street from the Moorea Lagoon Hôtel (PK 14). It all happens on Friday and Saturday nights from around 2200 (admission CFP 500-1000).

The disco at **Billy Ruta Bungalows** (tel. 56-12-54), at PK 28, Tiahura, is a nice, very Polynesian scene with a good music mix of Tahitian, French, American, reggae, etc. It's a fun place which gets very busy with some very talented dancers (Friday and Saturday from 2230).

See **Tahitian dancing** in the Sofitel Ia Ora's La Pérouse Restaurant (tel. 56-17-61) on Tuesday, Thursday, and Saturday at 2000. The Tahitian show at the Moorea Beachcomber Parkroyal (tel. 56-19-19) is on Wednesday and Saturday nights. Both Hôtel Bali Hai (tel. 56-13-59) and the Moorea Village Hôtel (tel. 56-10-02) present Polynesian dancing Sunday at lunchtime. The Tahitian feasts which come with the shows cost CFP 4000 and up, but you can often observe the action from the bar for the price of a drink.

Moorea has its own instant culture village, the **Tiki Theater** (B.P. 1016, Moorea; tel. 56-18-97, fax 43-20-06) at PK 31, Haapiti. The doors are open Tuesday to Saturday 1100-1500, with a charge of CFP 1000 to visit the village and see the small dance show at 1300. The guided tour of the village is informative and the staff enthusiastic, but sometimes they're a little disorganized so you might obtain some understanding about the show time before parting with your francs. Lunch is available in their a la carte restaurant. Line fishing from a *pirogue* is CFP 1500 extra. Tuesday, Thursday, Friday and Saturday nights at 1800 there's a big sunset show with a *tamaaraa* buffet and open bar (CFP 5800, reservations required). If you're not hungry it's possible to pay CFP 2000 for the show alone at 2000. If you've got CFP 110,000 *(sic)* to blow, a "royal" Tahitian wedding can be arranged at the village (bring your own husband/wife). The ceremony lasts two hours, from 1600 to sunset, and is a private party, with the village closed to the public. The bridegroom arrives by canoe and the newlyweds are carried around in procession by four "warriors." Otherwise there's the less extravagant "princely" wedding for CFP 80,000, photos included. Yes, it's kinda tacky, but that's show biz! (Such weddings are not legally binding.)

SERVICES AND INFORMATION

Services
The Banque Socredo, Banque de Polynésie, and Banque de Tahiti are near the Hôtel Bali Hai at Maharepa. The Westpac Bank is in Le Petit Village shopping mall opposite Club Med. None of these banks are open on Saturday.

The main **post office** (Monday to Thursday 0700-1500, Friday 0700-1400) is near the banks at Maharepa. Branch post offices are found at Afareaitu and Papetoai.

The **Tahiti Parfum** shop (tel. 56-34-61) in Le Petit Village will wash and dry six kg of laundry for CFP 1400 (same-day service if you get your wash in early). Look for the Lav'matic sign.

Information
The **Moorea Visitors Bureau** (B.P. 1019, Papetoai; tel. 56-29-09) has a poorly-marked kiosk next to the gas station in front of Le Petit Village (Monday to Saturday 0900-1800).

The boutique at the Hôtel Bali Hai offers a book-exchange service.

Health
The island's main hospital (tel. 56-11-97) is at Afareaitu.

Dr. Hervé Paulus (tel. 56-10-09) is at Le Petit Village near Club Med. Dr. Christian Jonville (tel. 56-32-32), who has his office behind the Banque de Polynésie at Maharepa, not far from the Hôtel Bali Hai, is fluent in English. In the same complex is a private dentist, Dr. Jean-Marc Thurillet (tel. 56-32-44). The island's pharmacy (tel. 56-10-51) is nearby.

TRANSPORT

Air Moorea and **Air Tahiti** (both tel. 56-10-34) are based at Moorea Temae Airport. Details of the air and ferry services from Tahiti are given in the "Getting Around" section of the main Introduction.

Trucks meet the ferries at Vaiare Wharf five times a day, charging CFP 200 to anywhere on the island. Although they don't go right around the island, the northern and southern routes meet at Club Med, so you could theoretically effect a circumnavigation by changing there, provided you caught the last *truck* back to Vaiare at 1545 from Club Med.

In mid-1994 an eight-seater minibus service along Moorea's north coast was launched by **Moorea Nui** (tel. 56-12-54). Minibuses depart the Sofitel Ia Ora and Résidence Linareva about every two hours Monday to Saturday (CFP 200 OW, children CFP 100, baggage CFP 50).

A taxi on Moorea is actually a minibus with a white letter **T** inside a red circle. Hitching is wearing thin with Moorea motorists, although it's still quite possible. If you need the ride you'll probably get it; just be prepared to do some walking.

Car Rentals and Tours
If you're staying at one of the luxury hotels, you'll do better dealing with a kiosk on the highway for rental cars and circle-island tours, as reservations desks inside the hotels tack on commissions.

There are four gasoline stations around Moorea: Mobil near Vaiare Wharf, Total at the airport access road, another Mobil near Motel Albert at Paopao, and another Total opposite Club Med. The maximum speed limit is 60 km per hour.

Pacificar (tel. 56-16-02) at Vaiare Wharf, the airport, and seven other locations on Moorea has cars at CFP 5800 for 24 hours, unlimited mileage and insurance included. Pacificar also rents scooters at CFP 3500 and bicycles for CFP 1000.

Good rates for rental cars and bicycles are also obtained at **Albert Activities Center** (B.P. 77, Moorea; tel. 56-13-53, fax 56-10-42), with locations opposite the Hôtel Bali Hai, Club Bali Hai, and Club Med. Unlimited-mileage cars begin at CFP 6000 for 24 hours, CFP 11,000 for 48 hours, including insurance.

Pierre Rent-A-Car (Pierre Danloue, tel. 56-12-58), which represents Avis on Moorea, has an office at the Total service station on the airport access road (and elsewhere). At CFP 7800 for 24 hours with unlimited mileage, plus CFP 1300 insurance, they're extremely expensive.

Local Tours
Albert Activities (tel. 56-13-53) runs a five-hour motorized aluminum canoe ride right around Moorea with a stop for snorkeling (gear provided), departing the Hôtel Bali Hai dock every Monday, Wednesday, and Friday at 0930 (CFP 4000 pp, minimum of four). For a free pickup inquire at one of the three Albert Activities centers around Moorea, or call the hotel at tel. 56-13-59.

Albert Activities does a three-hour circle-island bus tour daily at 0900 (CFP 1500) and a two-hour interior-island tour to the Belvédère at 1330

(CFP 1500). If you take both tours on the same day it will be just CFP 2000 (lunch not included).

Ron's Tours (B.P. 1097, Papetoai; tel. 56-35-80) specializes in hiking tours and mountain climbing, such as an ascent of Mt. Mouaputa (CFP 3500 pp, minimum of eight participants). Contact them through the Moorea Visitors Bureau kiosk in front of Le Petit Village.

Moorea Airport

Moorea Temae Airport (MOZ) is at the northeast corner of the island. No *trucks* service the airport, so unless you rent a car you'll be stuck with a rip-off taxi fare in addition to the airfare: CFP 1150 to the Hôtel Bali Hai or Vaiare Wharf, CFP 2100 to the Moorea Lagoon Hôtel, CFP 3500 to Club Med. You could also walk out to the main highway and wait for the boat *truck* (CFP 200), or just hitch. Thanks to intimidation from the taxi drivers, none of the hotels are allowed to offer airport pickups. This considered, we suggest you give Air Moorea a miss and take the ferry to/from Moorea. At a third the price of the plane, the scenic 30-minute catamaran ride to/from Tahiti may end up being one of the highlights of your visit. If you do fly, be sure to sit on the left side of the aircraft on the way to Moorea and on the right on the way to Papeete.

SOCIETY ISLANDS
The Leeward Islands

Huahine, Raiatea, Tahaa, Bora Bora, Maupiti

Mount Otemanu, Bora Bora

an early 19th-century view of Fare, Huahine

HUAHINE

Huahine, the first Leeward island encountered on the ferry ride from Tahiti, is a friendly, inviting island, 170 km northwest of Papeete. In many ways lush, mountainous Huahine has more to offer than overcrowded Bora Bora. The variety of scenery, splendid beaches, archaeological remains, and charming main town all call on you to visit. Huahine is a well-known surfing locale, with excellent lefts and rights in the passes off Fare. (Don't leave valuables unattended on the beaches here.)

It's claimed the island got its name because, when viewed from the sea, Huahine has the shape of a reclining woman—very appropriate for such a fertile, enchanting place. *Hua* means "phallus" (from a rock on Huahine Iti) while *hine* comes from *vahine* (woman). The almost entirely Polynesian population numbers under 5,000, yet some of the greatest leaders in the struggle for the independence of Polynesia, Pouvanaa a Oopa among them, have come from this idyllic spot.

In recent years Huahine has been discovered by international tourism, with several deluxe hotels and bungalow-style developments now operating on the island. Luckily Huahine is able to absorb these new properties fairly painlessly, as it's a much larger island than Bora Bora and the resorts are well scattered and tastefully constructed in the traditional Tahitian style. The island has also become a major port of call for locally chartered or cruising yachts which anchor just off the Hôtel Bali Hai. Backpackers pioneered Huahine in the mid-1980s, and there are still good facilities for them.

HISTORY

Archaeology

Archaeologists have found that human habitation goes back 1,300 years on Huahine; Maeva village was occupied as early as A.D. 850. In 1925 Dr. K.P. Emory of Hawaii's Bishop Museum

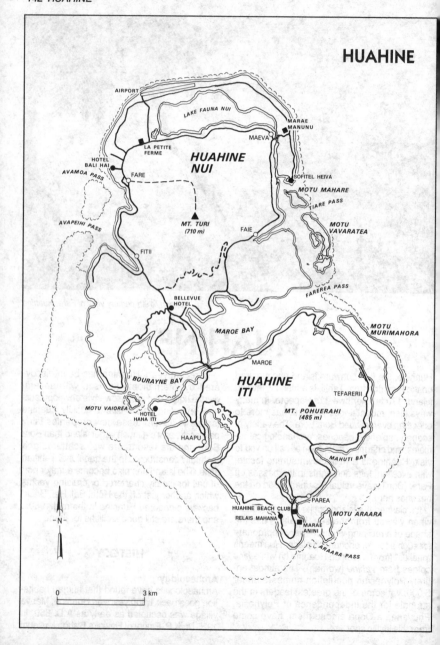

HUAHINE

ecorded 54 *marae* on Huahine, most of them built after the 16th century. In 1968 Prof. Yosihiko H. Sinoto found another 40. Huahine Nui was divided into 10 districts, with Huahine Iti as a dependency. As a centralized government complex for a whole island, Maeva, on the south shore of Lake Fauna Nui, is unique in Tahiti-Polynesia. Both of the great communal *marae* at Maeva and Parea have two-stepped platforms (*ahu*) that served as raised seats for the gods. Since 1967 about 16 *marae* have been restored, and they can be easily visited today. During construction of the Hôtel Bali Hai just north of Fare in 1972 a *patu* hand club was uncovered, proving that New Zealand's Maoris originated in this area.

History of the Leeward Islands

Roggeveen, coming from Makatea in the Tuamotus, discovered (but did not land on) Bora Bora and Maupiti on 6 June 1722. Captain Cook discovered the other Leeward Islands in July 1769, which was quite easy since the Tahitians knew them well. Cook had the Raiatean priest Tupaia on board the *Endeavour* as a pilot. Cook wrote: "To these six islands, as they lie contiguous to each other, I gave the names of Society Islands." Later the name was extended to the Windward Islands. In 1773 a man named Omai from Huahine sailed to England with Cook's colleague, Captain Furneaux, aboard the *Adventure;* he returned to Fare in 1777.

During the 19th century American whalers spent their winters away from the Antarctic in places like Huahine, refurbishing their supplies with local products such as sugar, vegetables, oranges, salted pork, and *aito,* or ironwood. These visits enriched the island economy, and the New England sailors presented the islanders with foreign plants as tokens of appreciation for the hospitality received.

Though Tahiti and Moorea came under French control in 1842, the Leeward Islands remained a British protectorate until 1887 when these islands were traded for fishing rights off Newfoundland and a British interest in what was then New Hebrides (today Vanuatu). Armed resistance to France, especially on Raiatea, was only overcome in 1897, and the English missionary group that had been there 88 years was asked to leave. Today 80% of the population of the Leewards remains Protestant.

Orientation

The unsophisticated little town of Fare, with its tree-lined boulevard along the quay, is joyfully peaceful after the roar of Papeete. A beach runs right along the west side of the main street and local life unfolds without being overwhelmed by tourism. The seven other villages on Huahine are joined by winding, picturesque roads which are fairly flat and easily managed by bicycle riders. A narrow channel crossed by a bridge slices Huahine into Huahine Nui and Huahine Iti (Great and Little Huahine, respectively). The story goes that the demigod Hiro's canoe cut this strait. The airstrip sits on an elevated barrier reef north of Lake Fauna Nui. White beaches line this cantaloupe- and watermelon-rich north shore.

frangipani
(Plumeria obtusa)

SIGHTS

Near Fare

After you've had a look around Fare, walk inland on the road that begins near the house marked "Oliveti" near the Total service station to see the beautiful *mape* (chestnut) forest up the valley. After the road becomes a trail follow the small stream into a forest laced with vanilla vines. By the stream is a long, bedlike rock known as Ofaitere, or "Traveling Rock." With a guide you could continue right to the summit of Mt. Turi (710 meters) in about three hours, but it's rough going.

Maeva

At Maeva, six km east of Fare, you encounter that rare combination of an easily accessible archaeological site in a spectacular setting. Here each of the 10 district chiefs of Huahine Nui had his own *marae,* and huge stone walls were erected to defend Maeva against invaders from Bora Bora (and later France). The plentiful small fish in Lake Fauna Nui supported large chiefly and priestly classes (ancient stone fish traps can still be seen under the bridge at the east end of the

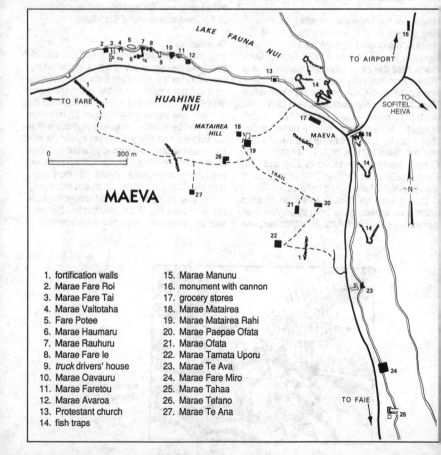

1. fortification walls
2. Marae Fare Roi
3. Marae Fare Tai
4. Marae Vaitotaha
5. Fare Potee
6. Marae Haumaru
7. Marae Rauhuru
8. Marae Fare Ie
9. *truck* drivers' house
10. Marae Oavauru
11. Marae Faretou
12. Marae Avaroa
13. Protestant church
14. fish traps
15. Marae Manunu
16. monument with cannon
17. grocery stores
18. Marae Matairea
19. Marae Matairea Rahi
20. Marae Paepae Ofata
21. Marae Ofata
22. Marae Tamata Uporu
23. Marae Te Ava
24. Marae Fare Miro
25. Marae Tahaa
26. Marae Tefano
27. Marae Te Ana

Marae Fare Miro at Huahine's Maeva

village). In the 1970s Prof. Y.H. Sinoto of Hawaii restored many of the structures strewn along the lakeshore and in the nearby hills.

On the shores of the lake is round-ended **Fare Potee** (1974), a replica of an old communal meeting house which now contains an historical exposition. In front of the building is a large map of the area.

From Fare Potee, walk back along the road toward Fare about 100 meters, to a **fortification wall** on the left. Follow this inland to an ancient well at the foot of the hill, then turn right and continue around the base of the hill till you find the trail up onto Matairea Hill. Just beyond a second fortification wall along the hillside is the access to **Marae Te Ana** on the right. The terraces of this monumental *marae* excavated in 1986 climb back up the hillside.

Return to the main trail and continue up to the ruins of **Marae Tefano** which are engulfed by an immense banyan tree. **Marae Matairea Rahi,** to the left, was the most sacred place on Huahine, dedicated to Tane, god of light. The backrests of Huahine's eight principal chiefs are in the southernmost compound of the *marae,* where the most important religious ceremonies took place. Backtrack a bit and keep straight, then go up the fern-covered hill to the right to **Marae Ofata,** which gives a magnificent view over the whole northeast coast of Huahine.

Continue southeast on the main trail past several more *marae* and you'll eventually cross another fortification wall and meet a dirt road down to the main highway near **Marae Te Ava.** Throughout this easy two-hour hike, watch for stakes planted with vanilla.

When you get back down to the main road, walk south a bit to see photogenic **Marae Fare Miro,** then backtrack to the bridge, across which is a **monument** guarded by seven cannon. Underneath are buried the French soldiers killed in the Battle of Maeva (1846), when the islanders successfully defended their independence against French marines sent to annex the island.

A few hundred meters farther along toward the ocean and to the left is two-tiered **Marae Manunu,** the community *marae* of Huahine Nui. In its base is the grave of Raiti, the last great priest of Huahine. When he died in 1915 a huge stone fell from the *marae.*

Maeva is accessible by infrequent *truck* from Fare (CFP 150), and there are two small stores in the village where you can get cold drinks. From **Faie,** south of Maeva, a very steep track crosses the mountains to Maroe Bay, making a complete circuit of Huahine Nui possible on foot (not feasible by rental car and dangerous even by bicycle). If you're driving, you can return to Fare via the airport road for a change of scenery.

Huahine Iti

Though the "July Bridge" joins the two islands, Huahine Iti is far less accessible than Huahine Nui. *Trucks* to **Parea** village (CFP 250) run only once a day, so you'll have to stay the night unless you rent a bicycle, scooter, or car. The hotels are very expensive, so you may want to bring a tent. Bourayne Bay, to the west of the interisland bridge, is one of the loveliest spots on the island.

On a golden beach on Point Tiva, one km south of Parea, is **Marae Anini,** the community *marae* of Huahine Iti. Look for petroglyphs on this two-tiered structure, dedicated to the god Oro, where human sacrifices once took place. (If you decide to camp near the *marae,* don't leave a mess. Search for the water tap by the road at the end of the path. Be aware of theft by dogs at night and small boys by day.) Surfing is possible in Araara Pass, beside the *motu* just off Marae Anini. Another nice beach with better swimming is a couple of km west.

This bridge links Huahine Nui to Huahine Iti.

Haapu village was originally built entirely over the water, for lack of sufficient shoreline to house it. The only grocery store on Huahine Iti is at Haapu, but three grocery trucks circle the island several times daily; the locals can tell you when to expect them.

Sports and Recreation

Pacific Blue Adventure (B.P. 193, Fare; tel. 68-87-21, fax 68-80-71) at Fare offers scuba diving at CFP 5000 a dive (night diving CFP 6500) and CMAS certification courses (CFP 30,000 including four dives, texts, and documentation). Trips leave at 0915 and 1415, depending on demand.

La Petite Ferme (B.P. 12, Huahine; tel. 68-82-98), between Fare and the airport, offers riding with Pascale, Yvan, and their 10 small, robust Marquesan horses. A two-hour ride along the beach is CFP 3500 pp, and they also offer a two-day ride and campout in the mountains or on the beach for CFP 13,500 pp, meals included. Call the day before to let them know you're coming. If riding is your main interest, it's possible to stay in their on-site guesthouse at CFP 3600 double or CFP 1500 pp dormitory, breakfast included. They also have a self-catering bungalow at CFP 5000/7500/9500 single/double/triple. This is the best horseback-riding operation in Tahiti-Polynesia.

PRACTICALITIES

ACCOMMODATIONS

Budget Accommodations

Several inexpensive lodgings await you in and around Fare (most of them levying a CFP 500 surcharge if you stay only one night). **Guynette's Lodging** (Alain and Hélène Guerineau, B.P. 87, Fare; tel. 68-83-75), also known as "Club Bed," on the waterfront to the left as you get off the boat, has an eight-bed CFP 1200 dorm and three rooms at CFP 3000/3500/4500 single/double/ triple, minimum stay two nights, maximum one month. Mosquito nets are provided in the fan-cooled rooms. You can cook your own meals in the communal kitchen here, and the meals prepared by the friendly staff are good value (order before 1400). It's a very clean place: no shoes or radios allowed in the house. Upon arrival peruse the list of rules and rates—applied rigorously (for example, it's lights out at 2200). Most readers say they liked the efficiency. Thankfully, the management doesn't allow overcrowding and will turn people away rather than pack them in for short-term gain. Recommended.

Nearby on the waterfront is decrepit three-story **Hôtel Huahine** (B.P. 220, Fare; tel. 68-82-69), at CFP 2500/3500/4500 single/double/triple, or CFP 1000 in a dorm. There's no surcharge for a one-night stay. It's not possible to lock the rooms and they have water problems. Don't order any meals here as the food is lousy and far too expensive, but they will let you sit in the restaurant and watch TV for the price of a beer.

Pension Martial et Enite (Enite Temaiana, B.P. 37, Fare; tel./fax 68-82-37) is an eight-room boardinghouse at the west end of the waterfront beyond the snack bar. Rooms with shared bath are CFP 5200 pp with half board, CFP 6300 pp with full board (two-night minimum stay, no room rentals without meals). In the event of a shortened stay, the pension will bill for the number of nights originally reserved. Middle-of-the-night arrivals mustn't knock on the door before 0700. French expats often stay here. Martial and Enite also serve meals to outsiders in their thatched cookhouse on the beach for CFP 2200, or CFP 3000 if shellfish is on the menu. Advance notice must be given, but the food is good (closed on Sunday).

Three good places to stay are between Fare and the airport, about 800 meters north of the wharf. Look for a signposted dirt road leading west from the main highway, just north of the Bali Hai. Chez Richard is on the left, and almost opposite it are the high thatched roofs of Chez Lovina. About a hundred meters further along on the same road is Chez Marie Louise

the back porch at Guynette's Lodging, Fare, Huahine

(see below). A reasonable beach for snorkeling is nearby at the end of this road.

Chez Richard (B.P. 121, Fare; tel. 68-87-86) caters to budget travelers with four pleasant shared-bath rooms at CFP 3000 single or double, and a four-bed dorm at CFP 1000 pp. Cooking is possible and their two bicycles are loaned free. Owner Richard Bowens will pick you up free at the airport if you call ahead, and he's usually present in search of guests when the interisland ships arrive.

Chez Lovina (Lovina Richmond, B.P. 173, Fare; tel. 68-88-06, fax 68-82-64) has five small *fares* with TV and shared bath at CFP 2500/4000 single/double. For families and groups, Chez Lovina has four oversized bungalows with cooking and bathing facilities at CFP 5000/6000/7000 single/double/triple, CFP 10,000 for up to five persons, CFP 15,000 for eight people, etc. Dormitory accommodations are CFP 1200 pp and camping is CFP 1000 pp. The layout of the communal toilets and showers can lead to exasperating situations. All guests have access to cramped cooking facilities (and mosquitoes). The minimum stay is two nights and discounts may be negotiable. Airport pickups are CFP 1000 pp; from the harbor it's CFP 400 pp.

One of the best budget places on Huahine is **Chez Marie Louise** (B.P. 5, Fare; tel. 68-81-10), with three neat little bungalows at CFP 2500/3500 double/triple. A larger bungalow with private bath, kitchen and TV is CFP 5000/6000 double/triple. Camping is CFP 1000 per tent. There's a large open communal kitchen. This place is run by a friendly German/Tahitian couple: Hans (a former French foreign legionnaire) scouts for guests at the harbor and airport, and provides free transfers in his rickety old car, while Marie-Louise greets newcomers with a large bowl of tropical fruit. This easygoing resort, just 100 meters from the beach, is perfect for a long, restful stay. Recommended.

The **Hôtel Bellevue** (B.P. 21, Huahine; tel. 68-82-76, fax 68-85-35), six km south of Fare, offers eight rooms in the main building at CFP 3500/4500/5000 single/double/triple and 15 bungalows for CFP 8000 double. The rooms are stuffy due to the lack of fans, and the poor lighting makes it hard to read in the evening. There's an expensive restaurant (meals CFP 3000 each) with a lovely view of Maroe Bay.

Roundtrip airport transfers are CFP 1000. Considering the expense, isolation, and absence of a beach (there is a swimming pool), the Bellevue has little going for it.

Upmarket Hotels

In recent years the American-owned **Hôtel Bali Hai** (B.P. 2, Fare; tel. 68-84-77, fax 68-82-77), just north of Fare, has faced closure due to labor disputes but it's now operating again under lease from the Moorea Bali Hai company. This was always the nicest of the Bali Hai chain, tastefully placed between a lake and the beach. The 10 rooms in the main building begin at CFP 12,000/14,000 single/double; the 34 bungalows cost 25% more in the garden, 50% more facing the beach. Cooking facilities are not provided but their restaurant serves excellent food and the largely French crowd is chic. The breakfast and dinner plan is CFP 3900 pp, airport transfers CFP 800 pp. Visit the lobby to see the showcase displaying artifacts found here by Dr. Yosihiko H. Sinoto of the Bishop Museum, Hawaii, who excavated the site during construction of the hotel in 1973-75. Marae Tahuea has been reconstructed on the grounds.

In October 1989 the exclusive **Sofitel Heiva Huahine** (B.P. 38, Huahine; tel. 68-86-86, fax 68-85-25) opened in a coconut grove on a *motu* just east of Maeva along a rough road. Striking neo-Polynesian paintings by the late artist/singer Bobby Holcomb highlight the decor in public areas, and ancient *marae* are preserved in the gardens. Unspoiled white beaches are all along this section of lagoon, and the Maeva archaeological area is only a 30-minute walk away. The 58 tastefully decorated rooms are CFP 21,000 single or double, the nine thatched beach bungalows 50% more. The breakfast and dinner plan is CFP 4800 pp, airport transfers CFP 1500 pp. One of the best Polynesian cultural shows you'll ever see usually takes place here on Monday, Thursday, and Saturday nights at 2000, complete with fire dancing, acrobatics, and coconut tree climbing. Pacificar has a desk at this hotel.

The US$12-million **Hôtel Hana Iti** (B.P. 185, Fare; tel. 68-87-41, fax 68-85-04) opened in 1992 on a verdant ridge high above Bourayne Bay. A three-room thatched bungalow complete with whirlpool spa will set you back CFP 58,000/63,000 double/triple or more. Breakfast and dinner are another CFP 7200 pp, return airport transfers CFP 2200 pp. Yes, this is the most expensive hotel in Tahiti-Polynesia, but each of the 26 traditional *fare* units is unique. Some perch on rocks, more stand on stilts, and a few are built into huge trees. The Hana Iti is owned by American meat-packing millionaire Thomas C. Kurth, who bought the property from Spanish singer Julio Iglesias. If you're a Hollywood star in search of an exotic hideaway, this is it.

The 22-unit **Relais Mahana** (B.P. 30, Huahine; tel. 68-81-54, fax 68-85-08), on a wide white beach near Parea, charges CFP 14,500 single or double, CFP 17,500 triple for a garden bungalow, CFP 2000 more for a beach bungalow. For breakfast and dinner add another CFP 3500 pp; roundtrip airport transfers are an extra CFP 1800 pp. This French-operated hotel has a certain snob appeal.

The 17-unit **Huahine Beach Club** (B.P. 39, Huahine; tel. 68-81-46, fax 68-85-86) at Parea is overpriced at CFP 19,000 for a large garden bungalow, CPF 4000 more for a beach bungalow. Breakfast and dinner are CFP 3800 pp, airport transfers CFP 1800 pp. Saturday night there's a Tahitian buffet with traditional dancing (CFP 3200). This well-constructed resort sits on a small beach between Parea village and Marae Anini, and there's also a swimming pool. Windsurfing, snorkeling, and fishing gear are loaned free. The Club can arrange cars through Kake Rent-A-Car, a necessity due to the lack of public transport.

OTHER PRACTICALITIES

Food
Food trailers congregate at Fare Wharf when a ship is due in. One trailer has a good selection of sandwiches and pastries. The numerous Chinese stores along the waterfront sell groceries and cold beer. The tap water on Huahine can be clouded after heavy rains.

Restaurant Te Manu (tel. 68-86-61), facing the boat landing in Fare, has basic Chinese fare and cheap beer. There's no sign outside, so ask.

Snack Temarara (closed Sunday) at the west end of the waterfront charges prices similar to those of the deluxe hotel restaurants, which is a little ridiculous. Temarara does have an unpre-

tentious terrace built over the lagoon, so drop in for a sunset beer. On Friday evening the place is crowded with Polynesians enjoying *kaina* (folkloric) music.

The **Restaurant Bar Orio** (closed Monday; tel. 68-83-03) at the east end of the waterfront is similar to Snack Temarara.

Noticeably cheaper than either of these is the **Tiare Tipanier Restaurant** (closed Monday; tel. 68-80-52), next to the Mairie (town hall) at the north entrance to Fare from the Bali Hai. They serve mahimahi with pepper sauce (CFP 1000), omelette (CFP 350), shrimp (CFP 1250), and hamburgers (CFP 350), and a large Hinano beer here is CFP 350.

Also check **Restaurant Te Moana** (tel. 68-88-63) on the beach next to Hôtel Bali Hai, which has a few thatched bungalows for rent.

Cultural Shows for Visitors
If you're staying in budget accommodations around Fare, you'll be able to witness the Polynesian dancing at the **Hôtel Bali Hai** (tel. 68-84-77) on Friday evening for the price of a drink or a meal. Drop by beforehand to check the program. There's also traditional dancing at the **Sofitel Heiva Huahine** and **Huahine Beach Club** certain nights, but you'll need motorized transportation to get there unless you're a guest.

Services
The Banque de Tahiti facing the waterfront is open weekdays 0745-1145/1330-1630. Banque Socredo, on the first street back from the Fare waterfront, opens Monday to Thursday 0730-1130/1330-1600, Friday 0730-1130/1330-1500.

The **post office** is opposite the access road to the Hôtel Bali Hai. The **gendarmerie** is opposite the hospital over the bridge at the south end of town.

The **laundromat** opposite Kake Rent-A-Car charges CFP 750 to wash and CFP 750 to dry (Monday to Thursday 0700-1600, Friday 0730-1500).

Public toilets and wash basins are in one of the yellow buildings on the waterfront (if open).

The useless **Comité du Tourisme** information office (weekdays 0800-1500, Saturday 0800-1000: B.P. 54, Fare; tel. 68-86-34, fax 68-87-34) shares a pavilion on the waterfront with Pacificar, Kake Rent-A-Car, and Pacific Blue Adventure.

TRANSPORT

Getting There

The **Air Tahiti** agent (tel. 68-82-65) is at the airport. For information on flights to Huahine from Papeete, Moorea, Raiatea, and Bora Bora see "Getting Around" in the main Introduction.

The Papeete cargo ships tie up to the wharf in the middle of town, where there's a large open pavilion at which you can sleep until dawn. *Taporo VI* arrives from Papeete bound for Raiatea, Tahaa, and Bora Bora around 0200 on Tuesday, Thursday, and Saturday, returning from Raiatea on its way to Papeete Tuesday, Thursday, and Friday afternoons. Northbound, the *Vaeanu* calls at Huahine on Tuesday and Saturday at 0230; southbound on Tuesday at 1830, and Thursday and Sunday at 1700. The *Raromatai Ferry* arrives from Papeete Wednesday and Saturday at 0030 or 0230, departing for Papeete again on Thursday at 1300 and Sunday at 2030 (nine hours, CFP 3800 deck). You can also take this ship to Raiatea, Tahaa, and Bora Bora (all CFP 1000) Wednesday and Saturday in the middle of the night.

Tickets for *Taporo VI* and *Vaeanu* go on sale at their offices four hours before sailing and you can buy one as the ship is loading. Tickets for the *Raromatai Ferry* are sold on board upon arrival. The *Vaeanu* office adjoins the yellow warehouse on the wharf. *Taporo VI* has an office next to Pacificar on the waterfront.

The high-speed monohull *Ono-Ono* (tel. 68-85-85) departs Huahine for Raiatea (one hour, CFP 1600) and Bora Bora (three hours, CFP 2800) Monday and Wednesday at 1230, Friday at 2000, Saturday at 1130. To Papeete (three hours, CFP 4300) it leaves Huahine Tuesday and Thursday at 1500, Sunday at 1700.

Getting Around

Getting around Huahine is not easy. You'll find *trucks* to anywhere on Huahine when a ship arrives; otherwise, they're irregular. Only one *truck* a day runs to Maeva, leaving Fare at 0900 (CFP 150). It's fairly easy to hitch back to Fare from Maeva. The bus to Parea leaves Fare on Monday, Tuesday, Thursday, and Friday at 1100, returning from Parea to Fare at 1400 (CFP 250 OW).

Car Rentals

Pacificar (tel. 68-81-81), on the Fare waterfront, rents small cars (from CFP 5200, plus CFP 1000 for insurance), scooters (CFP 3000), and bicycles (CFP 1000). **Kake Rent-A-Car** (B.P. 34, Fare; tel. 68-82-59, fax 68-80-59), beside the entrance to the Hôtel Bali Hai, is similar. Pacificar will rent to persons aged 18 and over, Kake 21 and over. Both companies charge identical rates and never give you the car with a full tank of gas, which means you have to waste time filling it up as soon as you get it. There are only two gas stations on Huahine, both in Fare: Mobil is open weekdays 0630-1700, Saturday 0700-1100, Sunday 0700-0900, while Total is open somewhat shorter hours.

Airport

The airport (HUH) is four km north of Fare. Make arrangements for the regular airport minibus (CFP 400 pp) at Pension Martial et Enite. Both Kake and Pacificar have counters at the airport.

an early 19th-century view of Raiatea

RAIATEA AND TAHAA
RAIATEA

Raiatea is the second largest high island of Tahiti-Polynesia. Its main town and port, Uturoa, is the business and administrative center of the Leeward Islands; the balance of the island's population of about 9,000 lives in eight flower-filled villages around the island: Avera, Opoa, Puohine, Fetuna, Vaiaau, Tehurui, Tevaitoa, and Tuu Fenua. The west coast of Raiatea south of Tevaitoa is old Polynesia through and through. Raiatea is traditionally the ancient Havai'i, the sacred isle from which all of eastern Polynesia was colonized. Today it's mostly worth visiting if you want to get off the beaten tourist track, though public transportation and budget accommodations are scarce. The island does offer good possibilities for scuba diving, charter yachting, and hiking, and the varied scenery is worth a stop.

The Land
Raiatea, 220 km northwest of Tahiti, shares a protected lagoon with Tahaa three km away. Legends tell how the two islands were cut apart by a mythical eel. About 30 km of steel-blue sea separates Raiatea from both Huahine and Bora Bora. Mount Temehani on mountainous Raiatea rises to 772 meters, and some of the coastlines are rugged and narrow. The highest mountain is Toomaru (1,017 meters). All of the people live on a coastal plain planted in coconuts, where cattle also graze.

No beaches are found on big, hulking Raiatea itself. Instead, picnickers are taken to picture-postcard *motus* in the lagoon. Surfing is possible at the eight passes that open onto the Raiatea/Tahaa lagoon, and windsurfers are active. The Leeward Islands (Îles Sous le Vent) are the most popular sailing area in Tahiti-Polynesia, and most of the charter boats are based at Raiatea.

History
Before European encroachment, Raiatea was the religious, cultural, and political center of Tahiti-Polynesia. Tradition holds that the great Polynesian voyagers to Hawaii and New Zealand departed from these shores.

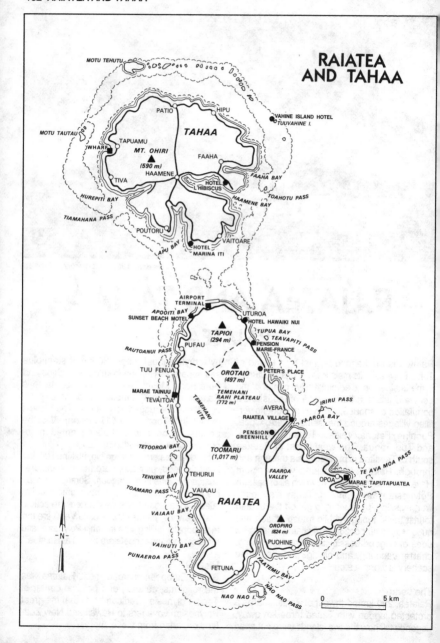

Raiatea was Captain Cook's favorite island; he visited three times. During his first voyage in 1769 he called first at Opoa from 20 to 24 July. After having surveyed Bora Bora from the sea, he anchored for a week in the Rautoanui Pass on the northwest coast of Raiatea, near the village of Tuu Fenua. During his second voyage Cook lay at anchor twice, first from 8 to 17 September 1773 and again from 25 May to 4 June 1774, both times at Rautoanui. His third visit was from 3 November to 7 December 1777, again at Rautoanui. It can therefore be said that Rautoanui (which he calls "Haamanino Harbour" in his journals) was one of Cook's favorite anchorages.

The last resistance to the French takeover on Raiatea lasted until 1897, when French troops and warships used arms to conquer the island. The native leader of the resistance, Teraupoo, was deported to New Caledonia.

SIGHTS

Everything is easy to find in Uturoa (pop. 3,200). The double row of Chinese stores along the main drag opens onto a colorful **market** which is most crowded on Wednesday and Friday mornings when the Tahaa people arrive by motorized canoe to sell their products here. The Sunday market is over by 0700. Beyond the market is the harbor, with a pleasant park alongside. All of the stores in Uturoa close for lunch 1200-1300.

For a view of four islands, climb **Tapioi Hill** (294 meters), the peak topped by a TV antenna behind Uturoa—one of the easiest and best climbs in Tahiti-Polynesia. Take the road beside the Gendarmerie Nationale up past the Propriété Privé sign (don't worry, visitors are allowed). The fastest time on record for climbing Tapioi is 17 minutes, but it's best to allow two or three hours to hike up and down.

Around the Island
It takes 5-10 hours to ride a bicycle around Raiatea (97 km), depending on how fast you go. The road down the east coast is paved to the head of Faaroa Bay, then the paved road cuts directly across the island to the south coast. Down the west coast, the road is paved as far as Tehurui. The bottom half of the circuminsular road is unpaved, but no problem for a car.

The road down the east coast circles fjordlike **Faaroa Bay,** associated with the legends of Polynesian migration. From the popular yacht anchorage in the middle of the bay there's a fine view of Toomaru, highest peak in the Leeward Islands. The Apoomau River drains the Faaroa Valley. (The boat trips occasionally offered up this river are not recommended, as the boat can only proceed a couple of hundred meters.)

Instead of crossing the island on the paved road, keep left and follow the coast around to a point of land just beyond Opoa, 32 km from Uturoa. Here stands **Marae Taputapuatea,** one of

Marea Taputapuatea on Raiatea is among the most sacred sites in Polynesia.

DAVID STANLEY

the largest and best preserved in Polynesia, its mighty *ahu* measuring 43 meters long, 7.3 meters wide, and between two and three meters high. Before it is a rectangular courtyard paved with black volcanic rocks. A small platform in the middle of the *ahu* once bore the image of Oro, god of fertility and war (now represented by a reproduction); backrests still mark the seats of high chiefs on the courtyard. Marae Taputapuatea is directly opposite Te Ava Moa Pass, and fires on the *marae* may have been beacons to ancient navigators. Human sacrifices and fire-walking once took place on the *marae*.

Marae Taputapuatea is said to retain its psychic power. Test this by writing down all your negative emotions, bad habits, unhappy memories, and self-doubts on a piece of paper. Then burn the paper(s) on the *marae*. The catharsis works best when done solo, beneath a full moon or on one of the three nights following it. The *tupapau* (spirits) are most active at this time, often taking the forms of dogs, cats, pigs, etc.

The only places to buy food in the southern part of Raiatea are the two Chinese grocery stores at **Fetuna** and another at **Vaiaau**. Behind Tevaitoa church, on the west side of Raiatea, is **Marae Tainuu,** dedicated to the ancient god Taaroa. Petroglyphs on a broken stone by the road at the entrance to the church show a turtle and some other indistinguishable figure.

Hiking

According to Polynesian mythology the god Oro was born from the molten rage of **Mt. Temehani** (772 meters), the cloud-covered plateau that dominates the northern end of the island. *Tiare apetahi,* a sacred white flower which exists nowhere else on earth and resists transplantation, grows on the slopes around the summit. The fragile blossom represents the five fingers of a beautiful Polynesian girl who fell in love with the handsome son of a high chief, but was unable to marry him due to her lowly birth. These flowers are now rare, so don't pick any! Small pink orchids also grow by the way.

Temehani can be climbed from Pufau, the second bay south of Marina Apooiti. Note a series of old concrete benches by the road as you come around the north side of the bay. The track inland begins at a locked gate, 700 meters south of the bridge, beyond the concrete bench-

es. It's private property, so ask permission to proceed of anyone you meet. You hike straight up through pine reforestation till you have a clear view of Temehani Rahi and Temehani Ute, divided by a deep gorge. Descend to the right and continue up the track you see on the hillside opposite. It takes about three hours to go from the main road to the Temehani Rahi Plateau. Friday and Saturday are the best days to go, and long pants and sturdy shoes are required. A guide up Temehani should charge about CFP 5000 for the group.

Reader Will Paine of Maidstone, England, sent us this:

The through hike from Pufau to Uturoa takes five or six hours on foot with beautiful views from high vantage points where the difficultly manageable jeep track becomes a path. The same trail is shared by the Temehani route until it splits up shortly after the ford/bathing pool on the higher reaches. Here take the left branch. Follow it down across a water catchment and up to a ridge. The Orotaio cone will come into view to the east and the path drops to a better 4WD track. From here it's just under two hours down to a gas station on the coastal road a few km south of Uturoa.

SPORTS AND RECREATION

Raiatea Plongée (B.P. 272, Uturoa; tel. 66-37-10, fax 66-26-25) is run by Patrice Philip, husband of Marie-France mentioned under "Accommodations" below. He'll take you to the century-old wreck of a 100-meter Dutch coal boat, the top of which is 18 meters down. The coral life is rather poor, but there's ample marinelife, including sharks, moray eels, barracudas, manta rays, and countless tropical fish. Patrice charges CFP 5000 for a one-tank dive. A trip right around Tahaa by motorized canoe with visits to two *motus* is CFP 4500 (eight-person minimum), snorkeling in a pass is CFP 3500, or you can just be dropped off on a nearby *motu* for CFP 800. PADI scuba certification (four dives) is CFP 35,000. A swimming pool on the premises is used for the lessons. We've had varying reports about Patrice's operation.

Hémisphere Sub (B.P. 492, Raiatea; tel. 66-11-66, fax 66-11-67), at the Marina Apooiti, offers scuba diving at CFP 4500 per dive. A five-dive CMAS certification course is CFP 24,000. There's diving daily at 0830 and 1430.

There's good swimming in a large pool open to the sea at the **Centre Nautique** *("la piscine")* on the coast just north of Uturoa.

The **Kaoha Nui Ranch** (Patrick Marinthe, B.P. 568, Uturoa; tel. 66-25-46) at PK 6, Avera, a few hundred meters north of Pension Manava, charges CFP 3000 for horseback riding (1.5 hours). You must reserve 24 hours in advance (closed Wednesday), and there's a two-person minimum.

Bareboating

The Moorings (B.P. 165, Uturoa; tel. 66-35-93, fax 66-20-94), a bareboat charter operation with 19 yachts, is based at Marina Apooiti, one km west of the airport. Leeward Island charter rates begin at US$500 a day, with food, drink, and three percent tax extra. This may seem like a lot, but split among a nautical-minded group it's comparable to a deluxe hotel room. Charterers are given a complete briefing on channels and anchorages, and provided with a detailed set of charts. All boats are radio-equipped and a voice from the Moorings is available to talk nervous skippers in and out. Travel by night is forbidden, but by day it's easy sailing.

Another company, **Tahiti Yacht Charters** (tel. 66-28-86, fax 66-28-85), also based at Marina Apooiti, has eight charter yachts available.

A third yacht charter operation, **A.T.M. Yachts South Pacific** (B.P. 705, Uturoa; tel. 66-23-18, fax 66-23-19), based at Faaroa Bay next to La Veranda Restaurant, is slightly cheaper than the Moorings. For more information on bareboat chartering see "Getting There" in the main Introduction to this book.

ACCOMMODATIONS

All of the places to stay are on the northeast side of Raiatea and we've arranged them below from north to south. The proprietors often pick up guests at the airport or harbor if they call ahead for reservations. Transfers are usually free, but ask.

The friendly **Sunset Beach Motel Apooiti** (Jean and Elianne Boubée, B.P. 397, Uturoa; tel. 66-33-47, fax 66-33-08) is in a coconut grove by the beach, five km west of Uturoa. Look on the point across the bay from Marina Apooiti, about 2.5 km west of the airport. The 16 comfortable, well-spaced bungalows with cooking facilities and private bath (hot water) are CFP 6000/7000/8000 single/double/triple—good value for families. Camping is CFP 1000 pp here and there's a large communal kitchen. Discounts of 10% a fortnight and 20% a month are available, but there's a CFP 2000 surcharge if you stay only one night. Bicycles are for rent and hitching into Uturoa is easy.

The former Hôtel Le Motu, conveniently located on the main street in the center of Uturoa, was destroyed by a hurricane in 1991, but the seven-room building was being rebuilt at press time, so check. Cooking facilities are not available.

Pension Marie-France (Patrice and Marie-France Philip, B.P. 272, Uturoa; tel. 66-37-10, fax 66-26-25), by the lagoon just beyond Magasin Andre Chinese store, 2.5 km south of Uturoa (yellow sign), caters to misplaced backpackers and scuba divers. The four rooms with shared bath are CFP 4000 single or double in back, or CFP 4500 single or double facing the lagoon. Five bungalows with kitchen and TV facing the lagoon are CFP 6000/7000/8000 single/double/triple. There's also a six-bed dormitory with cooking facilities at CFP 1000 pp (sheets provided only if you request them). There's a supplement of up to CFP 1000 if you stay only one night. Bicycles (CFP 1000 daily) and a washing machine are for rent, and there's even hot water (sometimes). The lagoon off Pension Marie-France is good for windsurfing, but they're a little pushy in the way they try to convince you to sign up for the half-day minibus tour of the island (CFP 3500) and other activities, so don't come expecting to rest. As soon as Marie-France senses you're not interested in taking any of her trips, she becomes rather abrupt. The meals served here are poor value. Airport transfers are CFP 500 pp each way (nothing here is free).

Pension Manava (B.P. 559, Uturoa; tel. 66-28-26), at PK 6, Avera, is run by Andrew and Roselyne Brotherson. This warm, sympathetic

JOHN WEBBER

Poetua, daughter of the chief of Raiatea, as painted by Captain Cook's artist, John Webber

couple rents a Polynesian-style bungalow at CFP 4000 pp with breakfast, CFP 6000 pp with half board, CFP 7000 pp with full board. A separate two-room building is CFP 3000 pp, and the four-bed dormitory with cooking facilities CFP 1000 pp. The meals served here are good. Excursions are free for bungalow guests; dormitory residents pay extra, for example, CFP 3500 pp (five-person minimum) for a boat trip around Tahaa.

Peter's Place (Peter Brotherson, tel. 66-20-01) at Hamoa, six km south of Uturoa and just beyond Pension Manava, is the backpacker's best choice on Raiatea. The eight neat double rooms in a long block are CFP 1100 pp and

you can pitch a tent in the large grassy area facing the rooms at CFP 700 pp. A large open pavilion is used for communal cooking but there are no grocery stores nearby, so bring food. Bicycles are for rent at CFP 1000 a day. Peter or his son Frame take guests on a hike up the valley to a picturesque waterfall with a tour of a vanilla plantation, swimming in the river, and fish feeding included at CFP 3000 per group. They can also guide you directly to the Temehani Plateau, taking about three hours up and two hours down (CFP 5000 per group). Highly recommended.

Pension Yolande Roopinia (B.P. 298, Uturoa; tel. 66-35-28) is in an attractive location facing the lagoon at PK 10, Avera. The four rooms are CFP 5000 single or double (private bath). Cooking facilities are provided, but you may be asked to take half pension (CFP 7000/13,000 single/double). You'll like the family atmosphere.

A hundred meters beyond Chez Yolande is the 12-unit **Raiatea Village Hôtel** (B.P. 282, Uturoa; tel. 66-31-62, fax 66-10-65), at the mouth of Faaroa Bay (PK 10). A garden bungalow with kitchenette and terrace is CFP 5350/6420 single/double, CFP 8560 for four. Airport transfers are CFP 1000 pp extra.

Pension Greenhill (Marie-Isabelle Chan, B.P. 598, Raiatea; tel./fax 66-37-64), at PK 12, is on the hillside directly above La Veranda Restaurant overlooking Faaroa Bay. The six rooms with private bath are CFP 6500/8000 single/double, including breakfast and dinner at the host's table (minimum stay two nights). Children under 10 are half price. Sightseeing trips and occasional boat rides are also included, though a minimum of four persons is required before they'll go. Getting into town is no problem—the pension minibus makes several trips a day and will arrange to pick you up later. Bicycles and the jacuzzi are at your disposal. Gourmet chef Jason makes dining a delight, while hostess Marie-Isabelle loves to sit and chat with guests. They'll pick you up free at the airport or wharf if you call ahead.

The new **Hôtel Te Moana Iti** (Irmine Ariitai, B.P. 724, Uturoa; tel. 66-21-82, fax 66-28-60), on the beach just beyond Marae Taputapuatea, 35 km from Uturoa, has seven tastefully decorated bungalows from CFP 8500/9500 double/triple, plus CFP 3000 for half board. The managers organize excursions to a *motu* and around the island, and they serve excellent if expensive food. There's good snorkeling off their wharf. The hotel's biggest drawback is its isolation, but they'll pick you up at the port or airport if you call ahead (CFP 2000 pp RT). It's good for a couple of days of relaxation.

Upmarket Hotel

The 36-room **Hôtel Hawaiki Nui** (B.P. 43, Uturoa; tel. 66-20-20, fax 66-20-23), 1.5 km south of Uturoa, is Raiatea's only luxury hotel. This is the former Raiatea Bali Hai, destroyed by a kitchen fire in 1992 and completely rebuilt in 1994. It's CFP 26,000 single or double for an overwater bungalow, CFP 17,000 for a lagoonside bungalow, or CFP 10,500 for a garden bungalow. There's Polynesian dancing once or twice a week. Firewalking, once commonly practiced on Raiatea, is now a dying art. The pit is just across the street from the Haviki Nui, so ask there if they'll be lighting anyone's fire.

FOOD AND SERVICES

Food

To escape the tourist scene, try **Bar Restaurant Maraamu,** also known as Chez Remy, in what appears to be an old Chinese store between the market and the wharf. The few minutes it takes to locate will net you the lowest prices in town. Coffee and omelettes are served in the morning, while the lunch menu tilts toward Chinese food. There's also *poisson cru* and a good selection of other dishes.

Snack Moemoea (closed Sunday; tel. 66-39-84), on the harbor, has hamburgers. **Le Quai des Pécheurs** (closed Monday; tel. 66-36-83), closer to the wharf, offers a view of the port.

Le Gourmet Restaurant (closed Sunday; tel. 66-21-51), next to the Westpac Bank in Uturoa, serves reasonable meals which are listed on the blackboard outside. It's a good choice for lunch (come early).

A more upmarket choice would be the **Jade Garden Restaurant** (open Wednesday to Saturday; tel. 66-34-40) on the main street which offers some of the best Chinese dishes this side of Papeete.

Entertainment

Friday, Saturday, and Sunday at 2200 the Moana Chinese Restaurant (tel. 66-27-49) opposite Uturoa Market becomes **Discotheque Le Zénith.**

The nicest place for a drink is Le Quai des Pécheurs, which transforms itself into **Disco Quaidep** on Friday and Saturday from 2200.

Services

Of Uturoa's four banks, the Banque de Tahiti and Banque Socredo charge a slightly lower commission on currency exchange than the Banque de Polynésie and the Westpac Bank.

The large modern **post office** (Monday to Thursday 0700-1500, Friday 0700-1400, Saturday 0800-1000) is opposite the new hospital just north of town, with the **gendarmerie** about 50 meters beyond on the left.

There are free **public toilets** *(sanitaires publics)* on the wharf behind Le Quai des Pécheurs.

A km west of the Sunset Beach Motel is **Raiatea Carenage Services** (tel. 66-22-96), a repair facility often used by cruising yachts. The only easily accessible slip facilities in Tahiti-Polynesia are here.

Beside the souvenir stalls opposite the wharf is a **tourist information** stand (B.P. 707, Raiatea; tel. 66-23-18), open Monday and Friday 0800-1100, Tuesday and Thursday 0730-1100/1400-1600, Wednesday 0800-1200.

TRANSPORT

Getting There and Away

The **Air Tahiti** office (tel. 66-32-50) is at the airport. Flights operate from Raiatea to Maupiti (CFP 5500) three times a week. For information on flights from Papeete, Huahine, and Bora Bora see "Getting Around" in the main Introduction.

You can catch the *Vaeanu, Taporo VI,* and *Raromatai Ferry* to Tahaa, Bora Bora, Huahine or Papeete twice weekly. Consult the schedule in "Getting Around" in the main Introduction. The agent for the *Taporo VI* is Les Mutuelles du Mans in the same block as Snack Moemoea. Tickets for the *Vaeanu* and *Raromatai Ferry* ferry are sold when the ship arrives.

The high-speed cruiser *Ono-Ono* (tel. 66-35-35) departs Raiatea for Bora Bora (1.5 hours, CFP 1600) Monday and Wednesday at 1345, Friday at 2115, Saturday at 1330. To Huahine (one hour, CFP 1600) and Papeete (4.5 hours, CFP 4800) it leaves Tuesday and Thursday at 1345, Sunday at 1545. Saturday at 1015 there's an extra trip only to Huahine.

A government supply ship, the *Meherio III,* shuttles twice a month between Raiatea and Maupiti, usually departing Raiatea on Thursday (CFP 1035 deck). The exact time varies, so check with the Capitainerie Port d'Uturoa (tel. 66-31-52) on the wharf.

Several village boats run between Raiatea and Tahaa on Wednesday and Friday mornings (CFP 500). The shuttle boat *Uporu* (tel. 65-61-01) departs Uturoa for Tahaa weekdays at 0930, 1400, and 1700, weekends at 0930 and 1700 (CFP 750 OW).

Getting Around

Getting around Raiatea is a problem as the only *trucks* leaving Uturoa go to Fetuna (CFP 250) and Opoa in the afternoon, but never on Sunday. Bicycle rentals are offered only by the hotels, and scooters are generally unavailable.

Pacificar (tel. 66-11-66, fax 66-11-67), at the Apooiti Marina, and **Raiatea Location** (tel. 66-34-06), between the airport and Uturoa, have cars beginning around CFP 5500, including mileage and insurance. Prices are often higher at peak periods. Apart from cars, Raiatea Location rents a four-meter boat with a six-horse-power motor at CFP 500 half day, CFP 8000 full day.

Garage Motu Tapu (Guirouard Rent-a-Car, B.P. 139, Uturoa; tel. 66-33-09), in a poorly marked building a few hundred meters east of the airport, has cars at CFP 6600 for 24 hours, insurance and mileage included.

Airport

The airport (RFP) is three km northwest of Uturoa. A taxi from the Uturoa market taxi stand to the airport is CFP 600 (double tariff late at night). Most of the hotels pick up clients at the airport free upon request. Pacificar and Raiatea Location both have car rental desks inside the terminal. The Air Tahiti reservations office is in a separate building adjacent to the main terminal. The friendly but unknowledgeable Tourist Board information kiosk at the airport is only open at flight times.

TAHAA

Raiatea's lagoonmate Tahaa is shaped like a hibiscus flower. It's a quiet island, with little traffic and few tourists. Mount Ohiri (590 meters), highest point on the island, gets its name from the demigod Hiro, who was born here. There aren't many specific attractions other than a chance to escape the crowds and hurried life on the other Society Islands. Notice the vanilla plantations. Beaches are scarce on the main island, so the pension owners arrange picnics on *motus* such as Tautau off Tapuamu. The *motus* off the northeast side of Tahaa have the finest white-sand beaches. The Tahaa Festival in late October includes stone fishing, with a line of canoes herding the fish into a cove by beating stones on the surface of the lagoon. The 4,000 Tahaa islanders are a little wary of outsiders as it's well off the beaten track.

Orientation
The administrative center is at Patio on the north coast, where the post office, Mairie (town hall), and police station share one compound. The ship from Papeete ties up to the wharf at Tapuamu. There's a large covered area at the terminal where you could spread a sleeping bag in a pinch. The Banque Socredo branch is also at Tapuamu. A new road crosses the mountains from Patio direct to Haamene where a second post office is found.

Sights
Several large sea turtles are held captive in a tank by the lagoon behind the community hall near the church in Tiva. You could walk right around the main part of Tahaa in about eight hours with stops, passing villages every couple of km. Haamene Bay, the longest of Tahaa's four fjords, catches the full force of the southeast trades.

PRACTICALITIES

Accommodations
The most convenient place to stay is **Chez Pascal** (Pascal Tamaehu, tel. 65-60-42). From the Tapuamu ferry wharf you'll see a small bridge at the head of the bay. Turn left as you leave the dock and head for this. Chez Pascal is the first house north of the bridge on the inland side. The rate is CFP 4000 pp for bed, breakfast, and dinner, or CFP 2000 pp without meals. Boat trips to a *motu* (CFP 4000 pp) and the loan of the family bicycle are possible.

The **Hôtel L'Hibiscus** (B.P. 184, Haamene; tel. 65-61-06, fax 65-65-65), or "Tahaa Lagon," is run by Leo and Lolita on the northeast side of windy Haamene Bay. L'Hibiscus has two classes of accommodations: six small bungalows with private bath at CFP 7850 double, or a small house nearby called Le Moana, accommodating four persons at CFP 1500 pp. Transfers from Raiatea are CFP 2500 pp return. You could also get there from Raiatea on the Haamene launch (Wednesday and Friday mornings) and ask to be dropped near the hotel.

Although the accommodations are satisfactory, the trick is that virtually everything you consume—even the water you drink—is charged extra at resort prices. Common drinking water is not available at L'Hibiscus; bottled water is CFP 350. The prices of the meals are fixed at CFP 3500 pp half pension, CFP 5000 full pension (not possible to order a la carte). Don't accept a "free welcome drink" from Leo or Lolita unless you don't mind having it added to your bill (which could be breathtaking). There are no cooking facilities, and the nearest store is three km away in Haamene (bring food and bottled water). The running water in the house may be turned off, although you can usually use the communal shower behind the restaurant. Lighting in the dorm could consist of a kerosene lamp.

The **Hôtel Marina Iti** (Philippe Robin, B.P. 888, Uturoa, Raiatea; tel. 65-61-01, fax 65-63-87) sits at the isolated south tip of Tahaa, opposite Raiatea on Tahaa's only sandy beach. The four clean, pleasant bungalows accommodating three persons are CFP 18,000 by the lagoon or CFP 12,000 in the garden. Meals are CFP 7000 extra for all three. Use of bicycles, canoe, and snorkeling gear is included, and scuba diving is available. Airport transfers are CFP 3000 pp. As you'll have guessed, the Marina Iti caters to an upmarket crowd here in connection with yacht cruises from Raiatea, and numerous cruising yachts anchor in the calm waters offshore.

It's also possible to stay at the **Hôtel Vahine Island** (B.P. 510, Uturoa; tel. 65-67-38, fax 65-67-70) on lovely Motu Tuuvahine off the northeast side of Tahaa. The 11 bungalows are overpriced at CFP 30,000 single or double on the beach or CFP 45,000 overwater. For three meals add CFP 8800 pp, for airport transfers CFP 2200 pp. Outrigger canoes, windsurfing, snorkeling, and fishing gear are free. Moorings are provided for yachts.

Food

The only nonhotel restaurant on Tahaa is **Snack Melanie** (tel. 65-63-06) in Patio. A grocery truck passes L'Hibiscus around 1000 on Monday, Tuesday, Thursday, and Saturday; the same truck calls at the Marina Iti about noon daily except Sunday.

TRANSPORT

There's no airport on Tahaa. Seven of the eight villages have small passenger launches, which leave for Raiatea at 0500 on Wednesday and Friday only, returning to Tahaa at 1000 these same days (CFP 500 OW). Make sure your boat is going exactly where you want to go.

The **Tahaa Transport Service** (tel. 65-61-01) runs the shuttle boat *Uporu* from Tapuamu Wharf and the Hôtel Marina Iti to Uturoa twice a day on weekdays and daily on weekends (CFP 750 OW), connecting with sailings of the high-speed cruiser *Ono-Ono*.

Taporo VI from Papeete, Huahine, and Raiatea calls at Tahaa on Tuesday, Thursday, and Saturday at 0700 and continues on to Bora Bora (southbound it doesn't stop at Tahaa). The *Vaeanu* departs Tahaa for Raiatea, Huahine, and Papeete Thursday and Sunday at noon; Saturday at 0830 it goes to Bora Bora. The *Raromatai Ferry* visits Tahaa on Wednesday and Saturday morning northbound, and Thursday morning and Sunday afternoon southbound. There's a telephone booth at Tapuamu Wharf where you could call your hotel to have them come pick you up.

Trucks on Tahaa are for transporting schoolchildren only, so you may have to hitch to get around. It's not that hard to hitch a ride down the west coast from Patio to Haamene, but there's almost no traffic along the east coast. Even car rentals are difficult on Tahaa (try the Marina Iti).

BORA BORA

Bora Bora, 260 km northwest of Papeete, is everyone's idea of a South Pacific island. Dramatic basalt peaks soar 700 meters above a gorgeous, multicolored lagoon. Slopes and valleys blossom with hibiscus. Some of the most perfect beaches you'll ever see are here, complete with topless sunbathers. Not only are the beaches good but there's plenty to see and do. The local population of 4,500 includes many skilled dancers. To see them practicing in the evening, follow the beat of village drums to their source.

Bora Bora is the only island of Tahiti-Polynesia which can be said to have reached a tourist glut. The relentless stream of cars, pickups, hotel *trucks,* and scooters up and down the main road from Vaitape to Matira approaches Tahitian intensity at times. The uncontrolled expansion of tourism continues as luxury resorts are thrown up around the island, creating the illusion of being in Hawaii or some West Indies hot spot. Yet many of the US$250-a-night hotels stand almost empty. Construction of a huge Hyatt Regency on a swampy shore at the far north end of the island was halted by a land dispute. Today the crumbling Hyatt ruins stand as a monument to bad planning and the perils of high-impact development.

The Land

Seven-million-year-old Bora Bora is made up of a 10-km-long main island, a few smaller high islands in the lagoon, and a long ring of *motus* on the barrier reef. Pofai Bay marks the center of the island's collapsed crater with Toopua and Toopuaiti as its eroded west wall. Mount Pahia's gray basalt mass rises 649 meters behind Vaitape and above it soar the sheer cliffs of Otemanu's mighty volcanic plug (727 meters). The wide-angle scenery of the main island is complemented by the surrounding coral reef and numerous *motus,* one of which bears the airport. Tiny Motu Tapu of the travel brochures was popularized in Murnau's 1928 film *Tabou.* Te Ava Nui Pass is the only entry through the barrier reef. Watch for dolphins near this channel as your ship enters Bora Bora's lagoon; whole colonies sometimes race the boats.

History

The letter *b* doesn't exist in Tahitian, so Bora Bora is actually Pora Pora (First Born). Bora Borans of yesteryear were indomitable warriors who often raided Maupiti, Tahaa, and Raiatea. "Discovered" by Roggeveen in 1722, Bora Bora was visited by Capt. James Cook in 1777. In 1895 the island was annexed by France.

In February 1942 the Americans hastily set up a refueling and regrouping base code-named "Bobcat" on the island to serve shipping between the U.S. west coast or Panama Canal and Australia/New Zealand. You can still see remains from this time, including eight huge naval guns placed here to defend the island

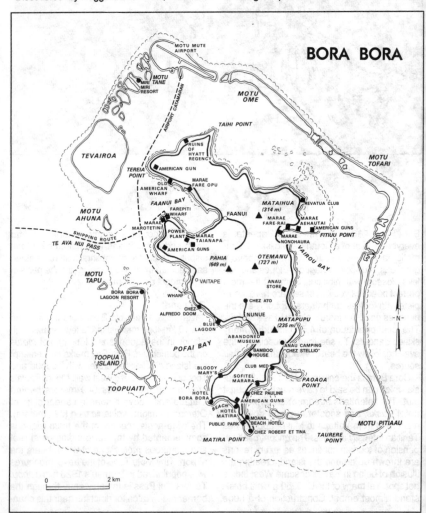

BORA BORA

against a surprise Japanese attack that never materialized. The big lagoon with only one pass offered secure anchorage for as many as 100 U.S. Navy transports at a time. A road was built around the island and an airfield constructed. The 4,400 American army troops also left behind 130 half-caste babies, 40% of whom died when the base closed in 1946 and the abandoned infants were forced to switch from their accustomed American baby formulas to island food. The survivors are now approaching ripe middle age. Novelist James A. Michener, a young naval officer at the time, left perhaps the most enduring legacy by modeling his Bali Hai on this "enchanted island," Bora Bora.

Orientation
You can arrive at Motu Mute airport and be carried to Vaitape Wharf by a fully enclosed catamaran, or disembark from a ship at Farepiti Wharf, three km north of Vaitape. Most of the stores, banks, and offices are near Vaitape Wharf. The best beaches are at Matira at the island's southern tip.

SIGHTS

Vaitape
Behind the Banque de Tahiti at Vaitape Wharf is the **monument to Alain Gerbault,** who sailed his yacht, the *Firecrest,* around the world solo from 1925 to 1929—the first Frenchman to do so. Gerbault's first visit to Bora Bora was from 25 May to 12 June 1926. He returned to Polynesia in 1933 and stayed until 1940.

To get an idea of how the Bora Borans live, take a stroll through Vaitape village: go up the road that begins beside the Banque Socredo.

Around the Island
The largely paved and level 32-km road around the island makes it easy to see Bora Bora by rented bicycle (it's unnecessary to rent a car). At the head of **Pofai Bay** notice the odd assortment of looted war wreckage across the road from Boutique Alain Linda, remnants of an abandoned museum. The seven-inch American gun dragged here from Tereia Point in 1982 is hard to miss. The locations of the other seven MK II naval guns remaining in situ on Bora Bora are given below. The forlorn, violated gun lying on its side at Pofai demonstrates the stupidity of those who would despoil historical monuments.

Stop at **Bloody Mary's Restaurant** to scan the goofy displays outside their gate, but more importantly to get the classic view of the island's soaring peaks across Pofai Bay as it appears in countless brochures. At photographer Erwin Christian's **Moana Art Boutique** just before Hôtel Bora Bora you can buy a postcard of the scene.

The finest beach on the island stretches east from Hôtel Bora Bora to Matira Point. Some of the best snorkeling on the island, with a varied multitude of colorful tropical fish, is off the small point at Hôtel Bora Bora, but you may want to enter from beyond the hotel grounds (near Hôtel Matira) and walk or swim back as the hotel staff don't appreciate strangers who stroll through their lobby to get to their beach. Beware of getting run over by a glass-bottom boat! Martine's Créations (tel. 67-70-79) just east of Hôtel Bora Bora has finely crafted black-pearl jewelry and designer beachwear.

Two **naval guns** sit on the ridge above Hôtel Matira. Take the overgrown trail on the mountain side of the road that winds around behind the bungalows from the east end of the property and keep straight ahead to the top of the ridge for good views of the lagoon and neighboring islands (10 minutes).

Bora Bora's most popular public beach is **Matira Beach Park** directly across the street from the Moana Beach Hôtel on Matira Point. At low tide you can wade from the end of Matira Point right out to the reef. Proceed north to the **Sofitel Marara,** a good place for a leisurely beer. Visitors are unwelcome at the new Club Med, and even the road is forced to climb over a hill to get around the resort. The two general stores at **Anau** can supply a cold drink or a snack.

On the north side of Vairou Bay the road begins to climb over a ridge. Halfway up the slope, look down to the right and by the shore you'll see the *ahu* of *Marae Aehautai,* the best of the three *marae* in this area. From the *marae* there's

one of eight U.S. naval guns left behind in 1945

a stupendous view of Otemanu and you should be able to pick out Te Ana Opea cave far up on the side of the mountain. The steep unpaved slope on the other side of this ridge can be dangerous if you're unaware, so slow down. At the bottom of the hill is a rough track along the north shore of Fitiuu Point. Follow it east till you find a jeep track up onto the ridge to two more of the American **seven-inch guns.** Unfortunately the municipality often uses this area for burning refuse, and the stench can make a visit to the guns almost unbearable.

From between Taihi Point and the Hyatt Regency ruins a steep jeep track climbs to **Popoti Ridge** (249 meters), where the Americans had a radar installation during WW II.

One American **naval gun** remains on the hillside above the rectangular water tank at Tereia Point. The housing of a second gun, vandalized in 1982, is nearby. The remains of several American concrete wharves can be seen along the north shore of **Faanui Bay.** Most of the wartime American occupation force was billeted at Faanui, and a few Quonset huts linger in the bush. **Marae Fare Opu,** just east of a small boat harbor, is notable for petroglyphs of turtles carved into the stones of the *ahu*. Turtles, a favorite food of the gods, were often offered to them on the *marae*. (Mindless guides sometimes highlight the turtles in chalk for the benefit of tourist cameras.)

Between Faanui and Farepiti Wharf, just east of the electricity-generating plant, is **Marae Ta-**

ianapa; its long *ahu* is clearly visible on the hillside from the road. The most important *marae* on Bora Bora was **Marae Marotetini,** on the point near Farepiti Wharf—west of the wharf beyond a huge banyan tree. The great stone *ahu*, 25 meters long and up to 1.5 meters high, was restored by Professor Sinoto in 1968 and is visible from approaching ships.

The last two **American guns** are a 10-minute scramble up the ridge from the main road between Farepiti Wharf and Vaitape. Go straight up the concrete road signposted Garderie Creche d'Enfants. If you reach Otemanu Tours (where you see several *trucks* parked), you've passed the road. At the end of the ridge there's a good view of Te Ava Nui Pass, which the guns were meant to defend. Maupiti is farther out on the horizon. The old Club Med near here was knocked out of service by a hurricane in December 1991.

Hiking

If you're experienced and determined, it's possible to climb **Mt. Pahia** in about four hours of rough going. Take the road inland beside the Banque Socredo at Vaitape and go up the depression past a series of mango trees, veering slightly left. Circle the cliffs near the top on the left side, and come up the back of Snoopy's head and along his toes. (These directions will take on meaning if you study Pahia from the end of Vaitape's wharf.) The trail is unmaintained and a local guide would be a big help (to hire one inquire at CETAD at the Collège de Bora Bora in Vaitape). Avoid rainy weather, in which the way will be muddy and slippery.

Despite what some tourist publications claim, **Otemanu,** the high rectangular peak next to pointed Pahia, has *never* been climbed. It's possible to climb up to the shoulders of the mountain, but the sheer cliffs of the main peak are inaccessible because clamps pull right out of the vertical, crumbly cliff face. Helicopters can land on the summit, but that doesn't count. Otemanu's name means "It's a bird."

SPORTS AND RECREATION

The **Bora Diving Center** (Anne and Michel Condesse, B.P. 182, Nanue; tel. 67-71-84, fax 67-74-83), on Pofai Bay opposite Bloody Mary's Restaurant, does open-water scuba diving every day at CFP 6000 and night dives for CFP 7500. Prices are negotiable if you book direct at their office (closed while they're out diving) and don't book through your hotel reception (there's a CFP 500-1000 surcharge if you're staying at Hôtel Bora Bora, Club Med or the Bora Bora Lagoon Resort). Hotel pickups are at 0830 and 1330.

Scuba diving can also be arranged through Claude Sibani's **Bora Bora Calypso Club** (B.P. 259, Bora Bora; tel. 67-74-64, fax 67-70-34) at the Bora Bora Beach Club. They charge CFP 6000 for a lagoon dive, CFP 6500 for an ocean dive, and go out daily at 0900 and 1400 from the Beach Club dock. Their specialty is diving with manta rays (worth doing to see the mantas, though you won't see much else in that area as the coral is all dead and the waters fished

out). Most scuba diving at Bora Bora is within the lagoon and visibility is sometimes limited.

Like Aitutaki in the Cook Islands, Bora Bora is famous for its lagoon trips. Prices vary depending on whether lunch is included, the length of the trip, the luxury of boat, etc., so check around. A seafood picnic lunch on a *motu,* reefwalking, and snorkeling gear are usually included, and you get a chance to see giant clams, manta rays, and the hand-feeding of small lagoon sharks. For example, the **Blue Lagoon Bar** (tel. 67-70-54, fax 67-79-10) on the north side of Pofai Bay offers a six-hour reef tour with shark feeding and lunch on a *motu* for CFP 4900 pp—it's said to be quite good. Their three-hour lagoon excursion without lunch is CFP 3000, hotel transfers included. Also see the Chez Nono listing which follows. Motorized canoe trips right around Bora Bora are also offered. An excursion of this kind is an essential part of the Bora Bora experience, so splurge on this one. (Several readers have written in to say they agree completely.)

Three-hour tours to the so-called **Bora Lagoonarium** (B.P. 56, Vaitape; tel. 67-71-34) on a *motu* off the main island occur daily except Saturday at 1400 (CFP 3000); you'll see more colorful fish than you ever thought existed. Call for a free hotel pickup.

Stellio (tel. 67-71-32) of the Anau camping ground mentioned below does an island tour by boat for CFP 3000 which includes shark feeding, clam viewing, snorkeling, reef walking, and picnic on a *motu* (bring your own lunch). For CFP 1000 return Stellio will drop you off on a *motu* where you can do your own thing. Chez Pauline also offers this service.

strand morning glory (Ipomoea pes-caprae)

PRACTICALITIES

ACCOMMODATIONS

There's an abundance of accommodations on Bora Bora and except at holiday times (especially during the July festivities), it's not necessary to book a room in advance. When things are slow, the hotel owners meet the interisland boats in search of guests. If someone from the hotel of your choice isn't at the dock when you arrive, get on the blue *truck* marked Vaitape-Anau and ask to be taken there. This should cost CFP 500 pp from Farepiti Wharf, CFP 300 pp from Vaitape Wharf, plus CFP 100 for luggage. However, if you're staying at a luxury resort you could be charged CFP 1800 pp return for airport transfers.

The luxury hotels add a seven percent tax to their room rates (often not included in the quoted price) but most of the budget places include the tax in their price. Be aware that the large hotels frequently tack a CFP 1000 commission onto rental cars, lagoon excursions, and scuba diving booked through their front desks. The campgrounds and pensions don't usually take such commissions. Bora Bora suffers from serious water shortages, so use it sparingly.

Camping and Dormitories

Backpackers often stay at **Chez Stellio** (B.P. 267, Bora Bora; tel. 67-71-32) at Anau on the east side of the island. Camping is CFP 1000 pp and there's a 10-bed guesthouse next to the lagoon at CFP 1500 pp. Double rooms are CFP 4000. Cooking facilities are provided (shortage of utensils). Stellio often hangs up big bunches of free bananas for guests, and his grandchildren do their part to keep the grassy camping area clean. This place is not on a beach, but Stellio owns land on idyllic Motu Vaivahia and for CFP 1000 pp he'll drop you off there for a day or two of Robinson Crusoe-style camping (take sufficient food and water). If you know how to swim, ask him about renting an outrigger canoe *(pirogue)*. Look for Stellio's blue Vaitape-Anau *truck* with "Vaiho" on the door at the wharf and you'll get a free ride to the camping ground when you first arrive, although upon departure everyone must pay CFP 300-500 pp, plus CFP 100 for luggage, for transfers back to the wharf. Stellio's a helpful, laid-back sort of guy and he'll probably offer you additional free rides in his school bus if he's going anyway and you're staying at his place. The trail up the hill across the street is a shortcut into town. Bora Bora is overrun by land crabs, funny little creatures that make camping exciting.

Despite fast-rising prices, many backpackers make the adjustment and stay at **Chez Pauline** (Pauline Youssef, B.P. 215, Vaitape; tel. 67-72-16, fax 67-78-14), on a white-sand beach between the Moana Beach and Sofitel Marara hotels, eight km from Vaitape. Pauline charges CFP 1600 pp to camp (own tent), CFP 2000 in the 10-bed dormitory, or CFP 5000 double in one of her eight small, closely packed beach cabins. The six thatched bungalows with kitchens are CFP 9000/11,500 double/triple. There are communal cooking facilities for campers but they become cramped when many guests are present. It's quite a hike to the grocery store at Anau, but the food truck circling the island passes daily except Sunday around 1100 (check with the receptionist). Due to rave reviews in the Australian guidebooks it can get crowded, and unlike Stellio's which is in the middle of a local village, Pauline's is strictly a tourist scene. An American reader's report: "We couldn't sleep the first night because the mattress was wet and had to move to another bungalow the next day. We were very upset after returning from dinner the second night to find that our bungalow had been broken into and all of my clothes were taken. We'd planned to spend 12 days on Bora Bora but left after four."

Budget Accommodations near Vaitape

Most of the budget places to stay in Vaitape village have closed in recent years, but you can still stay at **Chez Alfredo Doom** (tel. 67-70-31) at Tiipoto, a km south of Vaitape Wharf (just past the Jehovah's Witnesses church, across the street from the garage where you see several *trucks* parked—no sign). Their large thatched house with full cooking facilities, private bath, and plenty of space is fair value at CFP 5000/6000 double/triple for the whole building, but it's a little dark due to the low eaves. Still, if you'd rather stay near town and avoid the tourist ghetto at Matira Point, it's a good choice. The main drawbacks are the steady roar of traffic and a neighbor's radio. Bookings must be made through Madame Doom at the hamburger stand next to the Banque de Polynésie in Vaitape.

CETAD (B.P. 151, Bora Bora; tel. 67-71-47, fax 67-78-20), at the Collège de Bora Bora on the lagoon just north of Magasin Chin Lee in the center of Vaitape, rents a small five-bed bungalow with kitchenette and private bath at CFP 3000 for the first person, plus CFP 1000 for each additional person. It's often full.

At Nunue, right up below Otemanu's soaring peak is **Pension Chez Ato** (tel. 67-77-27), a secluded little hideaway with six rooms at CFP 2000 pp. Cooking facilities are provided and Ato can arrange guides for mountain hikes. Ato is a member of the environmental group *atu atu te natura* and he takes the concept of ecotourism seriously. It's a good way to experience a slice of Tahitian life, so long as you don't mind being away from the beach. Look for a paved road running inland from opposite a large stone engraved Bora 2000 at the head of Pofai Bay and follow it right up to the end (there's no sign). Recommended.

Budget Accommodations at Matira Point

On the Matira peninsula are two excellent alternatives to the upmarket hotels. **Chez Nono** (Noël Leverd, B.P. 282, Vaitape; tel. 67-71-38, fax 67-74-27) faces the beach across from the Moana Beach Hôtel. They have one large bungalow with cooking facilities (CFP 14,000), two smaller bungalows with private bath (CFP 7000), and a six-bedroom thatched guesthouse with shared kitchen at CFP 4000/5000 single/double per room. Ventilation spaces between the ceilings and walls mean you hear *everything* in the other rooms, but the atmosphere is amiable and all guests soon become good friends. Their garden is a pleasant place to sit but the bungalows occasionally experience a lot of noise from beach parties. The solar water heating only works when the sun is shining. Their boat tour around the island includes shark feeding and an excellent fish lunch. Noël isn't very attentive when you come to him with complaints, however.

Also good is **Chez Robert et Tina,** (tel. 67-72-92) two European-style houses with cooking facilities down the road from Chez Nono at the tip of Matira Point (CFP 3000/6000 single/double). Robert offers excellent lagoon trips at CFP 3000 pp without lunch.

Medium-Priced Hotels

Hôtel Matira (B.P. 31, Vaitape; tel. 67-70-51, fax 67-77-02) is one of the few medium-priced places offering cooking facilities. Their nine thatched bungalows with kitchenettes on the mountain side of the road are CFP 15,200/19,200 double/triple. The units without kitchens are CFP 3000 cheaper. The 16 thatched bungalows with kitchenettes in the annex right on the lagoon at the neck of Matira peninsula are a better value at CFP 17,000/21,000. The Matira's Chinese restaurant (closed Monday) is reasonable, and the beach is excellent. Airport transfers are CFP 1000 pp return.

The **Bora Bora Motel** (B.P. 180, Vaitape; tel. 67-78-21, fax 67-77-57) shares a white beach with the Sofitel Marara (see below). Their four studios with bedroom, living room, dining room, and kitchen are CFP 13,000 double; the three slightly larger apartments are CFP 17,000 double, extra persons are CFP 3000 each. These units built in 1991 are comfortable and spacious, a good compromise if you want to go upmarket while keeping to a budget.

Next door to the Bora Bora Motel is the **Bora Bora Beach Club** (B.P. 252, Nunue; tel. 67-71-16, fax 67-71-30), part of the Tahiti Resort Hotels chain. The nine four-unit, single-roof blocks total 36 rooms beginning at CFP 23,000 single, double, or triple (garden) or CFP 25,000 (beach)—highly overpriced for what you get, and a/c is CFP 4000 extra! Not all rooms have a fridge (check), and if your room is without a/c make sure your neighbors are in the same predicament, otherwise you could get the noise without the chill. There are no cooking facilities. Jackie Halter of Jackson, Wyoming, sent us this comment: "The bathroom was filthy, an active wasp nest was in our ceiling, the refrigerator was big enough to put a piece of fruit in, and the restaurant which we went to upon arrival because we were starving left a lot to be desired. The beach was so dirty we couldn't even walk along it in bare feet." Windsurfing, fishing, and snorkeling gear are loaned free to guests (that's why they call it a "club"). They also claim to provide free outrigger canoes but most have holes in them. Airport transfers are CFP 1800 pp return. Not recommended

The 16-room **Revatua Club** (B.P. 159, Vaitape; tel. 67-71-67, fax 67-76-59) on the northeast side of the island is isolated, beachless, and CFP 8900/10,400/11,700 single/double/triple, plus CFP 3800 pp for breakfast and dinner and CFP 800 pp for airport transfers. Its only draws are the excellent overwater French restaurant **Chez Christian**, which offers free transport for diners, and the bar. The mock-Victorian architecture is right out of Hollywood.

Cruising yachties are catered for by the **Yacht Club de Bora Bora** (B.P. 17, Vaitape; tel. 67-70-69) near Farepiti Wharf. They allow boats free use of their 17 moorings, and provide fresh water and showers. In turn, yachties are expected to splash out occasionally in their seafood restaurant. The club has three stuffy garden bungalows at CFP 10,000 double, but no beach (or cooking). During the night you could be visited by both mosquitoes and burglars. Their three floating bungalows with cooking facilities and solar electricity (CFP 20,000 for four persons) can be towed out and moored off a *motu*.

Upmarket Hotels

Hôtel Bora Bora (B.P. 1, Bora Bora; tel. 67-44-60, fax 60-44-66), which opened in June 1961, was the island's first large hotel. At CFP 60,000 single or double for an overwater bungalow, it's one of the most exclusive millionaire's playgrounds in the South Pacific. Standard rooms in this 55-unit resort begin at CFP 39,500 single or double, CFP 46,000 triple. Breakfast and dinner are CFP 6200 pp extra. Their beach is superb and the hotel restaurant's cuisine exceptional. The hotel's scuba diving concession is run by noted photographer Erwin Christian.

Japanese-owned **Hôtel Moana Beach Parkroyal** (B.P. 156, Bora Bora; tel. 67-73-73, fax 67-71-41) on a white-sand beach at Matira Point is also absurdly expensive. One of the 10 beachfront bungalows here will set you back CFP 40,500 single or double; the 30 overwater bungalows are an additional CFP 15,300 (children under 19 free). It's CFP 6200 pp extra for breakfast and dinner.

A less pretentious top-end resort is the **Hôtel Sofitel Marara** (B.P. 6, Bora Bora; tel. 67-74-01, fax 67-74-03). The Sofitel Marara (the name means "Flying Fish") was built in 1978 to house the crew filming Dino de Laurentiis' *Hurricane*; the film flopped but the hotel has been going strong ever since. The 64 bungalows begin at CFP 26,000 single or double, CFP 30,500 triple. It's open and informal, and instead of the Americans you hear at Hôtel Bora Bora and the

Japanese you see at the Moana Beach, the Marara caters to an international mix of tourists. The beach doesn't have the policed feel of the Bora Bora's and this is the only hotel on the main island with a swimming pool. The Marara's bar is fairly reasonable for such a swank place (happy hour is daily 1700-1800), but the restaurant isn't highly rated (and the service is incredibly slow).

In late 1993 a new 150-bungalow **Club Méditerranée** (B.P. 34, Bora Bora; tel. 60-46-04, fax 60-46-11) opened on Bora Bora. The circuminsular road had to be rerouted around this US$30-million enclave just north of the Sofitel, and as usual, security is tight. You don't just stroll in and rent a room at Club Med as only guests are allowed to set foot on these hallowed grounds, so book in advance at the Club Med office in Papeete's Vaima Center (tel. 42-96-99). The Bora Bora Club Med is more luxurious than Club Med Moorea, and as usual, all meals and nonmotorized nautical activities are included in the basic price (from CFP 22,000 pp, double occupancy). The gaudy orange and yellow bungalows face the beach.

The 80-unit, Japanese-owned **Hôtel Bora Bora Lagoon Resort** (B.P. 175, Vaitape; tel. 60-40-00, fax 60-40-01) on Toopua Island opposite Vaitape offers five-star facilities with prices to match. Beach bungalows start at an amazing CFP 52,000/60,500 double/triple (50% more for an overwater bungalow), plus another CFP 12,000 pp for all meals. A large sign at the landing announces that it's forbidden to bring your own food and drink into the resort. (French expatriates point to this resort, which opened in June 1993, as a good example of Japanese financial lunacy: the investors have sunk countless millions of dollars into the place, though it will revert to the local landowner in 30 years.)

FOOD

Budget Places to Eat
Pâtisserie-Bar Le Vaitape, across the street from the Banque de Polynésie in Vaitape, has reasonable beer prices and the *poisson cru* (CFP 700) is excellent but they don't have it every day (ask). They also serve ice cream but their coffee is terrible.

Snack Matira (tel. 67-77-32), opposite the college just north of Magasin Chin Lee, serves filling meals for CFP 700. Try the *maa tinito*.

The **Restaurant Manuia** at the Collège de Bora Bora (tel. 67-71-47) just north of Magasin Chin Lee in Vaitape is used to train students for employment at the large hotels. Since their aim is not profit, you can get a three-course meal with coffee and a carafe of wine for CFP 1200 here, but only on Wednesday and Friday 1130-1330 during the school year (mid-January to June and August to mid-December). It's a nice change of pace and excellent value.

Facing the beach just east of Hôtel Bora Bora are two reasonable places to eat. **Ben's Snack** (tel. 67-74-54) manages to turn out surprisingly good home-cooked pizza, lasagna, pasta, and omelettes, and the colorful American-Tahitian owners, Robin and Ben, add a Bohemian air to the place. Another snack bar (closed Monday), across the street and along a bit, offers hamburgers and *poisson cru* for noticeably lower prices.

Snack Chez Hinavai (tel. 67-79-26) near Chez Pauline has a few Chinese dishes and fairly reasonable meat and fish. **Snack La Bounty** (tel. 67-70-43) between Chez Pauline and the Sofitel is a simple open-air restaurant with good-quality food at medium prices.

The **Pofai Shoppe** on the road near Hôtel Bora Bora sells cold fruit drinks at normal prices (open daily).

Better Restaurants
Basically, there are two choices if you want to "eat out." **Bloody Mary's Restaurant** (closed Sunday; tel. 67-72-86) is the larger and better established with a tradition dating back to 1979. A board outside lists "famous guests," including Jane Fonda and Baron George Von Dangel. It remains good, with inexpensive pizza for lunch (1100-1500) and upmarket seafood for dinner (1830-2100). Beer is on tap all day (a pitcher of Hinano is CFP 750), so it's worth a stop on your way around the island at any time. Free hotel pickups for diners are available at 1830 or 1930 if you call ahead. Bloody Mary's offers free moorings to yachties who dine with them.

At dinner the newer **Bamboo House Restaurant** (tel. 67-76-24), also on Pofai Bay, does its best to challenge Bloody Mary's famous seafood and if you call, they'll also pick you up at your hotel. Both places are good, but pick Bloody Mary's if you only have time for one.

In 1995 **Restaurant Le Tiare** opened across the street from the Bora Bora Beach Club. In the evening the tables are all taken, which perhaps says something about the restaurants in the Beach Club and nearby Sofitel Marara.

Groceries

Bora Bora's largest supermarket is **Magasin Chin Lee,** north of Vaitape Wharf (just north of the large church) and opposite the island's Mobil gas station. It and another well-stocked grocery store in Vaitape are open Monday to Saturday 0600-1800. The Total service station is north again. The only other places to buy groceries are the two general stores at Anau, halfway around the island (closed Sunday). No grocery store is found at Matira, although a grocery truck passes this way around 1100 daily (except Sunday).

ENTERTAINMENT AND EVENTS

Entertainment

Le Récife Bar (B.P. 278, Vaitape; tel. 67-73-87), between Vaitape and Farepiti Wharf, is Bora Bora's after-hours club, open Friday and Saturday from 2230. Disco dancing continues almost until dawn, but expect loud, heavy-on-the-beat music with few patrons. Steer clear of the local drunks hanging around outside who can't afford the CFP 1000 cover charge.

Witness Polynesian dancing on the beach at **Hôtel Bora Bora** (tel. 67-44-60) by grabbing a barside seat before it starts at 2030 on Wednesday and Sunday nights.

Additional traditional dancing occurs after dinner Tuesday, Thursday, and Saturday nights at 2030 at the **Moana Beach Hôtel** (tel. 67-73-73).

You may feel more at home watching the Tahitian dance show at the **Hôtel Sofitel Marara** (tel. 67-74-01) every Tuesday, Friday and Saturday night at 2030; see it all for the price of a draught beer. On Saturday at 1830 they open the earth oven and a Tahitian feast begins. The floor show is good but the food is mediocre.

Events

The *Fêtes de Juillet* are celebrated at Bora Bora with special fervor. The canoe and bicycle races,

javelin throwing, flower cars, singing, and dancing competitions run until 0300 nightly. A public ball goes till dawn on the Saturday closest to 14 July. Try to participate in the 10-km foot race to prove that all tourists aren't lazy, but don't take the prizes away from the locals. If you win, be sure to give the money back to them for partying. You'll make good friends that way and have more fun dancing in the evening. The stands are beautiful because the best decorations win prizes, too.

SHOPPING AND SERVICES

Shopping

There are plenty of small boutiques around Vaitape selling black coral jewelry, pearls, pareus, T-shirts, designer beachwear, etc. The **Centre Artisanal** near Vaitape Wharf is a good place to buy a shell necklace or a pareu directly from the locals.

Services and Information

The four main banks all have offices near Vaitape Wharf but none are open on Saturday. The post office, gendarmerie, and health clinic *(Santé Publique)* are within a stone's throw of the wharf. **Pharmacie Fare Ra'au** is farther north.

Dr. Marie-Joseph Juen's private **Cabinet Médical** (tel. 67-70-62) behind the Banque de Polynésie is open weekdays 0700-1200/1500-1800, Saturday 0700-1200, Sunday 0900-1000. Dr. François Macouin has his private **dental clinic** (tel. 67-70-55) in the same building.

The helpful **tourist information office** (B.P. 144, Bora Bora; tel./fax 67-76-36) and public toilets are in the Centre Artisanal next to Vaitape Wharf. The unmarked **Air Tahiti** office (tel. 67-70-35) is beside the Banque de Tahiti on the wharf at Vaitape.

TRANSPORT

Getting There

Air Tahiti has a useful transversal flight direct from Bora Bora to Rangiroa (CFP 20,700) twice a week. For information on flights to Bora Bora from Papeete, Huahine, and Raiatea, see "Getting Around" in the main Introduction.

Ships from Raiatea and Papeete tie up at Farepiti Wharf, three km north of Vaitape. The shipping companies have no representatives on Bora Bora, so for departure times just keep asking. Drivers of the *trucks* are the most likely to know. You buy your ticket when the ship arrives. Officially the *Taporo VI* leaves for Raiatea, Huahine, and Papeete on Tuesday, Thursday, and Saturday at 1130. The *Vaeanu* departs Bora Bora for Raiatea, Huahine, and Papeete Tuesday at noon, Thursday at 0830, and Sunday at 0930. The *Raromatai Ferry* leaves for Tahaa, Raiatea, Huahine, and Papeete Thursday at 0700 and Sunday at 1430. Beware of ships leaving early.

The high-speed cruiser *Ono-Ono* (tel. 67-78-00) departs Bora Bora for Raiatea (1.5 hours, CFP 1600), Huahine (three hours, CFP 2800), and Papeete (six hours, CFP 5800) on Tuesday and Thursday at 1200, Sunday at 1400. On Saturday there's a trip to Raiatea and Huahine alone at 0830.

Getting Around
Getting around is a bit of a headache, as *truck* service is irregular and at lunchtime everything stops. Public *trucks* usually meet the boats, but many of the *trucks* you see around town are strictly for guests of the luxury hotels. If you do find one willing to take you, fares between Vaitape and Matira vary from CFP 300-500, plus CFP 100 for luggage. Taxi fares are high, so check before getting in.

Mataura Rent-A-Bike (tel. 67-73-16) just south of Vaitape rents bicycles at CFP 500 a day or CFP 800 for two days. At Chez Pauline bicycles are CFP 900 half day, CFP 1300 full day. Bora Bora is perfect for cycling as there's an excellent paved road right around the island (with only one unpaved stretch on the incline at Fitiuu Point), almost no hills, and lots of scenic bays to shelter you from the wind.

If you must rent a car, **Bora Rent-a-Car** (B.P. 246, Vaitape; tel. 67-70-03) opposite Vaitape Wharf has Renaults at CFP 6500 for a 0800-1700 day, CFP 7500 for 24 hours. The price includes insurance and unlimited km, valid driver's license required. They also have motor scooters for CFP 4500 0800-1700 or CFP 5500 for 24 hours. For service and price they're the best on the island. If driving at night, watch out for scooters and bicycles without lights. However, to better enjoy the scenery and avoid disturbing the environment, we suggest you dispense with motorized transport on little Bora Bora.

The **Yacht Club de Bora Bora** (tel. 67-70-69) rents small, two-person dinghies with six-horsepower outboard motors for CFP 3500 half day, CFP 6000 full day (gas extra). With an early start you could circumnavigate the island.

The **Blue Lagoon Bar** (tel. 67-70-54) also rents four-person motorboats at CFP 5000 half day, CFP 8000 full day, gasoline and insurance included.

Otemanu Tours (tel. 67-70-49), just north of Vaitape, offers a 2.5-hour minibus tour around Bora Bora daily except Sunday at 1400 (CFP 2000). **Jeep Safaris** (tel. 67-70-34) offers Land Rover tours up a steep ridge opposite Otemanu at CFP 4000.

Airport
Bora Bora's vast airfield (BOB) on Motu Mute north of the main island was built by the Americans during WW II. The first commercial flight from Paris to Tahiti-Polynesia landed here in October 1958 and until March 1961 all international flights used this airstrip; passengers were then transferred to Papeete by Catalina amphibious or Bermuda flying boat seaplanes.

Today, a 25-minute catamaran ride brings arriving air passengers to Vaitape Wharf (included in the plane ticket). The boat ride isn't as much fun as it sounds because you have to sit in a stuffy a/c cabin peeping at Bora Bora through salt-encrusted windows and are not allowed to stand on the upper deck. (Why doesn't Air Tahiti get smart and scrap their flash cat? It's hard to imagine a more anticlimactic way to arrive!)

When the catamaran from the airport arrives at Vaitape Wharf, all of the luxury hotels will have guest transportation waiting, but the budget places don't always meet the flights (the deluxe places don't bother meeting the interisland boats). As you arrive at the wharf, shout out the name of your hotel and you'll be directed to the right *truck* (they don't have destination signs).

The airport café serves a very good cup of coffee.

If you're flying to Bora Bora from Papeete go early in the morning and sit on the left side of the aircraft for spectacular views—it's only from the air that Bora Bora is the most beautiful island in the world!

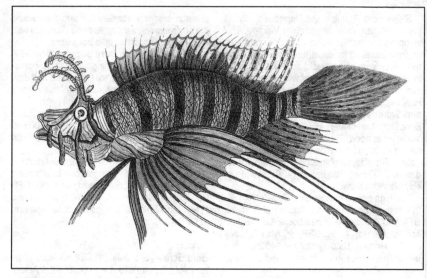

scorpion fish

MAUPITI

Majestic Maupiti (Maurua), 44 km west of Bora Bora, is the least known of the accessible Society Islands. Maupiti's mighty volcanic plug soars from a sapphire lagoon and the vegetation-draped cliffs complement the magnificent *motu* beaches. Almost every bit of level land on the main island is taken up by fruit trees, while watermelons thrive on the surrounding *motus*. Maupiti abounds in native seabirds, including frigate birds, terns, and others. The absence of Indian mynahs allows you to see native land birds almost extinct elsewhere.

The 1,000 people live in the adjacent villages of Vai'ea, Fararuru, and Pauma. Tourism is not promoted because there aren't any regular hotels, which can be an advantage! Maupiti was once famous for its black basalt stone pounders and fishhooks made from the seven local varieties of mother-of-pearl shell.

Sights

It takes only three hours to walk right around the island. The nine-km crushed-coral road,

lined with breadfruit, mango, banana, and hibiscus, passes crumbling *marae,* freshwater springs, and a beach.

Marae Vaiahu, by the shore a few hundred meters beyond Hotuparaoa Massif, is the largest *marae.* Once a royal landing place opposite the pass into the lagoon, the *marae* still bears the king's throne and ancient burials. Nearby is the sorcerers' rock: light a fire beside this rock and you will die. Above the road are a few smaller *marae.*

Terei'a Beach, at the west tip of Maupiti, is the only good beach on the main island. At low tide you can wade across from Terei'a to Motu Auira in waist-deep water. **Marae Vaiorie** is a double *marae* with freshwater springs in between.

As many as two dozen large *marae* are hidden in Maupiti's mountainous interior, and the island is known for its ghosts. A local guide will lead you to the 372-meter summit of Maupiti for around CFP 2500. With the proper encouragement he/she may show you the *marae* and tell the legends.

PRACTICALITIES

Accommodations

Several of the inhabitants take paying guests and they usually meet the flights and boats in search of clients. The absence of a regular hotel on Maupiti throws together an odd mix of vacationing French couples, backpackers, and "adventuresome" tourists in the guesthouses. You could camp on the white sands of Terei'a Beach, but water and *nonos* (insects) would be a problem. If you're set on camping, get across

to the airport *motu*, hike south, and look for a campsite there—you'll have to befriend someone to obtain water and, like Bora Bora, Maupiti experiences serious water shortages during the dry season.

Chez Mareta (Tinorua and Mareta Anua, tel. 67-80-25), in the center of Vai'ea village, is the house with the sloping blue roof a few minutes' walk from the Mairie (town hall). They offer mattresses on the floor in the upstairs double rooms for CFP 1000 pp, or for CFP 3000 pp including breakfast and dinner. A pleasant sitting room faces the lagoon downstairs. Upon request,

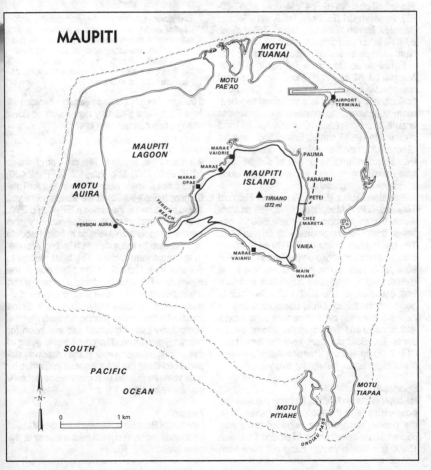

MAUPITI

MOTU TUANAI

MOTU PAE'AO

AIRPORT TERMINAL

MAUPITI LAGOON

MARAE VAIORIE

MARAE

MARAE OPAE

PAUMA

MAUPITI ISLAND

FARAURU

TIRIANO (372 m)

PETEI

MOTU AUIRA

TEREI'A BEACH

CHEZ MARETA

PENSION AUIRA

VAIEA

MARAE VAIAHU

MAIN WHARF

SOUTH

PACIFIC

OCEAN

-N-

0   1 km

MOTU TIAPAA

MOTU PITIAHE

ONOIAU PASS

they'll drop you on a *motu* for the day (beware of sunburn). Chez Mareta is okay for a couple of days, but not an extended stay. Agree on the price beforehand and check your bill when you leave. The church choir in the next building practices their singing quite loudly each night.

At **Pension Tamati** (Ferdinand and Etu Tapuhiro, tel. 67-80-10) the nine rooms cost CFP 2000 pp with breakfast. Unfortunately, tourists are usually given the inside rooms without proper ventilation, but communal cooking facilities are available.

Other places to stay in Vai'ea village are **Chez Floriette Tuheiava** (B.P. 43, Maupiti; tel. 67-80-85), **Pension Eri** (Eri Nohi, tel. 67-81-29), and **Pension Marau** (Tino and Marau Tehahe, tel. 67-81-19), all charging around CFP 4500 pp a night with half board, CFP 5500 with full board.

Fare Pae'ao (Jeannine Tavaearii, B.P. 33, Maupiti; tel. 67-81-01) on Motu Pae'ao is quiet and offers a superb white beach. It's CFP 6000 pp including all meals in a screened two-bedroom bungalow. Reservations are required to ensure an airport pickup (CFP 1000 pp RT) and a room. (In 1962 Kenneth Emory and Yoshihiko Sinoto excavated a prehistoric cemetery on Pae'ao and found 15 adzes of six different types, providing valuable evidence for the study of Polynesian migrations.)

Pension Auira (Edna Terai and Richard Tefaatau, B.P. 2, Maupiti; tel. 67-80-26) on Motu Auira, the *motu* opposite Terei'a Beach, has seven thatched bungalows with private bath. The garden variety are CFP 7000 pp a day including all meals; those on the beach are CFP 8000 pp. At those prices you'd expect fans in the rooms, reading lights, beach furniture, and nautical activities, but no such luck. The food is good but the beach could use a cleaning. At night the charming owner's pack of dogs makes a lot of noise and their inevitable excrement attracts flies. Boat transfers from the airport are CFP 2000 pp. In sum, Pension Auira is a wonderful experience, but not for everyone.

Services

No bank exists on Maupiti, so bring money. The **post office** is at the Mairie. The bakery is in the power plant on the edge of town and baguettes are baked and sold around 1100 and 1500. The island youths hang out here from

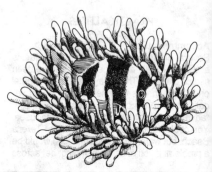

The clown- or damselfish (Amphiprion clarkii) nestles among the venomous tentacles of an anemone. A mucous secretion protects the fish from the creature's stinging cells, providing it with a safe refuge. Anemones gather plankton from the water, but also feed on mussels, snails, or barnacles that fall their way.

1000 on. There's a village disco in Fararuu village Friday and Saturday nights with no cover charge, and canned beer is sold.

Getting There

Air Tahiti has flights to Maupiti from Raiatea (CFP 5500 OW) and Papeete (CFP 12,400) three times a week. Reconfirm with the Air Tahiti agent (tel. 67-80-20) at the Mairie. Here you board the launch to the airport (CFP 400 pp OW).

For information on the twice-monthly government supply ship *Meherio III* from Papeete and Raiatea to Maupiti, see "Getting Around" in the main Introduction. The boat returns to Raiatea from Maupiti on the afternoon of the arrival day. The pass into Maupiti is narrow and when there's a southeast wind it can be dangerous—boats have had to turn back. Ships must enter the channel during daylight, thus the compulsory morning arrival and afternoon (or morning) departure. The coming and going of this ship is a major event in the otherwise unperturbed life of the Maupitians. If you arrive by boat you'll be treated with more respect than if you arrive by plane.

Airport

Like that of Bora Bora, Maupiti's airport (MAU) is on a small *motu*. You must take a launch to the main island (CFP 400).

OTHER LEEWARD ISLANDS

Tupai

Tupai or Motu Iti ("Small Island"), 13 km north of Bora Bora, is a tiny, privately owned coral atoll measuring 1,100 hectares. The facing horse-shoe-shaped *motus* enclose a lagoon. Ships must anchor offshore. The few dozen people who live here make copra from coconuts off the 155,000 trees. In 1990 opposition from traditional landowners blocked resort development here by a Japanese corporation and now the entire atoll is up for sale at US$50,000,000 (contact René Boehm, Neuer Wall 2-6, D-20354 Hamburg, Germany; fax 49-40-340568).

Maupihaa

To approach 360-hectare Maupihaa (Mopelia) in stormy weather is dangerous. The unmarked pass into the atoll's lagoon is a mere 10 meters wide and can only be found by searching for the strong outflow of lagoon water at low tide. Cruising yachts often anchor in the lagoon (no fresh water available here).

The notorious German raider *Seeadler* was wrecked on Maupihaa in 1917. Eventually Count Felix von Luckner was able to carry on to Fiji, where he was captured at Wakaya Island. Count von Luckner's journal, *The Sea Devil,* became a best-seller after the war.

In 1983 the pro-independence Pomare Party filed claim to Maupihaa on the ancestral rights of their leader, Joinville Pomare, a descendent of Queen Pomare IV. Party members occupied the atoll, and declared it and neighboring Manuae and Motu One to be an independent state. On Maupihaa they established a successful pearl farm, which attracted the interest of villagers on Maupiti who had claims of their own to the atoll. In 1991 the French colonial government took advantage of the opportunity to play one group of Polynesians against another by granting land concessions on Maupihaa to the Maupiti people, and on 5 September 1992 the eight Pomare pearl farmers were evicted from the atoll by 40 French gendarmes backed by a helicopter and a frigate. A day later settlers from Maupiti arrived on Maupihaa with the blessing of the deceitful French and took over the Pomare's pearl farm.

Manuae

Manuae (Scilly) is the westernmost of the Society Islands. This atoll is 15 km in diameter but totals only 400 hectares. Pearl divers once visited Manuae. In 1855 the three-masted schooner *Julia Ann* sank on the Manuae reef. It took the survivors two months to build a small boat, which carried them to safety at Raiatea.

Motu One

Motu One (Bellingshausen) got its second name from a 19th-century Russian explorer. Tiny 280-hectare Motu One is circled by a guano-bearing reef, with no pass into the lagoon.

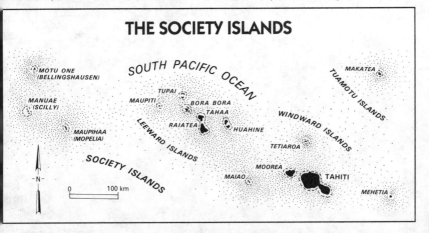

THE SOCIETY ISLANDS

(top) *les roulettes,* Papeete, Tahiti (Robert Leger); (bottom left) Tahitian dancer (Tahiti Tourisme); (bottom right) girl at Avatoru, Rangiroa (Robert Leger)

(top) flower vendors, Papeete Market, Tahiti (Tahiti Tourisme, Tini Colombel);
(bottom) frangipani (Richard Eastwood)

OUTER ISLANDS

Australs, Tuamotus, Gambiers, Marquesas

LES MARQUISES

Ils parlent de la morte comme tu parles d'un fruit
Ils regardent la mer comme tu regardes un puits
Les femmes sont lascives au soleil redouté
Et s'il n'y a pas d'hiver cela n'est pas l'été
La pluie est traversière elle bat de grain en grain
Quelques vieux chevaux blancs qui fredonnent Gauguin
Et par manque de brise le temps s'immobilise
Aux Marquises.
Du soir montent des feux et des points de silence
Qui vont s'élargissant et la lune s'avance
Et la mer se déchire infiniment brisée
Par des rochers qui prirent des prénoms affolés
Et puis plus loin des chiens des chants de repentance
Et quelques pas de deux et quelques pas de danse
Et la nuit est soumise et l'alizé se brise
Aux Marquises.
Leur rire est dans le coeur le mot dans le regard
Le coeur est voyageur l'avenir est au hasard
Et passent des cocotiers qui écrivent des chants d'amour
Que les soeurs d'alentours ignorent d'ignorer
Les pirogues s'en vont les pirogues s'en viennent
Et mes souvenirs deviennent ce que les vieux en font
Veux-tu que je te dise gémir n'est pas de mise
Aux Marquises.

— *Jacques Brel*

THE AUSTRAL ISLANDS

The inhabited volcanic islands of Rimatara, Rurutu, Tubuai, Raivavae, and Rapa, plus uninhabited Maria (or Hull) atoll, make up the Austral group. This southernmost island chain is a 1,280-km extension of the same submerged mountain range as that of the southern Cook Islands, 900 km northwest. The islands of the Australs seldom exceed 300 meters, except Rapa, which soars to 650 meters. The southerly location makes these islands notably cooler than Tahiti. Collectively the Australs are known as Tuhaa Pae, the "Fifth Part" or fifth administrative subdivision of Tahiti-Polynesia. It's still a world apart from tourism.

History

Excavations carried out on the northwest coast of Rurutu uncovered 60 round-ended houses arrayed in parallel rows, with 14 *marae* scattered among them, demonstrating the presence of humans here as early as A.D. 900. Ruins of *marae* can also be seen on Rimatara, Tubuai, and Raivavae. Huge stone tikis once graced Raivavae, but most have since been destroyed or removed. The terraced mountain fortifications, or *pa,* on Rapa are unique.

The Australs were one of the great art areas of the Pacific, represented today in many museums. The best-known artifacts are sculptured sharkskin drums, wooden bowls, fly whisks, and tapa cloth. Offerings that could not be touched by human hands were placed on the sacred altars with intricately incised ceremonial ladles. European contact effaced most of these traditions and the carving done today is crude by comparison.

Rurutu was spotted by Capt. James Cook in 1769; he found Tubuai in 1777. In 1789 Fletcher Christian and the *Bounty* mutineers attempted to establish a settlement at the northeast corner of Tubuai. They left after only three months, following battles with the islanders in which 66 Polynesians died. The European discoverer of Rapa was Capt. George Vancouver in 1791. Rimatara wasn't discovered until 1813, by the Australian captain Michael Fodger.

English missionaries converted most of the people to Protestantism in the early 19th century. Whalers and sandalwood ships introduced diseases and firearms, which decimated the Austral islanders. The French didn't complete their annexation of the group until 1900. Since then the Australs have gone their sleepy way.

The People
The 6,500 mostly Polynesian inhabitants are fishermen and farmers who live in attractive villages with homes and churches built of coral limestone. The rich soil and temperate climate stimulate agriculture with staple crops such as taro, manioc, Irish potatoes, sweet potatoes, leeks, cabbage, carrots, corn, and coffee. The coconut palm also thrives, except on Rapa. Today many Austral people live in Papeete.

Getting There
Air Tahiti has three flights a week to Rurutu and Tubuai, the only islands with airports. One flight operates Papeete-Tubuai-Rurutu-Papeete, the other two Papeete-Rurutu-Tubuai-Papeete. One-way fares from Tahiti are CFP 17,700 to Rurutu and CFP 19,800 to Tubuai. Rurutu-Tubuai is CFP 8100.

All the other Austral Islands are accessible only by boat. For information on the twice-monthly sailings of the *Tuhaa Pae II* from Papeete, see "Getting Around" in the main Introduction to this book.

RURUTU

This island, 572 km south of Tahiti, is shaped like a miniature replica of the African continent. For the hiker, mountainous, 32-square-km Rurutu is a more varied island to visit than Tubuai. Taatioe (389 meters) and Manureva (384 meters) are the highest peaks. A narrow fringing reef surrounds Rurutu, but there's no lagoon. The climate of this northernmost Austral island is temperate and dry. The history of Rurutu revolves around three important dates: 1821, when the gospel arrived on the island; 1970, when Cyclone Emma devastated the three villages; and 1975, when the airport opened.

In January and July Rurutuans practice the ancient art of stone lifting or *amoraa ofai*. Men get three tries to hoist a 130-kg boulder coated with *monoi* (coconut oil) up onto their shoulders, while women attempt a 60-kg stone. Dancing and feasting follow the event. The women of Rurutu weave fine pandanus hats, bags, baskets, fans, lamp shades, and mats. Rurutu's famous Manureva ("Soaring Bird") Dance Group has performed around the world. The main evening entertainment is watching dancers practice in the villages.

Sights
The pleasant main village, Moerai, boasts a post office, four small stores, two bakeries, and two banks. Two other villages, Avera and Hauti, bring the total island population to about 2,000. Electricity functions 24 hours a day. Neat fences and flower gardens surround the coral limestone houses. This is the Polynesia of 50 years ago: though snack bars have appeared, *trucks*

have yet to cover the 30-km coastal road. Beaches, waterfalls, valleys, and limestone caves beckon the explorer.

At **Moerai** village lies the tomb of French navigator Eric de Bisschop, whose exploits equaled, but are not as well known as, those of Thor Heyerdahl. Before WW II de Bisschop sailed a catamaran, the *Kaimiloa,* from Hawaii to the Mediterranean via the Indian Ocean and the tip of Africa. His greatest voyage was aboard the

Eric de Bisschop

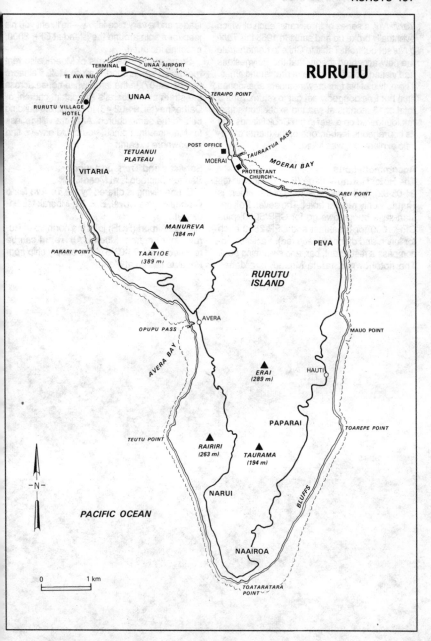

Tahiti Nui, a series of three rafts, each of which eventually broke up and sank. In 1956 the *Tahiti Nui* set out from Tahiti to Chile to demonstrate the now-accepted theory that the Polynesians had visited South America in prehistoric times. There, two of his four crewmembers abandoned ship but Eric doggedly set out to return. After a total of 13 months at sea the expedition's final raft foundered on a reef in the Cook Islands and its courageous leader, one of the giants of Pacific exploration, was killed.

Accommodations

The **Hôtel Rurutu Village** (B.P. 6, Moerai; tel. 94-03-92), on a beach just west of the airport, is Rurutu's only regular hotel. The seven Polynesian-style bungalows go for CFP 5000, plus CFP 1000 for breakfast and CFP 2500 each for lunch and dinner (if required). Facilities encompass a restaurant, bar, and swimming pool. The hotel owner, Iareta Moeau, is a dance leader and a very nice fellow—he'll rent you his jeep for a spin around the island at CFP 3000, gasoline included.

Some of the inhabitants of Moerai also rent rooms, so ask around. Talk to Metu Teinaore (tel. 94-04-07) in the large white house across the street from Moerai's Protestant church, or Catherine (tel. 94-02-43) in a concrete building behind the same church. At Avera village, ask for Maurice. In a pinch, you could always find somewhere to camp.

Services and Transportation

Banque Socredo is at Moerai.

Scuba diving is offered by the **Te Ava Ma'o Club** (Jacques Duval, B.P. 31, Moerai; tel. 94-02-29).

Unaa Airport (RUR) is at the north tip of Rurutu, four km from Moerai. **Air Tahiti** can be reached at tel. 94-03-57. The supply ship from Papeete ties up at Moerai.

TUBUAI

Ten-km-long by five-km-wide Tubuai, largest of the Australs, is 670 km south of Tahiti. Hills on the east and west sides of this oval 45-square-km island are joined by low land in the middle; when seen from the sea Tubuai looks like two islands. Mount Taitaa (422 meters) is its highest point. Tubuai is surrounded by a barrier reef; a pass on the north side gives access to a wide turquoise lagoon bordered by brilliant white-sand beaches. Picnics are often arranged on the small reef *motus*, amid superb snorkeling grounds.

The brisk climate permits the cultivation of potatoes, carrots, oranges, and coffee, but other vegetation is sparse. Several *marae* are on Tubuai, but they're in extremely bad condition, with potatoes growing on the sites. The *Bounty* mutineers attempted unsuccessfully to settle on Tubuai in 1789. Mormon missionaries arrived as early as 1844, and today there are active branches of the Church of Latter-day Saints in all the villages. The islanders weave fine pandanus hats, and some woodcarving is done at Mahu.

Most of the 1,900 inhabitants live in Mataura and Taahuaia villages on the north coast, though houses and hamlets are found all along the 24-km road around the island. A red dirt road cuts right across the middle of Tubuai to Mahu village on the south coast. Mataura is the administrative center of the Austral Islands, and the post office and Banque de Tahiti and Banque Socredo branches are here. *Trucks* haven't reached this island yet.

Accommodations and Food

Chez Taro Tanepau (tel. 95-03-82), by the lagoon near a small beach between Mataura and the wharf, has a two-bedroom house with cooking facilities at CFP 3000 single or double including breakfast (monthly rates available).

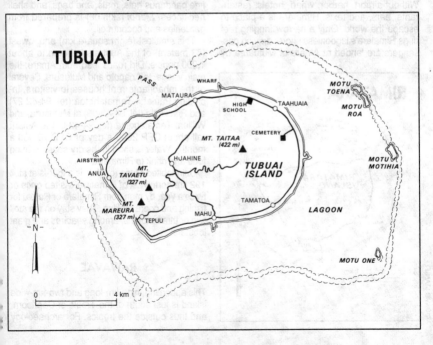

TUBUAI

PASS

MATAURA

WHARF

HIGH
SCHOOL

TAAHUAIA

CEMETERY

MOTU
TOENA

MOTU
ROA

MT. TAITAA
(422 m)

AIRSTRIP

HUAHINE

TUBUAI
ISLAND

MOTU
MOTIHIA

ANUA

MT.
TAVAETU
(327 m)

MT.
MAREURA
(327 m)

TEPUU

MAHU

TAMATOA

LAGOON

-N-

MOTU ONE

0   4 km

In past, Caroline Chung Tien (B.P. 94, Mataura; tel. 95-03-46) has rented rooms in her house next to Chung Tien store in Mataura.

In Taahuaia village, two km east of Mataura, **Chez Karine et Tale** (Karine Tahuhuterani, B.P. 34, Mataura; tel. 95-04-52) offers a complete house with cooking facilities at CFP 5000/7000/8500 single/double/triple. Other potential places to try in Taahuaia include Chez Ah Sing (Fabienne Nibel), Chez Victor Turina (B.P. 7, Mataura; tel. 95-03-27), and Chez Terii Turina (tel. 95-04-98), behind Chez Victor Turina (some of these may no longer be operating).

The **Ermitage Sainte Hélène** (Tihinarii Ilari, B.P. 79, Mataura; tel. 95-04-79) is at Mahu, eight km south of Matauru. There are three quiet houses with cooking facilities, and bicycles are

for rent. The Ermitage, named for Napoleon's isle of exile, is a nice place to stay if you don't mind preparing your own meals.

The **Manu Patia Restaurant** at the east end of Mataura has a nice verandah and reasonable prices. The two stores at Mataura bake bread.

Getting There

Tubuai Airport (TUB), in the northwest corner of the island, was opened in 1972. **Air Tahiti** (tel. 95-04-76) arrives from Rurutu and Papeete several times a week. Ships enter the lagoon through a passage in the barrier reef on the north side and proceed to the wharf at Mataura. Otherwise, the lagoon is too shallow for navigation.

OTHER AUSTRAL ISLANDS

RIMATARA

Without airport, harbor, wharf, hotels, restaurants, bars, and taxis, Rimatara is a place to escape the world. Only a narrow fringing reef hugs Rimatara's lagoonless shore; arriving passengers are landed at Amaru or Mutuaura by

RIMATARA

ANAPOTO

TERUAHU POINT

TIAVA PASS

RIMATARA ISLAND

AMARU

▲ UAHU (83 m)

IRIIRIROA POINT

MUTUAURA

-N-

0   1 km

© DAVID STANLEY

whaleboat. It's customary for newcomers to pass through a cloud of purifying smoke from beachside fires. The women of Rimatara make fine pandanus hats, mats, and bags, and shell necklaces. *Monoi* (skin oil) is prepared from gardenias and coconut oil.

This smallest (eight square km) and lowest (83 meters) of the Australs is home to about 1,000 people. Dirt roads lead from Amaru, the main village, to Anapoto and Mutuaura. Several of the inhabitants rent houses to visitors, including Paulette Tematahotoa (tel. 94-42-27) and Rita Hutia (tel. 94-43-09) at Mutuaura, and William Tematahotoa (tel. 94-43-06) at Amaru (all about CFP 2000 a day or CFP 70,000 a month). Water is short in the dry season. Bring food and drink to Rimatara.

Uninhabited Maria (or Hull) is a four-islet atoll 192 km northwest of Rimatara, visited once or twice a year by men from Rimatara or Rurutu for fishing and copra making. They stay on the atoll two or three months, among seabirds and giant lobsters.

RAIVAVAE

This appealing, nine-km-long and two-km-wide island is just south of the Tropic of Capricorn, and thus outside the tropics. For archaeology

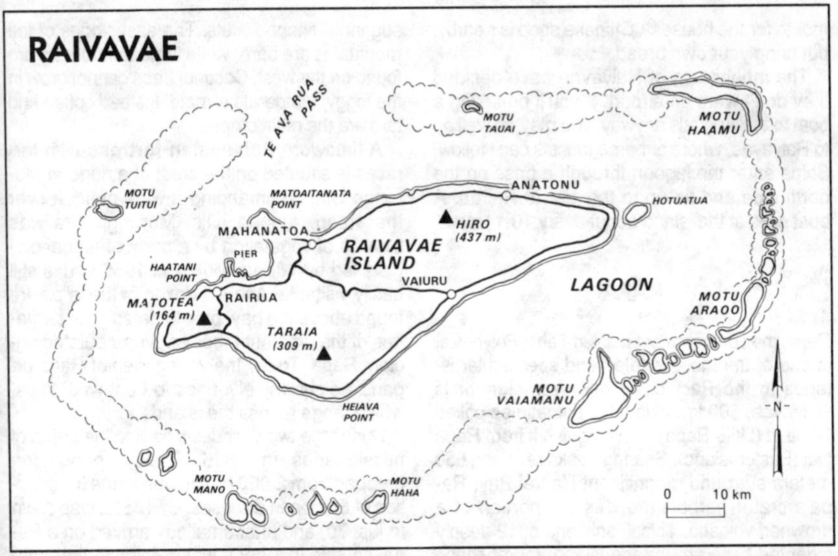
RAIVAVAE
TE AVA RUA PASS
MOTU TAUAI
MOTU HAAMU
MOTU TUITUI
MATOAITANATA POINT
ANATONU
HOTUATUA
HIRO (437 m)
MAHANATOA
RAIVAVAE ISLAND
PIER
HAATANI POINT
VAIURU
LAGOON
MATOTEA (164 m)
RAIRUA
MOTU ARAOO
TARAIA (309 m)
MOTU VAIAMANU
N
HEIAVA POINT
MOTU MANO
MOTU HAHA
0
10 km

and natural beauty, this is one of the finest islands in Polynesia. Fern-covered Mt. Hiro (437 meters) is the highest point on 16-square-km Raivavae. A barrier reef encloses an emerald lagoon, but the 20 small coral *motus* are all located on the southern and eastern portions of the reef. The tropical vegetation is rich: rose and sandalwood are used to make perfumes for local use.

A malignant fever epidemic in 1826 reduced the people of Raivavae from 3,000 to 120. The present population of around 1,250 lives in four coastal villages, Rairua, Mahanatoa, Anatonu, and Vaiuru, linked by a dirt road. A shortcut route direct from Rairua to Vaiuru crosses a 119-meter saddle, with splendid views of the island. The post office is in Rairua.

Different teams led by Frank Stimson, Don Marshall, and Thor Heyerdahl have explored the ancient temples and taro terraces of Raivavae. Many two- to three-meter-high stone statues once stood on the island, but most have since been destroyed, and two were removed to Tahiti where they can be seen on the grounds of the Gauguin Museum. One big tiki is still standing by the road between Rairua and Mahanatoa villages.

Annie Flores (tel. 95-43-28) runs a two-bedroom guesthouse with cooking facilities next to the Gendarmerie in Rairua, the main village. The charge is CFP 2000 a day or CFP 35,000 a

DAVID STANLEY

the famous tiki from Raivavae, now at Tahiti's Gauguin Museum

month for the house. A Chinese shop is nearby, but bring your own bread.

The inhabitants of Raivavae have decided they don't want an airport. If you'll be taking a boat to the Australs anyway, you may as well go to Raivavae, where airborne tourists can't follow! Ships enter the lagoon through a pass on the north side and tie up to the pier at Rairua. A boat calls at the island about every 10-14 days.

RAPA

Rapa, the southernmost point in Tahiti-Polynesia, is one of the most isolated and spectacular islands in the Pacific. Its nearest neighbor is Raivavae, 600 km away. It's sometimes called Rapa Iti (Little Rapa) to distinguish it from Rapa Nui (Easter Island). Soaring peaks reaching 650 meters surround magnificent Haurei Bay, Rapa's crater harbor, the western portion of a drowned volcano. This is only one of 12 deeply indented bays around the island; the absence of reefs allows the sea to cut into the 40-square-km island's outer coasts. Offshore are several

RAPA ITI

sugarloaf-shaped islets. The east slopes of the mountains are bare, while large fern forests are found on the west. Coconut trees cannot grow in the foggy, temperate climate. Instead coffee and taro are the main crops.

A timeworn **Polynesian fortress** with terraces is situated on the crest of a ridge at Morongo Uta, commanding a wide outlook over the steep, rugged hills. Morongo Uta was cleared of vegetation by a party of archaeologists led by William Mulloy in 1956 and is still easily visitable. About a dozen of these *pa* are found above the bay, built to defend the territories of the different tribes of overpopulated ancient Rapa. Today the young men of Rapa organize eight-day bivouacs to hunt wild goats, which range across the island.

During the two decades following the arrival of missionaries in 1826, Rapa's population dropped from 2,000 to 300 due to the introduction of European diseases. By 1851 it was down to just 70, and after smallpox arrived on a Peruvian ship in 1863 it was a miracle that anyone survived at all. The present population of about 550 lives at Area and Haurei villages on the north and south sides of Rapa's great open bay, connected only by boat.

To arrange a stay on Rapa is difficult. Write to Le Maire, Rapa, Îles Australes, four or five months in advance, stating your name, nationality, age, and profession. If you're granted a *certificat d'hébergement* it means the mayor is willing to arrange room and board for you with a local family, the price to be decided upon your arrival. For example, Tinirau Faraire in Area village rents a house at CFP 3500 a day. Then contact the Subdivision Administrative des Îles Australes, B.P. 82, Mataura, Tubuai (tel. 95-02-26), which may actually grant you a permit to go. The *Tuhaa Pae II* calls at Rapa every four to six weeks, so that's how long you'll be there.

Marotiri, or the "Bass Rocks," are 10 uninhabited islets 74 km southeast of Rapa. Amazingly enough, some of these pinnacles are crowned with man-made stone platforms and round "towers." One 105-meter-high pinnacle is visible from Rapa in very clear weather. Landing is difficult.

a Tuamotu outrigger

THE TUAMOTU ISLANDS

Arrayed in two parallel northwest-southeast chains scattered across an area of ocean 600 km wide and 1,200 km long, the Tuamotus are the largest group of coral atolls in the world. Of the 78 atolls in the group, 21 have one entrance (pass), 10 have two passes, and 47 have no pass at all. A total of around 12,500 people live on the 45 inhabited islands. Although the land area of the Tuamotus is only 726 square km, the lagoons of the atolls total some 6,000 square km of sheltered water. All are atolls: some have an unbroken ring of reef around the lagoon, while others appear as a necklace of islets separated by channels.

Variable currents, sudden storms, and poor charts make cruising this group by yacht extremely hazardous—in fact, the Tuamotus are popularly known as the Dangerous Archipelago, or the Labyrinth. Wrecks litter the reefs of many atolls. Winds are generally from the east, varying to northeast from November to May and southeast from June to October. A series of hurricanes devastated these islands between 1980 and 1983.

The resourceful Tuamotu people have always lived from seafood, pandanus nuts, and coconuts. They once dove to depths of 30 meters and more, wearing only tiny goggles, to collect mother-of-pearl shells. This activity has largely ceased as overharvesting has made the oysters rare. Today, cultured-pearl farms operate on Ahe, Aratika, Hikueru, Katiu, Kaukura, Manihi, Raroia, South Marutea, Takapoto, Takaroa, Takume, and Taenga. Cultured black pearls (*Pinctada margaritifera*) from the Tuamotus and Gambiers are world famous.

The scarcity of land and fresh water have always been major problems. Many of these dry, coconut-covered atolls have only a few hundred inhabitants. Though airstrips exist on 12 islands, the isolation has led many Tuamotuans to migrate to Papeete. The only regular hotels are on Rangiroa and Manihi. French military activity has largely closed the eastern Tuamotu to non-French tourism. Beware of eating poisonous fish all across this archipelago.

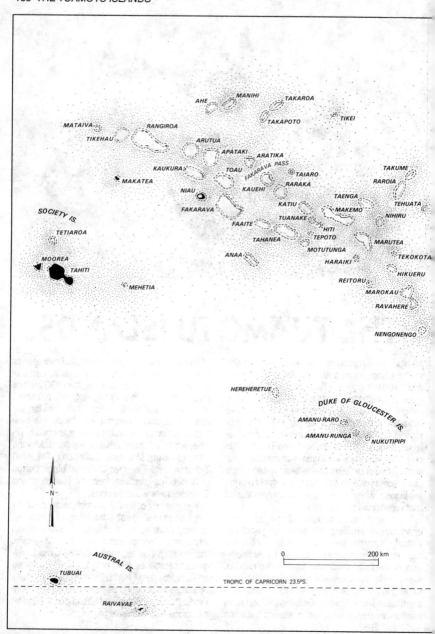

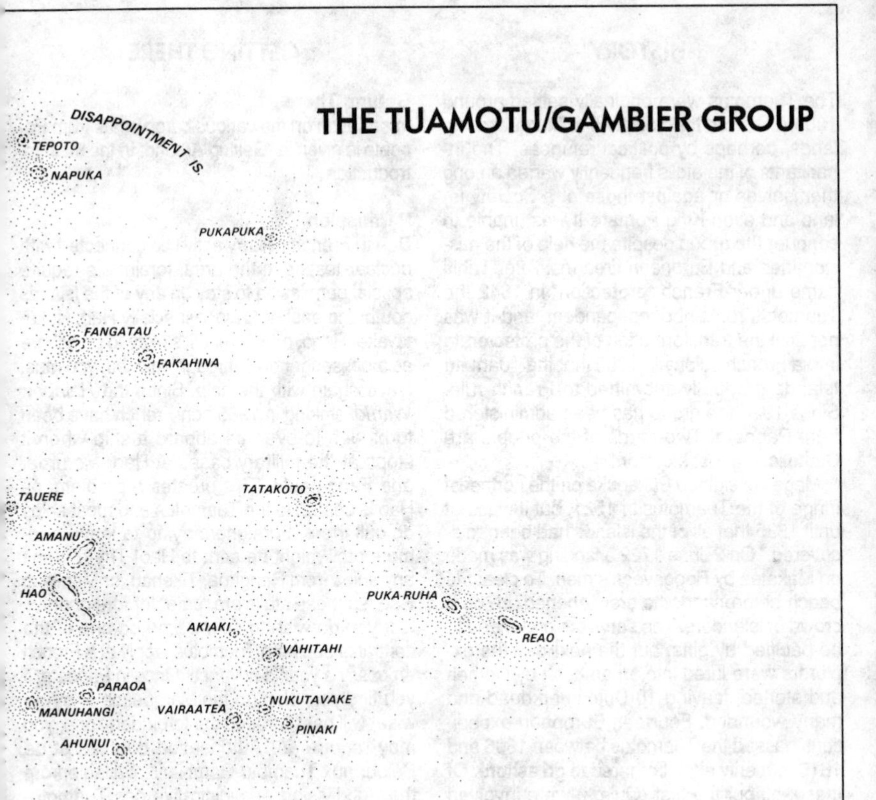

THE TUAMOTU/GAMBIER GROUP

DISAPPOINTMENT IS.
TEPOTO
NAPUKA

PUKAPUKA

FANGATAU
FAKAHINA

TAUERE
TATAKOTO

AMANU

HAO
PUKA-RUHA

AKIAKI
REAO
VAHITAHI

PARAOA
MANUHANGI
VAIRAATEA
NUKUTAVAKE
PINAKI

AHUNUI

VANAVANA TUREIA

BERTERO

TENARARO VAHANGA
TENARUNGA
TEMATANGI
MATUREI-VAVAO MARUTEA
MORUROA
MARIA

FANGATAUFA

GAMBIER IS. MINERVE

MANGAREVA

MORANE
TEMOE

TROPIC OF CAPRICORN
23.5°S.

© DAVID STANLEY

HISTORY

The Tuamotus were originally settled around 1000 A.D. from the Society and Marquesas islands, perhaps by political refugees. The inhabitants of the atolls frequently warred among themselves or against those of a Society island and even King Pomare II was unable to conquer the group despite the help of the missionaries and European firearms. After Tahiti came under French "protection" in 1842 the Tuamotus remained independent, and it was not until the transformation of the protectorate into a French colony in 1880 that the Tuamotu Islands gradually submitted to French rule. Since 1923 the group has been administered from Papeete. Two-thirds of the people are Catholic, the rest Mormon.

Magellan sighted Pukapuka on the northeast fringe of the Tuamotus in 1521, but it was not until 1835 that all of the islands had been "discovered." On 2 June 1722 a landing was made on Makatea by Roggeveen's men. To clear the beach beforehand, the crew opened fire on a crowd of islanders. The survivors pretended to be pacified by gifts, but the next day the explorers were lured into an ambush by women and stoned, leaving 10 Dutchmen dead and many wounded. Fourteen European expeditions passed the Tuamotus between 1606 and 1816, but only eight bothered to go ashore. Of these, all but the first (Quirós) were involved in skirmishes with the islanders.

Centuries later, a group of Scandinavians under the leadership of Thor Heyerdahl ran aground on Raroia atoll on 7 August 1947, after having sailed 7,000 km from South America in 101 days on the raft *Kon Tiki* to prove that Peruvian Indians could have done the same thing centuries before.

GETTING THERE

Getting There
Information on the various cargo boats from Papeete is given in "Getting Around" in the main Introduction.

Permission
Due to French military activities connected with nuclear testing in the area, foreigners require special permission to stay on any of the islands south and east of Anaa, especially Hao, Nukutavake, Reao, and Tureia. It's okay to go ashore as a passenger on a through ship, but you must leave again with the ship. Since the *Rainbow Warrior* sinking in 1985 non-French have been forbidden to even be aboard a ship when it stops at the military bases at Hao, Moruroa, and Fangataufa. This creates a problem, as Hao is central to the Tuamotus and most ships do call there. Foreigners trying to leave a remote atoll might be sent to Hao! There aren't any ships from Rangiroa, Tikehau, or Manihi to Hao, so those atolls are "safe" for foreigners.

If you do wish to spend time on one of the central or southern Tuamotus, apply at a French embassy a year in advance. Once in Papeete, if you find your ship (to the Marquesas or otherwise) will pass through the forbidden zone, you may require an "Autorisation d'Accès et de Séjour aux Tuamotu-Gambier," available from the Subdivision Administrative des Tuamotu-Gambier (B.P. 34, Papeete; tel. 41-94-14), behind the police station on Ave. Bruat. Take your boat ticket with you. They may send you back to the Police de l'Air et des Frontières, near the tourist office on the harbor or at the airport, and you'll need to know a little French—otherwise forget it. On departure day, get to the boat early enough to allow time for last-minute return visits to the above offices—you never know.

RANGIROA

Rangiroa, 200 km northeast of Papeete, is the Tuamotus' most populous atoll and the second largest in the world (after Kwajalein in the Marshall Islands). Its 1,020-square-km aquamarine lagoon is 78 km long, 24 km wide (too far to see), and 225 km around—the island of Tahiti would fit inside its reef. The name Rangiroa means "extended sky." Some 240 *motus* sit on this reef.

What draws people to Rangi (as everyone calls it) is the marinelife in the lagoon. You've never seen so many fish! Deep passages through the atoll's coral ring allow a constant exchange of water between the open sea and the lagoon, creating a most fertile habitat. While lagoons in the Society Islands are often murky due to runoff from the main volcanic islands and pollution from coastal communities, the waters of the Tuamotus are clean and fresh, with some of the best swimming and snorkeling in the South Pacific.

Orientation

Rangiroa's twin villages, each facing a pass 500 meters wide into the lagoon, house 1,400 people. Avatoru village on Avatoru Pass is at the west end of the airport island, about nine km from the airport itself. A paved 20-km road runs east from Avatoru past the airport and the Kia Ora Village Hôtel to Tiputa Pass. Tiputa village is just across the water.

Both villages have small stores; the town hall and gendarmerie are at Tiputa, and the health clinic and marine research center at Avatoru. Avatoru has better facilities, but Tiputa is less touristed and offers the chance to escape by simply walking and wading southeast. For yachts, the sheltered Tiputa anchorage by the Kia Ora Village Hôtel is recommended (as opposed to the Avatoru anchorage which is exposed to swells and chop). Far less English is spoken on Rangiroa than in the Society Islands.

SPORTS AND RECREATION

The strong tidal currents *(opape)* through Avatoru and Tiputa passes generate flows of three to six knots. It's exciting to shoot these 30-meter-deep passes on an incoming tide wearing a mask and snorkel, and the hotels offer this ac-

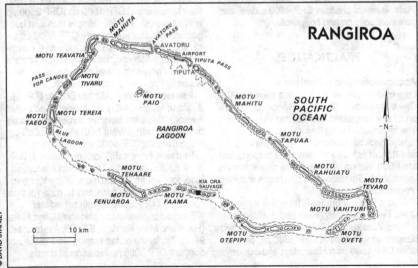

RANGIROA

MOTU MAHUTA
AVATORU PASS
AVATORU
AIRPORT
MOTU TEAVATIA
TIPUTA PASS
TIPUTA
PASS FOR CANOES
MOTU TIVARU
MOTU PAIO
MOTU MAHITU
SOUTH PACIFIC OCEAN
MOTU TEREIA
MOTU TAEOO
RANGIROA LAGOON
BLUE LAGOON
MOTU TAPUAA
MOTU TEHAARE
KIA ORA SAUVAGE
MOTU RAHUIATU
MOTU FAAMA
MOTU TEVARO
MOTU FENUAROA
MOTU VAHITURI
MOTU OTEPIPI
MOTU OVETE

0   10 km

N

© DAVID STANLEY

tivity (CFP 2000-3000) using a small motorboat. The marinelife is fantastic, and sharks are seen in abundance. They're *usually* harmless black-tip or white-tip reef sharks (don't risk touching them even if you see other divers doing so). Other popular excursions include a picnic to the Blue Lagoon at **Motu Taeoo** (CFP 5000 pp), and tiny mid-lagoon **Motu Paio**, a bird sanctuary (CFP 3500 pp).

Scuba diving is arranged by the friendly **Raie Manta Club** (Yves and Brigitte Lefèvre, B.P. 55, Avatoru; tel. 96-04-80, fax 96-05-60) with three branches at Rangiroa: near Rangiroa Lodge in Avatoru village, at Pension Teina et Marie at Tiputa Pass, and at the Kia Ora Village. Diving costs CFP 5000 pp for one tank, including a float through the pass. For regular customers the 11th dive is free. Every dive is different (falling, pass, undulating bottom, hollow, and night), and humphead wrasses, manta rays, barracudas, and lots of sharks are seen. A full day-trip to the Blue Lagoon is CFP 8000 for the boat, diving charges extra. PADI certification courses are offered. Divers come from all parts of the world to dive with Yves and his highly professional team.

The **Centre de Plongée Sous-Marine** (Bernard Blanc, B.P. 75, Rangiroa; tel. 96-05-55, fax 96-05-50), also known as "Rangiroa Paradive," is next to Chez Glorine at Tiputa Pass. Bernard charges CFP 4500 a dive, and he's very obliging and hospitable.

PRACTICALITIES

Accommodations at Avatoru

Low-budget travelers can pitch their tents at **Chez Tamatona** (B.P. 74, Rangiroa). There aren't any bungalows here but camping space is free for anyone taking their meals at Mr. Tamatona's snack bar (about CFP 1000 pp a day). To find it, turn left as you leave the airport, and after 500 meters you'll see the snack bar on the right. Mr. Tamatona is a good cook and very gregarious.

Also a five-minute walk from the airport is **Chez Felix et Judith** (Felix and Judith Tetua, B.P. 18, Avatoru; tel. 96-04-41) with six thatched bungalows with bath at CFP 2500 pp, plus another CFP 1500 pp for breakfast and dinner.

Chez Martine (Martine Tetua, B.P. 68, Avatoru; tel. 96-02-53), a km from the airport, has three bungalows with private bath and terrace (but no cooking) at CFP 2000 pp, plus another CFP 2000 pp for half board.

The **Raira Lagon** (Bruno and Hinano Chardon, B.P. 87, Avatoru; tel. 96-04-23, fax 96-05-86) near the Rangiroa Beach Club, a km west of the airport, offers three thatched bungalows with private bath and fridge (but no cooking facilities) at CFP 4500 pp with breakfast, CFP 6000 with half board. Nonguests also can order meals here.

About two km from the airport is **Pension Cécile** (Alban and Cécile Sun, B.P. 31, Avatoru; tel. 96-05-06) where the three bungalows with half board are CFP 4500 pp (no cooking).

In 1994 a new place opened beside the lagoon, two km west of the airport. **Pension Tuanake** (Roger and Iris Terorotua, B.P. 21, Avatoru; tel. 96-04-45) has two thatched bungalows with bath at CFP 6000/8000 pp half/full board. The meals are large enough to make lunch redundant and camping is possible on the front of the property near the road (separate facilities from the bungalows).

Chez Nanua (Nanua and Marie Tamaehu, B.P. 54, Avatoru; tel. 96-03-88), between the airport and Avatoru village, is an old favorite of low-budget travelers who are allowed to pitch their tents here at CFP 1000 pp (CFP 2500 pp with all meals). The four simple thatched bungalows with shared bath are CFP 3500 pp including all meals (small). You eat with the owners—a little fish and rice every meal. There's no electricity, communal cooking, or running water, but you're right on the beach.

Pension Hinanui (Mareta Bizien, B.P. 16, Avatoru; tel. 96-04-61), on a quiet beach near Avatoru, three km from the airport, has three bungalows with private bath at CFP 3000 pp without meals, CFP 5000 with half board.

Pension Herenui (Victorine Sanford, B.P. 31, Avatoru; tel. 96-04-71), right in Avatoru village, four km from the airport, offers four bungalows with private bath and terrace (but no cooking) at CFP 3000 pp with breakfast.

The two overwater bungalows at **Chez Mata** (Henri and Mata Sanford, B.P. 33, Avatoru; tel. 96-03-78), by the ocean four km west of the airport, are CFP 5000 pp including all meals.

The son of the Nanua mentioned previously operates **Chez Punua et Moana** (Punua and Moana Tamaehu, B.P. 54, Avatoru; tel. 96-04-73) in Avatoru village. The four bungalows with shared bath are CFP 2000 pp, or CFP 3500 pp including all meals. It can be a little noisy due to the activities of the surrounding village. Punua also has eight small huts on Motu Teavahia where you can stay for CFP 3500 pp including all meals, plus CFP 3500 pp for boat transfers. This is the solution for those who really want to get away.

Chez Henriette (Henriette Tamaehu, tel. 96-04-68) by the lagoon in Avatoru village is a four-bungalow place charging CFP 2500 pp for a bed, CFP 5000 with half pension, CFP 6000 full pension. The food is excellent (especially the banana crepes) but it can be a little noisy.

Rangiroa Lodge (Jacques and Rofina Ly, tel. 96-02-13), near the wharf in Avatoru village, has six rooms with shared bath in a main building at CFP 2000 pp (plus CFP 200 for a fan, if desired). This is one of the few places with communal cooking facilities, though they also prepare meals upon request. The snorkeling just off the lodge is outstanding and they'll loan you gear if you need it. If you book ahead they'll provide free airport transfers.

The **Tuamotel** (Anna Lucas, B.P. 29, Avatoru; tel. 96-02-88), on the airport island back toward Tiputa Pass, has a large bungalow with cooking facilities at CFP 4000 pp.

Pension Teina et Marie (Tahuhu Maraeura, B.P. 36, Avatoru; tel. 96-03-94, fax 96-04-44) at Tiputa Pass has rooms with shared bath upstairs in a concrete house and seven bungalows with private bath at CFP 2000 pp. There are no communal cooking facilities but meals can be ordered. Both Marie and Glorine (see below) prepare meals for nonguests who reserve.

A sister of the Henriette mentioned previously runs the popular **Chez Glorine** (Glorine To'i, tel. 96-04-05), also at Tiputa Pass, five km from the airport. The six thatched bungalows with private bath (cold water) are CFP 5500 pp including all meals (specialty fresh lagoon fish). Bicycle rentals are available.

Accommodations at Tiputa
Chez Lucien (Lucien and Esther Pe'a, B.P. 69,

Tiputa; tel. 96-03-55) in Tiputa village offers three traditional bungalows with private bath at CFP 2000 pp for a bed only, or CFP 4000 with half board.

Pension Estall (Ronald Estall, B.P. 13, Tiputa; tel. 96-03-16) also in Tiputa village has four Polynesian-style bungalows with private bath, CFP 5000 pp complete pension.

The **Mihiroa Village** (Maurice Guitteny, no phone), in a coconut grove on Tiputa Island, has four large bungalows with bath at CFP 4500 pp to sleep, or CFP 6000 pp with half board. Boat transfers from the airport are CFP 1000 pp during the day or CFP 2000 pp at night.

Upmarket Hotels
Just west of the airport is the friendly 20-unit **Rangiroa Beach Club** (B.P. 17, Avatoru; tel. 96-03-34), formerly known as "La Bouteille à la Mer." A thatched garden bungalow will set you back CFP 18,000 single, double, or triple, and for a CFP 2000 more, you can have a beach bungalow. Children under 12 sharing a room with their parents are free. Their restaurant serves excellent food (CFP 4500 pp for breakfast and dinner) and the bar functions daily 1200-1400/1800-2000 (try one of Lionel's Mai-Tais). The beach is poor and protective footwear should be used. Snorkeling and fishing gear are loaned free, and all land and water tours are arranged.

The **Miki Miki Village** (B.P. 5, Avatoru; tel./fax 96-03-83), also known as the Rangiroa Village, is an 11-bungalow resort near Avatoru village: CFP 9200/15,000/19,550 single/double/triple, including breakfast and dinner. Extras are a small "bungalow tax" and CFP 600 pp for airport transfers.

Rangiroa's top resort is the snobbish **Kia Ora Village** (B.P. 1, Tiputa; tel. 96-03-84, fax 96-04-93), established in 1973 near Tiputa Pass, about two km east of the airport by road. The 30 thatched beach bungalows are CFP 32,000/35,000 double/triple; breakfast and dinner CFP 5300 pp extra. Yachties are not especially welcome here. In 1991 the Kia Ora Village began offering accommodation in five A-frame bungalows at "Kia Ora Sauvage" on Motu Avaerahi on the far south side of the lagoon. It's CFP24,000 pp a night including all meals, plus CFP 7500 pp for return bus transfers.

The **Village Sans Souci** (Sara Nantz, B.P. 22, Avatoru; tel. 96-03-72) is an escapist's retreat on Motu Mahuta, an islet to the west of Avatoru Pass. The package rates are CFP 7500 pp per night including all meals, with a minimum stay of three nights. The breakfast and desserts offered here are meager and they make you wait until 1930 for dinner. Add CFP 16,000 for return boat transfers from the airport. Despite the price, the 14 thatched bungalows are very simple, with communal shower and toilet stalls (cold water). Scuba diving is possible. It's remarkably overpriced for what you get and not recommended.

Services
The Banque de Tahiti has a branch at Avatoru. Banque Socredo has branches in both villages, but the one at the Mairie (town hall) in Tiputa is only open on Monday and Thursday afternoons. **Post offices** are found in Avatoru, Tiputa, and the airport.

Getting There
Air Tahiti (tel. 96-03-41) flies Tahiti-Rangiroa daily (CFP 13,300 OW). Wednesday and Sunday a flight arrives direct from Bora Bora (CFP 20,700); on Friday it goes back. There's service three times a week from Rangiroa to Manihi (CFP 8600). From Rangiroa to the Marquesas (CFP 25,000), on Saturday there's an ATR 42 flight to Nuku Hiva (46 passengers); the Wednesday flight from Rangiroa to Hiva Oa via Napuka is on a 19-passenger Dornier 228. Seats on flights to the Marquesas should be booked well in advance.

Schooners (goelettes) from Papeete (CFP 3000 OW) take 23 hours to get there from Tahiti, but 72 hours to return (not direct). One cargo boat, the *Dory,* departs Papeete for Rangiroa every Monday at 1300, the most regular connection. To return, ask about the copra boat *Rairoa Nui* which is supposed to leave Rangiroa Wednesday at 0230 and arrive at Papeete Thursday at 0500 (CFP 3000 including meals and a bunk—men only). For more information on transport to the Tuamotus, see the main Introduction to this book.

Airport
The airstrip (RGI) is about five km from Avatoru village by road, accessible to Tiputa village by boat. Some of the pensions offer free transfers; others charge CFP 500-1000.

OTHER ISLANDS AND ATOLLS

MANIHI

Manihi is the other Tuamotu atoll commonly visited by tourists lured by its white-sand beaches and cultured black pearls. You can see right around the 10-by-22-km Manihi lagoon; Tairapa Pass is at the west end of the atoll. Many of the *motus* are inhabited. The 50,000 resident oysters outnumber the 500 local inhabitants a hundred to one. Due to the pearl industry the people of Manihi are better off than those on the other Tuamotu Islands. The 50 houses of Turipaoa village, shaded by trees and flowers, share a sandy strip across the lagoon from the airstrip.

Accommodations

The **Hôtel Kaina Village Noa Noa** (B.P. 2460, Papeete; tel. 96-42-73, fax 96-42-72), located on the airport *motu* and owned by Air Tahiti was completely rebuilt in 1995. The 30 overwater bungalows here begin at CFP 23,000 single or double, plus CFP 5600 pp for breakfast and dinner. There's a beachfront swimming pool, floodlit tennis courts, and scuba diving at the Kaina Village.

Pension Le Keshi (Robert and Christine Meurisse, tel. 96-43-13), on Motu Taugaraufara, has seven small bungalows with private bath (cold water) at CFP 8000 pp with all meals. Airport transfers are CFP 500 return. Reservations are recommended.

Less expensive lodging may be available with some of the 400 inhabitants of Turipaoa village, but this is uncertain and Tahitian-tourist relations on Manihi have been rather spoiled by upmarket tourism. Unless you're willing to pay the sort of prices just mentioned, it's strongly suggested you pick another atoll.

Getting There

You'll need a boat to go from Manihi airport (XMH) to Turipaoa, which can be expensive unless you've arranged to be picked up. Most Air Tahiti (tel. 96-43-34) flights from Papeete or Bora Bora are via Rangiroa. Boats from Papeete also call here.

OTHERS

The Japanese-owned Beachcomber Parkroyal hotel chain is building a 40-bungalow resort called Eden Beach on Rangiroa's neighbor, **Tikehau**, so expect to hear a lot more about that almost circular atoll in future. Local residents of Tuterahera village, two km from the airstrip, provide less opulent accommodations with shared cooking facilities at around CFP 2000 pp without meals or CFP 5000 full board. Contact Nini Hoiore (tel. 96-22-70), Colette Huri (tel. 96-22-47), Maxime Metua (tel. 96-22-38), or Habanita Teriiatetoofa (tel. 96-22-48). Scuba diving is available on Tikehau with the **Raie Manta Club** (B.P. 9, Tikehau; tel. 96-22-53).

Makatea is an uplifted atoll with a lunar surface eight km long and 110 meters high. Gray cliffs plunge to the sea. Phosphate was dug up here by workers with shovels from 1917 to 1966 and exported to Japan and New Zealand by a transnational corporation that pocketed the profits. At one time 2,500 workers were present. The mining was abandoned in 1966 but many buildings and a railway remain. Numerous archaeological remains were found during the mining.

Ahe, 13 km west of Manihi, is often visited by cruising yachts, which are able to enter the 16-km-long lagoon. The village is on the southeast side of the atoll. Facilities include two tiny stores, a post office, and a community center where everyone meets at night. Despite the steady stream of sailing boats, the people are very friendly. All of the houses have solar generating panels supplied after a hurricane in the early 1980s. Only a handful of small children are seen in the village; most are away at school on Rangiroa or Tahiti. Many families follow their children to the main islands while they're at school, so you may even be able to rent a whole house. As well as producing pearls, Ahe supplies oysters to the pearl farms on Manihi. A local government boat runs between Ahe and Manihi on an irregular schedule.

In 1972 the private owner of **Taiaro,** Mr. W.A. Robinson, declared the atoll a nature reserve and in 1977 it was accepted by the United Nations as a biosphere reserve. Scientific missions studying atoll ecology sometimes visit Taiaro, the only permanent inhabitants of which are a caretaker family.

The shark-free lagoon at **Niau** is enclosed by an unbroken circle of land. Yachts can enter the lagoon at **Toau,** though the pass is on the windward side. A leper colony once on **Reao** is now closed.

Takapoto and **Takaroa** atolls are separated by only eight km of open sea, and on both the airstrip is within walking distance of the village. On the outer reef near Takaroa's airstrip are two wrecks, one a four-masted sailing ship here since 1906. Due to the fact that all 400 inhabitants of Teavaroa village on Takaroa belong to the Mormon church, their village is often called "little America." Pearl farming is carried out in the Takaroa lagoon, which offers good anchorage. The yachtie log at Takaroa's town hall is a testimony to the splendid character of the atoll's inhabitants. The snorkeling 30 meters across the pass is second to none.

For information on lodging with the inhabitants on Anaa, Arutua, Fakarava, Kaukura, Mataiva, Takapoto, Takaroa, and Tikehau, ask at Tahiti Tourisme in Papeete. Prices average CFP 2000 pp for a room only, or CFP 5000 pp including all meals. All these atolls receive regular Air Tahiti flights from Tahiti and offer a less commercialized environment than heavily promoted Rangiroa and Manihi.

Interisland boats call about once a week, bringing imported foods and other goods and returning to Papeete with fish. If you come by boat, bring along a good supply of fresh produce from the bountiful Papeete market, as such things are in short supply here. It's very difficult to change money on the atolls, so bring enough cash. All the Tuamotu atolls offer the same splendid snorkeling possibilities (take snorkeling gear), though scuba diving is only developed

on Rangiroa and Manihi. The advantage of the outer atolls is that the people will be far less impacted by packaged tourism. On these it should be easy to hitch rides with the locals across to *le secteur* (uninhabited *motus*) as they go to cut copra or tend the pearl farms. You don't really need maps or guides to these outer atolls—you'll soon know all you need to know.

The Lost Treasure of the Tuamotus
During the War of the Pacific (1879-83) four mercenaries stole a large quantity of gold from a church in Pisco, Peru. They buried most of the treasure on **Pinaki** or **Raraka** atolls in the Tuamotus before proceeding to Australia, where two were killed by aboriginals and the other two were sentenced to 20 years of imprisonment for murder. Just prior to his death the surviving mercenary told prospector Charles Howe the story.

In 1913 Howe began a 13-year search which finally located part of the treasure on an island near Raraka. He reburied the chests and returned to Australia to organize an expedition which would remove the gold in secret. Before it could set out, however, Howe disappeared. Using Howe's treasure map, diver George Hamilton took over in 1934. Hamilton thought he found the cached gold in a pool but was unable to extract it. After being attacked by a giant octopus and moray eel, Hamilton abandoned the search and the expedition dissolved. As far as is known, the US$1.8 million in gold has never been found.

The legend of the hidden treasure is still very much alive and traces of old diggings can be seen in a dozen places, mostly around the only passage (which is too shallow for even dinghies to enter). Pinaki is only inhabited until the end of the copra harvest in October and excavations are prohibited before then because they cause rain, the last thing anyone trying to make copra would want. Only landowners are allowed to dig for treasure, so a foreigner would have to marry a local first. At night the treasure is guarded by the spirits of two whites and a black (who were killed after burying the gold).

THE NUCLEAR TEST ZONE

The nuclear test zone (Centre d'Expérimentations du Pacifique) is at the southeastern end of the Tuamotu group, 1,200 km from Tahiti. The main site is 30-km-long Moruroa atoll, but Fangataufa atoll 37 km south of Moruroa is also being used. In 1962 the French nuclear testing sites in the Algerian Sahara had to be abandoned after that country won its independence, so in 1963 French president Charles de Gaulle announced officially that France was shifting the program to Moruroa and Fangataufa. Between 1966 and 1992 a confirmed 175 nuclear bombs, reaching up to 200 kilotons, were set off in the Tuamotus at the rate of six a year and a cost to French taxpayers of millions of dollars each. By 1974 the French had conducted 44 *atmospheric* tests, 39 over Moruroa and five over Fangataufa.

Way back in 1963, the U.S., Britain, and the USSR agreed in the Partial Test Ban Treaty to halt nuclear tests in the atmosphere. France chose not to sign. On 23 June 1973, the World Court urged France to discontinue the nuclear tests, which might drop radioactive material on surrounding territories. When the French government refused to recognize the court's jurisdiction in this matter, New Zealand Prime Minister Norman Kirk ordered the New Zealand frigate *Otago* to enter the danger zone off Moruroa, and on 23 July Peru broke diplomatic relations with

France. On 15 August French commandos boarded the protest vessels *Fri* and *Greenpeace III*, attacking and arresting the crews.

In 1974, with opposition mounting in the Territorial Assembly and growing world indignation, French president Giscard D'Estaing ordered a switch to the *underground* tests. The French forward support base on Hao atoll (pop. 1,200), 500 km north of Moruroa, allowed the French military to fly materials directly into the area without passing through Faa'a Airport.

On 8 April 1992, as the Greenpeace *Rainbow Warrior II* confronted French commandos off Moruroa, French Prime Minister Pierre Bérégovoy suddenly announced that nuclear testing was being suspended for one year. President Boris Yeltsin had already halted Russian nuclear testing in October 1991, and in October 1992 U.S. president George Bush followed suit by halting underground testing in Nevada. Despite the French moratorium, the testing facilities were maintained at great expense, and in June 1995 newly elected President Jacques Chirac ordered the testing to resume without bothering to consult the Polynesians.

Chirac is a ruthless opportunist with a long history of using Pacific islanders as pawns in personal power games. While serving as prime minister in May 1988 he sent French troops to free a group of hostages held by independence activists on the island of Ouvéa in New Caledonia, resulting in a massacre of 19 islanders, several of whom were murdered in cold blood after their capture. This arrogant man declared that the tests would go ahead despite widespread objections.

On 9 July 1995 the Greenpeace vessel *Rainbow Warrior II* reached Moruroa again, almost 10 years to the day since its predecessor was sunk by French terrorists at Auckland, New Zealand. Oscar Temaru, the mayor of Faa'a, Tahiti-Polynesia's largest city, called on Pacific countries to boycott the South Pacific Games scheduled to be held on Tahiti in August, and official protests and demonstrations have occurred around the world, all of it falling on Chirac's deaf ears.

Moruroa

Obviously, an atoll, with its porous coral cap sitting on a narrow basalt base, is the unsafest place in the world to stage underground nuclear explosions. It's unlikely this was ever intended. Moruroa was chosen for its isolated location, far from major population centers that might be affected by fallout. By 1974, when atmospheric testing had to cease, the French military had a huge investment there. So rather than move to a more secure location in France or elsewhere, they decided to take a chance. Underground testing was to be carried out in Moruroa's basalt core, 500-1,200 meters below the surface of the atoll.

On 10 September 1966 President de Gaulle was present at Moruroa to witness an atmospheric test of a bomb suspended from a balloon. Weather conditions caused the test to be postponed and the following day conditions were still unsuitable, as the wind was blowing in the direction of inhabited islands to the west instead of toward uninhabited Antarctica to the south. De Gaulle complained that he was a busy man and could afford to wait no longer, so the test went ahead, spreading radioactive fallout across the Cook Islands, Niue, Tonga, Samoa, Fiji, and Tuvalu. Tahiti itself was the most directly affected island, but the French authorities have never acknowledged this fact.

Two serious accidents occurred within weeks of each other in 1979. On 6 July, an explosion and fire in a laboratory bunker on Moruroa killed two and injured four others. For two weeks after the accident, workers in protective suits tried to clean up the area contaminated with plutonium by the explosion. On 25 July, a nuclear device became stuck halfway down an 800-meter shaft. When the army engineers were unable to move the device, they exploded it where it was, causing a massive chunk of the outer slope of the atoll to break loose. This generated a huge tidal wave, which hit Moruroa, overturning cars and injuring seven people. After the blast, a crack 40 centimeters wide and two km long appeared on the surface of the island. As a precaution against further tidal waves and hurricanes, refuge platforms were built at intervals around the atoll. For an hour before and after each test all personnel must climb up on these platforms.

Right from the beginning, contaminated debris including scrap metal, wood, plastic, and clothing had carelessly been stored in plastic bags on the north side of the atoll. On 11 March 1981, a hurricane washed large quantities of this nuclear waste into the lagoon and surrounding sea, and that August another storm spread more material from the same dump. Enough radioactive debris to fill 200,000 44-gallon drums is still lying on the north side of the atoll.

By 1981 Moruroa was as punctured as a Swiss cheese and sinking two cm after every test, or 1.5 meters between 1976 and 1981. With the atoll's 60-km coral rim dangerously fractured by drilling shafts, the French switched to underwater testing in the Moruroa lagoon in 1981, in order to be closer to the center of the island's core. By 1988 the 108 underground blasts had weakened the geological formations beneath Moruroa so severely that French officials announced that henceforth the largest underground tests would take place on nearby Fangataufa atoll, despite the additional cost involved. The military base remained on Moruroa, and small groups of workers and technicians were sent over to Fangataufa every time a test was made there.

The French government claims it owns Moruroa and Fangataufa because in 1964 a standing committee of the Territorial Assembly voted three to two to cede the atolls to France for an indefinite period. This was never ratified by the full assembly, and French troops had occupied the islands before the vote was taken anyway.

Impact

In 1983 the French government invited a delegation of scientists from Australia, New Zealand, and Papua New Guinea to visit Moruroa. Significantly, they were not permitted to take samples from the northern or western areas of the atoll, nor of lagoon sediments. The scientists reported that "if fracturing of the volcanics accompanied a test and allowed a vertical release of radioactivity to the limestones, specific contaminants would, in this worst case, enter the biosphere within five years."

On 21 June 1987 the famous French underwater explorer Jacques Cousteau was present for a test at Moruroa and the next day he took water samples in the lagoon, the first time such independent tests had been allowed. Two samples collected by Cousteau nine km apart contained traces of cesium-134, an isotope with a half-life of two years. Though French officials claimed the cesium-134 remained from atmospheric testing before 1975, a September 1990 *Review of the Calypso Water Samples* by Norm Buske of Search Technical Services (HCR Box 17, Davenport, WA 99122, U.S.A.) has proven that this is not scientifically feasible, and leakage from underground testing is the only possible explanation. In 1990 a computer model of Moruroa developed by New Zealand scientists indicated that radioactive groundwater with a half-life of several thousand years may be seeping through fractures in the atoll at the rate of 100 meters a year and, according to Prof. Manfred Hochstein, head of Auckland University's Geothermal Institute, "in about 30 years the disaster will hit us." In December 1990 Buske found traces of cesium-134 in plankton collected in the open ocean, outside the 12-mile exclusion zone. Buske's findings indicate that the release of contamination into the Pacific from the numerous cracks and fissures has already started, yet despite the 1992 pause in testing, the French government continues its cover-up operations and no independent studies are allowed.

Unlike the U.S., which has paid millions of dollars in compensation money to the Marshallese victims of its nuclear testing program, the French government has refused to even acknowledge the already-apparent effects of its 44 atmospheric tests. From 1963 to 1983, no public health statistics were published. Now the rates of thyroid cancer, leukemia, brain tumors, and stillbirths are on the upswing in Tahiti-Polynesia, and the problem of seafood poisoning (ciguatera) in the nearby Gambier Islands is clearly related. French nonresponse to these first side effects demonstrates vividly how they plan to deal with the more serious environmental consequences yet to come.

The Issue

France is the only nuclear state to have conducted tests *under* a Pacific island. France has not limited itself to testing atomic and hydrogen devices: numerous neutron bombs have also been exploded. The French have always maintained that their tests are harmless and that every precaution has been taken. And yet, such underground tests could be carried out much more effectively, safely, and cheaply in France itself! The claim that the tests are "safe" is disproved by the very choice of the test site, on the opposite side of the globe from their homeland.

French radioactivity will remain in the Tuamotus for thousands of years, and the unknown future consequences of this program are the most frightening part of it. Virtually every South Pacific country has strongly condemned the tests on numerous occasions, and the island people have protested, yet it remains official U.S. government policy not to condemn French nuclear testing in the region. Thus the U.S. must share responsibility with France for this shameful practice. And even with the Cold War over and the need for this type of weaponry gone, little has been done to convert the Partial Test Ban Treaty into a Comprehensive Test Ban Treaty and permanently end all nuclear testing worldwide.

By ordering the resumption of nuclear testing, Jacques Chirac has demonstrated his total disregard for public opinion in the South Pacific and around the world. For him, the islands and their inhabitants are expendable. Thanks to several years of waffling by presidents Mitterrand and Clinton, who failed to irreversibly break the insane chain of nuclear testing when they had the chance, Polynesia is being subjected to a new and catastrophic round of environmental terrorism in the Tuamotus for the glory of France.

an early 19th-century engraving of Mangarevans aboard a craft with sail

THE GAMBIER ISLANDS

The Gambier (or Mangareva) Islands are just north of the Tropic of Capricorn, 1,650 km southeast of Tahiti. The archipelago, contrasting sharply with the atolls of the Tuamotus, consists of 10 rocky islands enclosed on three sides by a semicircular barrier reef 65 km long. In all, there are 22 square km of dry land. The Polynesian inhabitants named the main and largest island Mangareva, or "Floating Mountain." Unlike the Marquesas, where the mountains are entirely jungle-clad, the Gambiers have hilltops are covered with tall *aeho* grass.

Aside from Mangareva, small groups of people live only on Taravai and Kamaka islands. Makaroa is a barren, rugged 136-meter-high island. In a cliffside cave on the island of Agakauitai the mummies of 35 generations of cannibal kings are interred. A local seabird, the *karako,* crows at dawn like a rooster.

A dramatic intensification of the ciguatera problem in the Gambiers is believed to be linked to reef damage or pollution originating at the nuclear-testing facilities on Moruroa, 400 km east. During the atmospheric testing series (until

1974), Mangarevans had to take refuge in French-constructed fallout shelters whenever advised by the military. Before each of the 41 atmospheric tests, French warships would evacuate the 3,000 persons from Moruroa, usually to Mangareva, Hao, and Fakarava. Upon arrival the ships were washed down with seawater, spreading radioactive contamination into the lagoons, and the French never made the slightest attempt to clean up after themselves. Between 1971 and 1980 the annual incidence of ciguatera remained above 30%, peaking at 56% in 1975. Each of the 500-600 inhabitants has suffered five to seven excruciating attacks of seafood poisoning. Lagoon fish can no longer be eaten.

Now, increases in birth defects, kidney problems, and cancer among the inhabitants are being covered up by the authorities. It's believed that a decisive factor in the French decision to launch a terrorist attack on Greenpeace's *Rainbow Warrior* in 1985 was a report indicating that the ship intended to proceed to Mangareva with doctors aboard to assess the radiation exposure of residents.

HISTORY

Mangareva, which was originally settled from the Marquesas Islands around A.D. 1100, was shortly afterwards the jumping-off place for small groups that discovered and occupied Pitcairn and Henderson islands. In 1797 Capt. James Wilson of the London Missionary Society's ship *Duff* named the group for English Admiral Gambier. France made the Gambiers a protectorate in 1844 and annexed the group in 1881.

Mangareva was the area of operations for a fanatical French priest, Father Honoré Laval of the Congregation for the Sacred Hearts, who ruled here for nearly 40 years. Upon hearing whalers' tales of rampant cannibalism and marvelous pearls, Laval left his monastery in Chile and with another priest reached the Gambiers in 1834.

An old Mangarevan prophecy had foretold the coming of two magicians whose god was all-powerful. Laval toppled the dreaded stone effigy of the god Tu on the island's sacred *marae* with his own hands. He single-handedly imposed a ruthless and inflexible moral code on the islanders, recruiting them as virtual slaves to build a 1,200-seat cathedral, convents, and triumphal arches, with the result that he utterly destroyed this once vigorous native culture and practically wiped out its people. During Laval's 37-year reign the population dropped from 9,000 to 500. You can still see his architectural masterpiece—the Cathedral of St. Michael with its twin towers of white coral rock from Kamaka and altar shining with polished mother-of-pearl—a monument to horror and yet another lost culture. In 1871 Laval was removed from Mangareva by a French warship, tried for murder on Tahiti, and declared in-

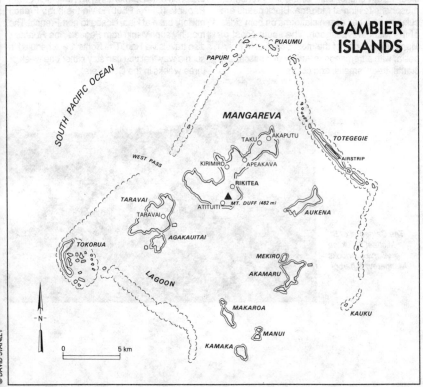

GAMBIER ISLANDS

sane. He lies buried in a crypt before the altar of St. Michael's Cathedral, Mangareva.

For a glimpse of the Gambiers half a century ago and a fuller account of Père Laval, read Robert Lee Eskridge's *Manga Reva, The Forgotten Islands* (see the Resources chapter at the end of this book).

Orientation

The population of the Gambiers is around 650. Rikitea, on 6.5-by-1.5-km Mangareva, is the main village. A post office, seven small shops, a gendarmerie, an infirmary, schools, and a cathedral three times as big as the one in Papeete make up the infrastructure of this administrative backwater.

The tomb of Gregorio Maputeoa, the 35th and last king of Mangareva (died 1868), is in a small chapel behind the church (below the school). On the opposite side of Rikitea is a huge nuclear-fallout shelter built during the French atmospheric testing at Moruroa. Black pearls are cultured on a half dozen platforms on both sides of the Mangareva lagoon. The south coast of Mangareva is one of the most beautiful in Polynesia, with a tremendous variety of landscapes, plants, trees, smells, and colors.

PRACTICALITIES

Due to the nearby French nuclear-testing facilities, the entry of foreigners to the Gambier Islands is restricted. For information write: Subdivision Administrative des Tuamotu-Gambiers, B.P. 34, Papeete (tel. 41-94-14). Of course, this is unnecessary if you're French.

There are no hotels, restaurants, or bars at Rikitea, but you can always arrange accommodations with the village people. Madame Duval (tel. 97-82-64) at one of the shops near the wharf can provide a room with hot showers and all meals at CFP 6000 pp. Mr. Jean Anania (nicknamed "Siki") offers speedboat charters and fishing trips.

The airstrip (GMR) is on Totegegie, a long coral island eight km northeast of Rikitea. The expensive, twice-monthly Air Tahiti flight from Papeete (CFP 41,500) is via the huge French military base at Hao, closed to non-French. The monthly supply ship from Papeete, the *Ruahutu*, also travels via Hao. The flights are scheduled in such a way that you can stay either one week or three weeks in the Gambiers.

The Cathedral of St. Michael at Rikitea village overlooks Mangareva's harbor.

ANSELM ZANKERT

a Marquesan meae at Nuku Hiva in the early 19th century

THE MARQUESAS ISLANDS

The Marquesas Islands are the farthest north of the high islands of the South Pacific, on the same latitude as the Solomons. Though the group was known as Te Fenua Enata ("The Land of Men") by the Polynesian inhabitants, depopulation during the 19th and 20th centuries has left many of the valleys empty. Ten main islands form a line 300 km long, roughly 1,400 km northeast of Tahiti, but only six are inhabited today: Nuku Hiva, Ua Pou, and Ua Huka in a cluster to the northwest, and Hiva Oa, Tahuata, and Fatu Hiva to the southeast. The administrative centers, Atuona (Hiva Oa), Hakahau (Ua Pou), and Taiohae (Nuku Hiva), are the only places with post offices, banks, gendarmes, etc. The total population is just 7,500.

The expense and difficulty in getting there has kept most potential visitors away. Budget accommodations are scarce and public transport is nonexistent, which makes getting around a major expense unless you're really prepared to rough it. Of the main islands, Hiva Oa is ap-preciably cheaper than Nuku Hiva, and getting to town from Hiva Oa airport is much easier. Cruising yachts from California often call at the Marquesas on their way to Papeete, even though ocean swells reaching the shorelines make the anchorages rough. This is paradise, however, for surfers and hikers. Multitudes of waterfalls tumble down the slopes, and eerie overgrown archaeological remains tell of a golden era long gone. If you enjoy quiet, unspoiled places, you'll like the Marquesas, but one month should be enough. The Marquesas have been left behind by their remoteness.

The Land

These wild, rugged islands feature steep cliffs and valleys leading up to high central ridges, sectioning the islands off into a cartwheel of segments, which creates major transportation difficulties. Reefs don't form due to the cold south equatorial current. The absence of protective reefs has prevented the creation of coastal plains, so no roads go around any of the islands. Most of the people live in the narrow, fertile river valleys. The interiors are inhabited only by hundreds of wild horses, cattle, and goats, which have destroyed much of the original vegetation. A Catholic bishop introduced the horses from Chile in 1856, and today they're almost a symbol of the Marquesas. The islands are abundant with lemons, tangerines, oranges, grapefruit, bananas, mangos, and papayas. Taro and especially breadfruit are the main staples. Birdlife is rich, and the waters around the Marquesas teem with lobster, fish, and sharks.

The subtropical climate is hotter and drier than that of Tahiti. July and August are the coolest months. The deep bays on the west sides of the islands are better sheltered for shipping, and the humidity is lower there than on the east sides, which catch the trade winds. The precipitation is uneven, with drought some years,

FIELD MUSEUM OF NATURAL HISTORY, CHICAGO

Stilt footrests: The Marquesans once staged races and mock battles on stilts with the participants attempting to knock one another off balance.

heavy rainfall the others. The southern islands of the Marquesas (Hiva Oa, Tahuata, Fatu Hiva) are green and humid; the northern islands (Nuku Hiva, Ua Huka, Ua Pou) are brown and dry.

HISTORY

Pre-European Society

Marquesan houses were built on high platforms *(paepae)* scattered through the valleys (still fairly easy to find). Each valley had a ceremonial area *(tohua)* where important festivals took place. Archaeologists have been able to trace stone temples *(meae,* called *marae* elsewhere in Tahiti-Polynesia), agricultural terraces, and earthen fortifications *(akaua)* half hidden in the jungle, evocative reminders of a vanished civilization. Then as now, the valleys were isolated from one another by high ridges and turbulent seas, yet warfare was vicious and cannibalism an important incentive. An able warrior could attain great power. Local hereditary chiefs exercised authority over commoners.

The Marquesans' artistic style was one of the most powerful and refined in the Pacific. The ironwood war club was their most distinctive symbol, but there were also finely carved wooden bowls, fan handles, and tikis of stone and wood, both miniature and massive. The carvings are noted for the faces: the mouth with lips parted and the bespectacled eyes. Both men and women wore carved ivory earplugs. Men's entire bodies were covered by bold and striking tattoos, a practice banned by the Catholic missionaries. Stilts were used by boys for racing and mock fighting. This was about the only part of Polynesia where polyandry was common. There was a strong cult of the dead: the bodies or skulls of ancestors were carefully preserved. Both Easter Island (around A.D. 500) and Hawaii (around A.D. 700) were colonized from here.

European Contact

The existence of these islands was long concealed from the world by the Spanish, to prevent the English from taking possession of them. The southern group was found by Álvaro de Mendaña in July 1595 during his second voyage of exploration from Peru. He named them Las Marquesas de Mendoza after his benefactor, the Spanish viceroy. The first island sighted (Fatu Hiva) seemed uninhabited, but as Mendaña's *San Jerónimo* sailed nearer, scores of outriggers appeared, paddled by about 400 robust, light-skinned islanders. Their hair was long and loose, and they were naked and tattooed in blue patterns. The natives boarded the ship, but when they became overly curious and bold, Mendaña ordered a gun fired, and they jumped over the side.

Then began one of the most murderous and shameful of all the white explorer's entries into the South Pacific region. As a matter of caution, Mendaña's men began shooting natives on sight, in one instance hanging three bodies in the shore camp on Santa Cristina (Tahuata) as a warning. They left behind three large crosses, the date cut in a tree, and over 200 dead Polynesians.

The northern Marquesas Islands were "discovered" by Joseph Ingraham of the American trading vessel *Hope* on 19 April 1791. After that, blackbirders, firearms, disease, and alcohol reduced the population. American whalers called frequently from 1800 onwards. Although France took possession of the group in 1842, Peruvian slavers kidnapped some Marquesans to South America in 1863 to work the plantations and mines. Those few who returned brought a catastrophic smallpox epidemic. The Marquesans clung to their warlike, cannibalistic ways until 95% of their number had died—the remainder adopted Catholicism. (The Marquesas today is the only island group of Tahiti-Polynesia with a Catholic majority.) From 80,000 at the beginning of the 19th century, the population fell to about 15,000 by 1842, when the French "protectors" arrived, and to a devastated 2,000 by 1926.

The Marquesas Today

Slowly the Marquesas are catching up with the rest of the world—VCRs are the latest introduced

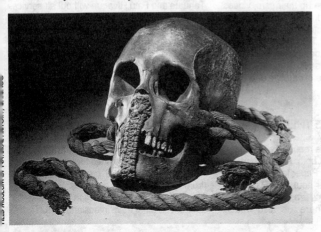

The Marquesans preserved the skulls of their ancestors.

Madisonville, Nuku Hiva: On 19 Nov. 1813, Captain David Porter of the U.S. frigate Essex took possession of Nuku Hiva, Marquesas Islands, for the United States.

species. Cruise ships are also finding their ways into the group. Yet the islands remain very untouristy. Though there are many negative attitudes toward the French and on Tahiti talk for independence is heard, the Marquesans realize that without French subsidies their economy would collapse and they would become even more distant from the Tuamotus, Tahiti, and "civilization." Making copra would no longer be an economic activity and far fewer supply ships would call at the islands. Hospitalization, drugs, and dental care are provided free by the government and a monthly family allowance of US$100 is paid for each child under 16—quite a bundle if you have eight kids, as many do! If the Marquesans had to give up their cars, videos, and U.S. frozen chicken, many would abandon the already underpopulated islands.

During the Heiva or Tiurai festival in July, races, games, and dance competitions take place on the different islands. The older women prove themselves graceful dancers and excellent singers.

GETTING THERE

A visit to the Marquesas requires either lots of money or lots of time, or both. An **Air Tahiti** 46-seat ATR 42 flies from Papeete to Nuku Hiva four times a week (four hours, CFP 37,800). Two of the ATR 42 flights are via Hiva Oa, another via Rangiroa. There are also weekly Dornier 228 flights from Rangiroa to Hiva Oa via Napuka in the Tuamotus (CFP 25,000), but the plane is always full. Stopovers on Napuka cost CFP 19,000 extra!

Dornier flights between Nuku Hiva and Ua Huka and Ua Pou operate weekly, connecting with one of the ATR 42 flights from Papeete. Fares from Nuku Hiva are CFP 5000 to Ua Pou, CFP 5000 to Ua Huka, and CFP 8600 to Atuona. No flight goes straight from Ua Pou to Ua Huka—you must backtrack to Nuku Hiva. (Ua Huka airport was closed in 1994, so check.) Get a through ticket to your final destination, as flights to Nuku Hiva, Hiva Oa, Ua Pou, and Ua Huka are all the same price from Papeete. Tahuata and Fatu Hiva are without air service. All flights are heavily booked.

Three ships, the *Aranui, Tamarii Tuamotu,* and *Taporo V,* sail monthly from Papeete, calling at all six inhabited Marquesas Islands. The *Aranui* and *Taporo V* are the easiest to use, as they follow a regular schedule and no special permission is required. To come on the *Tamarii Tuamotu* you may have to go through the procedure described under "Permission" under "Getting There" in the Tuamotu Islands chapter.

The freighter *Aranui* is the more convenient and comfortable, if you can afford it. The roundtrip voyages designed for tourists flown in from Europe and the U.S. cost cruise-ship prices (from US$1560 return on deck). See "Getting Around" in the main Introduction to this book for details. The other main interisland boat, *Taporo*

V, is cheaper at CFP 17,000 deck OW to Hiva Oa, but it's basic. Food is included in the passages and it's not necessary to reserve deck passage on these boats. The ships tie up to the wharves at Taiohae, Atuona, Vaipaee, and Hakahau; at Tahauta and Fatu Hiva, passengers must go ashore by whaleboat. In stormy weather, the landings can be dangerous.

NUKU HIVA

Nuku Hiva is the largest (339 square km) and most populous (2,250 inhabitants) of the Marquesas. In 1813 Capt. David Porter of the American raider *Essex* annexed Nuku Hiva for the United States, though the act was never ratified by Congress. Porter built a fort at the present site of Taiohae, which he named Madisonville for the U.S. president of his day. Nothing remains of this or another fort erected by the French in 1842. Sandalwood traders followed Porter, then whalers. Herman Melville's *Typee,* written after a one-month stay in the Taipivai Valley in 1842, is still the classic narrative of Marquesan life during the 19th century.

Taiohae (population 1,500) on the south coast is the administrative and economic center of the Marquesas. It's a modern little town with a post office, a hospital, a town hall, a bank, five grocery stores, and street lighting. Winding mountain roads lead northeast from Taiohae to Taipivai and Hatiheu villages, where a few dozen families reside. In the center of the island Mt. Tekao (1,224 meters) rises above the vast, empty Toovii Plateau.

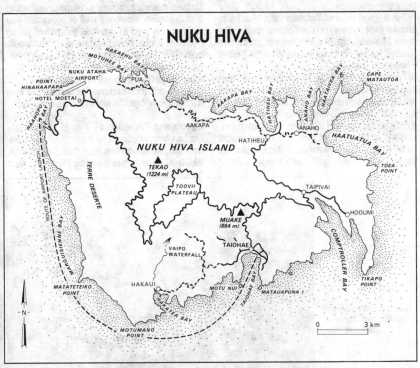

Though open to the south, Taiohae's deep harbor offers excellent anchorage, and cruising yachts are often seen here. A nominal "water fee" is charged (don't take on water if it's been raining). Take care with the drinking water at Taiohae. (One reader suggested that yachts should take on clean spring water at Hakatea Bay, although an extension tube would be necessary.)

SIGHTS

Vestiges of an **old prison** can still be seen in Taiohae. Many stone- and wood-carvers continue to work on Nuku Hiva, making wooden tikis, bowls, ukuleles, ceremonial war clubs, etc. Some items are on display at the Banque Socredo. Other woodcarvings may be viewed in the **Catholic cathedral** (1974) at Taiohae. Ask to see the small collection of artifacts at the bishop's residence.

For a good view of Taiohae Bay, hike up to **Muake** (864 meters) on the Taipivai road. From there lifts are possible with market gardeners headed for the agricultural station on the **Toovii Plateau** to the west.

Taipivai is a five-hour, 17-km walk from Taiohae. Herman Melville spent a month here, with his tattooed sweetheart Fayaway, in 1842. In his novel, *Typee* (his spelling for Taipi), he gives a delightful account of the life of the great-great-grandparents of the present forlorn and decultured inhabitants. The huge *tohua* of Vahangekua at Taipivai is a whopping 170 by 25 meters. Great stone tikis watch over the *meae* of Paeke, also near Taipivai. Vanilla grows wild. At Hooumi, a fine protected bay near Taipivai, is a truly magical little church.

Above **Hatiheu** on the north coast, 29 km from Taiohae, are two more tikis and a reconstructed *meae*. **Anaho,** 45 minutes east of Hatiheu on foot, is one of the most beautiful of Nuku Hiva's bays, with a fine white beach and good snorkeling. Unfortunately, it's infested with *nono* sand flies. Even better white-sand beaches face Haatuatua and Haataivea bays beyond Anaho. No one lives there, though wild horses are seen.

At Hakaui, west of Taiohae, a river runs down a steep-sided valley. Fantastic 350-meter **Vaipo Waterfall,** highest in the territory, drops from the plateau at the far end of the valley, four km from the coast. It's a two-hour walk from Hakaui to the waterfall with a few thigh-high river crossings after rains (guide not required). The trail passes many crumbling platforms, indicating that the valley was once well populated. If you swim in the pool at the falls beware of falling pebbles. A boat from Taiohae to Hakaui would cost CFP 12,500 and up return, but an overgrown switchback trail also crosses the 535-meter ridge from Taiohae to Hakaui. You'll need to be adventurous and good at finding your own way to follow it (allow eight hours each way).

Sports and Recreation
Scuba diving is offered by Xavier Curvat's **Centre Plongée Marquises** (B.P. 100, Taiohae; tel. 92-00-88). Xavier has explored the archipelago

Hakaui on Nuku Hiva's south coast, home of the Taioa tribe

(top left) Lake Vaihiria, Tahiti (David Stanley); (top right) a *motu* (Tahiti Tourisme, Tini Colombel); (bottom) Vaitepiha Valley, Tahiti (David Stanley)

(top) Tetiaroa atoll (Tahiti Tourisme)
(bottom) sunset over Moorea (Paul Bohler)

thoroughly during his 15 years in the Marquesas and his local knowledge is unequaled. One-week catamaran tours with him can be booked through Ocean Voyages in California (see "Getting There" in the main Introduction). Though there's no coral to be seen here, the underwater caves and spectacular schools of hammerhead sharks compensate.

Horseback riding is offered by Sabine and Louis Teikiteetini (B.P. 171, Taiohae), who can be contacted locally through Nuku Hiva Town Hall. Rides from Taiohae to Taipivai are possible.

PRACTICALITIES

Accommodations in Taiohae

The least expensive place is **Chez Fetu** (Cyprien Peterano, B.P. 22, Taiohae; tel. 92-03-66), on a hill behind Kamake Store, a five-minute walk from the wharf in Taiohae. The three bungalows with private bath, kitchen, and terrace cost CFP 2000/4000/5000 single/double/triple, or CFP 50,000 a month.

The **Hôtel Moana Nui** (Charles Nombaerts, B.P. 9, Taiohae; tel. 92-03-30, fax 92-00-02), in the middle of Taiohae, has seven rooms with private bath above their restaurant/bar. Bed and breakfast is CFP 3000/3500 single/double, other meals CFP 2500 each. Cars, scooters, and bicycles are for rent.

In 1993 the **Hôtel Nuku Hiva Village** (Bruno Gendron, B.P. 82, Taiohae; tel. 92-01-94, fax 92-05-97) opened in Taiohae village with 15 thatched *fares* with private bath arrayed along the west side of Taiohae Bay opposite the yacht anchorage. The rates are CFP 6500/7500/8500 single/double/triple, plus CFP 3500 pp a day for breakfast and dinner. Excursions by 4WD, horseback riding, and scuba diving can be arranged.

The **Keikahanui Inn** (B.P. 21, Taiohae; tel. 92-03-82, fax 92-00-74), just beyond the Nuku Hiva Village, is owned by American yachties Rose and Frank Corser (ask to see Maurice's logbooks). They have five screened Polynesian bungalows with private bath: CFP 8500/10,500/11,500 single/double/triple, breakfast included. Other meals in the dining room are CFP 2500 each. You can buy Fatu Hiva tapa at the inn.

Accommodations around the Island

The **Hôtel Moetai Village** (Guy Millon, tel. 92-04-91) near Nuku Ataha Airport has five bungalows with private bath (cold water): CFP 2500/3500/4500 single/double/triple for bed and breakfast, other meals CFP 2500.

At Taipivai village, **Chez Martine Haiti** (B.P. 60, Taiohae; tel. 92-01-19) has two bungalows with private bath at CFP 2000 pp, or CFP 4000 pp with half board. You could also camp on Taipivai's football field (ask).

In Hatiheu village, **Chez Yvonne Katupa** (B.P. 199, Taiohae; tel. 92-02-97) offers five bungalows without cooking facilities or hot water at CFP 1800 pp, breakfast included. A small restaurant nearby serves fried fish for CFP 1500, lobster for CFP 2500. Also at Hatiheu, ask if Clarisse Omitai still provides accommodations.

You can also stay on the white-sand beach at Anaho Bay, two km east of Hatiheu on horse or foot. **Pension Anaho** (Léopold and Louise Vaianui, B.P. 202, Taiohae; tel. 92-04-25) consists of a three-room house with cooking facilities and two bungalows at CFP 2000 pp, meals available. Or ask if Marie Foucaud at Anaho still rents bungalows.

Buying and Selling

Get bread at Ropa's Bakery and supplies from Maurice McKitrick's store. Yachties who figure they'll need fuel when they get to the Marquesas should write a letter to Maurice c/o the Keikahanui Inn and ask him to order an extra drum or two from Papeete. Things to bring to trade with the locals include perfume, earrings, reggae tapes, T-shirts, and surfing magazines, for which you'll receive tapas, tie-dyed pareus, and all the fruit you can carry. A small crafts center is on the ocean side near Maurice's store. War clubs, wooden bowls, and ukuleles are the most popular items.

Services and Information

Taiohae has a Banque Socredo branch. Tourist information is mailed out by the **Syndicat d'Initiative** (Debora Kimitete, B.P. 23, Taiohae).

Don't have your mail sent c/o poste restante at the local post office as it will be returned via surface after 15 days. Instead have it addressed c/o the Keikahanui Inn, B.P. 21, Taiohae, Nuku Hiva. From 1600-1800 you can also receive telephone calls and faxes through the inn (tel. 92-03-82, fax 92-00-74), but remember that the Corsers are running a restaurant and your patronage will be appreciated.

Getting Around
There are no *trucks* from Taiohae to other parts of the island, though you can hitch fairly easily. Island tours by Land Rover or speedboat can be arranged, but get ready for some astronomical charges (for example, CFP 15,000 for a visit to Hatiheu). Most car rentals are with driver only and thus cost taxi prices. To rent a car without driver for something approaching normal prices, ask at the **Hôtel Moana Nui** (tel. 92-03-30) or

check with Alain Bigot (tel. 92-04-34).

Airport
Nuku Ataha Airport (NHV) is in the Terre-Déserte at the northwest corner of Nuku Hiva, 53 km from Taiohae along a twisting dirt road across the Toovii Plateau (two hours). A restaurant and hotel are near the terminal. The main drawback to flying into Nuku Hiva is the cost of airport transfers, which run CFP 3000 each way by 4WD vehicle by day (CFP 5000 pp by night), or CFP 6900 pp each way by helicopter (10 minutes). At last report, the boat service between Taiohae and the airport wasn't operating. The **Air Tahiti** number is tel. 92-03-41.

The passion flower (passiflora) got its name from the symbolic resemblance between its flower and Jesus's wounds, crown of thorns, etc.

HIVA OA

Measuring 40 by 19 km, 315-square-km Hiva Oa (pop. 1,750) is the second largest of the Marquesas. Mount Temetiu (1,276 meters) towers above Atuona to the west. The administrative headquarters for the Marquesas group has switched back and forth several times: Taiohae was the center until 1904, then it was Atuona until 1944, when Taiohae once more took over. The town may be the center of the southern cluster of the Marquesas, but it's quieter still than Taiohae. The Marquesas Festival of Arts takes place in Atuona every December.

Atuona was made forever famous when Paul Gauguin came to live here in 1901. Despite the attentions of his 14-year-old mistress, Vaeoho, he died of syphilis a year later at age 55 and is buried in the cemetery above the town. When Tioka, Gauguin's neighbor, found him stretched out with one leg hanging over the side of his bed, he bit him on the head as the Marquesans do to see if he really was dead. No, there was no doubt. *"Ua mate Koke!"* he cried, and disappeared. Gauguin was constantly in conflict with the colonial authorities, who disapproved of his heavy drinking sessions with the locals. Just a week before his death, Gauguin was summarily convicted of "libel of a gendarme in the course of his official duties," fined, and sentenced to three months in prison.

The famous Belgian *chanson* singer Jacques Brel and his companion Maddly Bamy came to the Marquesas aboard his 18-meter yacht, the *Askoy II,* in 1975. Jacques decided to settle at Atuona and sold his boat to an American couple. Maddly, who had been a dancer on her native Guadeloupe, gave dancing lessons to the local girls, while Jacques ran an open-air cinema. His plane, nicknamed *Jojo,* was kept at Hiva Oa airport for trips to Papeete, 1,500 km southwest. The album *Brel 1977* on the Barclay label includes one of his last songs, "Les Marquises." In 1978, chain-smoker Brel died of lung cancer and was buried in Atuona cemetery near Gauguin.

SIGHTS

Gauguin's thatched "Maison du Jouir" (House of Pleasure) has been reconstructed next to the museum in central Atuona. The view of Atuona from the **graveyard** is good (take the first left fork in the road as you climb the hill from the gendarmerie), but the beach at Atuona is poor. A **lighthouse** on the point looks across Taaoa,

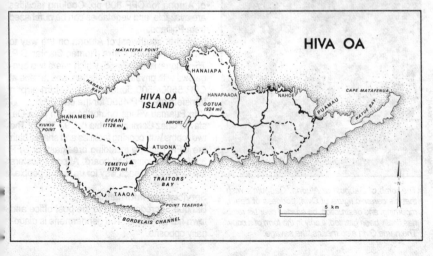

or "Traitors'," Bay. Polynesian ruins may be found up the Vaioa River, just west of Atuona.

For better swimming, take the road five km south along the bay to **Taaoa.** A big *meae* (temple) is found a kilometer up the river from there.

A second village, **Puamau,** is on the northeast coast, 40 km from Atuona over a winding road. It's a good eight-hour walk from Atuona to Puamau, up and down all the way. Five huge stone tikis and Meae Takaii can be seen in the valley behind Puamau, a 10-minute walk from Chez Bernard. One stands over two meters high.

At **Hanaiapa,** ask for William, who keeps a yachties' log. He's happy to have his infrequent visitors sign and is generous with fresh fruit and vegetables. **Hanamenu** in the northwest corner of Hiva Oa is now uninhabited, but dozens of old stone platforms can still be seen. If you'd like to spend some time here as a hermit, ask for Ozanne in Atuona, who has a house at Hanamenu he might be willing to rent. To the right of Ozanne's house is a small, crystal-clear pool.

RICHARD A. GOODMAN

The tomb of Gauguin at Atuona. Gauguin's wish that his ceramic figure of Oviri, goddess of death, mourning, and destruction, be erected over his tomb has finally been granted, if only in the form of a copy. The name Oviri also means "the savage."

PRACTICALITIES

Accommodations
Pension Gauguin (André Teissier, B.P. 34, Atuona; tel. 92-73-51) in central Atuona consists of a two-story house with four rooms downstairs, a common room and kitchen upstairs (CFP 5000/9000 single/double with half board).

The **Temetiu Village** (Gabriel Heitaa, B.P. 52, Atuona; tel. 92-73-02) overlooking Takauku Bay, near of Atuona on the way to the airport, has three bungalows with bath (cold water) at CFP 5000/9000 single/double with half pension. Airport transfers at both of the above are CFP 2000 pp return.

Atuona's upmarket place, the **Motel Hanakee Tahauku** (Serge Lecordier, B.P. 57, Hiva Oa; tel. 92-71-62, fax 92-72-51), has five stylish A-frame bungalows on the hillside toward the airport at CFP 12,840/19,260/21,400 single/double/triple. Breakfast and dinner are CFP 3200 pp extra, airport transfers CFP 3600 pp return. Each bungalow contains a TV, VCR, washing machine, kitchen, and bathtub.

Also ask if Jean Saucourt (tel 92-73-33) at Atuona still rents his bungalow with cooking facilities.

The budget traveler's best friend, **Philippe Robard** (B.P. 46, Atuona; tel. 92-74-73), takes guests in his large bungalow four km southwest of Atuona for CFP 800 pp. Cooking facilities are available, and vegetables can be purchased from Philippe.

Further southwest of Atuona on the way to Taaoa is **Pension Maire** (Roméo Ciantar, B.P. 75, Atuona; tel. 92-74-55) which offers two bungalows with private bath, kitchen, and terrace at CFP 5500/6500 double/triple. Return airport transfers are CFP 4500 for the car.

In Puamau village on northeastern Hiva Oa, stay at **Chez Bernard Heitaa** (tel. 92-72-27). The two rooms with cooking facilities and shared bath are CFP 1500 pp including breakfast, or CFP 3500 pp including half board. Airport transfers are CFP 15,000 each way for up to four people.

Services and Information
Banque Socredo is next to the post office and town hall at Atuona. The gendarmerie is diagonally opposite.

Marquesan model Tohotaua served as the model for "Girl with a Fan."
The photo was taken by Gauguin's friend Louis Grelet.

The Hiva Oa Visitors Bureau (B.P. 62, Hiva Oa; tel./fax 92-75-10) is at the local museum.

Yachting Facilities

Yachts anchor behind the breakwater in Tahauku Bay, two km east of the center of town. The copra boats also tie up here. A shower stall and laundry tub are provided on the wharf, and there's plenty of good water. Of the five small stores in Atuona, only Duncan's (the blue one) sells propane; diagonally across the street from Duncan's is a hardware store. Yachties should stock up on fresh vegetables at Atuona.

Getting Around

To rent a four-passenger Land Rover from Atuona to Puamau will run you CFP 20,000. Inquire at Atuona Town Hall. Roméo Ciantar (tel. 92-74-55) and Location David (Augustine Kaimuko, tel. 92-72-87) also rent cars.

Airport

The airstrip (AUQ) is on a 441-meter-high plateau, 13 km northeast of Atuona. In 1991 the runway was upgraded to allow it to receive direct ATR 42 flights from Papeete (via Nuku Hiva). Weekly flights by the smaller Dornier 228 aircraft continue to arrive from Rangiroa. **Air Tahiti** is at tel. 92-73-41.

It's a two-hour walk from the airport to Atuona (or you can hitch). According to the Comité du Tourisme, the taxi fare from the airport to Atuona is CFP 3600 pp RT, but the actual amount collected by the various hotels seems to vary, so check when booking.

OTHER MARQUESAS ISLANDS

UA HUKA

Goats and wild horses range across the plateaus and through the valleys of 81-square-km Ua Huka (pop. 550). Mount Hitikau (884 meters) rises northeast of Hane village. The tiny island of Teuaua, off the southwest tip of Ua Huka, is a breeding ground for millions of *kaveka* (sternas). Vaipaee is the main village of the island, although the clinic is at Hane.

Archaeological excavations by Prof. Y.H. Sinoto in 1965 dated a coastal site on Ua Huka to A.D. 300, which makes it the oldest in Tahiti-Polynesia; two pottery fragments found here suggest that the island was probably a major dispersal point for the ancient Polynesians. Small tikis may be visited in the valley behind Hane. The botanical garden in Hane is also worth a look. In Vaipaee is a small **museum** of local artifacts and

seashells, the only museum in the Marquesas. Woodcarvers are active in the village.

Accommodations

Chez Alexis (Alexis Scallamera, tel. 92-60-19) in Vaipaee village, seven km from the airport, is a four-room house with shared bath at CFP 1500 pp, or CFP 4000 with full board. Return airport transfers are CFP 1500 for the car. Alexis can arrange horseback riding and boat excursions.

Also in Vaipaee, ask if Laura Raioha (tel. 92-60-22), nicknamed "Tati Laura," and Miriama Fournier still rent rooms with cooking facilities.

A more isolated place to stay is **Chez Joseph Lichtle** (tel. 92-60-72) at Haavei Beach, 15 minutes west of Vaipaee by boat (CFP 2500 pp return). It's also possible to hike here along a rough track. There's a white sandy beach with good swimming, and no other families live here. The pension consists of two bungalows with

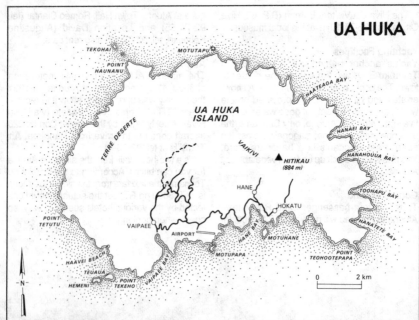

bath and two houses with two or three rooms at CFP 1500 pp, or CFP 4500 with full board. Communal cooking facilities should also be available. Joseph and Laura are reputedly the best cooks in the Marquesas, and their son Leon, mayor of Ua Huka, is extremely helpful. You can also rent a horse from Joseph.

In Hane village, the **Auberge Hitikau** (Céline Fournier, tel. 92-60-68) offers four rooms with shared bath in a concrete building (no cooking) at CFP 2000/3000 single/double. Food is available at their restaurant.

Ask if Madame Vii Fournier of Hane rents rooms in her two-bedroom house with cooking facilities.

Also worth checking is **Chez Maurice et Delphine** (Maurice and Delphine Rootuehine, tel. 92-60-55) at Hokatu village, where rooms in a three-bedroom house with shared bath and kitchen are CFP 1000 pp (CFP 3000 with all meals).

Getting There
The airstrip (UAH) is on a hilltop between Hane and Vaipaee, closer to the latter. (At last report this airport was closed, so check.) Ships tie up to a wharf at Vaipaee.

UA POU

This island lies about 40 km south of Nuku Hiva. Several jagged volcanic plugs loom behind Hakahau, the main village on the northeast coast of 120-square-km Ua Pou. One of these sugarloaf-shaped mountains inspired Jacques Brel's song, "La Cathédrale." Mount Oave (1,203 meters), highest point on Ua Pou, is often cloud-covered. The population of 2,000 is almost the same as Nuku Hiva's. In 1988, 500 French foreign legionnaires rebuilt the breakwater at Hakahau, and yachts can now tie up to the concrete pier.

A track goes right around the island. The road leads south from Hakahau to a beach beyond Hohoi. On 112-meter-high Motu Oa off the south coast, millions of seabirds nest. The villages of Hakatao and Hakamaii on the west coast are only accessible by foot, hoof, or sea. In Hakahetau village are two new churches, one Catholic, the other Protestant. The first stone

church in the Marquesas was erected at Hakahau in 1859, and the present church has a finely carved pulpit shaped like a boat.

Accommodations
Just a three-minute walk from the wharf at Hakahau is **Chez Marguerite Dordillon** (B.P. 17, Hakahau; tel. 92-53-15), where guests are accommodated in a two-room house with cooking facilities at CFP 2000 pp. Airport transfers are CFP 2000 each way for the car.

Chez Samuel et Jeanne Marie (Samuel and Jeanne Teikiehuupoko, B.P. 19, Hakahau; tel. 92-53-16), a km from Hakahau Wharf, has two two-room houses with cooking facilities at CFP 1500 pp. There's a CFP 500 pp surcharge if you want hot water and another CFP 500 is collected if you stay only one night.

Pension Vaikaka (Valja Klima, B.P. 16, Hakahau; tel. 92-53-37), two km south of Hakahau Wharf, is CFP 2500/4000 single/double in the one bungalow (CFP 500 pp discount beginning on the fourth night).

You could also inquire at the Collège de Ua Pou in Hakahau where **CETAD** (B.P. 9, Hakahau; tel. 92-53-83) has a bungalow for rent to visitors.

Also in Hakahau, ask is Marguerite Kaiha-Schaffer (tel. 92-53-76), Rosalie Tata (who also operates a restaurant), and local taxi driver Jules Hituputoka (tel. 92-53-33) still rent rooms to visitors.

Further afield, **Pension Paeaka** (Marie-Augustine Aniamioi, B.P. 27, Hakahau; tel. 92-53-96) at Haakuti village has a one-room house with cooking facilities at CFP 1000 pp a day or CFP 25,000 a month.

Shopping

A boutique sells local carvings and beautiful hand-painted pareus. Four woodcarvers work in Hakahau village—just ask for *les sculpteurs*. If you're buying, shop around at the beginning of your stay, as many items are unfinished and there'll be time to have something completed for you; the same carvings cost three times as much on Tahiti. On the right just past the bakery (great baguettes!) is the home of Jacob Teikitutoua (tel. 92-51-48), who makes ukuleles.

Services and Information

Banque Socredo, a post office, a gendarmerie, and six or seven stores are at Hakahau.

Motu Haka (Georges Teikiehuupoko, B.P. 54, Hakahau; tel. 92-53-21) is a cultural organization which promotes Marquesan language instruction, archaeological projects, and traditional arts while rejecting cultural domination by Tahiti.

Getting There

Ua Pou's Aneou airstrip (UAP) is on the north coast, five km from Hakahau on a very rough road over a ridge. You can reach **Air Tahiti** at tel. 92-53-41.

Friday at 0730 a launch from Nuku Hiva to Ua Pou departs Ua Pou for the return at 1600 (1.5 hours each way, CFP 6000 RT).

TAHUATA

Fifteen km long by nine km wide, 61-square-km Tahuata is the smallest of the six inhabited islands of the Marquesas. The population is about 700.

On the west coast is the main village, Vaitahu, where a new Catholic church was completed in 1988. The anchorage at Hana Moe Noa just

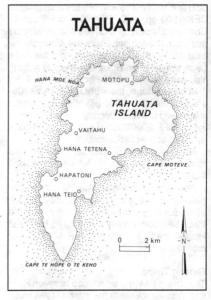

north of Vaitahu is protected from the ocean swells. The water here is clear, as no rivers run into this bay. It was here that Mendaña first anchored in 1595, followed by Captain Cook in 1774. Here too, Admiral Dupetit-Thouars took possession of the Marquesas in 1842 and established a fort, provoking armed resistance by the islanders.

Archaeological sites exist in the Vaitahu Valley. Hapatoni village, farther south, is picturesque, with a *tamanu*-bordered road and petroglyphs in the Hanatahau Valley behind. White-sand beaches are found on the north side of the island.

Accommodations

The only official place to stay is **Chez Naani** (François and Lucie Barsinas, tel. 92-92-26) in Vaitahu village. A room in this four-room concrete house with communal cooking facilities is CFP 1500 pp (or CFP 3350 pp with half board).

Getting There

There's no airport on Tahuata, which is only six km south of Hiva Oa across Bordelais Channel. To charter a six-passenger boat between the islands is CFP 15,000 (one hour). Small boats leave Hiva Oa for Tahuata almost daily, so ask around at the harbor on Takauku Bay near Atuona. The launch *Te Pua Omioi,* belonging to the Commune of Tahautu, leaves Atuona on Thursday and Friday at 1230. Take supplies with you.

FATU HIVA

Fatu Hiva was the first of the Marquesas to be visited by Europeans (Mendaña called in 1595). In 1937-38 Thor Heyerdahl spent one year on this southernmost island with his young bride Liv and wrote a book called *Fatu Hiva,* describing their far from successful attempt "to return to a simple, natural life." Fatu Hiva (80 square km) is far wetter than the northern islands, and the vegetation is lush. Mount Tauaouoho (960 meters) is the highest point.

This is the most remote of the Marquesas, and no French officials are present. With 500 inhabitants, Fatu Hiva has only two villages, Omoa and Hanavave. It takes about five hours to walk the 17-km trail linking the two, up and

the Cannilie Kai *at Bay of Virgins, Fatu Hiva*

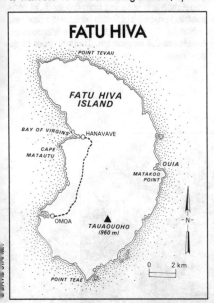

FATU HIVA

FATU HIVA ISLAND

POINT TEVAII

BAY OF VIRGINS — HANAVAVE

CAPE MATAUTU

OUIA

MATAKOO POINT

OMOA

▲ TAUAOUOHO (960 m)

N

0   2 km

POINT TEAE

down over the mountains amid breathtaking scenery. Surfing onto the rocky beach at Omoa can be pretty exciting! Hanavave on the Bay of Virgins offers one of the most fantastic scenic spectacles in all of Polynesia, with tiki-shaped cliffs dotted with goats. Horses and canoes are for hire in both villages.

Today a revival of the old crafts is taking place in Fatu Hiva, and it's again possible to buy not only sculptures but painted tapa cloth. Hats and mats are woven from pandanus. *Monoi* oils are made from coconut oil, gardenia, jasmine, and sandalwood. Fatu Hiva doesn't have any *nonos,* but lots of mosquitoes. If you plan on staying awhile, get some free anti-elephantiasis pills at a clinic.

Yachting Facilities
Yachts usually anchor in the Bay of Virgins (from January to September); the swell can be uncomfortable at times, but the holding is good in about six fathoms. Yachties trade perfume, lipstick, and cosmetics for the huge Fatu Hiva grapefruits.

Cruising yachts often make Fatu Hiva their first landfall in Polynesia, but this is technically illegal, as the island is not a port of entry. If the village chief uses his radio to report your presence to the gendarme at Atuona, you'll probably pay a CFP 5000 fine when you check in at Hiva Oa.

Accommodations and Food
Several families in Omoa village take paying guests. **Marie-Claire Ehueinana** (tel. 92-80-16) takes guests in her two-room house at CFP 1500 pp a day or CFP 35,000 a month. **Norma Ropati** (tel. 92-80-13) has four rooms at CFP 2000 pp with breakfast or CFP 5000 with all meals. **Cécile Gilmore** (tel. 92-80-54) has two rooms with shared kitchen at CFP 2500 pp or CFP 4000 with all meals). Other residents of Omoa who have accommodated visitors in past include Jean Bouyer, Kehu Kamia, François Peters, and Joseph Tetuanui (tel. 92-80-09). A bakery and four or five small stores are also in Omoa.

Getting There
There's no airstrip on Fatu Hiva but a speedboat, or *bonitier,* travels once a week from Fatu Hiva to Atuona (CFP 3500 OW), leaving Atuona at 1500 on Friday. The trip takes just over three hours and the boat carries eight people, mail, and videocassettes.

MOTANE

Motane (Mohotani) is an eight-km-long island rising to 520 meters about 18 km southeast of Hiva Oa. The depredations of wild sheep on Motane turned the island into a treeless desert. When the Spaniards "discovered" it in 1595, Motane was well-wooded and populated, but today it's uninhabited.

EIAO

Uninhabited Eiao and Hatutu islands, 85 km northwest of Nuku Hiva, are the remotest of the Marquesas. Eiao is a 40-square-km island, 10 km long and 576 meters high, with landings on the northwest and west sides. The French once used Eiao as a site of deportation for criminals or "rebellious" natives. In 1972 the French Army drilled holes 1,000 meters down into Eiao to check the island's suitability for underground nuclear testing, but deemed the basalt rock too fragile for such use. Wild cattle, sheep, pigs, and donkeys forage across Eiao, ravaging the vegetation and suffering from droughts. In contrast, the profusion of fishlife off Eiao is incredible.

Hatutu, the northernmost of the Marquesas, measures 6.4 square km. Thousands of birds nest here.

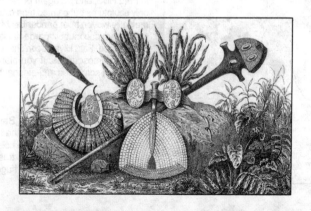

M.G.L. DOMENY DE RIENZI

RESOURCES

GUIDEBOOKS

Box, Ben, ed. *South American Handbook*. Trade & Travel Publications, 6 Riverside Court, Lower Bristol Road, Bath BA2 3DZ, England (fax 44-1225/469461). Highly recommended for anyone combining a trip to Latin America with Tahiti-Polynesia via Easter Island.

Danielsson, Bengt. *Tahiti, Circle Island Tour Guide*. Singapore: Les Editions du Pacifique, 1986. A kilometer-by-kilometer ride around the island with *the* expert.

Davock, Marcia. *Cruising Guide to Tahiti and the French Society Islands*. Stamford, CT: Wescott Cove Publishing, 1985. A large-format, Spiral-bound guide for yachties.

Fisher, Jon. *Uninhabited Ocean Islands*. Loompanics Unlimited, Box 1197, Port Townsend, WA 98368, U.S.A. This unique book and Fisher's other work, *The Last Frontiers on Earth,* are essential reading for anyone considering relocating to the South Pacific. Write Loompanics for a free copy of "The Best Book Catalog in the World."

Hammick, Anne. *Ocean Cruising on a Budget*. Camden, ME: International Marine Publishing. Hammick shows how to sail your own yacht safely and enjoyably over the seas while cutting costs. Study it beforehand if you're thinking of working as crew on a yacht.

Health Information For International Travel. An excellent reference published annually by the Centers for Disease Control, U.S. Public Health Service. Available from the Superintendent of Documents, U.S. Government Printing Office, Washington, DC 20402, U.S.A.

Hinz, Earl R. *Landfalls of Paradise: The Guide to Pacific Islands*. Honolulu: University of Hawaii Press. With 97 maps and 40 tables, this is the only genuine yacht cruising guide to all 32 island groups of Oceania.

Laudon, Paule. *Randonnées en Montagne, Tahiti-Moorea*. Les Editions du Pacifique. The French-language guide describes 30 hikes ranging in difficulty from "easy" to "mountain-climbing experience required." For each hike, the author has provided a map, a brief description of the hike, the time required, the altitude gained, and an indication of the type of flora and fauna to be seen. The descriptions can be a little confusing (even if your French is good), yet it's a must for anyone serious about discovering the interior of these islands.

Ryan, Paddy. *The Snorkeler's Guide to the Coral Reef*. Honolulu: University of Hawaii Press, 1994. Covers everything from the Red Sea to the Pacific Ocean.

Schroeder, Dr. Dirk. *Staying Healthy in Asia, Africa, and Latin America*. Chico, CA: Moon Publications, 1995. Order a copy of this book if you'd like to acquire a degree of expertise in tropical medicine.

Stanley, David. *South Pacific Handbook*. Chico, CA: Moon Publications, 1996. Covers the entire region in the same manner as the book you're reading.

DESCRIPTION AND TRAVEL

de Bovis, Edmond. Robert D. Craig, trans. *Tahitian Society Before the Arrival of the Europeans*. Honolulu: University of Hawaii Press, 1980. These observations of a French naval officer on the history, customs, religion, and government of Tahiti, were written in 1850.

Danielsson, Bengt. *Forgotten Islands of the South Seas*. London: Allen and Unwin, 1957.

A fascinating tale of life and love in the Marquesas Islands.

Danielsson, Bengt. *From Raft to Raft.* New York: Doubleday and Co., 1960. The story of one of the greatest sea adventures of modern times: Eric de Bisschop's raft voyage from Tahiti to South America and back, as told by one of the survivors.

Dodd, Edward. *Polynesia's Sacred Isle.* New York: Dodd, Mead and Co., 1976. An excellent account of Raiatea, its culture and history, based on the author's own researches, together with a vivid account of his many sojourns on the island.

Ellis, William. *Polynesian Researches.* Rutland, VT: Charles E. Tuttle Co., 1969. An early missionary's detailed observations of Tahiti during the years 1817-25.

Eskridge, Robert Lee. *Manga Reva: The Forgotten Islands.* Honolulu: Mutual Publishing. The autobiography of a wandering American painter in the Gambiers in 1927.

Finney, Ben R. *Hokule'a: The Way to Tahiti.* New York: Dodd, Mead, 1979. The story of the *Hokule'a*'s 1976 voyage from Hawaii to Tahiti.

Heyerdahl, Thor. *Fatu Hiva: Back to Nature.* New York: Doubleday, 1974. In 1936 Heyerdahl and his wife Liv went to live on Fatu Hiva. This book describes their year there.

Heyerdahl, Thor. *Kon Tiki.* Translated by F.H. Lyon. Chicago: Rand McNally, 1950. Convinced that the mysterious origin of the Polynesians lies in the equally mysterious disappearance of the pre-Incan Indians of Peru, the author finds that only by repeating their feat of sailing some 6,500 km across the Pacific in a balsa raft can he substantiate his theory.

Kyselka, Will. *An Ocean in Mind.* Honolulu: University of Hawaii Press, 1987. Analyzes the learning techniques of Nainoa Thompson, who successfully navigated without the use of modern navigational equipment the recreated traditional Polynesian sailing vessel, *Hokule'a,* during its second roundtrip journey between Hawaii and Tahiti in 1980.

Stevenson, Robert Louis. *In the South Seas.* New York: Scribner's, 1901. The author's account of his travels through the Marquesas, Tuamotus, and Gilberts by yacht in the years 1888-90.

Theroux, Paul. *The Happy Isles of Oceania.* London: Hamish Hamilton, 1992. The author of classic accounts of railway journeys sets out with kayak and tent to tour the Pacific. Theroux has caught the mood of paradise in a way that makes his book really satisfying to read.

Thompson, Reverend Robert. Robert D. Craig, ed. *The Marquesas Islands.* Honolulu: University of Hawaii Press, 1980. Thompson's account, written in 1841, is a valuable record of the Marquesas just before their rapid decline.

Watson, Thomas F., Jr. *Pacific Passage.* Camden, ME: International Marine Publishing. The story of voyage through Polynesia under sail with extensive notes on navigation, yacht handling, trip planning, and natural history.

GEOGRAPHY

Atlas of French Polynesia. Editions ORSTOM, 72 route d'Aulnay, 93143 Bondy Cedex, France. A major thematic atlas summarizing the geography, population, and history of the territory.

Crocombe, Ron, and Nancy Pollock, eds. *French Polynesia.* Suva: Institute of Pacific Studies, 1988. Overview of the history, customs, land, economy, development, migration, media, and politics.

Ridgell, Reilly. *Pacific Nations and Territories.* Published by Bess Press, Box 22388, Honolulu, HI 96823, U.S.A. One of the few high school geography textbooks on the region.

NATURAL SCIENCES

Bruner, Phillip L. *Field Guide to the Birds of French Polynesia.* Honolulu: Bishop Museum Press, 1972.

Crawford, Peter. *Nomads of the Wind.* London: BBC Books, 1993. A beautifully illustrated natural history of Polynesia which grew out of a five-part television series.

Hargreaves, Bob, and Dorothy Hargreaves. *Tropical Blossoms of the Pacific.* Ross-Hargreaves, Box 11897, Lahaina, HI 96761, U.S.A. A handy 64-page booklet with color photos to assist in identification; a matching volume is titled *Tropical Trees of the Pacific.*

Hinton, A.G. *Shells of New Guinea and the Central Indo-Pacific.* Australia: Jacaranda Press, 1972. A photo guide to identification.

Martini, Frederic. *Exploring Tropical Isles and Seas.* Englewood Cliffs, N.J.: Prentice-Hall, 1984. A fine introduction to the natural environment of the islands.

Merrill, Elmer D. *Plant Life of the Pacific World.* Rutland, VT: Charles E. Tuttle Co., 1981. First published in 1945, this handy volume is a useful basic reference.

Mitchell, Andrew W. *A Fragile Paradise: Man and Nature in the Pacific.* London: Fontana, 1990. Published in the U.S. by the University of Texas Press under the title, *The Fragile South Pacific: An Ecological Odyssey.* Andrew Mitchell, an Earthwatch Europe deputy director, utters a heartfelt plea on behalf of all endangered Pacific wildlife is this brilliant book.

Pratt, Douglas. *A Field Guide to the Birds of Hawaii and the Tropical Pacific.* Princeton, N.J.: Princeton University Press, 1986. The best in a poorly covered field.

Tinker, Spencer Wilkie. *Fishes of Hawaii: A Handbook of the Marine Fishes of Hawaii and the Central Pacific Ocean.* Hawaiian Service, Inc., Box 2835, Honolulu, HI 96803, U.S.A. A comprehensive, indexed reference work.

Whistler, W. Arthur. *Polynesian Herbal Medicine.* Available at US$32.95 from Publications Office, National Tropical Botanical Garden, Box 340, Lawai, Kauai, HI 96765, U.S.A. This book discusses traditional and contemporary herbal medicinal practices in Polynesia.

HISTORY

Beaglehole, J.C. *The Life of Captain Cook.* Camden, ME: International Marine Publishing. A well-written account of Cook's achievements in the context of the era in which Cook lived. Beaglehole also edited Cook's three volumes of journals.

Bellwood, Peter. *Man's Conquest of the Pacific.* New York: Oxford University Press, 1979. One of the most extensive studies of the prehistory of Southeast Asia and Oceania ever published.

Bellwood, Peter. *The Polynesians: Prehistory of an Island People.* London: Thames and Hudson, 1987. A well-written account of the archaeology of Polynesian expansion.

Buck, Peter H. *Vikings of the Pacific.* Chicago: University of Chicago Press, 1959. A popular narrative of Polynesian migrations.

Clark, Thomas Blake. *Omai, First Polynesian Ambassador to England.* Honolulu: University of Hawaii Press, 1969. Catches the atmosphere of the cultural impact of Polynesia on the West, in that pristine dawn before the counterimpact of the West on Polynesia.

Danielsson, Bengt. *What Happened on the Bounty.* London: Allen and Unwin, 1963. A reappraisal of Captain Bligh, whom Hollywood has unfairly cast as a tyrant. The subsequent fate of the mutineers is also given in depth.

Ferdon, Edwin A. *Early Tahiti As The Explorers Saw It.* University of Arizona Press, 1981.

Ferdon's reconstruction of Tahitian society at the time of European contact.

Henningham, Stephen. *France and the South Pacific: A Contemporary History*. Honolulu: University of Hawaii Press, 1992. This lucid book brings French policy in the South Pacific into clear focus.

Howe, K.R. *Where the Waves Fall*. Honolulu: University of Hawaii Press, 1984. This history of the South Seas from first settlement to colonial rule maintains a steady and sympathetic focus on the islanders themselves.

Howarth, David. *Tahiti: A Paradise Lost*. New York: Penguin Books, 1985. A readable history of European exploration in the Society Islands until the French takeover in 1842.

Langdon, Robert. *The Lost Caravel*. Sydney: Pacific Publications, 1975. The author proposes that Spanish castaways from Magellan's fleet gave a totally new direction to Polynesian culture, an audacious theory that has met with little approval among professional anthropologists and historians.

Langdon, Robert. *Tahiti: Island of Love*. Australia: Pacific Publications, 1979. A popular history of Tahiti since the European discovery in 1767.

Moorehead, Alan. *The Fatal Impact*. New York: Harper & Row, 1966. European impact on the South Pacific from 1767 to 1840, as illustrated in the cases of Tahiti, Australia, and Antarctica.

Newbury, Colin. *Tahiti Nui: Change and Survival in French Polynesia, 1767-1945*. Honolulu: University of Hawaii Press, 1980. Describes major events, while providing many details of the social and economic processes.

Oliver, Douglas L. *Return to Tahiti: Bligh's Second Breadfruit Voyage*. Honolulu: University of Hawaii Press, 1988. Offers insights on the inhabitants of Tahiti and their customs at the time of European contact.

Oliver, Douglas L. *The Pacific Islands*. Honolulu: University of Hawaii Press, 1989. A new edition of the classic 1951 study of the history and economies of the entire Pacific area.

PACIFIC ISSUES

Buske, Norm. *Cesium-134 at Moruroa: Review of the Calypso Water Samples*. Search Technical Services, HCR Box 17, Davenport, WA 99122-9404, U.S.A. This report dated September 1990 provides clearest proof yet that radiation is leaking from the underground nuclear testing at Moruroa.

Buske, Norm. *Radioactivity in Plankton*. This June 1991 report describes the *Rainbow Warrior II*'s 1990 scientific mission to Moruroa which found traces of radioactivity outside the 12-mile exclusion zone. Although the French government has attempted to discredit Buske's findings, they have refused all requests to date for an independent scientific survey of their former nuclear test site.

Danielsson, Bengt, and Marie-Thérèse Danielsson. *Poisoned Reign: French nuclear colonialism in the Pacific*. Penguin Books, 1986. An updated version of *Moruroa Mon Amour*, first published in 1977.

Hamel-Green, Michael. *The South Pacific Nuclear Free Zone Treaty: A Critical Assessment*. Canberra: Peace Research Center, Australian National University, 1990. Hamel-Green demonstrates how Australia forced through a toothless treaty designed to appease regional antinuclear sentiment, then was humiliated when the U.S. refused to sign.

Robie, David. *Blood on Their Banner*. London: Zed Books, 1989. Robie, a well-known New Zealand journalist specializing in the islands, examines the nationalist struggles in New Caledonia and other Pacific territories. In the U.S., it's available from Zed Books, 171 1st Ave., Atlantic Heights, NJ 07716; in Britain from Zed Books, 57 Caledonian Rd., London N1 9BU; in Australia from Pluto Press, Box 199, Leichhardt, NSW 2040. Highly recommended.

Robie, David, ed. *Tu Galala: Social Change in the Pacific*. Wellington: Bridget Williams Books, 1992. Distributed in Australia by Pluto Press (address above). In this book, Robie has collected a series of essays examining the conflicting influences of tradition, democracy, and westernization, with special attention to environmental issues and human rights. The chapter on Tahiti-Polynesia is by Bengt and Marie-Thérèse Danielsson.

Weingartner, Erich. *The Pacific: Nuclear Testing And Minorities*. London: Minority Rights Group, 1991. A recent survey of the various environmental, political, and social issues facing the peoples of the Pacific. Available from Cultural Survival, 46 Brattle St., Cambridge, MA 02138, U.S.A.

SOCIAL SCIENCE

Cizeron, Marc, and Marianne Hienly. *Tahiti: Life on the Other Side*. Suva: Institute of Pacific Studies, 1985. Four lower-income urban Tahitians describe their experiences, and community leaders reflect on what must be done to help the Tahitian poor.

Danielsson, Bengt. *Love in the South Seas*. Honolulu: Mutual Publishing. Sex and family life of the Polynesians, based on early accounts as well as observations by the noted Swedish anthropologist.

Danielsson, Bengt. *Work and Life on Raroia*. Danielsson spent 18 months on this atoll observing Tuamotu life and this book is still the only detailed history of the Tuamotu Islands.

Levy, Robert. *Tahitians: Mind and Experience in the Society Islands*. Chicago: University of Chicago Press, 1973. Levy's study, based on several years of field work on Tahiti and Huahine, includes an intriguing examination of the *mahu* (transvestite) phenomenon.

Marshall, Don. *Raivavae*. New York: Doubleday and Co., 1961. The author, who is a professional anthropologist, did field work on this high island in the Austral group in 1957-58, to find out what was left of the old orgiastic pagan religion and sexual rites.

Oliver, Douglas L. *Ancient Tahitian Society*. Honolulu: University of Hawaii Press, 1975. Sets out to describe what Tahitian society was like immediately before, and immediately after, contact with peoples of literate, industrial societies.

Oliver, Douglas L. *Native Cultures of the Pacific Islands*. Honolulu: University of Hawaii Press, 1988. Intended primarily for college-level courses on precontact anthropology, history, economy, and politics of the entire region.

Oliver, Douglas L. *Two Tahitian Villages*. Honolulu: University of Hawaii Press, 1983. What is learned about this developing Polynesian society is useful to the study of other human societies.

LANGUAGE

Anisson du Perron, Jacques, and Mai-Arii Cadousteau. *Dictionaire Moderne, Tahitien-Français et Français-Tahitien*. Papeete: Stepolde, 1973.

Tryon, Darrell T. *Conversational Tahitian*. Canberra: Australian National University Press, 1970.

Tryon, Darrell T. *Say It In Tahitian*. Sydney: Pacific Publications, 1977. For lovers of the exotic, an instant introduction to spoken Tahitian.

LITERATURE

Burdick, Eugene. *The Blue of Capricorn*. Honolulu: Mutual Publishing. Stories and sketches of the Pacific by the coauthor of *The Ugly American*.

Day, A. Grove. *The Lure of Tahiti*. Honolulu: Mutual Publishing, 1986. Fifteen choice extracts from the rich literature of "the most romantic island in the world."

Hall, James Norman. *The Forgotten One and Other True Tales of the South Seas.* Honolulu: Mutual Publishing. A book about writers and intellectuals who sought refuge on the out-of-the-world islands of the Pacific.

Hall, James Norman, and Charles Bernard Nordhoff. *The* Bounty *Trilogy.* New York: Grosset and Dunlap, 1945. Retells in fictional form the famous mutiny, Bligh's escape to Timor, and the mutineers' fate on Pitcairn.

Lay, Graeme. *Motu Tapu.* Auckland: Pasifika Press, 1990. Short stories of the South Pacific. Lay has also written a travelogue called *Passages—Journeys in Polynesia* (Auckland: Tandem Press, 1993).

Loti, Pierre. *The Marriage of Loti.* Honolulu: University of Hawaii Press, 1976. This tale of Loti's visits to Tahiti in 1872 helped create the romantic myth of Polynesia in contemporary Europe.

Maugham, W. Somerset. *The Moon and Six-pence.* Story of a London stockbroker who leaves his job for Tahiti and ends up leading an artist's primitive life that isn't as romantic as he hoped.

Maugham, W. Somerset. *The Trembling of a Leaf.* Honolulu: Mutual Publishing. The responses of a varied mix of white men—colonial administrator, trader, sea captain, bank manager, and missionary—to the people and nature of the South Pacific. Maugham is a masterful storyteller, and his journey to Samoa and Tahiti in 1916-1917 supplied him with poignant material.

Melville, Herman. *Typee, A Peep at Polynesian Life.* Evanston, Ill.: Northwestern University Press, 1968. In 1842 Melville deserted from an American whaler at Nuku Hiva, Marquesas Islands. This semifictional work tells of Melville's four months among the Typee people. A sequel, *Omoo,* relates his observations on Tahiti at the time of the French takeover.

Michener, James A. *Return to Paradise.* New York: Random House, 1951. Essays and short stories. Michener's *Tales of the South Pacific,* the first of over 30 books, won the Pulitzer Prize for fiction in 1948. A year later it appeared on Broadway as the long-running musical *South Pacific.*

Stone, William S. *Idylls of the South Seas.* Honolulu: University of Hawaii Press, 1971. Stone uses the same narrator, Tetua, to recount 10 myths and legends of Tahiti.

THE ARTS

Barrow, Terence. *The Art of Tahiti.* London: Thames and Hudson, 1979. A concise, well-illustrated survey of works of art from the Society, Austral, and Cook islands.

Danielsson, Bengt. *Gauguin in the South Seas.* New York: Doubleday, 1966. Danielsson's fascinating account of Gauguin's 10 years in Polynesia.

Gauguin, Paul. *Noa Noa.* A Tahitian journal kept by this famous artist during his first two years in the islands.

Guiart, Jean. *The Arts of the South Pacific.* New York: Golden Press, 1963. A well-illustrated coffee-table art book, with the emphasis on the French-dominated portion of Oceania. Consideration is given to the cultures that produced the works.

Kaeppler, Adrienne L. *Polynesian Dance.* Honolulu: Bishop Museum Press, 1983. Describes the traditional dances of Hawaii, Tahiti, the Cook Islands, Tonga, and Niue.

Linton, Ralph, and Paul S. Wingert. *Arts of the South Seas.* New York: Museum of Modern Art, 1946. Although dated, this book provides a starting point for the study of the art of Polynesia.

DISCOGRAPHY

Music lovers will be happy to hear that authentic Pacific music is becoming more readily available on compact disc. In compiling this selection we've tried to list noncommercial recordings which are faithful to the traditional music of the islands as it exists today, and island music based on Western pop has been avoided. Most of the CDs below can be ordered through specialized music shops; otherwise write directly to the publishers.

Coco's Temaeva (S 65808). Manuiti Productions, B.P. 755, Papeete, Tahiti (fax 689/43-27-24). Founded by Coco Hotahota in 1962, Temaeva has won more prizes at the annual Heiva i Tahiti festivals than any other professional dance troupe.

Fanshawe, David, ed. *Heiva i Tahiti: Festival of Love* (EUCD 1238). ARC Music. Fanshawe has captured the excitement of Tahiti's biggest festival in these pieces recorded live in Papeete in 1982 and 1986. Famous groups led by Coco Hotahota, Yves Roche, Irma Prince, and others are represented.

Fanshawe, David, ed. *Spirit of Polynesia* (CD-SDL 403). Saydisc Records, Chipping Manor, The Chipping, Wotton-U-Edge, Glos. GL12 7AD, England. An anthology of the music of 12 Pacific countries recorded between 1978 and 1988. Over half the pieces are from Tahiti-Polynesia and the Cook Islands. A *Spirit of Melanesia* sequel is planned.

Nabet-Meyer, Pascal, ed. *The Tahitian Choir, Vol. I* (Triloka Records 7192-2). Triloka Inc., 7033 Sunset Blvd., Los Angeles, CA 90028, U.S.A. Recorded at Rapa Iti in 1991.

Nabet-Meyer, Pascal, ed. *The Tahitian Choir, Vol. II* (Shanachie 64055). Choral singing and chanting from Rapa Iti in the Austral group (recording date not provided).

South Pacific Drums (PS 65066). Manuiti Productions, B.P. 755, Papeete, Tahiti (fax 689/43-27-24). A compilation of 39 of the best percussion recordings in Manuiti's archives—an excellent introduction to the traditional music of Polynesia.

REFERENCE BOOKS

Craig, Robert D. *Dictionary of Polynesian Mythology*. Westport, CT: Greenwood Press, 1989. Aside from hundreds of alphabetical entries listing the legends, stories, gods, goddesses, and heroes of the Polynesians, this book charts the evolution of 30 Polynesian languages.

Craig, Robert D. *Historical Dictionary of Polynesia*. Metuchen, NJ: Scarecrow Press, 1994. This handy volume contains alphabetical listings of individuals (past and present), places, and organizations, plus historical chronologies and bibliographies by island group. A similar work on Melanesia is in preparation.

Douglas, Ngaire, and Norman Douglas, eds. *Pacific Islands Yearbook*. Australia: Angus & Robertson Publishers. Despite the name, a new edition of this authoritative sourcebook has come out about every four years since 1932. Copies may be ordered through *Pacific Islands Monthly*, G.P.O. Box 1167, Suva, Fiji Islands.

The Far East and Australasia. London: Europa Publications. An annual survey and directory of Asia and the Pacific. Provides abundant and factual political and economic data; an excellent reference source.

Fry, Gerald W., and Rufino Mauricio. *Pacific Basin and Oceania*. Oxford: Clio Press, 1987. A selective, indexed Pacific bibliography, which actually describes the contents of the books, instead of merely listing them.

Jackson, Miles M., ed. *Pacific Island Studies: A Survey of the Literature*. Westport, CT: Greenwood Press, 1986. In addition to comprehensive listings, there are extensive essays that put the most important works in perspective.

Taylor, Clyde R. *A Pacific Bibliography: Printed Matter Relating to the Native Peoples of Polynesia, Melanesia and Micronesia*. Oxford: Clarendon Press, 1965. Extensive.

BOOKSELLERS AND PUBLISHERS

Some of the titles listed above are out of print and not available in regular bookstores. Major research libraries should have a few, otherwise write to the specialized antiquarian booksellers or regional publishers listed below for their printed lists of recycled or hard-to-find books on the Pacific. Sources of detailed topographical maps or navigational charts are provided in the following section.

Antipodean Books, Maps, and Prints. Antipodean Books, Box 189, Cold Spring, NY 10516, U.S.A. (tel. 914/424-3867, fax 914/424-3617). A complete catalog of out-of-print and rare items.

Australia, the Pacific and South East Asia. Serendipity Books, Box 340, Nedlands, WA 6009, Australia (tel. 61-9/382-2246, fax 61-9/388-2728). The largest stocks of antiquarian, secondhand, and out-of-print books on the Pacific in Western Australia. Free catalogs are issued regularly.

Boating Books. International Marine Publishing Co., TAB Books, Blue Ridge Summit, PA 17294-0840, U.S.A. (tel. 800/822-8158, fax 717/794-5291). All the books you'll ever need to teach yourself how to sail.

Books from the Pacific Islands. Institute of Pacific Studies, University of the South Pacific, Box 1168, Suva, Fiji Islands. Their specialty is books about the islands written by the Pacific islanders themselves.

Books, Maps & Prints of Pacific Islands. Colin Hinchcliffe, 12 Queens Staith Mews, York, YO1 1HH, England (tel. 44-1904/610679, fax 44-1904/641664). An excellent source of antiquarian books, maps, and engravings.

Books on Oceania, Africa, Archaeology & Anthropology, & Asia. Michael Graves-Johnston, Bookseller, Box 532, London SW9 0DR, England (fax 44-171/738-3747).

Books Pasifika Catalogues. Box 68-446, Newton, Auckland 1, New Zealand (fax 64-9/377-9528). A good starting point for New Zealanders.

Books & Series in Print. Bishop Museum Press, Box 19000-A, Honolulu, HI 96817-0916, U.S.A. An indexed list of books on the Pacific available from Hawaii's Bishop Museum. A separate list of "The Occasional Papers" lists specialized works.

Hawaii and Pacific Islands. The Book Bin, 228 S.W. 3rd St., Corvallis, OR 97333, U.S.A. (tel./fax 503-752-0045). An indexed mail-order catalog of hundreds of rare books on the Pacific. If there's a particular book about the Pacific you can't find anywhere, this is the place to try.

Hawaii: New Books. University of Hawaii Press, 2840 Kolowalu St., Honolulu, HI 96822, U.S.A. This catalog is well worth requesting if you're trying to build a Pacific library.

Moon Handbooks. Moon Publications Inc., Box 3040, Chico, CA 95927, U.S.A. Write for a copy of this free catalog of Moon travel handbooks or, in you live in the U.S., dial (800) 345-5473.

Pacificana. Messrs Berkelouw, "Bendooley," Old Hume Highway, Berrima, NSW 2577, Australia (tel. 61-48/771-370, fax 61-48/771-102). A detailed listing of thousands of rare Pacific titles. Payment of an annual subscription of A$25 entitles you to 25 catalogs a year. They also have stores in Sydney (19 Oxford St., Paddington, NSW 2021, Australia; tel. 61-2/360-3200) and Los Angeles (830 North Highland Ave., Los Angeles, CA 90038, U.S.A.; tel. 213/466-3321).

Pacificana. Books of Yesteryear, Box 257, Newport, NSW 2106, Australia (fax 61-2/918-0545). Another source of old, fine, and rare books on the Pacific.

Pacific and Southeast Asia—Old Books, Prints, Maps. Catalog No. 39. Bibliophile, 24 Glenmore Rd., Paddington, NSW 2021, Australia (tel. 331-1411, fax 361-3371).

Société des Océanistes Catalogue. Musée de l'Homme, 75116, Paris, France. Many scholarly works (in French) on Polynesia are available from this body.

Tales of the Pacific. Mutual Publishing, 1127 11th Ave., Mezzanine B, Honolulu, HI 96816, U.S.A. (tel. 808/732-1709, fax 808/734-4094). The classics of Pacific literature, available in cheap paperback editions.

The 'Nesias' & Down Under: Some Recent Books. The Cellar Book Shop, 18090 Wyoming, Detroit, MI 48221, U.S.A. (tel./fax 313/861-1776). A wide range of in-print and out-of-print books on the Pacific.

MAP PUBLISHERS

Defense Mapping Agency Catalog of Maps, Charts, and Related Products: Part 2—Hydrographic Products, Volume VIII, Oceania. National Ocean Service, Distribution Branch, N/CG33, 6501 Lafayette Ave., Riverdale, MD 20737, U.S.A. A complete index and order form for nautical charts of the Pacific. The National Ocean Service also distributes nautical charts put out by the National Oceanic and Atmospheric Administration (NOAA).

Liste des Cartes Disponibles. Service de l'Urbanisme, 11 rue du Commandant Destremeau, B.P. 866, Papeete, Tahiti. The main source of recent topgraphical maps of Tahiti-Polynesia.

PERIODICALS

Atoll Research Bulletin. Washington, D.C.: Smithsonian Institution. A specialized journal and inexhaustible source of fascinating information (and maps) on the most remote islands of the Pacific. Consult back issues at major libraries.

The Centre for South Pacific Studies Newsletter. Centre for South Pacific Studies, The University of New South Wales, Kensington, NSW 2033, Australia. A useful bimonthly publication which catalogs scholarly conferences, events, activities, news, employment opportunities, courses, scholarships, and publications across the region.

Commodores' Bulletin. Seven Seas Cruising Assn., 1525 South Andrews Ave., Suite 217, Fort Lauderdale, FL 33316, U.S.A. (fax 305/463-7183; US$53 a year worldwide by airmail). This monthly bulletin is chock-full of useful information for anyone wishing to tour the Pacific by sailing boat. All Pacific yachties and friends should be Seven Seas members!

The Contemporary Pacific. University of Hawaii Press, 2840 Kolowalu St., Honolulu, HI 96822, U.S.A. (published twice a year, US$30 a year). Publishes a good mix of articles of interest to both scholars and general readers; the country-by-country "Political Review" in each number is a concise summary of events during the preceding year. The "Dialogue" section offers informed comment on the more controversial issues in the region, while recent publications on the islands are examined through book reviews. Those interested in current topics in Pacific island affairs should check recent volumes for background information. Recommended.

Europe-Pacific Solidarity Bulletin. Published monthly by the European Center for Studies Information and Education on Pacific Issues, Box 151, 3700 AD Zeist, The Netherlands (fax 31-3404/25614).

German Pacific Society Bulletin. Feichtmayr Strasse 25, D-80992 München, Germany. At DM 70 a year, Society membership is a good way for German speakers to keep in touch. News bulletins in English and German are published four times a year, and study tours to various Pacific destinations are organized annually.

Globe Newsletter. The Globetrotters Club, BCM/Roving, London WC1N 3XX, England. This informative travel newsletter, published six times a year, provides lots of practical information on how to tour the world "on the cheap." Club membership includes a subscription to *Globe,* a globetrotter's handbook, a list of other members, etc. This is *the* club for world travelers.

In Depth. Box 90215, Austin, TX 78709, U.S.A. (tel. 512/891-9812). A consumer protection-oriented newsletter for serious scuba divers. Unlike virtually every other diving publication, *In Depth* accepts no advertising, which allows them to tell it as it is.

Islands Business Pacific. Box 12718, Suva, Fiji Islands (annual airmailed subscription US$45 to North America, US$55 to Europe, A$35 to Australia, NZ$55 to New Zealand). A monthly newsmagazine with the emphasis on political, economic, and business trends in the Pacific.

Journal of Pacific History. Division of Pacific and Asian History, RSPAS, Australian National University, Canberra, ACT 0200, Australia. Since 1966 this publication has provided reliable scholarly information on the Pacific. Outstanding.

Journal of the Polynesian Society. Department of Maori Studies, University of Auckland, Private Bag 92019, Auckland, New Zealand. Established in 1892, this quarterly journal contains a wealth of material on Pacific cultures past and present written by scholars of Pacific anthropology, archaeology, language, and history.

Pacific Affairs. University of British Columbia, 2029 West Mall, Vancouver, B.C. V6T 1Z2, Canada (quarterly).

Pacific AIDS Alert. Published monthly by the South Pacific Commission, B.P. D5, Nouméa Cedex, New Caledonia. An informative news-oriented publication dedicated to limiting the spread of sexually transmitted diseases.

Pacific Arts. Pacific Arts Association, c/o Dr. Michael Gunn, PAA Secretary/Treasurer, c/o A.A.O.A., The Metropolitan Museum of Art, 1000 5th Ave., New York, NY 10028, U.S.A. (fax 212/570-3879). For US$40 PAA mem-

bership, you will receive their annual magazine "devoted to the study of all the arts of Oceania" and four issues of their newsletter.

Pacific Islands Monthly. G.P.O. Box 1167, Suva, Fiji Islands (annual subscription A$42 to Australia, US$45 to North America, and A$63 to Europe; fax 679/303-809). Founded in Sydney by R.W. Robson in 1930, *PIM* is the granddaddy of regional magazines. In June 1989, the magazine's editorial office moved from Sydney to Suva.

Pacific Magazine. Box 25488, Honolulu, HI 96825, U.S.A. (every other month; US$15 annual subscription). This business-oriented newsmagazine, published in Hawaii since 1976, will keep you up-to-date on what's happening in the South Pacific and Micronesia. Recommended.

Pacific News Bulletin. Pacific Concerns Resource Center, Box 803, Glebe, NSW 2037, Australia (A$12 a year in Australia, A$25 a year elsewhere). A 16-page monthly newsletter with up-to-date information on nuclear, independence, environmental, and political questions.

Pacific Research. Research School of Pacific and Asian Studies, Coombs Building, Australian National University, Canberra, ACT 0200, Australia (fax 61-6/249-0174; A$25 a year). This monthly periodical of the Peace Research Center publishes informative articles on regional conflicts.

Pacific Studies. Box 1979, BYU-HC, Laie, HI 96762-1294, U.S.A. (quarterly, US$30 a year). Funded by the Polynesian Cultural Center and published by Hawaii's Brigham Young University.

South Sea Digest. G.P.O. Box 4245, Sydney, NSW 2001, Australia (A$150 a year in Australia, A$175 overseas). A private newsletter on political and economic matters, published every other week. It's a good way of keeping abreast of developments in commerce and industry.

Tahiti Pacifique. B.P. 368, Moorea (fax 689/56-30-07). A newsmagazine in French focusing on economic and political events in Tahiti-Polynesia.

Tok Blong Pasifik. South Pacific Peoples Foundation of Canada, 415-620 View St., Victoria, BC V8W 1J6, Canada (fax 604/388-5258; C$25 a year). This quarterly of news and views focuses on regional environmental, development, human rights, and disarmament issues. Recommended.

Travel Matters. Moon Publications Inc., Box 3040, Chico, CA 95927, U.S.A. Write for a free subscription to this useful quarterly publication.

The Washington Pacific Report. Pacific House, Suite 400, 1615 New Hampshire Ave. NW, Washington, DC 20009-2520, U.S.A. (published twice a month, US$159 a year domestic, US$184 outside U.S. postal zones). An insider's newsletter highlighting strategic, diplomatic, and political developments involving the insular Pacific.

AN IMPORTANT MESSAGE

Authors, editors, and publishers wishing to see their publications listed here should send review copies to: David Stanley, c/o Moon Publications Inc., P.O. Box 3040, Chico, CA 95927, U.S.A.

GLOSSARY

afa—a *demi* or person of mixed Polynesian/European blood

ahimaa—a Tahitian underground or earth oven; called an *umu* in Samoa

ahu—a Polynesian stone temple platform

aparima—a Tahitian hand dance

archipelago—a group of islands

arii—a Polynesian high chief

Arioi—a pre-European religious society which traveled among the Society Islands presenting ceremonies and entertainments

atoll—a low-lying, ring-shaped coral reef enclosing a lagoon

bareboat charter—chartering a yacht without crew or provisions

barrier reef—a coral reef separated from the adjacent shore by a lagoon

bêche-de-mer—sea cucumber; trepang; edible sea slug; in Tahitian, *rori*

blackbirder—a European recruiter of slave labor during the 19th century

breadfruit—a large, round fruit with starchy flesh grown on an *uru* tree *(Artocarpus altilis)*

cassava—manioc; the starchy edible root of the tapioca plant

CEP—Centre d'Expérimentations du Pacifique; the Moruroa nuclear test zone

ciguatera—a form of fish poisoning caused by microscopic algae

CMAS—Confédération Mondiale des Activités Subaquatiques

coir—coconut husk sennit used to make rope, etc.

confirmation—A confirmed reservation exists when a supplier acknowledges, either orally or in writing, that a booking has been accepted.

copra—dried coconut meat used in the manufacture of coconut oil, cosmetics, soap, and margarine

coral—a hard, calcareous substance of various shapes comprised of the skeletons of tiny marine animals called polyps

coral bank—a coral formation over 150 meters long

coral head—a coral formation a few meters across

coral patch—a coral formation up to 150 meters long

cyclone—Also known as a hurricane (in the Caribbean) or typhoon (in the north Pacific). A tropical storm which rotates around a center of low atmospheric pressure; it becomes a cyclone when its winds reach 64 knots. In the northern hemisphere cyclones spin counter-clockwise, while south of the equator they move clockwise. The winds of cyclonic storms are deflected toward a low-pressure area at the center, although the "eye" of the cyclone may be calm.

DGSE—Direction Générale de la Sécurité Extérieure; the French CIA

direct flight—a through flight with one or more stops but no change of aircraft, as opposed to a nonstop flight

dugong—a large plant-eating marine mammal; called a manatee in the Caribbean

EEZ—Exclusive Economic Zone; a 200-nautical-mile offshore belt of an island nation or seacoast state which controls the mineral exploitation and fishing rights

endemic—native to a particular area and existing only there

fafa—a "spinach" of cooked taro leaves

farani—French; *français*

FIT—foreign independent travel; a custom-designed, prepaid tour composed of many individualized arrangements

fringing reef—a reef along the shore of an island

gendarme—a French policeman on duty only in rural areas in France and French overseas territories

guano—manure of seabirds, used as a fertilizer

lagoon—an expanse of water bounded by a reef

leeward—downwind; the shore (or side) sheltered from the wind; as opposed to windward

le truck—a truck with seats in back used for public transportation

LMS—London Missionary Society; a Protestant group which spread Christianity from Tahiti (1797) across the Pacific

maa Tahiti—Tahitian food

maa Tinito—Chinese food

mahimahi—dorado, Pacific dolphin (no relation to the mammal)

mahu—a male transvestite, sometimes also a homosexual

makatea—an uplifted reef around the coast of an elevated atoll

mama ruau—actually "grandmother," but also used for the Mother Hubbard long dress introduced by missionaries

mana—authority, prestige, virtue, "face," psychic power, a positive force

manahune—a commoner or member of the lower class in pre-Christian society

mangrove—a tropical shrub with branches that send down roots forming dense thickets along tidal shores

manioc—cassava, tapioca, a starchy root crop

maohi—a native of Tahiti-Polynesia

marae—a Tahitian temple or open-air cult place, called *meae* in the Marquesas

Melanesia—the high island groups of the western Pacific (Fiji, New Caledonia, Vanuatu, Solomon Islands, Papua New Guinea)

Micronesia—chains of high and low islands mostly north of the equator (Carolines, Gilberts, Marianas, Marshalls)

monoi—perfumed coconut oil

motu—a flat reef islet

Oro—the Polynesian god of war

ORSTOM—Office de la Recherche Scientifique et Technique d'Outre-Mer

otea—a ceremonial dance performed by men and women in two lines

overbooking—the practice of confirming more seats, cabins, or rooms than are actually available to ensure against no-shows

pa—an ancient stone fortress

PADI—Professional Association of Dive Instructors

pandanus—screw pine with slender stem and prop roots. The sword-shaped leaves are used for plaiting mats and hats. In Tahitian, *fara*.

papa'a—a white foreigner

parasailing—being carried aloft by a parachute pulled behind a speedboat

pareu—a Tahitian saronglike wraparound skirt or loincloth

pass—a channel through a barrier reef, usually with an outward flow of water

passage—an inside passage between an island and a barrier reef

pelagic—relating to the open sea, away from land

peretane—Britain, British

pirogue—an outrigger canoe, in Tahitian *vaa*

poe—a sticky pudding made from bananas, papaya, pumpkin, or taro mixed with starch, baked in an oven, and served with coconut milk

poisson cru—raw fish marinated in lime, in Tahitian *ia ota,* in Japanese *sashimi*

Polynesia—divided into Western Polynesia (Tonga and Samoa) and Eastern Polynesia (Tahiti-Polynesia, Cook Is., Hawaii, Easter I., and New Zealand)

pupu—a traditional dance group

raatira—a chief, dance leader

reef—a coral ridge near the ocean surface

scuba—self-contained underwater breathing apparatus

sennit—braided coconut-fiber rope

shareboat charter—a yacht tour for individuals or couples who join a small group on a fixed itinerary

shoal—a shallow sandbar or mud bank

shoulder season—a travel period between high/peak and low/off-peak

subduction—the action of one tectonic plate wedging under another

subsidence—geological sinking or settling

tahua—in the old days a skilled artisan; today a sorcerer or healer

tamaaraa—a Tahitian feast

tamure—a new name for 'ori Tahiti, a very fast erotic dance

tapa—a cloth made from the pounded bark of the paper mulberry tree *(Broussonetia papyrifera)*. It's soaked and beaten with a mallet to flatten and intertwine the fibers, then painted with geometric designs; called *ahu* in old Tahitian.

tapu—taboo, sacred, set apart, forbidden, a negative force

taro—a starchy tuber *(Colocasia esculenta)*, a staple food of the Pacific islanders

tavana—the elected mayor of a commune (from the English "governor")

tifaifai—a patchwork quilt based on either European or Polynesian motifs

tiki—a humanlike sculpture used in the old days for religious rites and sorcery

tinito—Tahitian for "Chinese"

toere—a hollow wooden drum hit with a stick

trade wind—a steady wind blowing toward the equator from either northeast or southeast, depending on the season

trench—the section at the bottom of the ocean where one tectonic plate wedges under another

tridacna clam—Eaten everywhere in the Pacific, the clam varies between 10 cm and one meter in size

tropical storm—a cyclonic storm with winds of 35-64 knots

tsunami—a fast-moving wave caused by an undersea earthquake

vigia—a mark on a nautical chart indicating a dangerous rock or shoal

windward—the point or side from which the wind blows, as opposed to "leeward"

zoreille—a recent arrival from France; from *les oreilles* (the ears); also called a *métro*

zories—rubber shower sandals, thongs, flip-flops

CAPSULE TAHITIAN VOCABULARY

ahiahi—evening
aita—no
aita e peapea—no problem
aita maitai—no good
aito—ironwood
amu—eat
ananahi—tomorrow
arearea—fun, to have fun
atea—far away
atua—god
avae—moon, month
avatea—midday (1000-1500)

e—yes, also *oia*
e aha te huru?—how are you?
e hia?—how much?

faraoa—bread
fare—house
fare iti—toilet
fare moni—bank
fare rata—post office
fenua—land
fetii—parent, family
fiu—fed up, bored

haari—coconut palm
haere mai io nei—come here
haere maru—go easy, take it easy
hauti—play, make love
he haere oe ihea?—where are you going?
hei—flower garland, lei
here hoe—number-one sweetheart
himaa—earth oven
himene—song, from the English "hymn"
hoa—friend

ia orana—good day, may you live, prosper
i nanahi—yesterday
ino—bad
ioa—name
ite—know

maeva—welcome
mahana—sun, light, day
mahanahana—warm

maitai—good, I'm fine; also a cocktail
maitai roa—very good
manava—conscience
manu—bird
manuia—to your health!
mao—shark
mauruuru—thank you
mauruuru roa—thank you very much
miti—salt water
moana—deep ocean
moemoea—dream
moni—money

nana—goodbye
naonao—mosquito
nehenehe—beautiful
niau—coconut-palm frond
niu—coconut tree

oa oa—happy
ora—life, health
ori—dance
oromatua—the spirits of the dead
otaa—bundle, luggage
oti—finished

pahi—boat, ship
pape—water, juice
parahi—goodbye
pareu—sarong
pia—beer
pohe—death
poipoi—morning
popaa—foreigner, European
potii—teenage girl, young woman

raerae—effeminate
roto—lake

taata—human being, man
tahatai—beach
tamaa maitai—bon appetit
tamaaraa—Tahitian feast
tamarii—child
tane—man, husband
taofe—coffee
taote—doctor
taravana—crazy

tiare—flower
toetoe—cold
tupapau—ghost

ua—rain
uaina—wine

uteute—red

vahine—woman, wife
vai—water
veavea—hot

NUMBERS

hoe—one
piti—two
toru—three
maha—four
pae—five
ono—six
hitu—seven
vau—eight
iva—nine
ahuru—ten
ahuru ma hoe—11
ahuru ma piti—12
ahuru ma toru—13
ahuru ma maha—14
ahuru ma pae—15
ahuru ma ono—16
ahuru ma hitu—17

ahuru ma vau—18
ahuru ma iva—19
piti ahuru—20
piti ahuru ma hoe—21
piti ahuru ma piti—22
piti ahuru ma toru—23
toru ahuru—30
maha ahuru—40
pae ahuru—50
ono ahuru—60
hitu ahuru—70
vau ahuru—80
iva ahuru—90
hanere—100
tauatini—1,000
ahuru tauatini—10,000
mirioni—1,000,000

CAPSULE FRENCH VOCABULARY

Useful Phrases and Words

bonjour—good day

bonsoir—good evening

salut—hello

Je vais à . . .—I am going to . . .

Où allez-vous?—Where are you going?

Jusqu'où allez-vous?—How far are you going?

Où se trouve . . .?—Where is . . .?

C'est loin d'ici?—Is it far from here?

Je fais de l'autostop.—I am hitchhiking.

À quelle heure?—At what time?

horaire—timetable

hier—yesterday

aujourd'hui—today

demain—tomorrow

Je désire, je voudrais . . .—I want . . .

J'aime . . .—I like . . .

Je ne comprends pas.—I don't understand.

une chambre—a room

Vous êtes très gentil.—You are very kind.

Où habitez-vous?—Where do you live?

Il fait mauvais temps.—It's bad weather.

gendarmerie—police station

Quel travail faites-vous?—What work do you do?

la chômage, les chômeurs—unemployment, the unemployed

Je t'aime.—I love you.

une boutique, un magasin—a store

le pain—bread

le lait—milk

le vin—wine

casse-croûte—snack

conserves—canned foods

fruits de mer—seafood

café très chaud—hot coffee

l'eau—water

plat du jour—set meal

Combien ca fait?—How much does it cost?

Combien ca coûte?

Combien? Quel prix?

auberge de jeunesse—youth hostel

la clef—the key

la route, la piste—the road

la plage—the beach

la falaise—the cliff

cascade—waterfall

grottes—caves

Est-ce que je peux camper ici?—May I camp here?

Je voudrais camper.—I wish to camp.

le terrain de camping—campsite

Devrais-je demander la permission?—Should I ask permission?

s'il vous plaît—please

oui—yes

merci—thank you

cher—expensive

bon marché—cheap

merde—shit

Numbers

un—1

deux—2

trois—3

quatre—4

cinq—5

six—6

sept—7

huit—8

neuf—9

dix—10

onze—11

douze—12

treize—13

quatorze—14

quinze—15

seize—16

dix-sept—17

dix-huit—18

dix-neuf—19
vingt—20
vingt et un—21
vingt-deux—22
vingt-trois—23
trente—30
quarante—40
cinquante— 50

soixante— 60
soixante-dix—70
quatre-vingts—80
quatre-vingt-dix—90
cent—100
mille—1,000
dix mille—10,000
million—1,000,000

PLEASE HELP US

Well, you've heard what *we* have to say, now we want to hear what *you* have to say! How did the book work for you? Your experiences were unique, so please share them. Let us know which businesses deserve a better listing, what we should warn people about, and where we're spot on. It's only with the help of readers like yourself that we can make *Tahiti-Polynesia Handbook* a complete guide for *everyone*. The address is:

David Stanley,
c/o Moon Publications Inc.,
P.O. Box 3040,
Chico, CA 95927, U.S.A.
e-mail: travel@moon.com

INDEX

Bold page numbers indicate the primary reference. Page numbers in *italics* indicate information in maps, charts, special topics, captions, or illustrations.

ABOUT THE AUTHOR

A quarter century ago, David Stanley's right thumb carried him out of Toronto, Canada, onto a journey that has so far wound through 168 countries, including a three-year trip from Tokyo to Kabul. His travel guidebooks to the South Pacific, Micronesia, Alaska, and Eastern Europe opened those areas to budget travelers for the first time.

During the late 1960s, David got involved in Mexican culture by spending a year in several small towns near

David Stanley atop Tahiti's Mt. Aorai

Guanajuato. Later he studied at the universities of Barcelona and Florence, before settling down to get an honors degree (with distinction) in Spanish literature from the University of Guelph, Canada.

In 1978 Stanley linked up with future publisher Bill Dalton, and together they wrote the first edition of South Pacific Handbook. Since then, Stanley has gone on to write additional definitive guides for Moon Publications, including Micronesia Handbook, Fiji Islands Handbook, Tahiti-Polynesia Handbook, and early editions of Alaska-Yukon Handbook. His books have informed a generation of budget travelers.

Stanley makes frequent research trips to the areas covered in his guides, jammed between journeys to the 79 countries and territories worldwide he still hasn't visited. To maintain his independence, Stanley does not accept subsidized travel arrangements or "freebies" from any source. In travel writing David Stanley has found a perfect outlet for his restless wanderlust. His zodiac sign is Virgo.

MOON TRAVEL HANDBOOKS
THE IDEAL TRAVELING COMPANIONS

Moon Travel Handbooks provide focused, comprehensive coverage of distinct destinations all over the world. Our goal is to give travelers all the background and practical information they'll need for an extraordinary, unexpected travel experience.

Every Handbook begins with an in-depth essay about the land, the people, their history, art, politics, and social concerns—an entire bookcase of cultural insight and introductory information in one portable volume. We also provide accurate, up-to-date coverage of all the practicalities: language, currency, transportation, accommodations, food, and entertainment. And Moon's maps are legendary, covering not only cities and highways, but parks and trails that are often difficult to find in other sources.

Below are highlights of Moon's Asia and the Pacific Travel Handbook series. Our complete list of Handbooks covering North America and Hawaii, Mexico, Central America and the Caribbean, and Asia and the Pacific, are listed on the order form on the accompanying pages. To purchase Moon Travel Handbooks, please check your local bookstore or order by phone: (800) 345-5473 Monday-Friday 8 a.m.-5 p.m. PST.

MOON OVER ASIA
THE ASIA AND THE PACIFIC TRAVEL HANDBOOK SERIES

> "Moon guides are wittily written and warmly personal; what's more, they present a vivid, often raw vision of Asia without promotional overtones. They also touch on such topics as official corruption and racism, none of which rate a mention in the bone-dry, air-brushed, dry-cleaned version of Asia written up in the big U.S. guidebooks."
> —*Far Eastern Economic Review*

BALI HANDBOOK by Bill Dalton, 428 pages, **$12.95**
"This book is for the in-depth traveler, interested in history and art, willing to experiment with language and food and become immersed in the culture of Bali." — Great Expeditions

BANGKOK HANDBOOK by Michael Buckley, 222 pages, **$13.95**
"Helps make sense of this beguiling paradox of a city . . . very entertaining reading." —*The Vancouver Sun*

FIJI ISLANDS HANDBOOK by David Stanley, 200 pages, $13.95
"If you want to encounter Fiji and not just ride through it, this book is for you." —*Great Expeditions*

HONG KONG HANDBOOK by Kerry Moran, 300 pages, **$15.95**
Hong Kong has been called "the most cosmopolitan city on earth," yet it's also one of the few places where visitors can witness Chinese customs as they have been practiced for centuries. Award-winning author Kerry Moran explores this unusual juxtaposition of tradition and modern life in *Hong Kong Handbook*. Moran traces the history and cultural development of the British Colony, and anticipates the changes to come in 1997, when this fascinating city reverts to Chinese rule.

INDONESIA HANDBOOK by Bill Dalton, 1,300 pages, **$25.00**
"Looking for a fax machine in Palembang, a steak dinner on Ambon or the best place to photograph Bugis prahus in Sulawesi? Then buy this brick of a book, which contains a full kilogram of detailed directions and advice." —*Asia, Inc. Magazine*

"One of the world's great guides." —*All Asia Review of Books*

"The classic guidebook to the archipelago."
—*Condé Nast Traveler*

JAPAN HANDBOOK by J.D. Bisignani, 952 pages, **$22.50**
"The scope of this guide book is staggering, ranging from an introduction to Japanese history and culture through to the best spots for shopping for pottery in Mashie or silk pongee in Kagoshima." —*Golden Wing*

"More travel information on Japan than any other guidebook."
—*The Japan Times*

MICRONESIA HANDBOOK by David Stanley, 345 pages, **$11.95**
"Remarkably informative, fair-minded, sensible, and readable . . . Stanley's comments on the United States' 40-year administration are especially pungent and thought-provoking." —*The Journal of the Polynesian Society*

NEPAL HANDBOOK by Kerry Moran, 378 pages, **$12.95**
"This is an excellent guidebook, exploring every aspect of the country the visitor is likely to want to know about with both wit and authority." —*South China Morning Post*

NEW ZEALAND HANDBOOK by Jane King, 571 pages, **$18.95**

"Far and away the best guide to New Zealand." —*The Atlantic*

OUTBACK AUSTRALIA HANDBOOK by Marael Johnson, 370 pages, **$15.95**

"Well designed, easy to read, and funny" —*Buzzworm*

PHILIPPINES HANDBOOK by Peter Harper and Laurie Fullerton, 638 pages, **$17.95**

"The most comprehensive travel guide done on the Philippines. Excellent work." —*Pacific Stars & Stripes*

SOUTHEAST ASIA HANDBOOK by Carl Parkes, 1,100 pages, **$21.95**

"Plenty of information on sights and entertainment, also provides a political, environment and cultural context that will allow visitors to begin to interpret what they see." —*London Sunday Times*

"Carl Parkes is the savviest of all tourists in Southeast Asia." —Arthur Frommer

SOUTH KOREA HANDBOOK by Robert Nilsen, 586 pages, **$14.95**

"One of a small number of guidebooks that inform without being pedantic, and are enthusiastic yet maintain a critical edge . . . the maps are without parallel." —*Far Eastern Economic Review*

SOUTH PACIFIC HANDBOOK by David Stanley, 778 pages, **$19.95**

"Off to Kiribati? Moon's tribute to the South Pacific, by David Stanley, is next to none." —*Ubique*

TAHITI-POLYNESIA HANDBOOK by David Stanley, 246 pages, **$13.95**

"If you can't find it in this book, it is something you don't need to know." —*Rapa Nui Journel*

THAILAND HANDBOOK by Carl Parkes, 568 pages, **$16.95**

". . . stands out for its attention to detail and accuracy." —*Meetings & Conventions Magazine*

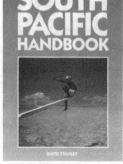

TIBET HANDBOOK   by Victor Chan, 1,100 pages, **$30.00**
"Not since the original three volume Murray's Handbook to India, published over a century ago, has such a memorial to the hot, and perhaps uncontrollable passions of travel been published. . . . This is the most impressive travel handbook published in the 20th century." —*Small Press Magazine*

"Shimmers with a fine madness."   —*Escape Magazine*

VIETNAM, CAMBODIA & LAOS HANDBOOK
by Michael Buckley, 650 pages, **$18.95**
Available January 1996.
The new definitive guide to Southeast Asia's hottest travel destination from a travel writer who knows Asia like the back of his hand. Michael Buckley combines the most current practical travel information—much of it previously unavailable—with the perspective of a seasoned adventure traveler. Good maps to the region are rare, but this comprehensive guidebook includes 75 of them.

STAYING HEALTHY IN ASIA, AFRICA, AND LATIN AMERICA
by Dirk G. Schroeder, ScD, MPH, 200 pages, **$11.95**

"Your family doctor will not be able to supply you with this valuable information because he doesn't have it."

—*Whole Earth Catalog*

"Read this book if you want to stay healthy on any journeys or stays in Asia, Africa, and Latin America."

—*American Journal of Health Promotion*

TRAVEL MATTERS

Travel Matters is Moon Publications' free quarterly newsletter, loaded with specially commissioned travel articles and essays that tell it like it is. Recent issues have been devoted to Asia, Mexico, and North America, and every issue includes:

Feature Stories: Travel writing unlike what you'll find in your local newspaper. Andrew Coe on Mexican professional wrestling, Michael Buckley on the craze for wartime souvenirs in Vietnam, Kim Weir on the Nixon Museum in Yorba Linda.

Transportation: Tips on how to get around. Rick Steves on a new type of Eurail pass, Victor Chan on hiking in Tibet, Joe Cummings on how to be a Baja road warrior.

Health Matters: Articles on the most recent findings by Dr. Dirk Schroeder, author of *Staying Healthy in Asia, Africa, and Latin America.* Japanese encephalitis, malaria, the southwest U.S. "mystery disease" . . . forewarned is forearmed.

Book Reviews: Informed assessments of the latest travel titles and series. The Rough Guide to *World Music*, Let's Go vs. Berkeley, Dorling Kindersley vs. Knopf.

The Internet: News from the cutting edge. The Great Burma Debate in rec.travel.asia, hotlists of the best WWW sites, updates on Moon's massive "Road Trip USA" exhibit.

There are also booklists, Letters to the Editor, and anything else we can find to interest our readers, as well as Moon's latest titles and ordering information for other travel products, including Periplus Travel Maps to Southeast Asia.

To receive a free subscription to *Travel Matters,* call (800) 345-5473, write to Moon Publications, P.O. Box 3040, Chico, CA 95927-3040, or e-mail travel@moon.com.

Please note: subscribers who live outside the United States will be charged $7.00 per year for shipping and handling.

MOON TRAVEL HANDBOOKS

ASIA AND THE PACIFIC

Bali Handbook (3379)	$12.95
Bangkok Handbook (0595)	$13.95
Fiji Islands Handbook (0382)	$13.95
Hong Kong Handbook (0560)	$15.95
Indonesia Handbook (0625)	$25.00
Japan Handbook (3700)	$22.50
Micronesia Handbook (3808)	$11.95
Nepal Handbook (3646)	$12.95
New Zealand Handbook (3883)	$18.95
Outback Australia Handbook (3794)	$15.95
Philippines Handbook (0048)	$17.95
Southeast Asia Handbook (0021)	$21.95
South Korea Handbook (3204)	$14.95
South Pacific Handbook (3999)	$19.95
Tahiti-Polynesia Handbook (0374)	$13.95
Thailand Handbook (3824)	$16.95
Tibet Handbook (3905)	$30.00
*Vietnam, Cambodia & Laos Handbook (0293)	$18.95

NORTH AMERICA AND HAWAII

Alaska-Yukon Handbook (0161)	$14.95
Alberta and the Northwest Territories Handbook (0676)	$17.95
Arizona Traveler's Handbook (0536)	$16.95
Atlantic Canada Handbook (0072)	$17.95
Big Island of Hawaii Handbook (0064)	$13.95
British Columbia Handbook (0145)	$15.95
Catalina Island Handbook (3751)	$10.95
Colorado Handbook (0137)	$17.95
Georgia Handbook (0609)	$16.95
Hawaii Handbook (0005)	$19.95
Honolulu-Waikiki Handbook (0587)	$14.95
Idaho Handbook (0617)	$14.95
Kauai Handbook (0013)	$13.95
Maui Handbook (0579)	$14.95
Montana Handbook (0544)	$15.95
Nevada Handbook (0641)	$16.95
New Mexico Handbook (0153)	$14.95

Northern California Handbook (3840)	$19.95
Oregon Handbook (0102)	$16.95
Texas Handbook (0633)	$16.95
Utah Handbook (0684)	$16.95
Washington Handbook (0552)	$15.95
Wyoming Handbook (3980)	$14.95

MEXICO

Baja Handbook (0528)	$15.95
Cabo Handbook (0285)	$14.95
Cancún Handbook (0501)	$13.95
Central Mexico Handbook (0234)	$15.95
*Mexico Handbook (0315)	$21.95
Northern Mexico Handbook (0226)	$16.95
Pacific Mexico Handbook (0323)	$16.95
Puerto Vallarta Handbook (0250)	$14.95
Yucatán Peninsula Handbook (0242)	$15.95

CENTRAL AMERICA AND THE CARIBBEAN

Belize Handbook (0370)	$14.95
Caribbean Handbook (0277)	$16.95
Costa Rica Handbook (0358)	$18.95
Jamaica Handbook (0129)	$14.95

INTERNATIONAL

Egypt Handbook (3891)	$18.95
Moon Handbook (0668)	$10.00
Moscow-St. Petersburg Handbook (3913)	$13.95
Staying Healthy in Asia, Africa, and Latin America (0269)	$11.95

* New title, please call for availability

PERIPLUS TRAVEL MAPS

All maps $7.95 each

Bali	Hong Kong	Singapore
Bandung/W. Java	Java	Vietnam
Bangkok/C. Thailand	Ko Samui/S. Thailand	Yogyakarta/C. Java
Batam/Bintan	Penang	
Cambodia	Phuket/S. Thailand	

WHERE TO BUY MOON TRAVEL HANDBOOKS

BOOKSTORES AND LIBRARIES: Moon Travel Handbooks are sold worldwide. Please write to our sales manager for a list of wholesalers and distributors in your area.

TRAVELERS: We would like to have Moon Travel Handbooks available throughout the world. Please ask your bookstore to write or call us for ordering information. If your bookstore will not order our guides for you, please contact us for a free title listing.

> **Moon Publications, Inc.**
> **P.O. Box 3040**
> **Chico, CA 95927-3040 U.S.A.**
> **Tel: (800) 345-5473**
> **Fax: (916) 345-6751**
> **E-mail: travel@moon.com**

IMPORTANT ORDERING INFORMATION

PRICES: All prices are subject to change. We always ship the most current edition. We will let you know if there is a price increase on the book you order.

SHIPPING AND HANDLING OPTIONS: Domestic UPS or USPS first class (allow 10 working days for delivery): $3.50 for the first item, 50 cents for each additional item.

EXCEPTIONS:

Tibet Handbook and *Indonesia Handbook* shipping $4.50; $1.00 for each additional *Tibet Handbook* or *Indonesia Handbook*.

Moonbelt shipping is $1.50 for one, 50 cents for each additional belt.

Add $2.00 for same-day handling.

UPS 2nd Day Air or Printed Airmail requires a special quote.

International Surface Bookrate 8-12 weeks delivery: $3.00 for the first item, $1.00 for each additional item. Note: Moon Publications cannot guarantee international surface bookrate shipping. Moon recommends sending international orders via air mail, which requires a special quote.

FOREIGN ORDERS: Orders that originate outside the U.S.A. must be paid for with either an international money order or a check in U.S. currency drawn on a major U.S. bank based in the U.S.A.

TELEPHONE ORDERS: We accept Visa or MasterCard payments. Minimum order is US$15.00. Call in your order: (800) 345-5473, 8 a.m.-5 p.m. Pacific Standard Time.

ORDER FORM

Be sure to call (800) 345-5473 for current prices and editions or for the name of the bookstore nearest you that carries Moon Travel Handbooks • 8 a.m.–5 p.m. PST.
(See important ordering information on preceding page.)

Name: _____ Date: _____

Street: _____

City: _____ Daytime Phone: _____

State or Country: _____ Zip Code: _____

QUANTITY	TITLE	PRICE

Taxable Total_____

Sales Tax (7.25%) for California Residents_____

Shipping & Handling_____

TOTAL_____

Ship: ☐ UPS (no P.O. Boxes) ☐ 1st class ☐ International surface mail

Ship to: ☐ address above ☐ other _____

Make checks payable to: **MOON PUBLICATIONS, INC**. P.O. Box 3040, Chico, CA 95927-3040 U.S.A. We accept Visa and MasterCard. **To Order**: Call in your Visa or MasterCard number, or send a written order with your Visa or MasterCard number and expiration date clearly written.

Card Number: ☐ **Visa** ☐ **MasterCard**

☐ ☐ ☐ ☐ ☐ ☐ ☐ ☐ ☐ ☐ ☐ ☐ ☐ ☐ ☐ ☐

Exact Name on Card: _____

Expiration date:_____

Signature:_____

F/95–A

THE METRIC SYSTEM

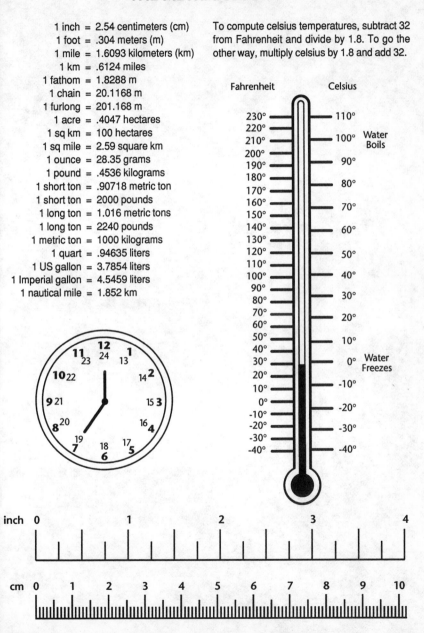

1 inch = 2.54 centimeters (cm)
1 foot = .304 meters (m)
1 mile = 1.6093 kilometers (km)
1 km = .6124 miles
1 fathom = 1.8288 m
1 chain = 20.1168 m
1 furlong = 201.168 m
1 acre = .4047 hectares
1 sq km = 100 hectares
1 sq mile = 2.59 square km
1 ounce = 28.35 grams
1 pound = .4536 kilograms
1 short ton = .90718 metric ton
1 short ton = 2000 pounds
1 long ton = 1.016 metric tons
1 long ton = 2240 pounds
1 metric ton = 1000 kilograms
1 quart = .94635 liters
1 US gallon = 3.7854 liters
1 Imperial gallon = 4.5459 liters
1 nautical mile = 1.852 km

To compute celsius temperatures, subtract 32 from Fahrenheit and divide by 1.8. To go the other way, multiply celsius by 1.8 and add 32.

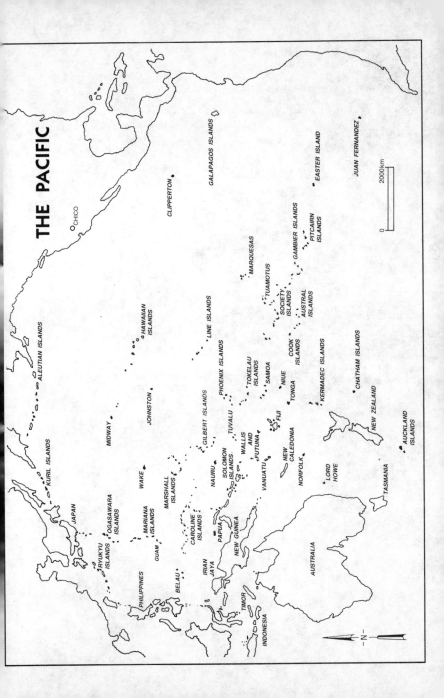